POLISH POLITICS

EDGE OF THE ABYSS

EDITED BY
JACK BIELASIAK
AND
MAURICE D. SIMON

PRAEGER SPECIAL STUDIES • PRAEGER SCIENTIFIC

New York • Philadelphia • Eastbourne, UK
Toronto • Hong Kong • Tokyo • Sydney

Library of Congress Cataloging in Publication Data
Main entry under title:

Polish politics.

    Includes index.
    1. Poland—Politics and government—1980–   —Ad–
dresses, essays, lectures. I. Bielasiak, Jack.
II. Simon, Maurice David.
DK4442.P646 1984   943.8'056   83-24759
ISBN 0-03-069633-X

Published in 1984 by Praeger Publishers
CBS Educational and Professional Publishing,
a Division of CBS Inc.
521 Fifth Avenue, New York, NY 10175 USA

456789 052 9876545321

Printed in the United States of America
on acid-free paper

To our Parents

and to

Jean and Judy

Preface

The actions of the Polish workers in August 1980, the birth of Solidarity, and the changes brought about by the independent trade union into the life of Poland seized the imagination of the world. The imposition of the state of war on December 13, 1981 put a sudden end to that process of change and presented the outside world with a very different view of the country. The aim of this volume is to explain the sixteen months of the Polish renewal by concentrating on the reasons for the 1980-81 upheavals, analyzing the economic, social, and political developments between the outburst of the strikes and the state of war declaration, and exploring the aftermath of these developments in martial law Poland.

The rapid pace of events, the magnitude of the changes, and the intensity of feelings associated with the Polish crisis rendered the writing of the individual chapters and the editing of the volume a difficult and hazardous task. Developments in Poland often outstripped our ability to keep abreast of events and to present the facts in their full context. Adjustments, updates, and rewrites were continually necessary. As a result, the present volume has been slow in coming to fruition. The original idea for the work must be credited to Professor Jim Morrison, who guided it through the initial stages. When commitments abroad prevented him from continuing his task, we took over as editors and sought to move the project forward. In this we were helped considerably by the dedication and patience of the authors, who understood well the difficulties associated with a study of contemporary Polish politics. For this we are most grateful to them.

All the contributors to the book are close observers of Polish affairs. Most of us have recently spent considerable periods of time pursuing research in Poland. Our firsthand observations of life in that country over the past few years, as well as our scholarly activities, have guided our examination of the 1980-81 events. The studies that follow stand up well to the passage of time and provide a comprehensive analysis of the sixteen months of Polish history associated with Solidarity and political renewal. The essays progress from an examination of economic to social to political issues. The introductory chapter by Jack Bielasiak traces the evolution of conflicts between the state and society in postwar Poland and argues that there is a sequential pattern to the crises with each cataclysm influencing subsequent manifestations of social breakdown.

The next three chapters concentrate on the economic problems that were the most direct catalysts for the expression of popular discontent. After its accession to power in 1970 the Gierek administration embarked on an ambitious program of economic growth to establish greater support among the people. The essence of the strategy was renovation of industry through new technology and improvements in the supply of consumer goods—programs financed by credits from the West. While successful in the first half of the decade, this economic policy soon fell prey to domestic inefficiencies and deteriorations in the international economy. David M. Kemme presents a general overview of the economic policy decisions that contributed to the breakdown of the system at the turn of the decade and concludes that this was a consequence of the sustained failure to introduce meaningful reforms. Despite some improvements in the economy over the past year, the commitment to reform is again the weak link in the Polish economy. The foreign economic policy of the government was also heavily politicized, and as Marcin Sar shows such intervention into economic decisions created severe dislocations for industry. The interference operated at both the national and enterprise levels and involved institutional as well as informal methods. The resulting deterioration in economic performance only served to increase political involvement, thereby creating a vicious cycle with high economic costs. The agricultural sector of the Polish economy, probably more than any other policy area, has been subject to a highly complex interrelationship of political, social, and economic issues. Andrzej Korbonski argues that as a result official agrarian policy has been a mix of pragmatism and dogmatism. The absence of an effective, organized group to represent the interests of the peasantry aggravated the mistakes of the government. The recognition of Rural Solidarity in May 1981 altered the situation, but only briefly. The peasant organization was outlawed as a result of martial law.

The regime's attempt to save the deteriorating economic situation was to once again place the burden on the Polish population, by increasing prices. As in prior cases, this attempt met with resistance on the part of the workers, who perceived the policy as unjust. The protests and strikes in the summer of 1980 turned into a national movement that saw the emergence of an independent trade union. The formation of Solidarity introduced a major dilemma for the Communist regime, since the ruling Communist party already claimed to be the representative of the working class. The most important issue thus became how to reconcile the leading role of the Polish United Workers' Party (PUWP) claim with the representation of workers' interests in an autonomous union. By 1980 the Polish working class had become well cognizant of the fact that its needs were not sufficiently represented through the official channels and institutions. Christine M. Sadowski shows how prior forms of workers' organizations, including factory councils, workers' councils, and strike committees, were coopted by the government. These experiences of industrial labor led to the free trade union movement as a means to obtain greater influence over their economic well-being. The concern with economic welfare was very much present in the policies of Solidarity. As David S. Mason demonstrates, this issue took the form of a genuine commitment on the part of the union for greater social and economic equality. The potential for agreement between the party and Solidarity on the policy issue of egalitarianism was in fact much greater than on the procedural issue of participation in policy formulation. The threat to the supremacy of the party, however, outweighed the concern with substantive policies among the political leadership, producing a stalemate in the Polish polity and economy. Survey data taken during the crisis period, and analyzed here by T. Anthony Jones, David Bealmear, and Michael D. Kennedy, reveal that the public indeed blamed the regime and the party for the quality of their lives and did not trust the officials' promises for improvements.

The advent of Solidarity and the ensuing mobilization of Polish society penetrated all social and political groups in the country, including the Communist party. The desire for autonomy and self-organization was expressed by most strata of the population and, together with the agreements of August 1980, introduced an unprecedented degree of participatory democracy into the life of the nation. The involvement of all social groups in socioeconomic, and ultimately political, issues altered significantly during the period of renewal. Barbara A. Misztal and Bronislaw Misztal trace the general changes befalling the sociopolitical elites of Poland as a result of this process. Most important, a new elite appeared on the scene, that of Solidarity. While the commitment to democracy and self-organization was very strong within the union, the charismatic nature of the movement and the initial spontaneity of action introduced an element of self-selection into leadership positions. This trend coexisted with a later development stressing representation and delegation of powers within Solidarity. The ultimate counter-

action against the appearance of an alternative group commanding the loyalty of society was the militarization of the traditional
Communist elite, with the military assuming unprecedented
political power.

The interplay between the Communist power elite and the
social movement represented by Solidarity affected all groupings
within society. Jane Leftwich Curry and Joanna Preibisz view
the role of the Polish intelligentsia during this period as primarily
that of advisors or onlookers, while the workers carried forth
the process of change. The failure of the intellectuals to play
a leading role in Poland's social revolution, despite theoretical
assumptions depicting this stratum as the mainstay of revolutionary activity, was due to structural aspects of Polish society and
the policies of the Gierek regime. At the same time, its inability
to provide workable solutions to the dilemmas faced by the nation
after August 1980 further fragmented and frustrated the intelligentsia. The position of the Catholic church, as Dieter Bingen
demonstrates, was subject to similar pressures. For the first
time in the postwar history of Poland, the church was not the
sole representative of the nation's interests vis-à-vis the party,
for Solidarity had undertaken that role as well. Nonetheless
the church had to use its moral authority to assure the well-
being of the nation and, therefore, act to prevent dangerous
confrontations between the state and society. This necessitated
a mediating role between these two forces that rendered the
moral and political authority of the church more precarious.

As with the other organizations, the ruling Communist
party did not remain immune to the developments introduced
by the formation of Solidarity. Perhaps most significant was
the penetration of the spirit of reform into the party's rank
and file, many of whom joined Solidarity and sought to democratize
the operations of the PUWP through the formation of horizontal
structures. As pointed out by Z. Anthony Kruszewski, it was
the danger of the party's transformation that strengthened the
position of the apparatus and contributed to a course of action
aimed at destroying reform. By that time, however, the party's
position was so weak as to force it to rely on the military as
the only political force capable of restoring the status quo ante.
In fact the erosion of the political vitality of the party had enabled the military to assume gradually a more prominent role
in the administration of the state. Paul C. Latawski shows that
in this task the military was aided by its image as an efficient
institution, well respected by the population. Both these
factors, the popular esteem and administrative experience,
enabled the armed forces to usher in very effectively direct

military rule over the entire country on the night of December 13, 1981.

The course of the Polish renewal was not influenced exclusively by the interactions of the various social groups and political organizations. On the contrary, outside forces were very much a felt presence in the Polish drama. While the external influences were not always direct, Soviet and East European interests and concerns were consistently present in the unfolding Polish drama. Howard E. Frost demonstrates that the Soviets became involved from the very beginning and that they were motivated by a desire to assure the political stability of Poland at minimal economic and military costs to themselves. The expressions of concern by the Soviet Union and other East European states became evermore forceful as the process of change gained momentum in Poland. Roger E. Kanet's comprehensive examination of the attitudes and actions of Poland's allies reveals clearly that the latter viewed the developments in Poland as a threat to the very foundation of socialism and the existence of the Communist states. For this reason they were willing to engage in a constant barrage of denunciations against what they termed the antisocialist counterrevolution.

Despite the veiled threats of external intervention to put an end to the Polish transformation, it was the Polish military that acted to curb the process of change by imposing the state of war on December 13, 1981. In his declaration to the nation, General Jaruzelski stated that the nation had come to the edge of the abyss and that martial law was necessary to restore economic and political stability. The post-December reality of the Polish political scene is described by Maurice D. Simon in the concluding chapter. Whether that reality has changed substantially through the formal lifting of martial law on July 22, 1983 remains questionable in view of the fact that many of the provisions first introduced by the military government have now been encoded into civil law.

Contents

List of Tables

List of Abbreviations

CCTU	Central Council of Trade Unions
CMEA	Council for Mutual Economic Assistance
CPSU	Communist Party of the Soviet Union
DP	Democratic Party
FEP	Foreign Economic Policy
FJN	National Unity Front
FYP	Five-Year Plan
GDR	German Democratic Republic
KKP	National Consultative Commission
KOR	Committee for the Defense of Workers
KPN	Confederation for an Independent Poland
KSS "KOR"	Committee for Social Self-Defense
MKS	Interfactory Strike Committee
MO	Citizens' Militia
MPA	Main Political Administration
PCI	Italian Communist Party
PKOZRiN	Polish Committee for the Defense of Life, Family and Nation
PPN	Polish League for Independence
PPR	Polish Workers' Party
PUWP	Polish United Workers' Party
ROPCiO	Movement for the Defense of Human and Civil Rights
UPP	United Peasants' Party
WOG	Large Economic Organization
WRON	Military Council of National Salvation
WSW	Military Security Service
WTO	Warsaw Treaty Organization

1.

The Evolution of Crises in Poland

Jack Bielasiak

The history of Poland, to a degree paralleled by few other nations, has been shaped by periodic and profound crises. Cataclysmic incidents often propelled the country into the forefront of world events and at times were even responsible for the disappearance of the state from the geopolitical map of the globe. During the postwar history of Poland, crises altered the relationship between the regime and the people and affected the course of socialist construction. The workers' strikes of August 1980 once again introduced a critical period in the development of the nation, culminating in prolonged social, economic, and political tensions—tensions that persist well beyond the imposition of martial law on December 13, 1981.

This latest upheaval in the history of Poland is the culmination of a process that has seen repeated confrontations between the state and civil society. In October 1956, March 1968, December 1970, June 1976, and August 1980 events occurred that affected profoundly the relationship between the ruled and the rulers. Each successive clash had the effect of defining anew the basis of political power and social evolution in Poland, and each upheaval had the consequence of limiting the political options available to the state to stabilize the national situation. The consequence of such a historical pattern is a crisis legacy that defines the contemporary condition of Polish politics.

This chapter is an analysis of the evolution of conflicts between the state and society in postwar Poland. Its primary intent is to examine the nature of the opposition to the communist regime emanating from society during the various periods of national disruption and to evaluate the responses of the government and the party to the crises. The focus is on the types of issues and demands surfacing during the different conflicts and on the tactics employed by the regime to neutralize the expressions of popular discontent. The essential argument here is that there is a sequential pattern in the postwar cataclysms of Poland, with each crisis influencing subsequent manifestations of state-society conflict and regime strategies of crisis management.

THE POLISH OCTOBER AND REVISIONISM

The course of postwar development in socialist Poland was determined by the conflict within the Communist Party during 1947-48.[1] As in the rest of Eastern Europe, the confrontation centered around the exigencies of international communism in relation to domestic priorities and the applicability of the Soviet model to Poland. Although the situation in Warsaw was not as extreme as in the other capitals of the socialist camp (for it did not culminate in show trials and executions) the intraparty debate was more intense than in the other states of East Europe. At the time Wladyslaw Gomulka was the most outspoken proponent of national communism, advocating a gradual transformation of Polish society that took into account specific national traditions and conditions. Gomulka's Polish way to socialism resisted the Soviet imposition of ideological conformity in the region and instead favored policies giving priority to domestic considerations on such issues as collectivization, the formation of the Comintern, and emulation of the Soviet experience.

In the wake of the Soviet Union's push for consolidation and uniformity in Eastern Europe in 1948, Gomulka's political stand was denounced as rightist-nationalist deviation at Central Committee meetings of the Polish party. The defeat of Gomulka's approach to the building of socialism signified for Poland, as for the other bloc countries, a faithful adherence to the Stalinist mode of economic and social development.[2] Society was to undergo a revolutionary and rapid transformation imposed from above by the political authorities, and the political center emerged as the supreme intervening instrument in civil society. Equally important, because of traditional resentment, was the identification of official Polish policies with Soviet preferences and the loss of national autonomy in the conduct of socioeconomic affairs. The selection, or rather imposition, of this Soviet-type pattern of development had profound consequences, for the issues present in the 1948 conflict resurfaced several times in subse-

quent crisis situations. At these times, they took both socioeconomic and political forms. In the first instance, it meant
popular dissatisfaction with the emphasis placed on accumulation
and industrialization and the neglect of consumption investments
and consumer demands. In the political arena, the opposition
was to the intervention of political authorities in all aspects of
citizens' lives and to Soviet dominance over Polish affairs.

The first major societal crisis in Poland occurred in the
mid-1950s in the wake of the destalinization efforts throughout
the communist world and found expression in two streams of
opposition to the ruling elite and its ideology. [3] The first consisted of an intellectual ferment demanding sociocultural freedoms
and the depoliticization of private lives. The second centered
on economic issues through spontaneous actions by workers
rejecting centrally imposed programs. The movement of the
intellectuals was foremost a crisis of conscience aimed at the
reformation of state socialism into a more humane variant. [4]
This challenge to the existing political structure emanated from
the literary circles' demands for an end to strict controls over
the means of expression. The intelligentsia's campaign resulted
in a cultural thaw that penetrated the political establishment
and influenced the course of destalinization in Poland. The
implementation of a gradual process of liberalization resulted
in greater freedom in cultural and intellectual activities. Idealism
and humanism, as well as nationalism, were the prevailing themes
in the discussions of the clubs of Catholic and Marxist intelligentsia and in the writings of journalists and writers. This
intellectual ferment embodied a new spirit of change and a
belief in the transformation of the socialist system.

The second manifestation of social unrest during this period
occurred among the industrial labor class. [5] The source of the
workers' discontent lay in poor material conditions and a resultant
need to improve both the consumption and working environments
of manual laborers. The most extreme attempt to improve these
conditions took place in June 1956 in Poznan, where strikes and
rioting by workers led to a confrontation with the political
authorities and the violent suppression of the demonstrators.
Nonetheless, the workers' uprising contributed to a legitimization of labor's grievances and facilitated the formation of workers'
councils in enterprises throughout the country. This attempt
to institutionalize self-management can be taken as a reflection
of the workers' aspiration to influence the economic situation
through their participation in organizations representing the
genuine interests of industrial labor. In this sense, the workers'
self-management movement paralleled the intellectuals' faith in

the reformation of the existing socialist institutions and the creation of a Polish socialism deviating from the Soviet model.

While the two currents of dissatisfaction of the mid-1950s remained essentially separate—one permeated by sociopolitical concerns and the other embodying material goals—both found a common ground in a national consciousness directed against Soviet interference and Stalinist controls. The pressures for change during the destalinization process focused on greater national autonomy and culminated in an outburst of nationalism on the part of intellectuals and workers in October 1956. At the time the subordination of other issues to the patriotic feelings of the population facilitated the resolution of the 1956 crisis. The return to power of Gomulka was equated with a restoration of the Polish road to socialism and the fulfillment of the 1948 national aspirations. The reappearance of stability in the country after the Polish October was therefore accomplished by means of a nationalistic and personalized solution that found expression in the leadership of Gomulka. The new ruling elite was viewed by the people as a symbol of independence from Soviet and Stalinist domination, and its advent to power was perceived as a resolution of all the fundamental social and economic problems of society. Nonetheless, as the post-1956 period made clear, the initial popular support for Gomulka allowed him to consolidate the political situation without significantly altering the dominance of the state over society. Many gains of the Polish October attained by intellectuals and workers were eliminated in the late 1950s by the imposition of new limits on cultural expression, the cooptation of workers' councils into the system of economic management, and an emphasis on the monopolistic role of the Polish United Workers' Party (PUWP) in society. Gomulka's little stabilization, while rejecting the coercive, revolutionary transformation of society, returned to an authoritarian mode of rule aimed at the preservation of the status quo and culminating in a neglect of the country's important problems.[6]

At the same time, one must recognize that the transition from Stalinism to the new system represented an important political thaw leading to social improvements. In effect, this gave rise to the belief that changes could be introduced by the party and result in important alterations in the political system of communism. Specifically, this view was held by prominent Marxist intellectuals, who foresaw the possibility of gradual changes emanating from within the PUWP.[7] The ideological concept of revisionism held that socialism with a human face could be introduced from above, through the absorption of democratic ideals by the central political authority. The advocates of the revisionist strategy worked from within the party to bring about reforms within the communist organization to cause the broader evolution of society at large. The failure of the revisionist attempt to transform the nature of Polish communism became evident during the 1968 crisis. The events of that year, born in the continuing socioeconomic stagnation of the country and the influence of the Prague spring, were initiated by students against the government's interference in cultural life.[8] The consequent national-chauvinistic campaign launched by several party circles against the "Zionist" influence among the students was expanded to an antiintellectual, anti-revisionist stand. Under the circumstances, the Marxist intelligentsia could not maintain its hope for the enlightenment of party leaders favoring civil liberties and social democratization. The consequence of the 1968 crisis was the elimination of an alternative ideological formulation of socialism within the Polish party and the break of Marxist humanists from the party organization.[9] It also marked the end of the revisionist strategy of political transformation by means of a trickling down of reforms from the authoritarian center to the entire social environment.

The 1968 conflict remained, essentially, restricted to the upper strata of Polish society, featuring a confrontation between the intelligentsia and the political bureaucracy. The protests were limited in scope, found no popular support, and remained isolated from the concerns of the working people. The fundamental issues of the time, intellectual freedoms and humanist Marxism, were of little direct relevance to the lives of the masses. For that reason, the intellectual movement for the betterment of socialist conditions in Poland found no echo in the activities of the working class. The focus of the latter's interests continued to be economic.

DECEMBER 1970 AND THE NEW POLITICAL STYLE

The economic situation in the second half of the 1960s was worsening extensively in view of the government's failure to respond to management problems, a manifestation of Gomulka's propensity to maintain the existing political equilibrium. The 1968 crisis altered the situation in that criticism from several political quarters forced recognition of the need for changes in the status quo. The party leadership had to respond by showing a new initiative that took the form of an attempt to rationalize economic structures and practices.[10] The innovations were aimed at improving efficiency by altering the wage fund

in favor of white-collar employees and by lowering price subsidies of foodstuffs. The reforms hit hardest at the working
class, who had to spend a large proportion of available income
on necessities and whose wages became less certain. The result
was open defiance in December 1970 by the labor class of the
Baltic coast against the new policies, and the spread of social
discontent throughout the nation.

The workers in the shipyards of Szczecin, Gdansk, and
Gdynia organized strike committees dominated by shop-floor
activists, who were well aware of mismanagement and production
shortcomings. The principal aim of the strikers was to improve
their material and social benefits and to guarantee these gains
by obtaining better access for labor to policymaking in the
workplace.[11] The demands of the strikers thus focused on
issues of economic well-being; insofar as political concerns were
present, they were essentially reflections of the desire to improve
workers' participation in decisions over the work environment
and material conditions. In this regard, the calls for a change
in the functioning of the trade unions were outweighed by the
concern for improvements of wages and consumption. This
concentration on economic issues explains to a large extent why
the December actions by industrial workers were not supported
by other social groups. White-collar employees were, after all,
the beneficiaries of the economic reforms opposed by the working
class. The intelligentsia was more concerned with civil rights
issues and tended to understate the importance of economic
dissatisfaction. In addition, intellectuals and students were
alienated from workers as a consequence of the latter's failure
to act during the March 1968 crisis. As a result the workers
bore the burden of defiance virtually alone, a defiance that
became nonetheless very intense as strikes and riots spread
throughout the country during December and culminated in a
confrontation between the authorities and industrial labor that
saw 45 official deaths and hundreds of injuries.

Faced with the danger of a major, generalized workers'
revolt the ruling elite acted by removing Gomulka from the
leadership of the PUWP and introducing a new team of leaders.
However, what had proved a successful tactic in 1956 to placate
popular discontent was not sufficient in 1970. In the first place,
the issue of national autonomy was no longer as relevant and
could not be used to appeal for the support of the working class.
The Polish October had provided the country with greater
autonomy in pursuing a Polish "road" in the construction of
socialism, as evident by private agriculture and the position
of the Catholic church. The course followed since 1956 could

not be blamed exclusively on the imposition of external constraints. Furthermore, even though such constraints still
existed they could not be brought into the open by the regime
precisely because the Polish government was already operating
within the tolerable limits of autonomy. The Czechoslovak events
of 1968 made clear the boundaries of an independent socialist
course to all communist states within the bloc, and the new
Polish government was not in a position to exploit the autonomy
issue for its own advantage. The resolution of the 1956 crisis
through the nationalist strategy in fact limited the options available in 1970.

Not only was it impossible for Gierek to duplicate the
popular support of the Gomulka of 1956, but it was also difficult
to use a new personalized style of leadership to bring the country
out of the 1970 crisis. Again, the failure of Gomulka to fulfill
the expectations of the nation signified that the people would
no longer give their confidence to the regime based on changes
in leadership. Instead, the regime had to initiate visible policy
reforms addressing the substantive issues of discontent to
terminate popular turmoil. The failure of the new team to introduce policy changes conforming to the demands of the workers
resulted in a new wave of discontent, work stoppages, and
strikes in the first weeks of 1971.[12] The confidence of the
population in its political power came from the ability to affect
personnel changes at the very top and from the visible extension
of workers' movement throughout the country. Faced with the
strong resolve of the working class to hold out for alteration
of the economic program, the Gierek leadership had to give in
on substantive issues in order to end the social crisis. By
February 1971, both the wage reforms and price increases
imposed by the previous administration were revoked. The
confrontation between the working class and the regime culminated
in the victory of the people on specific policy differences.

The primary task of the Gierek government after its accession to power was the containment of disintegration in the social
fabric. While the open defiance of the workers was arrested
through the repeal of unpopular economic reforms, the need to
establish more positive support among the people for the leadership required more extensive and substantive changes. The
strategy of the new team to acquire political legitimacy and end
the crisis-infused social situation was dual in nature, consisting
first of efforts to improve economic growth and achieve social
reconciliation and, on the basis of these policies, consolidate
the political situation and the party's power.

The first half of the 1970s was devoted to the accomplishment of these tasks. Of primary importance was the resolution of economic problems, for the alleviation of social tensions depended to a large extent on fostering the well-being of the population. With that goal in mind, the Gierek leadership embarked on a program of rapid modernization to improve the overall economic conditions and, by the same process, provide the masses with better material benefits.[13] The essence of the strategy was the renovation of the industrial infrastructure through the infusion of new technology and machinery, coupled with a program of extensive wage increases, a freeze on prices, and a commitment to better supplies of consumer goods. Both the modernization of industry and the rise in mass consumption were achieved by turning to the West for economic aid and financing. In the short term at least, this strategy of economic development was indeed successful. By 1974 the standard of living had improved significantly, resulting in greater popular satisfaction and a diffusion of tensions.

The initial period of the Gierek regime was also characterized by an attempt to establish a "new political style," a response to the workers' call for greater involvement in policy deliberations. This program called for a social reconciliation between the people and the authorities through direct contacts between leaders and the masses, consultations between politicians and experts, and a normalization of relations between the state and the church. These efforts, however, took place simultaneously with the regime's drive to consolidate its position within the system. The thrust of this program was to strengthen the interventionist capabilities of the party in all social sectors.[14] The administrative reforms of 1973-75 substantially strengthened the power of the party bureaucrats in society, as well as consolidated power in the central leadership vis-à-vis political cadres in the periphery. The consequence was a growing isolation of the top party leaders from the masses and, once again, misperceptions about the mood of the people.

1975-76: THE NEW POLITICAL ACTIVISM

The gulf between the political leadership and social groups became clearly visible in 1975-76 and culminated once again in a major political crisis. In the first instance, the cause was the ideological offensive launched by the regime to ascertain the leading role of the party during the period of building developed socialism. The effort of the Gierek regime was aimed at demonstrating that the pragmatism of the past five years was not to be confused with the dispersion of political authority or the neglect of socialist transformation. To emphasize this position, the government chose the symbolic but significant act of revising the Polish Constitution. The response to the leadership's offensive was a strong opposition by the church and the intellectual community to the constitutional changes, leading to a major confrontation between the government and elite sectors of society, as well as the formation of a strong public opinion against the judicial reforms.[15] The regime was therefore forced to tone down the proposed changes and compromise with the opponents of the new constitution. Despite this settlement, the amendment process offered an opportunity for dissenting groups to express their dissatisfaction with the new, heavy-handed approach of the Gierek leadership and to resist further encroachments on social autonomy. The episode marked the beginning of an open schism between the intellectual circles and the ruling elite and considerably augmented the social discontent within the country.

The situation worsened further as a result of the government's attempt to introduce changes in the economic sector. Here the leadership's motivation reflected the growing difficulties of the economy and the need to prevent a deterioration of the situation. Given the commitment to political consolidation and centralization, changes in the economy focusing on decentralization measures were not acceptable to the ruling elite. Instead reforms had to take place within the existing structure of management and emphasize cost efficiency and improved productivity. In practice, this meant an end to subsidies of foodstuffs. The implementation of the price increases was announced on June 24, 1976, without any significant attempt to rally public support for the measure. Insofar as consultations on the policy were held, they involved party aktifs who were isolated from mainstream opinions and who tended to provide information sought out by the political center. The consequence is well known; in response to the price increase, strikes and demonstrations occurred in Ursus and Radom, and then spread to other parts of the country.[16] Well aware of the December 1970 course of events, which culminated in a change of leadership, the Gierek team immediately rescinded the price increases. The workers had once again demonstrated their ability to affect the policy preferences of the ruling elite.

Both the constitutional and the economic crises had the effect of eroding much of the credibility and support that the Gierek leadership had attained in the previous five years. The heavy-handed tactics of the government drove a wedge between the political leadership and the intellectual elite and then between the party and the workers. From 1976 on, the level of social tensions increased markedly in Poland and in turn profoundly altered the political reality of the nation.

The situation was further aggravated by the government's attempt, after the immediate June crisis passed, to reassert its commanding position. Arrests, trials, dismissals from work, and other punishment of activists involved in the June events occurred. This time, however, the workers were not left to face the political authority by themselves. The Committee for the Defense of Workers (KOR) was formed in September 1976 by a group of intellectuals for the expressed purpose of helping the mistreated workers and their families. The movement acted as a catalyst for the proliferation of political dissent and the articulation of opposition to the authorities throughout the country. After its successful action on behalf of the workers and the regime's amnesty of arrested strikers, KOR reconstructed its organization as the Committee for Social Self-Defense—KSS "KOR"—to act in the name of the entire society. Other activists in the intellectual community united in movements representing their own concerns and views, giving rise to strong and vocal dissident activities in post-1976 Poland.[17]

The proliferation of intellectual dissent and its linkages to the working class further politicized the working masses. To a large extent, the rise of activism among the labor class was a direct consequence of the successful defiance by workers of government policies in 1970 and 1976. These rebellions created among the workers both an awareness of their power and a consciousness of their interests. The failure of the government to provide laborers with genuine channels for the expression of these interests resulted in a rejection of official trade unions and self-management conferences as vehicles for workers' demands. To remedy the situation, already in 1978, worker activists organized Free Trade Union movements to provide industrial labor with autonomous and representative institutions.[18] A similar trend appeared in the Polish countryside, where peasant self-help societies were created. These organizational efforts demonstrated clearly a determination by the working people to make their interests known.

The growing schism between the population and the political authorities in turn contributed to a more activist role of the Catholic church, already evident at the time of the 1975-76 constitutional debate. At times of turmoil, the church had always acted to help resolve the problems faced by Poland; the

contemporary intensity of social tensions necessitated the intervention of the episcopate to alleviate the problems and conflicts
present in society. It is true that the church's stand in favor
of the workers' right to a decent life and human rights for all
societal sectors was matched by calls for responsibility by the
people to the nation. Nonetheless, in the eyes of the church's
hierarchy, such responsibility could be attained only on the
basis of the regime's recognition of diverse interests and values
in society.[19]

The 1975-76 crises made obvious to various social groups
the futility of pursuing a dialogue with the regime within the
accepted channels of political discourse. The consequence was
the activization of social and political groups outside the party's
rule. To a large extent, the capacity of these interests to step
beyond the existing political boundaries was facilitated by the
fact that for the first time since 1956 a congruence of dissatisfaction emerged among several strata of the population. The
government's tactics of political consolidation created opposition
among intellectuals, workers, peasants, and the church; the
regime's need to back off from its stand to safeguard stability
demonstrated to the people the utility of making their demands
known. From then on the willingness of various public sectors
to organize for the defense of their interests and to articulate
them openly expanded rapidly. These moves were successful
since the authorities' ability to respond had been eroded by
their own previous mismanagement and since discontent reached
not one but several groups simultaneously.

The late 1970s thus witnessed not only a growing dissatisfaction among the major social strata but also an increased
willingness to express their discontent in political action.
While these groups were separated by different policy aims,
they had a common goal in the attempt to extend their autonomy
in the system and provide for the expression of different values
and opinions in society. The congruence of dissatisfaction
among the intellectuals, the bishops, and the workers was
directed at the expansion of civil liberties within the political
system. All were concerned with the introduction of social
justice, tolerance of different beliefs, and freedom of expression.
For that reason, an open discussion of the issues and an increase
in the flow of information became the critical concern for each
group's activities.

The penetration of society by the presentation of alternative
views to the official language was a vital aim of the newly politicized groups. This policy was consequential to the rejection
of a reformist strategy of change, whereby the positive develop-

ment of society was tied to the internal reformation of the political authorities. The 1968 antiintellectual and 1976 constitutional crises had destroyed this approach among large segments of the Marxist and Catholic intelligentsia. Instead, the dissidents turned to a policy seeking change through the combined pressures of society upon the government. Appeals to society and agitation from below replaced appeals to the political authorities for enlightened change. The belief was that the direction of political and economic development could be influenced by open criticism of government failures, by polemics with official views, by protests and pressures on the regime.[20] In this way, society at large was made more aware of the issues at stake and was able to lend its support and strength to the cause of change. The leadership's problems with economic performance and growing social distrust made it especially vulnerable. The state-society relationship was thus altered in favor of social autonomy, creating in turn new opportunities for change.

Faced by increased social and political pressures, the regime's primary concern was to prevent an erosion of its political power. The fear of the Polish leaders was that in conditions of social instability, acquiescence to the demands of the spontaneous political forces or the introduction of major reforms in the system would only aggravate the situation.[21] The example of Czechoslovakia in 1968 undoubtedly played a significant role here, for the absorption of reformist views into the official system had led to a rapid disintegration of control by the party. During the late 1970s, the Polish leaders preferred to maintain a firm line between official and reformist policies to avoid such a situation.

This attitude characterized the refusal to introduce major economic reforms, despite the deterioration of economic conditions in the last four years. The government feared that decentralization measures were a threat to the political status quo, especially in the precarious social situation of the late 1970s. For that reason, the commitment to the existing economic structures and practices remained entrenched. The inability of the political authorities to impose a solution by increasing prices and its unwillingness to restructure the management system resulted in a crisis situation in the economy. The negative growth rate for 1979 and the 95 percent service debt ratio to repay loans from the West testified to the severity of the situation and forced the leadership into action.

1980: THE ROAD TO SOLIDARITY

Readjustments in the material sphere became pressing by 1980. The government had to lower reliance on Western goods, improve production efficiency, and end the demand spiral by alleviating price subsidies and curtailing wage increases. The problem with such a strategy of economic rationalization was that it was bound to have a negative effect on the population's standard of living. The government, based on the 1970 and 1976 experiences, was well aware that such economic measures could result in major disruptions that could further damage the already tense and fragile situation. The regime thus proceeded with great caution, this time seeking to inform the public about the needs for economic changes.

The process involved an austerity and unity campaign launched in conjunction with the Eighth Party Congress in February 1980.[22] The goal of the leadership was to make the people cognizant of the need to absorb economic setbacks in the near future and to lower their material expectations. While austerity was depicted as the immediate future, the solution to these difficult conditions was pictured as depending on the unity of the nation and cooperation among all groups. Apparently, the government's hope was that appeals to patriotic duty would bring forth the people's acceptance of the economic changes. To prevent a repetition of the violent outbreaks of December 1970 and June 1976, a propaganda campaign was waged in the first months of 1980. By the second half of 1980, the government thought it was ready to take the necessary steps to implement the economic rationalization plan. On July 1, it announced price increases directed at meat products.

The regime's hopes for a peaceful transition to a new economic order were quickly dashed, as the workers openly resisted the price increases by going on strike. From July 1 on workers in several factories throughout the country walked out from their jobs and demanded a rise in wages to compensate for the higher prices. The movement of work stoppage spread rapidly to other enterprises during the coming weeks, and the government was ultimately faced with an open defiance aimed at altering not only the economic policies but also the political distribution of power.[23] In assuming this stand, Polish workers demonstrated that they had learned from the prior actions against the political authorities, and now applied this knowledge to challenge the position of the regime.

Without doubt the crisis of 1980 had its roots in the events of the past decade. Primary among the causes of discontent was the deterioration in the economic well-being of the population, marked by a downturn in consumer satisfaction during the post-1975 period.[24] In addition inequalities in social consumption became ever more visible during this time, contributing to a widening gap between a privileged elite and the working people. The material hardships and the decline in mobility opportunities for the labor class in turn engendered social frustration expressed through growing dissatisfaction with the socioeconomic policies of the government. These feelings were accentuated by the fact that the Polish working class was relatively young and educated, but lacked the recourse to participate meaningfully in enterprise affairs. As a result labor activism outside the official system increased, and informal workers' committees acted to obtain better material and working conditions. All of the above factors provided the working class with the causes and the means to demonstrate its discontent in the summer of 1980.

However, the crisis was not formed solely by the conditions prevailing at the turn of the decade. To a large extent, the 1980 manifestation of workers' dissatisfaction was also influenced by the experience of the labor class in the prior societal outbursts, as well as by the resolutions and outcomes of the 1956, 1970, and 1976 crises. The latter events functioned as a learning experience; the workers applied their new knowledge, affecting the form, content, and course of the 1980 crisis.

Previous outbreaks of labor unrest were primarily actions manifested through street demonstrations and violent clashes directed at the symbols of the party's authority. In these circumstances the demonstration of workers' power, although quite evident, was diffuse and momentary. Moreover, this form of workers' discontent was subject to direct opposition and suppression by the authorities, as shown by the events of December 1970. Similarly, outbursts of violence in June 1976 made the working class vulnerable to accusations of antisocial behavior and to regime reprisals aimed at labor activists. The striking fact about the events of 1980 is that spontaneous, on the street worker outbursts did not take place. Instead, the contemporary workers' movement engaged in orderly, organized sit-in strikes, occupied the factories, arrested economic production, and offered the workers greater protection from counteractions by the government. Apparently the working class had become cognizant of the vulnerability of open defiance outside the workplace, and instead engaged in a more effective form of resistance to governmental policies.

The ability to devise such a course of action in the summer of 1980 was directly related to the attempts in the late 1970s to organize the working class in the defense of its interests and to the links that had been formed during that period between the workers and the intellectual community. The activities of the committees to create free unions and the information on blue-collar issues provided by the independent publication Robotnik effectively contributed to the rise of awareness on the part of the labor class and created the preconditions necessary to infuse greater discipline within the workers' movement. In this regard, the relationship that developed between worker activists and dissident intellectuals in the aftermath of the latter's intervention on behalf of the persecuted strikers of June 1976 played a vital role. [25] In the first place, the labor class could draw on the experience and skills of the intelligentsia to articulate its views for economic and social change. Second, the workers were also able to use the information networks of the dissident organizations to make their demands known. At no time was this more visible than during the initial phase of the 1980 strikes, when KOR helped to inform the nation and the world about the activities of the striking workers. The dissemination of this information helped to rally the support of other social groups to the labor class, thereby strengthening the movement.

The disciplined and organized form of the workers' action also had an impact on the content of the demands presented by the labor class. The very organization of the sit-in strike signified that workers were interacting constantly, were able to engage in discussion of the issues, and. were exposed to new ideas. The net result of the new activism was not only that workers became more cognizant of their unity and strength, but also that the situation became increasingly politicized. The economic problems of the nation became linked to the political structures and policies of the regime, so that the resolution of the economic grievances of the population became tied directly to an alteration of the political conditions. This tendency to move beyond exclusive economic concerns was reinforced by the experience of former clashes between workers and the government.

The working class had been well aware of its ability to alter policies through its intervention in national affairs, especially of its ability to exercise a veto power in 1970 and 1976. However, while the overt manifestation of workers' discontent succeeded in stopping announced policies and even changing the leadership of the party, the impact of the workers' action was essentially "negative" for it was not extended to influence the future content of the regime's program. This afforded the government with the opportunity to change the most visible aspect of its program (i.e., price increases) but make only vague promises of future changes. The long-term consequence was the continuance of prior problems and policies, as well as the erosion of workers' gains through hidden inflation, substitution of goods, and material shortages. Most important was the inability of the population to seek redress from the worsening conditions short of new outbreaks of workers' discontent, for no autonomous organization existed to represent and articulate workers' interests. The workers' councils formed in 1956 were absorbed within the factory management system, and the 1970 strike committees and 1976 activists each were rapidly suppressed.

The awareness by the working class that its previous intervention did not lead to substantial improvements had two primary consequences in the summer of 1980. In the first instance, the linkage between the satisfaction of economic demands and political changes was made explicit. The fulfillment of material needs and the improvement of economic conditions was viewed as dependent on the acquisition of political leverage by the workers.[26] In practice, this signified the creation of workers' organizational strength independent of the party and the state, and gave rise to demands aimed at institutionalizing workers' power. The attainment of this goal was tied to a second aspect of the workers' actions: the articulation of specific demands for change in the economic, social, and political spheres and a timetable for the implementation of the changes. The history of vague promises, as well as the politicization ensuing from the disciplined sit-in strikes, culminated in a concretization of the 1980 crisis. A list of specific economic and political demands, formulated by the shipyard workers of the Baltic coast, became the most visible act in the new manifestation of workers' discontent.[27]

In the face of these changes in the nature of the working class movement, the options of the Polish government became much more limited. Prior failures to carry out reforms and improve the situation meant that in 1980 the regime could not appease the workers solely by promises of future improvements or changes in the political leadership. Instead the return to work of blue-collar labor was contingent on the satisfaction of the program outlined by the striking workers. These demands were not only economic in nature but also addressed important sociopolitical issues, including the establishment of independent trade unions, the recognition of the right to strike, better access to the mass media, and the implementation of an economic reform and a new censorship law. Defying the initial attempts by the government to deal with the striking workers in separate negotiations, and thereby divide the labor movement, the strikers forced the regime's recognition of an Interfactory Strike Committee (MKS) in Gdansk to represent the workers in negotiations with the political authorities.[28] Discussion between the two sides covered all the points presented by the workers, including both the economic and sociopolitical issues. The final outcome of the negotiations, the accords of August 31, 1980, was a victory for the working class, which won the rights to form independent trade unions and to strike. The workers also extracted specific obligations from the government on a variety of issues, ranging from wage reforms to the relaxation of censorship.

THE 1980-81 RENEWAL

The signing of the August 31 agreement did not, however, resolve the conflict between the industrial workers and the political establishment. On the contrary, from the very beginning, the new leadership of Stanislaw Kania, who had become First Secretary of the PUWP on September 6, 1980, sought to limit the capacity of the workers and other social groups to challenge the authority of the state. The strategy adopted by the regime was to recognize the Gdansk agreements as the manifestation of a new state-society relationship, but to assure the party's dominance in this new development.

The articulation of an official program of renewal by the political leadership was therefore an attempt to limit the process of sociopolitical change in Poland.[29] This concept of renewal recognized the mistakes of the past and the need for changes as steps necessary for improving the condition of Poland. Precisely because the regime had recognized this fact and was committed to socioeconomic reforms, the leadership argued that it was in a position to direct the program of change. The aim was to safeguard the leading role of the party and assure its position as the instrument of social, economic, and political change. Renewal, according to this definition, was a process of social adjustment articulated and implemented from above by the regime. Most important, this meant the maintenance of the PUWP's supervision over all social activities in the country, so as to prevent autonomous forces from impinging on the party's leading position.

The official view of renewal was at odds with the position of Solidarity leaders and their advisors, who looked upon the post-August process of change as the culmination of workers' and other groups' involvement in societal issues. The new activism of the population was to be institutionalized through the self-organization of workers, peasants, students, and professionals into autonomous associations, facilitating the representation of mass interests in policymaking. The Gdansk accords were perceived in this context as a new social contract between the workers and the government that recognized the existence of independent social organizations. Furthermore, the new organizations would act on behalf of the Polish people and their interests independent of the regime's controls.

The concept of renewal advanced by Solidarity, however, did not seek to ignore the reality of political power in Poland. On the contrary, with the articulation of the self-limiting revolution the movement explicitly recognized the geopolitical position of the country and the limits Soviet concerns imposed on the social transformation of Poland. Solidarity thus rejected the notion of seeking political power alongside the Communist Party, and instead restricted its aims to influence the course of post-August social and economic development.[30] In this capacity, the movement's role was to express society's will vis-à-vis the party and act as a constraining force on the political authorities. The fulfillment of this task by Solidarity required the institutionalization of the social compact between the regime and the people and the introduction of regularized procedures for the interaction between the autonomous social organizations and the party-state apparatus.

From the very beginning, however, the party leadership adopted a containment policy toward the self-organization of Polish social groups to prevent the increased involvement of citizens in policy.[31] The regime's strategy in the months following the August agreement was to place continuous obstacles in the path of Solidarity and the implementation of the summer accords. Delays and vacillations in negotiations as well as intimidation against organizing efforts of the population were characteristic of the authorities' activities. The first crisis came in October 1980, when the regime unilaterally inserted "the leading role of the party" phrase in Solidarity's bylaws in order to officially subordinate the union to the power of the communist organization. The refusal of Solidarity to accept this limitation on its activities precipitated a general warning strike that forced the leadership to back down and accept a compromise whereby the party's leading role was recognized only in an appendix to Solidarity's charter.

The incident over the registration of Solidarity was symbolic of the leadership's attitude to the workers' movement. At each step in the process of change, the communist organization sought to contain the popular forces and reassert its political power. The most effective weapon at the disposal of the regime appeared to be delay, and as a result most of the 21 points of agreement negotiated at Gdansk remained unfulfilled. After another confrontation between the government and the trade union, free Saturdays were finally provided in January 1981. Progress on other issues, including access to the media and reform of the economy, as well as questions raised by other groups, such as the registration of a Rural Solidarity or an educational reform law, remained stalled and involved renewed confrontations between the political authorities and social groups. It became increasingly clear that the party leadership was resistant to the ongoing pluralization of society.

Despite the official attempt to limit the renewal process to terms acceptable to the ruling elite, the Solidarity movement continued to attract broad popular support that endangered to an unprecedented degree the existing system of power. The union succeeded in attracting over 10 million members, the vast majority of the Polish work force—including rank and file members of the PUWP. Following the successful example of Solidarnosc, peasants, students, and intellectuals organized to demand further changes.

The government's failure to regularize the access of social groups to policy influence and to provide solutions to substantive problems markedly increased the level of tension in Polish society in the winter of 1980-81. Faced with a government that had in effect gone on strike, Solidarity was forced to prod the political authorities into action. The only means at the disposal of the trade union were work stoppages, which were increasingly used to force negotiations with the government and assure the satisfaction of society's demands. The strike emerged as a weapon arousing governmental response, and, under the circumstances, workers' actions proliferated. The consequence was a cycle of conflicts between the workers' movement and the government.

In view of the stalemate between the state and society and the popular support for Solidarity, the party itself could not remain immune to the forces of change. Increasingly, throughout the winter and spring of 1980-81, the membership of the PUWP advocated significant innovations within the communist organization as a way of forcing the political leadership into action. The movement for "horizontal linkages" was a grass roots initiative against the PUWP apparatus that sought to transform the party's methods of operation.[32] To achieve that end, the horizontal movement advocated the creation of institutional links among the primary party organizations that would bypass the controlling mechanisms of the political center. The movement gained momentum in the period preceding the gathering of the PUWP Congress, as advocates of horizontal linkages attempted to affect more directly the selection of delegates and the policy discussions.

Strong opposition to these attempts at democratization of party life occurred at the mid-level of the PUWP. The party apparatus perceived, quite correctly, the proposals for horizontal linkages as a direct attack on its position in the communist organization. The party bureaucracy therefore rallied in defense of the status quo to maintain its political power and economic privileges. The opposition to change was demonstrated not only by bureaucratic resistance to any social or economic innovation, but also by the formation of party groups advocating a strongly orthodox method of political rule in the party and society.

Under these circumstances the political leadership itself became increasingly divided over how to retain the cohesion of the PUWP and assure its leading position in society. In turn, the growing divisions within the party organization and the political leadership created further difficulties in the resolution of the crisis. By the spring of 1981, the PUWP had ceased to be a cohesive force capable of articulating, much less of implementing, a program designed to solve the acute economic and social problems. The inability of the regime to respond to the continuing crisis further alarmed the Soviet leadership, which increased its pressures on their Polish counterparts. Through a mass media campaign and troop maneuvers the Soviets attempted to shift the PUWP to a more hard-line position. When these efforts failed, the Communist Party of the Soviet Union (CPSU) sent a letter on June 5, 1981 to the Central Committee of the Polish party denouncing Kania's methods of leadership and his inability to deal with the social unrest.[33] The intent of the Soviet pressures was to prevent the PUWP Congress from turning into a national forum for the horizontal movement that would culminate in the approval of a reformist course for the party. Indeed there was a general feeling of anticipation among the Polish population that the party congress would break the impasse existing in Poland and commit the leadership to a genuine reconciliation with society. Expectations ran high as well for major policy innovations that would contribute to a breakthrough of the economic and social stalemate.

The Ninth Extraordinary PUWP Congress met on July 14-22, 1981.[34] The reality of the congress proved to be different from the population's hopes and demonstrated that the pressures against major reforms and innovations had a positive effect. It is true that, on the surface at least, the congressional debate and electoral results seemed to indicate a democratization of the party. Nonetheless, this view had to be tempered by the lack of any other significant changes in the communist organization and its political course. Particularly telling was the congress' failure to address in any meaningful way substantive policy issues. The leadership of the party did not introduce the necessary economic reforms to meet the continuing decline in productivity and the standard of living, nor did it provide for new social policies aimed at invigorating the renewal process. The lack of progress on these critical substantive issues of economic reform and social reconciliation dashed the hopes of society for a meaningful solution to the country's problems. Instead the lack of policy innovations at the PUWP Congress served to confirm the population's perception that the party was committed to a renewal beset by deliberate delays and open to sabotage by opponents of the Gdansk agreements.

From that moment on, the stalemate between the party and society became more entrenched and a rapid deterioration in the situation occurred in the fall of 1981. With the growing realization that the regime was unable and incapable of addressing the major national problems, society itself took on greater initiatives. The activism of the grass root elements in Solidarity and other social groups increased, as hunger marches and factory and university strikes proliferated.

These actions, however, were essentially negative in nature and contributed to the instability and crisis atmosphere of the country. In the face of governmental intransigence, Solidarity needed more positive means of affecting the course of socio-economic development. Above all, a regularized mechanism enabling the social movement to initiate policy and maintain control over its execution was necessary. To fulfill that need the Solidarity trade union launched a comprehensive program of enterprise self-management. In that course, the leadership of Solidarity responded to earlier ad hoc, grass root initiatives within the work force that presented self-management as a solution to the continuing chaos of the sociopolitical order. The system favored by the trade union was based on a broad definition of self-management, providing social enterprises with considerable productive, distributive, and social tasks.[35] Among other features the program called for factory governance by

workers' councils and the selection of enterprise directors by
the work force—bypassing the nomenklatura system of appointments controlled by the party.

The self-management stance of Solidarity had to be viewed
as an effort to provide a new framework for the resolution of
the state-society impasse. The willingness to take on a more
responsible role in economic management and social governance
was testimony to the acute frustration, prevalent within the
ranks of Solidarity, with the regime's inaction. At the same
time, the self-management proposal was an expression of the
need to provide a workable alternative to the socioeconomic and
political stagnation befalling the country. The frustration was
clearly evident at the first session of the Solidarity congress,
held on September 5-10, 1981. The gathering witnessed demands for a referendum on the self-management issue and produced a politically sensitive "Letter to the Working People of
Eastern Europe" as an expression of the Polish workers' struggle
to improve the life of all working people. The second session
of Solidarity, on September 26-October 7, went beyond the
mood of defiance to approve a program concerned primarily
with the reconstruction of the Polish economy through a mobilizing
effort of the entire society. [36] While depicting the self-management
scheme as the only viable solution, the resolution also appealed
for a genuine dialogue with the political authorities and called
for an anticrisis agreement between Solidarity and the government.

The advocacy of a self-management system by the trade
union, however, was perceived by the political leadership as a
further attempt to limit the prerogatives of the party's leading
role in society. The response of the PUWP was to consolidate
its position toward society. From September on, the leadership's policies became bolder as the PUWP took a firm stand in
negotiations with Solidarity and resisted social pressures. The
regime in fact adopted a more offensive political stand, turning
to a veritable mass media blitz to denounce counterrevolutionary
activities, criticize openly the policies advocated by Solidarity,
calling for law and order, and even talking about a crackdown. [37]
The new hardening of the party's policies was confirmed by the
replacement of Stanislaw Kania as first secretary of the PUWP
by the prime minister, General Jaruzelski. The October 18,
1981 Central Committee meeting that approved the change in
leadership made clear in its deliberations and resolution the
party's intent to prevent a further erosion of its power by
focusing the blame for the crisis on Solidarity and demanding
a tougher position by the PUWP's leadership. In fact, the intent

was to replace what was generally perceived as weak leadership by a strong man capable of exercising more effective control over the party and society.

Despite the new firmness of the regime, the social discontent was too deep and the party too weak to enable the new leadership to restore the leading role of the party and contain the social forces of change, at least not without the use of force. Ultimately indeed the regime had to have recourse to coercion, as it put an end to the Polish renewal on the night of December 13, 1981.[38] The imposition of a state of war on the Polish people by its government, by means of a police and military action, nonetheless did not restore stability to Polish society. On the contrary, the martial law actions revealed the extent of the gap between the state and society—a gap that the Polish renewal was not only incapable of closing but indeed widened.

The dynamics of the interaction between the political authorities and Solidarity during the sixteen months between August 1980 and December 1981 were ultimately responsible for the failure of the Polish renewal. From the very beginning, the government's search for a solution to the 1980 social discord was influenced by the course of prior state-society conflicts and their resolution. The regime was thus forced to embark on a strategy of crisis management that culminated in the intensification of the conflicts between the state and the social movement. The political leadership never adhered to the notion of a social contract between the state and society, for it did not trust the self-limiting aspects of Solidarity. The movement was instead perceived as a threat to the power of the party-state apparatus, which refused to cooperate in a meaningful way with the new social movement. In turn, this made it impossible for Solidarity to keep within the self-defined limits of social action. Faced with the government's failure to adhere to its side of the agreement, Solidarity had to go beyond the concept of the self-limiting revolution and adopt a strategy providing for a more direct role in policy making.

CONCLUSION

Throughout the history of socialist Poland major sectors of society rejected the regime's claim to exclusive political power. Lacking proper institutional channels to voice their discontent, however, social forces had to express their frustrations in overt challenges to the authority of the Communist Party. Time and time again, this led to open political crises in October 1956, March 1968, December 1970, June 1976, and August 1980. In these instances, society challenged the course of socialist construction in Poland. In response, the political authorities promised to work in a new political style and revise the country's socioeconomic and political development.

The evolution of the crises and the methods for their resolution took on a sequential pattern, with each conflict affecting the subsequent social upheaval. This trend was dictated by the government's failure to live up to its promises of change, for in each societal breakdown the regime reverted to the old style of political rule after the passing of the crisis. Faced with such a pattern of intransigence, society learned to demand specific alterations in the socioeconomic and political program rather than to seek general and undefined changes. In turn, regime options for the termination of crises became more limited with each upheaval, for the government had to respond to specific demands through substantive reforms rather than long-term, unclear intentions.

The 1980 crisis marked an end of the use by the regime of socialist imagery and promises for future improvement to solve the conflict between the state and society. Instead a new form of confrontation, over concrete economic, social, and political programs, created a new political reality in Poland. The impetus for this change was the fact that for the first time since 1956 a major current of dissatisfaction swept society. This discontent had been fostered in the 1970s by the willingness of social groups to present demands outside accepted channels of political expression. What had previously been private frustrations and aspirations emerged into the open, and criticisms of the regime became a new standard in the politics of Poland by the late 1970s. The consequence was an expansion in the scope of the 1980 crisis, represented by the politicization of diverse social groups.

This situation in turn limited the political capacities of the government. Unlike the Polish October, there were no obvious programs or leadership alternatives. Recourse to a nationalistic solution was very limited, for no major shift in the position of Poland within the socialist bloc was possible. Similarly, innovative social and economic policies could not be undertaken without a restructuring of the system—a step that the party organization and its leadership found unacceptable (even if it were amenable, given the external pressures). Changes in political leadership also proved inadequate for the resolution of the tension. The nation was well aware of the prior violations of the social trust by leaders who had promised to rule in a new political style. The consequence has been the formalization of the impasse between the political authority and society. In the present situation, neither side is capable of fully imposing its understanding of the country's needs and policy solutions on the entire system. The price of this condition is the perpetuation of social and political tensions.

ACKNOWLEDGMENTS

I would like to thank Jean Robinson, Myron Rush, and Barbara Hicks for comments and suggestions on earlier drafts of this chapter.

NOTES

1. M. K. Dziewanowski, The Communist Party of Poland, 2nd ed (Cambridge, Mass.: Harvard University Press, 1976), pp. 108-222; Jan B. de Weydenthal, The Communists of Poland (Stanford: Hoover Institution, 1978), pp. 53-56; Zbigniew Brzezinski, The Soviet Bloc (Cambridge, Mass.: Harvard University Press, 1967), pp. 51-64, 96-97.

2. For the difference in the approaches, see the discussion at the Central Committee plenum of the Polish Workers' Party (PPR) on August 31-September 3, 1948, in Nowe Drogi 2, September-October 1948.

3. Evaluation of the Stalinist period, from different viewpoints, can be obtained from the July and October 1956 Central Committee plenums, Nowe Drogi 10 (July-September 1956) and Trybuna Ludu, October 21, 1956 and October 22, 1956.

4. Adam Bromke, Poland's Politics: Idealism vs. Realism (Cambridge, Mass.: Harvard University Press, 1967), pp. 86-103.

5. Edmund Makowski, ed., Wydrzenia Czerwcowe w Poznaniu 1956 (Poznan: UAM, 1981).

6. de Weydenthal, The Communists, Chap. 6.

7. Adam Michnik, "The New Evolutionism," Survey 22 (Summer/Autumn 1976):167-169. See also the analyses by Adam Bromke, Idealism a Realism (Chicago: Polonia, 1977); Marek Tarniewski, Evolucia czy Rewolucja (Paris: Instytut Literacki, 1975); Jack Bielasiak, "Introduction" to Poland Today (Armouk, N.Y.: M. E. Sharpe, 1981), pp. vii-xxiv.

8. See the discussion and documents in Peter Raina, Political Opposition in Poland 1954-1977 (London: Poets and Painters Press, 1978), Chap. 5.

9. Michnik, "The New Evolutionism," pp. 169-174; Adam Bromke, "Poland's Idealism and Realism in Retrospect," Canadian Slavonic Papers 31 (March 1979):76-91; Stefan Kisielewski, "O podwojnym mysleniu i dzialaniu," Kultura 3 (March 1980): 102-106.

10. A. Ross Johnson, "Polish Perspectives, Past and Present," Problems of Communism 20 (July-August 1971):60-66; Jan B. de Weydenthal, "The Workers' Dilemma of Polish Politics: A Case Study," East European Quarterly 13 (1979):102-104.

11. Rewolta Szczecinska i jej Znaczenie (Paris: Instytut Literacki, 1971).

12. Poznan 1956-Grudzien 1970 (Paris: Instytut Literacki, 1971), pp. 19-66.

13. Adam Bromke, "Poland under Gierek: A New Political Style," Problems of Communism 21 (September-October 1971): 20-22; Zbigniew M. Fallenbuchl, "The Polish Economy in the 1970s," in U.S. Congress, Joint Economic Committee, East European Economies Post-Helsinki (Washington: GPO, 1977), pp. 816-846. For the rapid rise in wages, for example, see Mieczyslaw Kabaj, "Efektywnosc wzrostu plac," Nowe Drogi 2 (February 1980):128-142.

14. Bromke, "Poland under Gierek," pp. 7-14; Jack Bielasiak, "Party Leadership and Mass Participation in Developed Socialism," in Developed Socialism, Jim Seroka and Maurice Simon, eds. (Boulder, Colo.: Westview, 1983), pp. 121-153; Adam Lopatka and Zbyslaw Rykowski, eds., Formy Panstwa Socjalistycznego (Wroclaw: Ossolinskich, 1977).

15. Dissent in Poland 1976-77 (London: Association of Polish Students and Graduates in Exile, 1977), pp. 11-24; Raina, Political Opposition, pp. 210-218.

16. Dissent in Poland, pp. 50-78; KOR, Wypadki Czerwocowe i Dialalnosc KOR (London: Aneks, 1977).

17. A comprehensive documentation of KOR activities can be found in Ruch Oporu (Paris: Instytut Literacki, 1977); Dissent in Poland, pp. 79-146. For surveys of dissent in Poland, see Adam Bromke, "The Opposition in Poland," Problems of Communism 27 (September-October 1978):37-51; Raina, Political Opposition, pp. 119-344; Joanna M. Preibisz, ed., Polish Dissident Publications (New York: Praeger, 1982).

18. Jack Bielasiak, "Workers and Mass Participation in 'Socialist Democracy'," pp. 88-107, and Jan B. de Weydenthal, "Poland: Workers and Politics," pp. 108-167, both in Blue Collar

Workers in Eastern Europe, Jan F. Triska and Charles Gati, eds. (London: George Allen and Unwin, 1981). For declarations of the free trade union movement see "Polish Documents: The Strike Movement" in Adrian Karatnycky, Alexander J. Motyl, and Adolph Sturmthal, Workers' Rights, East and West (New Brunswick: Transaction Books, 1980), pp. 111-133.

19. Adam Michnik, Kosciol, Lewica, Dialog (Paris: Instytut Literacki, 1977); Stanislaw Markiewiez, Panstwo i Kosciol w Polsce Ludowej (Warsaw: Ludowa Spoldzielnia Wydawnicza, 1981); Ruch Oporu, pp. 113-152; Dissent in Poland, pp. 147-164.

20. Michnik, "The New Evolutionism"; Bromke, "Poland's Idealism"; Bielasiak "Introduction"; and the statements in Ruch Oporu; Dissent in Poland; and Raina, Political Opposition, pp. 229-ff.

21. George Blazynski, Flashpoint Point (New York: Pergamon Press, 1979), pp. 308-356; the discussion in "Uwagi a Sytuaci Gospodarczej Kraju," Aneks 20 (1979):10-84.

22. See the reports presented to the Eighth Congress of the PUWP, Trybuna Ludu, February 8, 12, 13, and 14, 1980.

23. August 1980: The Strikes in Poland (Munich: Radio Free Europe Research, 1980).

24. Zbigniew M. Fallenbuchl, "The Polish Economy at the Beginning of the 1980's," in U.S. Congress, Joint Economic Committee, East European Economic Assessment (Washington, D.C., GPO, 1981), pp. 33-71; Jack Bielasiak, "Inequalities and Politicization of the Polish Working Class" in Communism and the Politics of Inequalities, Daniel N. Nelson, ed. (Lexington, Mass.: Lexington Books, 1983), pp. 221-247.

25. For an account of this relationship in the shipyards, see Jadwiga Staniszkis, "The Evolution of Forms of Working-Class Protest in Poland: Sociological Reflections on the Gdansk-Szczecin Case, August 1980," Soviet Studies 33 (April 1981): 204-231.

26. August 1980: The Strikes in Poland, pp. 47-98.

27. For the list of demands, see the New York Times, August 29, 1981. A complete documentation of the agreements between the strikers and the Polish government is contained in Protokoly Porozumien Gdansk, Szczecin, Jastrzebie (Warsaw: KAW, 1980).

28. August 1980: The Strikes in Poland, pp. 77-86; "Wolny ruch zawodowy w Polsce," Kultura 4 (April 1981):99-103.

29. See, for example, the address of First Secretary Stanislaw Kania at the Sixth Plenum of the PUWP Central Committee, Trybuna Ludu, October 5, 1980. Also the discussion with Stefan Olszowski, Trybuna Ludu, February 27, 1981.

30. Jadwiga Staniszkis, "Samoograniczajaca Sie Rewolucja," Kultura (Warsaw, March 22, 1981); "Polish Peaceful Revolution: An Anatomy of Polarization," Journal of Peach Research 19 (1982):181-195; Halina Bortnowska, "The Dialectics of Solidarity," Cross Currents 31 (Fall 1981):334-342; Grazyna Pomian, Polska 'Solidarnosci' (Paris: Instytut Literacki, 1982).

31. See the report of Tadeusz Grabski to the Eighth Plenum of the PUWP Central Committee, as well as the discussion at the meeting, Trybuna Ludu, February 10, 1981.

32. M. Ksiezarczyk, "Forum Porozumienia Partyjnego w Toruniu," Zycie Warszawy, April 16, 1981; and Lech Witkowski, "Partia: Zjednoczenie w Dzialaniu," Polityka, February 7, 1981.

33. For the text of the Soviet letter, see Trybuna Ludu, June 11, 1981. For a discussion of Soviet concerns, see Seweryn Bialer, "Poland and the Soviet Imperium," Foreign Affairs 59 (1980):522-539.

34. "Dziewiaty Nadzwyczajny," Zycie Partii 8 (1981):3-23; reports on the deliberations in Trybuna Ludu, July 15, 16, 17, 18-19, and 20, 1981.

35. Siec Wiodacych Zakladow Pracy, "Dokumenty i Opracowania," NTO 8 (July 1981):67-78; and the discussions, "O Samorzadzie Bez Nerwos," Zycie Warszawy, July 23, 1981; and "Samorzadna Rzeczypospolita" Tygodnik Solidarnosc, October 30, 1981.

36. "I Krajowy Zjazd Delegatow," Tygodnik Solidarnosc, September 11, September 18, October 2, and October 9, 1981; and "Program NSZZ "Solidarnosc," Tygodnik Solidarnosc, October 16, 1981.

37. Andrew Arato, "Empire vs. Civil Society: Poland 1981-82," Telos 50 (Winter 1981-82):19-48.

38. "Proklamacja Wojskowej Rady Ocalenia Narodowego," Zolnierz Wolnosci, December 14, 1981.

2.

The Polish Crisis:
An Economic Overview

David M. Kemme

The current political and economic crises have deep roots.
The failure of the Gierek development strategy and the retreat
from economic reform in the 1970s are simply echoes of earlier
failure and retreat. The establishment of free trade unions
and the strikes of 1980-81 were certainly not the cause of the
economic crisis but a reaction of the public to the crisis and
the government and party's inability to alleviate it. The economic system itself—overly centralized and bureaucratic—along
with the generally poor economic policy decisions made in the
mid-1970s must be considered the primary causes. The traditional development strategy of the Soviet-type centrally planned
economy, emphasizing development of heavy industry (predominately capital and energy intensive industries), neglecting
agriculture, the consumer goods sector and services, contributed
greatly to the structural imbalances that were alleviated in the
past only via foreign trade. The failure to develop strong
export markets to finance these necessary imports lies at the
foundation of the severe balance of payments problem today.
And these foreign trade constraints prevent the Polish authorities
from ameliorating popular discontent via short run increases in
consumer goods, in part imported, which traditionally have
shadowed a change in political leadership. In this examination
of the Polish economic crisis, first a very general economic
history of the postwar period of industrialization till 1970 is
presented. A more detailed analysis of the crisis of the 1970s
prior to the declaration of martial law is then presented, and
the last section offers an overview of the current, postmartial
law, period and prognosis.

INDUSTRIALIZATION AND EXTENSIVE DEVELOPMENT

The Polish economy, devastated during World War II, underwent a period of reconstruction until 1949. The three-year plan for 1947 to 1949 was more a forecast of production, given the existing capacities, than an actual plan. The primary goals were to increase the standard of living above the prewar level and strengthen state control. This was achieved through three measures: nationalization of most industry enabled the direct transfer of resources to key branches of production to take place and brought about a more rapid start-up of production in those branches; realignment of the Polish borders brought Western territories from Germany, which had a more technologically advanced industrial base and agricultural territory with a highly developed infrastructure, in exchange for less developed agricultural territory ceded to the Soviet Union; and extensive use of resources—increasing employment and utilizing industrial capacity that was idle during the interwar period.

The six-year plan from 1950 to 1955 assumed an imperative or command nature that the three-year plan did not. At this time national plans were drawn up using material balances and balances of equipment and plant capacities. The central planning board used prices only to facilitate control of enterprise management, and they did not necessarily reflect relative scarcities. The plan itself appeared overly optimistic and only in one area, the growth of industrial output, were planned aggregate targets achieved. However, the extensive development pattern that dominates the Polish economy yet today was firmly implanted.

The evaluation of the plan and its results is difficult since plan targets often changed or were extremely vague and prices used in calculations had little or no meaning. Not only did prices cause difficulty in evaluating plan fulfillment but they were also the source of many allocation problems. Many plants and entire branches of industry were unprofitable, but this was concealed by distorted prices. By early 1953 Polish economists began to realize the potential of prices as a means of influencing the production decisions of enterprises and improving the allocation of investment goods.[1] The economy was undergoing a rapid rate of industrialization, and economic growth was quite high as a result of the classical, Stalinist, extensive development strategy, which emphasized rapid rates of growth of factor inputs. However, the glaring inefficiency of Polish firms at the microeconomic level and the misallocation of investment resources brought about the discussion of economic reforms.

The debate on economic reforms was intense from 1955 to 1957 as information on the growth of real wages, estimated at an average of only 4 percent for the entire six-year-plan period, was particularly disturbing to the central planners.[2] Further, riots broke out in June 1956 in Poznan and brought much attention to the shortcomings of the economic and political system.[3] Shortly afterward a majority of the Politburo decided to continue a policy of democratization and the Polish United Workers' Party (PUWP) Central Committee approved a program of political and economic reforms. These reforms, initially scheduled to be in effect for the first Five-Year Plan (FYP), 1956-1960, included both price reform as well as decentralization. The number of centrally rationed inputs was decreased and the compilation of material balances was decentralized, as economic ministries, industrial associations, and supply organizations compiled their own balances independently of the central planning board.[4] These systemic changes were not, however, sufficient to improve the efficiency of the economic system.

The five-year plan itself was one of transition, completing the first wave of investment begun in the six-year plan and, in 1958-59, beginning a new investment effort in anticipation of the second five-year plan. The initial period, 1956-57, was marked by growth in personal income and agricultural production. Consumption accounted for nearly 80 percent of national income (consumption also accounted for 78 percent of the increase in national income during 1956-57). However, the share of consumption declined continuously after 1956. Much of the increase in agricultural output may be attributed to the reform of the government's agricultural policy. The collectivization drive had reached its peak in 1955, with only 8 percent of total agricultural output being produced by collectives. In 1956 the Polish government returned to a policy favoring private agriculture and disbanding the collective. The positive benefits of a return to private agriculture were offset, however, as implementation of reform policies in other areas slowed and investment allotted to agriculture decreased.

The reform movement had begun to lose momentum by 1957-58 and the reforms that were implemented were only partially successful. First, the 1956 realignment of prices, which provided more realistic scarcity relationships, brought on inflationary pressures. By 1958 many pre-1956 leaders had returned to prominent government posts after Wladyslaw Gomulka replaced Bierut as first secretary of the Polish United Workers' Party.[5] They then argued for a return to central control to combat these inflationary pressures. Second, industrial associations, created in 1958, organized enterprises on an operational basis rather than the bureaucratic hierarchy. It was the intention of the reform-minded central planners that these associations were to be the basic plan executive. However, there was substantial institutional resistance from enterprises and a tendency within the planning hierarchy to do it the old way. And third, there was a substantial increase in investment that favored transportation, communications, and heavy industry. This relative neglect of agricultural investment further neutralized any gains that may have resulted from the decollectivization of agriculture. Economic inefficiency at the industry level still persisted and the growth in real wages stagnated throughout the 1960s.

The 1961-65 Five-Year-Plan was intended to catch up with the West, and the actual performance of the economy during the second five-year plan featured two distinct periods: 1961 and 1962, in which there was an increase in investment and employment, continuing the targets and goals of the last five-year plan, a high level of production of producer goods, poor agricultural performance, and a surge in the balance of payments deficit; 1964 and 1965 (with 1963 as a transition period), marked by major changes in the plan, most notably a redirection of investment expenditures, lower growth of employment, and increased growth of consumer goods.

The overly ambitious targets, based on the assumption that intensive growth factors could be utilized as a result of the 1956-58 reforms, could not be met. Higher rates of productivity were assumed and built into the plan,[6] but many of the reform proposals had been set aside by the Gomulka leadership. Extensive patterns of growth reemerged, as in the previous plan periods, and growth in factor productivity was disappointing. Further, it was expected that during 1961-65 both real wages and consumption would grow at the same rate: planned at 23 percent over the five-year period.[7] However, real wages grew by just 7.8 percent, or an average annual rate of about 1.5 percent. Real incomes increased only for a small percent of the population, most notably for those families for whom the number of hours employed increased.[8] Distorted relative prices at the retail level led to scattered shortages of consumer goods and food products. The low rates of growth of productivity, low rates of growth of real wages, and continuing inefficiency at the enterprise level brought the discussion of economic reforms back to center stage.

A new wave of reforms was thus initiated by the Fourth Congress of PUWP in June 1964.[9] The economic reforms and

the Third Five-Year Plan (1966-1970) had several common goals:
(1) to change the industrial structure of the economy, bringing
it closer to that of the advanced West European countries; (2)
to expand the production of exports and improve the profitability
of foreign trade; and (3) to improve the generation of technology
and utilization of research and development.[10] The reforms
stressed partial remedies and emphasized that improvements
were to be a continuous process. Specifically, the reforms
attempted to improve the system of success indicators and
managerial incentives, thereby increasing the role of industrial
associations, and decrease the role of ministries.[11]

The Third Five-Year Plan called for further development
of the natural resource base and higher rates of growth of
investment, especially in the machine building and chemical
industries. The actual performance of the economy can again
be broken into distinct periods. The first, 1966 to 1968, was
marked by above-plan growth in national income and industrial
output, which grew at a yearly average of about 8 percent.[12]
Again, this was brought about largely through high rates of
investment and employment—extensive development—rather
than increases in technological change or factor productivity.
There was also much better than average performance in agriculture as overall output grew by about four percent per year.

In the second period, from 1969 to 1970, a severe drought
and harsh winter in 1969 resulted in a decrease in agricultural
output and increased imports of grain. As a result of the increased imports of grain and above-plan imports of machinery
there was a marked deterioration in the balance of payments.
The agricultural failure could not be alleviated by imports as
shortages of food products (at relatively low, heavily subsidized,
prices) persisted. By late 1970 the rate of growth of national
income had fallen and investment was below planned levels.[13]

The performance of the economy in the earlier subperiod
was generally quite acceptable with one exception. The reforms
of the 1964-66 period gave enterprises much more discretion in
investment and hiring decisions. As a result firms were often
spending at greater than planned levels. By 1968 difficulties
in supplying inputs to industry were beginning to arise as shortages and inflationary pressures began to build. These finally
brought about pressures for a return to administrative control[14]
as plan failures in many industrial sectors resulted from shortages of semifabricates and electricity.[15] Also, new reforms
designed to alleviate these supply problems and encourage
enterprises to stay within planned spending were being designed
and implemented during 1969 and 1970 for the operation of the

1971-75 five-year plan. These reforms, however, were relatively short lived.

The 1969-70 reforms had two distinct features. The first was the change in the planning system (announced in April 1969) and management methods (announced somewhat later). The most notable changes dealt with (1) the financial system (a new system of bonus criteria from which the enterprise could choose and new methods of financing research and development);[16] (2) reform-realignment of transfer prices for domestic goods, to be implemented in stages (and for imported goods the transfer price was linked to the world market price); and (3) a radical reform of the incentive system (which related all potential pay raises for 1971-75 to the 1970 level of enterprise wage funds).[17]

The second distinct feature of the 1969-70 reforms was their antiinflationary, anticonsumer nature. The reform of the incentive system was intended to slow the growth of nominal wages, thought to be the cause of much of the inflationary pressure.[18] As a result, the expansion of employment was slowed as redundant workers were dismissed and planned increases in employment in several sectors were halted. Although it was argued that these measures were necessary to increase productivity, most workers viewed the new system simply as a means of decreasing wages. On December 13, 1970, a reform of retail prices was announced that included an average 8 percent increase in the price of foodstuffs, which was to be offset in part by a decline in prices of manufactured consumer goods. The reaction of the population was quick, as the next day dockworkers and shipyard workers in Gdansk went on strike in protest. The strike was joined by others and violence erupted. The local party headquarters were burned and shops wrecked. The riots quickly spread to Gdynia, Elblag, and Szczecin. By the end of the week order was restored only by deployment of troops and tanks. The events caused a crisis in the party leadership and within days Edward Gierek was elected first secretary of the Polish United Workers' Party, replacing Wladyslaw Gomulka and beginning a new period in the economic history of Poland.[19]

During the 1947-70 period the Soviet-type system of central planning was firmly established in Poland. The only growth strategy for which it is suited—extensive development—was initially successful in providing a rapid recovery from the devastation of World War II. Repeated economic failures due to the lack of incentives to strive for economic efficiency led to continual demands for economic reform. With each five-year plan came a new set of proposals for improvement of management, finance, and industrial organization to increase efficiency and factor productivity but each reform was soon supplanted by a return to central control. The only lasting feature of any of the reform programs was the realignment of prices, which initially restored market equilibrium but soon became a constraint on the efficient functioning of the economy. Finally, the population's response to the price changes in 1969-70—only a focal point for more general dissatisfaction with the economic system and general living conditions—led to the change in political leadership and a new growth strategy.

GIEREK'S NEW ECONOMIC MANEUVER

The development policy and the economic system that dominated the 1950s and 1960s was clearly inadequate. The ability of the system to mobilize and redirect resources was not questioned but the efficient utilization of those resources could not be guaranteed. Gierek immediately initiated a New Economic Maneuver designed to bring an immediate increase in the standard of living and set a new course in the development strategy of Poland. Immediate, short run improvements in the standard of living were brought about by increasing wages and pensions in the lowest income brackets and completely eliminating the new system of bonuses (which depressed wages). In addition, the increase in food prices was cancelled but the reduction in prices of certain consumer goods of industrial origin was maintained.[20] Further improvements in the standard of living were expected as a new agriculture policy evolved. The new policy, designed to increase agricultural output, included the following measures: (1) for the first time the government granted formal certification of property rights to owners of agricultural land and removed legal barriers to the sale and inheritance of land; (2) in 1972, workers in the rural economy were included in the national health insurance program; (3) obligatory and contractual delivery prices for agricultural products were raised in 1971, and obligatory deliveries were entirely eliminated in 1972; (4) the steep progressivity of farm land taxes was eliminated; and (5) credit for the purchase of equipment and fertilizers became more readily available.[21] All of these combined with favorable weather to increase income in the agricultural sector by over 10 percent in 1971 and over 9 percent in 1972.

In addition to the measures intended to increase the standard of living, major reforms in the system of planning and management were implemented in 1972 and 1973 to replace those of the 1969-70 period, and a new development strategy was formulated. The systematic changes were based on several assumptions: (1) that different development strategies need different systems of planning and management; (2) the reforms would again be only a part of the continuous process of improving the economic system; (3) a system of economic parameters determined by the central planners would steer the economy; and (4) the scale of management should be enlarged, and closer links between production, research and development, and marketing should be established.[22]

Gierek's development strategy called for both high levels of investment expenditures to modernize the productive capacity of the economy and build a strong export sector and high levels of production of consumer goods in order to improve the standard of living and increase labor productivity. Increased imports of advanced machinery and Western credits to finance them were the foundation of this investment drive. In order to increase the utilization of these high technology imports, expand the domestic research and development effort, and improve labor productivity, a new system of planning and management was also implemented.

The new system depended heavily upon the Wielkie Organizacje Gospodarcze (WOGs) or Large Economic Organizations, associations of many enterprises or industrial complexes in which more of the day-to-day planning and operational decisions were to be made. In addition, more control over investment funds was granted to each WOG as not only the producing enterprises but also research and development institutions and internal and foreign trade organizations were placed under its jurisdiction. Control of the WOGs by the ministries was ensured since long term parameters governing the level of tax-free profits kept by the WOG, as well as guidelines for the participation in foreign trade for each WOG, were set by planners at the ministries or the Planning Commission. The system was still highly centralized since central planners continued to set most prices, the rates of interest and amortization, foreign trade coefficients, subsidies for the production of normally unprofitable goods, price equalization subsidies and taxes on exports and imports, and so forth.[23]

The annual rates of growth of national income and of production in every sector showed substantial increases in the 1970-74 period. However, there was a substantial fall in agricultural output due to poor weather conditions in 1974 and 1975. Agricultural output recovered and grew rapidly in 1976 and 1977 alleviating this setback. The success in terms of economic growth may be attributed to two major factors: again there was extensive development as both fixed capital and labor grew substantially in the industrial sector and there was a tremendous increase in imports of machinery and equipment from the West, leaving Poland with substantial hard currency debts to repay.

The success of Gierek's New Economic Maneuver was hardly complete. Inflationary pressures began to develop and the growth of exports was not enough to alleviate Poland's hard currency debt, which had reached $10.2 billion by the end of 1976.[24] This was in part due to the fact that the length of time for investment projects to become operational had nearly doubled, delaying the production of goods and the repayment (via export) of much of the accumulating debt. Further, potential export goods were selected not by the WOG but from above and price distortions made it impossible to determine their profitability. Although the share of national income going to consumption increased from 62.2 percent in 1975 to 68.5 percent in 1977, there was a slowing in the rate of growth of real wages from 8.5 percent in 1975 to 3.9 percent in 1976 and 2.3 percent in 1977 and a corresponding increase in the cost of living.

The slowing in the rate of growth of real wages and price increases to alleviate shortages of consumer goods and lessen the growing subsidies on food products again led to worker unrest. The announcement of price increases on June 25, 1976 triggered riots in Ursus, Radom, and other locations throughout Poland.[25] These riots succeeded in forcing the government to roll back the scheduled price increases and contributed to growing political unrest. Dissident intellectuals banded with workers to protest both political and economic conditions in a movement that marked the conception of Solidarity.[26] There was also evidence of growing excess demand in both 1976 and 1977 that was impossible to remove without price increases.[27]

In addition to these internal pressures for economic reform, Poland, by 1976-77, had reached the second phase of Gierek's development strategy. It was necessary to generate large amounts of exports to repay the loans from the West that financed the initial phase of the development program. The need for increased efficiency and rational prices had become acute. And again during two conferences in late 1978, new reform proposals were made as economists in Poland recognized the basic flaws of the WOG system, which had little practical impact on the system of planning and management.[28]

The plan for the 1976-80 period emphasized the need to address the growing problem of the hard currency debt. More resources were to be devoted to the expansion of exports and imports were to be curtailed. The agricultural sector along with the production of consumer goods and housing was to be emphasized as well. Investment in other sectors was to be reduced to facilitate growth in these areas and the Modified Economic and Financial System, a new set of reforms, was implemented to induce enterprises to eliminate inefficiencies and reduce the material intensity of production. The new operating system, an extension of the 1973 reforms, remained in operation and was extended to cover more of the economy, despite the fact that planners overruled the rules of operation—reverting to direct controls or administrative commands—whenever plan fulfillment was endangered.[29]

The balance of payments began to improve in 1977 primarily due to an increase in world prices (exports increased by 9.8 percent in nominal terms but decreased by 0.2 percent in real terms) and import restrictions (imports fell by 4.6 percent in current prices, 10.6 percent in constant prices).[30] Import restrictions continued in 1978 and 1979 and the reductions were felt in nearly all branches of the economy. Due to the tremendous investment drive of the early 1970s there was a gap between the existing productive capacity and the ability of the economy to provide essential inputs. This major structural imbalance was the result of serious planning errors in the mid-1970s and nearly uncontrolled investment expenditures by the large economic organizations.[31] Import constraints, then, were critical. In 1978 many sectors could not meet plan targets. The rate of growth of output in socialist industry fell from 9.3 percent in 1975 to 2.5 percent in 1978.[32]

Although the plan for 1979 was carefully prepared and set relatively modest goals, the results were disappointing. National income fell by 2 percent, investment declined by 8.2 percent (actually less than planned), and gross agricultural production declined (in part due to poor weather) by 1.4 percent. In the realm of foreign trade, exports with the dollar area increased 12.9 percent, imports increased by 5.6 percent, and the deficit on the balance of trade fell to $1.17 billion (all in current prices). The net hard currency indebtedness reached a staggering $20.5 billion. The expansion of energy intensive industries also left Poland as a net importer of energy and fuels for the first time. There were declines in production in nearly every category of basic materials, fuels, and energy. The fundamental restructuring of production toward exports and consumer goods was not achieved. Economic results for 1979 were released just before the Eighth Party Congress and forced the resignation of Premier Piotr Jaroszewicz and Deputy Premier Jan Szydlak (who had earlier been responsible for rejecting the more progressive reform proposals).

The plan for 1980 continued with only modest retrenching. Investment was to fall by about 8 percent but it was expected that national income would increase 1.4 percent and industrial output would increase 4 percent. The results, however, were quite another story. National income (net domestic material product) fell by 4 percent and weather caused a disaster in agriculture as crop output fell by 25 to 30 percent from the already low 1979 level.[33] Although the trade deficit with the dollar area narrowed, the hard currency debt rose by $3.2 billion and two thirds of the new borrowings were applied to interest payments. Although output was being maintained at levels close to capacity, exports to the West in real terms actually declined. These resources flowed instead to the heavily subsidized consumer goods sector.

Again the central authorities attempted to alleviate the imbalance on consumer good markets by increasing food prices and in August 1980 the social turmoil led to the creation of Solidarity, which later brought about huge unplanned wage increases exacerbating the excess demand for consumer goods as well as overall macrobalance.

It is clear that the economic crisis that began in 1978, worsened in 1979, and finally reached unbelievable depths by 1981 was not a by-product of the Solidarity trade union movement, but that Solidarity was the consequence of the continued ineptness of central planners and the refusal of the central authorities to enact and implement meaningful economic reforms in the preceding two and a half decades. During the 1970s Gierek's development strategy—to increase productivity via high technology imports with payment for these imports via exports from these now more efficient industrial branches—had failed. The investment front was too large and the gestation period for new plants lengthened and prevented the development of profitable exports. The changes in the system of planning and management were superficial and there were no incentives to provide efficient utilization of resources at the enterprise level. Within only a few years the strategy had reverted to the familiar pattern of extensive development and central control.

THE SOLIDARITY PERIOD AND MARTIAL LAW

The economy continued to deteriorate in nearly every activity. The reform discussion took on a new sense of urgency as the government had little popular support and was trying desperately to consolidate its position. The growth of Solidarity as a social force continued and the leadership of Solidarity played a major role in the reform discussions. Gierek was replaced by Stanislaw Kania as First Secretary of PUWP, and the new government was pressured into preparing a recovery program as well as new economic reforms. The reform proposals were first discussed at the PUWP Ninth Extraordinary Party Congress in July 1981 and Premier Jaruzelski endorsed the quick implementation of the proposals. The new program emphasized, among other things, halting the declines in production, improving the supply of consumer goods, reallocating large portions of the work force, and alleviating the imbalances of the foreign sector.

The revised 1981 plan was pessimistic to say the least.[34] It envisaged industrial production to be only 87.3 percent of the 1980 level. Foreign trade turnover and national income produced were planned at 83.7 percent and 84.9 percent of the 1980 levels, respectively. Coal production was planned at 168 million metric tons versus 193 million in 1980. Despite these lowered targets, plan fulfillment was not expected in industry or for exports to the hard currency area (and therefore imports from this area were to be constrained even further). Only agricultural production was expected to grow.

In 1981 the economic situation had reached truly crisis levels. By September the value of production sold by socialized industry fell 14 percent compared to September 1980, 18 percent compared to September 1979. On a year-to-year basis in September 1981 average employment had fallen 0.4 percent while wage fund expenditures had increased 27.6 percent, worsening the so-called inflationary gap.[35] For the first eight months of 1981 total income of the population was 30,000 million zlotys greater than the value of goods produced. Free market prices for agricultural products increased rapidly while contractual deliveries to the state declined. Some thirty-eight thousand people were unemployed actually seeking work, half of them recent graduates. Coal production, a crucial export, fell 19.1 percent for the first three-quarters of the year to 121.7 million metric tons. Total exports fell 15.4 percent and imports fell 10.1 percent; imports from the West falling 24.7 percent and from the socialist area increasing 3.1 percent. In agriculture the production results were more positive: for example, grain production was 19.7 million tons, 1.4 million more than 1980, sugar production reached 1.72 million tons versus 1.04 million in 1980, and potatoes harvested was 42.6 million tons, nearly a third more than 1980. At the same time livestock herds were growing as deliveries of both crops and livestock to the state declined.[36] By the end of the third quarter of 1981 the disastrous economic results had set the stage for drastic political actions.

With the continued decline in the production of consumer goods, the diversion of agricultural products to the free market, and the rapid growth in incomes, shortages, open inflation, and lengthy queues soon developed. The number of goods rationed, ranging from staples such as flour, sugar, soap, and rice to items like alcohol, cigarettes, and chocolate, to items for babies—diapers, lotion, formula—and children's clothing, increased and the rations per person or family declined. Popular discontent was clearly evident and the removal of large numbers of trams and buses from service due to shortages of spare parts in November aggravated the situation. The number of active strikes and strike alerts grew and the time for confrontation with Solidarity was near.

The Solidarity leadership had refused to accept the price reforms—desperately needed to restore macrobalance—until assurances that the economic reforms would truly be meaningful. Solidarity demanded a greater role for workers in self-management of the enterprise and inter alia removal of the nomenklatura system for selection of management in enterprises. Two bills (the bill on workers self-management and the bill on the state enterprise[37]) of the nine bills making up the reform were passed by the Sejm (Polish parliament) prior to General Jaruzelski's declaration of martial law on December 13, 1981, but were immediately suspended. The remaining seven bills were passed and implemented in January 1982 along with portions of these two.[38]

Despite the political and economic turmoil of this period the Planning Commission developed an annual plan (released in September) that included the basic indexes for 1982: industrial output was to be 100 percent of 1981 ending the decline, national income 99 percent of 1981, and sales of consumer goods, in real terms, 102 percent of 1981. In the agricultural sector output was expected to increase along with investment in food processing complexes, housing, and the fuel and power industry.

The declaration of martial law and the tremendous uncertainty due to the implementation of the reforms shattered these plans. The operation of the economy during the first half of 1982 reverted to a system of Stalinist central directives as nearly 70 percent of industry and all of transportation and communications were controlled by military commissars. A series of quarterly plans was issued along with nine operational programs to ensure the production of crucial factor inputs in agriculture, medical and basic health services, and primary products such as coal and rolled steel products. The few enterprises that had a choice opted for inclusion in the operational plans rather than independent operation (as the bill on the state enterprise allowed) because the operational programs guaranteed some minimum levels of inputs. Military authority was relaxed to a small degree by mid-year and the implementation of the bill on self-management and the establishment of workers' councils had resumed.

Economic performance in 1982 continued the decline evidenced in 1981 until the third quarter of the year, when in August an increase in industrial production (in constant prices) was recorded after twenty-five straight months of decline (since July 1980). Table 2.1 illustrates the monthly changes in industrial production, employment and labor productivity. In October 1982 industrial output increased 5 percent over the very low levels of 1981, while employment continued to fall. Not only did total employment fall but some 44,000 persons changed jobs. Despite the increases in production in August through October, the overall volume of sold industrial output from January to October 1982 was 4 percent less than the same period in 1981 and 16 percent lower than the same period in 1979. By the end of October housing construction had also begun to increase on a month-to-month comparison, but the housing plan was only 58 percent complete and 21 percent fewer flats had been built when compared to the same period in 1981. Further, during the first seven months of 1982 only one third of planned investment projects were completed.

The new principles of price formation created three types of prices in addition to prices for the small free market sector: contractual prices, basically free market prices between producers (but these in fact may be heavily influenced by price formation guidelines of appropriate ministries); regulated prices (based on production costs plus a mark-up to be reviewed by a national price board); and official prices (set by central authorities). The new system of price formation and the price reform introduced in February 1982 resulted in a tremendous increase in the overall level of prices, illustrated in Table 2.2, which began to narrow the inflationary gap. [39]

The objectives of the reform after martial law were: (1) to increase the efficiency of management (that is, increase the efficient use of raw and intermediate inputs and increase the quality of production)—a problem now decades old; (2) to restore balance on the consumer goods markets; and (3) to provide a

TABLE 2.1

Economic Performance in 1982: Percentage Change from the Corresponding Month of 1981

	January	February	March	April	May	June	July	August	September
Industrial production (constant prices)	-13.8	-10.7	-6.4	-6.3	-2.7	-2.8	-3.6	+1.0	+4.0
Employment	-4.6	-4.8	-5.0	-5.7	-5.6	-5.8	-5.9	-5.5	-5.5
Labor productivity (constant prices)	-9.6	-6.2	-1.5	-0.7	+3.1	+3.2	+2.4	+7.1	+10.0

Source: "Report by the Government Plenipotentiary Minister on the Implementation of Economic Reform in the First Half of 1982," Rzeczpospolita Economic Reform Supplement, No. 1, October 26, 1982.

TABLE 2.2

Price Indexes, 1982

	January	February	March	April	May	June
Prices of consumer goods and services						
In general	115.7	140.9	106.5	103.2	102.3	99.9
Food only	111.7	192.6	103.6	103.0	104.2	98.1
Nonfood, total	107.8	129.7	116.1	104.2	101.0	100.6
Clothing	101.2	115.7	125.3	105.2	103.4	101.1
Household appliances	132.6	151.9	119.7	106.8	101.5	101.9
Services	112.7	121.1	101.9	106.0	102.2	104.9

Note: Previous month = 100.

Source: "Report by the Government Plenipotentiary Minister on the Implementation of Economic Reform in the First Half of 1982," Rzeczpostpolita Economic Reform Supplement, No. 1, October 26, 1982.

44

more just distribution of income, now defined as one with greater correlation between the individual's wages and his or her share of work or, for an enterprise, greater correlation between enterprise income and productivity. [40] It is also important to note that the foundation for all planning and regulation of the economy as a result of the reform is the nine acts of the Sejm rather than governmental decrees. A total of 753 acts issued by the Council of Ministers and the Presidium were rescinded, replaced by these nine acts of parliament. The impact of the reform of the economic system has been greatest in the sphere of planning and the reorganization of enterprises. Indirect stimuli—prices and taxes—are more important and the enterprise has more independence under the new system. There has been a limited restructuring of the organization of the national economy, with a movement away from centralization, as employment of central administrative personnel fell 6 percent, and administrative personnel at sectoral ministries fell 35 percent. [41] Local state-administrative bodies have assumed more responsibility with respect to local economic operations.

These appear to be positive movements but the declaration of martial law has suppressed the movement toward self-management and lessened the influence of workers on enterprise functioning. Formally the reform replaced the zjednoczenia, a compulsory monopolistic industrial group to which enterprises belonged (which comprised an intermediate level of management), with associations of enterprises. The dissolution of these groups is nearly complete and by the end of the year the ministerial plenipotentiary for separate production areas will also be dissolved. However, the associations that enterprises are joining are already taking on the obligatory characteristics of the zjednoczenia and many ministries are endowing these associations with middle-management duties and powers that the zjednoczenia had.

In many sectors of the economy quota-based central administration of raw and intermediate materials is still the rule and the rationing of consumer products persists. Further, there has been a segmentation of the consumer goods market. Miners and young married couples, for example, receive special privileges in the form of additional rations or low-interest loans to purchase furniture. The burden of the costs of the reform are uneven and much of the population views the decrease in the standard of living as a consequence of the reform itself rather than a result of the economic crisis of the 1978-81 prereform period.

The major goals of the three-year plan, 1983-85, were recently outlined in "The Program of Overcoming Crisis and

Stabilizing the Economy" approved in July by the Ninth Party Congress. [42] The major goals include many of the same goals as the 1982 annual plan: (1) to check the decline in industrial production and initiate its growth; (2) to restore market equilibrium; (3) to reduce state expenditures and subsidies and complete major investment projects; (4) to redeploy the workforce in an efficient manner; and (5) to restore balance of payments equilibrium by increasing exports. The functioning of the economy and future socioeconomic change will, however, be shaped predominately by the employees and enterprise staffs. The most important factors are yet to be determined: how the principles of the reform are translated into operation—the crucial aspect that resulted in the failure of every previous reform; the introduction of a pay or incentive system to link wages and productivity—never before attempted; and the resumption of self-management—the most novel concept in the Polish economic reform. [43]

POSTSCRIPT

In 1983 there were both positive and negative developments in the Polish economy. The most heartening development is that the overall economic decline has been arrested and it appears the economy reached its low point in early 1982. Industrial output in the first quarter of 1983 was 2 percent greater than the fourth quarter of 1982 but 11 percent above the very low levels of the first quarter of 1982. Manufacturing sectors showed the greatest increase, in part because those sectors were most depressed. At the same time employment in the socialized sector continued to fall—by 54,600 employees—and industrial output per worker increased 13 percent over the first quarter of 1982. Average earnings increased 27.5 percent while consumer goods delivered to the marketplace increased 16 percent in constant prices (still well below 1979 levels). Although there is an official antiinflationary campaign, the price reform of early 1982 appears to have eliminated a large part of excess money balances that would contribute to the inflationary pressures. As a result of the price reforms several unofficial sources report that real incomes of the population have fallen to 60-70 percent of the 1981 level.

In agriculture there has been favorable weather and it appears there will be an excellent harvest for the second year in a row. However, procurement of animals for slaughter in May 1983 was down 10.4 percent from May 1982, and purchases of poultry fell by 56.8 percent from 1982 levels (already low due to the U.S. sanctions).

Foreign trade has increased from the 1982 levels. For the first five months of 1983 exports were 15.2 percent and imports, 17.8 percent higher than the first five months of 1982 (22.6 and 15.9 percent, respectively, for the socialist bloc and 7.2 and 9.5 percent, respectively, for the West). With respect to trade with the West exports and imports for the first five months of 1983 were 23.2 and 45.8 percent less than the first five months of 1980, a period of more normal trade patterns. Although there has been a marked improvement from 1982 levels, plan targets for the first quarter of 1983 were not met. Imports from the Council of Mutual Economic Assistance (CMEA) region and exports to the CMEA region were 25.5 billion zlotys and 3.6 billion zlotys, respectively, short of the plan target while imports from the West and exports to the West were 9.4 billion zlotys and 23.6 billion zlotys short of the plan targets.

The most disappointing developments were not in the area of economic performance but in the area of economic reform. The 1981/82 reform proposals were more comprehensive than the WOG industrial reforms of the 1970s, since the current proposals touch every branch of the economy and call for a radical change in the operations of the center (elimination of the associations and less comprehensive planning at the Planning Commission and ministerial levels), which was left untouched by previous reforms. The implementation of the reform has not been satisfactory. The structure of the economic system (that is, degree of decentralization) has not yet met the goals of the reform. The new economic associations, the plenipotentiaries for operational programs, represent a compromise between enterprise autonomy and the former associations as a link to the center, with most of the command elements of the center being transferred to the new plenipotentiaries. Quarterly plans are still the dominant economic force and limit the role of enterprise autonomy.

In the area of self-financing, the amount of profit is being used as an economic indicator but it is not the sole indicator of enterprise performance. Unprofitable enterprises are still heavily subsidized and there appears to be few enterprises in danger of bankruptcy. Subsidies amounted to 597,100 million zlotys (70.9 percent of state budget aid) and were granted to 3,097 enterprises in 1982. The resource allocative effects of using profits as an economic indicator appear to be nonexistent. The greatest differences between the reform proposals and reality lie in the area of self-management. The suspension then

reinstatement of the principles of self-management has led to a
situation in which neither management nor workers are interested
in developing self-management even though workers' councils
exist in most enterprises. The participation of workers' councils in enterprise management was minimal in 1982 and apparently
in no case was the enterprise plan submitted to the workers'
council for approval or comment.

It appears that through the first half of 1983 there has
been positive development with respect to economic performance
but little change with respect to the economic system. The
implementation of the reform proposals has been disappointing
and the most significant aspects, enterprise autonomy, self-
financing and self-management, are yet to be implemented.
There is still substantial debate concerning the reform, its
implementation, and its effectiveness. The atmosphere may
change significantly in the future, however, and conditions
for meaningful economic reform may arise.

NOTES

1. See John Michael Montias, Central Planning in Poland
(New Haven, Conn.: Yale University Press, 1962), for a discussion of the problems Polish planners encountered in setting
prices of producer goods in this period.
2. See George R. Feiwel, Poland's Industrialization Policy:
A Current Analysis (New York: Praeger, 1971), for more details
of the growth of consumption and income during this period.
3. The Poznan riots were first denounced by Moscow
and then Warsaw as "provocation inspired by imperialist circles."
But the Polish official attitude changed abruptly on July 1, as
the disturbances were attributed to the general neglect of the
standard of living by the planning authorities. See J. G.
Zielinski, Economic Reforms in East European Industry: Poland
(New York: Oxford University, 1973), for further details.
4. This period is labeled the period of thought "toward
a grand design" by Zielinski as much of the discussion concerns
transition to a new economic model or system. See his work
and Montias, Central Planning, for further discussion.
5. See Zielinski, Economic Reforms, for further details.
6. In fact, as much as 84 percent of the increase in
industrial output was to be obtained solely through an increase
in labor productivity achieved by technical progress and a more
rational and more intensive use of inputs. See Feiwel, Industrial
Policy, Chapter 7 for details.

7. Feiwel, Industrial Policy, p. 321.
8. Ibid., p. 322.
9. See J. G. Zielinski, "New Polish Reform Proposals,"
Soviet Studies 32 (1980):16.
10. Zbigniew Fallenbuchl, "The Polish Economy in the
1970s," in East European Economies Post-Helsinki (Washington,
D.C.: JEC, USGPO, 1977), pp. 818-28.
11. See Zielinski, Economic Reforms, for a more detailed
analysis of the 1964-66 reform period.
12. Feiwel, Poland's Industrialization, p. 403. Only
Bulgaria and Rumania had higher rates of growth at any time
during the 1961-68 period.
13. Ibid., Table 96, p. 432.
14. Zielinski, Economic Reforms, p. 17.
15. See Feiwel, Poland's Industrialization, p. 402. In
1968 the requirements for electricity grew by 11 percent while
generating capacity was hindered by delays in commissioning
new plants and work stoppages at power plants. Further, in
the semifabricates, auxiliary materials, and castings and forgings
sectors output did not keep pace with demand. Some of these
shortages were made up by increased imports.
16. Enterprise managers could select one of the following
four bonus criteria for evaluating the enterprises' performances:
(1) the decrease in unit costs of production, (2) final cost
levels, (3) volume of production, or (4) rate of profitability.
17. Polish enterprises were pressured into revealing all
wage fund reserves in 1969-70 so that under the new incentive
system nominal wages were not likely to increase over the next
two years. See J. G. Zielinski, Economic Reforms, for further
details.
18. The planners were attempting to restrain aggregate
demand but much of the inflationary pressure could be attributed
to plan failures and shortages in particularly crucial areas (semifabricates), which reduced aggregate supply (especially of consumer goods and services). See Zielinski, Economic Reforms.
19. See Zbigniew Pelczynski, "The Downfall of Gomulka,"
Canadian Slavonic Papers 15 (1973):1-23, for an excellent day-
by-day description of the political events leading to Gierek's
election to the secretarial post.
20. In addition to these economic measures there were
further concessions to popular sentiments. These included
rebuilding of the old royal castle in Warsaw and normalization
of relations with the Catholic church. See Vincent G. Chrypinski,
"Political Changes Under Gierek," Canadian Slavonic Papers 15
(1973):36-51, for further details with regard to political conces-

sions, and Zbigniew Fallenbuchl, "The Polish Economy at the Beginning of the 1980s," East European Economic Assessment, Part 1, Country Studies (Washington, D.C.: JEC, USGPO, 1980), pp. 33-71, for a more complete description of the new economic measures implemented.

21. See Witold Lipski, "Changes in Agriculture," Canadian Slavonic Papers 15 (1973):101-107, for a more detailed description of the changes in agricultural policy.

22. See Fallenbuchl, The Polish Economy, for more details.

23. See Heinrich Machowski, "Poland," in The New Economic Systems of Eastern Europe, Hans-Hermann Hohman, et al., eds. (Berkeley and Los Angeles: University of California Press, 1975), pp. 79-104; Andrzej Tyminski, "Changes in the Price System for Producer Goods in Poland (1971-1976)," Soviet Studies 29 (1977):429-448; and Fallenbuchl, The Polish Economy, for further details of the new system.

24. Joan Parpart Zoeter, "Eastern Europe: The Growing Hard Currency Debt," in East-European Economies Post-Helsinki (Washington, D.C.: JEC, USGPO, 1977), p. 1356.

25. See Walter D. Conner, "Dissent in Eastern Europe: A New Coalition?" Problems of Communism 29 (1980):1-17.

26. See Jadwiga Staniszkis, "On Some Contradictions of Socialist Society: The Case of Poland," Soviet Studies 30 (1981): 167-187.

27. See Stanislaw Gomulka, "Poland's Economic Situation in the Second Half of the 1970s," Osteuropa-Wirtschaft 24 (1979): 13-23.

28. Zielinski, New Polish Reforms, notes that there were two conferences discussing a reform of the system of economic planning and guidance. The first conference was held in Wroclaw, in September 1978 and the second in Warsaw in November 1978.

29. See Fallenbuchl, The Polish Economy, p. 52, for further details.

30. Ibid.

31. See John Michael Montias, "Poland: Roots of the Economic Crisis," Association for Comparative Economic Studies Bulletin 24 (1982):1-19, for several accounts of nearly unbelievable investment disasters, often associated with incompetent party functionaries.

32. Fallenbuchl, The Polish Economy, p. 53. Also see Zbigniew Fallenbuchl, "Poland's Economic Crisis," Problems of Communism 31 (1982):1-21.

33. See Montias, Poland, for details.

34. Zycie Gospodarcze, September 20, 1981.

35. Trybuna Ludu, October 15, 1981.

36. Trybuna Ludu, April 5, 1982.

37. See David M. Kemme, "The Foundation of Economic Reform in Poland: The Bill on Self-Management of the Employees of the State-Owned Enterprise," UNC-G Working Paper Series (November 1981).

38. Portions of the bill on self-management were suspended and are just now being reimplemented. The establishment of workers' councils was halted for those enterprises that had not yet established councils and the authority of those that were established was suspended. This authority has been restored in some sectors of industry—less strategic—and the formation of new workers' councils had begun by June 1982. The power of the workers' council to remove the enterprise director is one provision of this bill that has not been restored. The remaining bills dealt with banking and the new charter for the National Bank of Poland, finance, taxation, planning, statistics, price formation, and foreign trade.

39. Note that the price indexes reported in Table 2.2 are official price indexes and subject to the common criticisms of all price indexes with respect to their calculation.

40. Trybuna Ludu, December 23, 1981.

41. But already by October 1982 there have been requests by these administrative organizations for an increase in staffing. See Rzeczpospolita: Economic Reform Supplement, No. 1, October 26, 1982.

42. Trybuna Ludu, July 1981.

43. By September 15, 1982 three hundred self-managing workers' councils had been established but their effectiveness and influence on enterprise operations are still unknown.

BIBLIOGRAPHY

Adam, Jan. "The Recent Reform of the Incentive System in Poland." Osteuropa Wirtschaft 20 (1965):169-184.

Bozyk, Pawel, et al. "Polish Economic Development for the Seventies." Jahrbuch der Wirtschaft Osteuropas 4 (1973): 211-232.

Bromke, A. "Beyond the Gomulka Era." Foreign Affairs 49 (1971):480-492.

____. "A New Juncture in Poland." Problems of Communism 25 (1976):1-17.

____. "Poland Under Gierek, A New Political Style." Problems of Communism 21 (1972):1-19.

____. "Polish Foreign Policy in the 1970's." In Gierek's Poland, edited by Adam Bromke and John W. Strong, pp. 192-204. New York: Praeger, 1973.

Bromke, Adam, and Strong, J. W., eds. Gierek's Poland. New York: Praeger, 1973.

Chrypinski, Vincent C. "Political Changes Under Gierek." Canadian Slavonic Papers 15 (1973):36-51.

Conner, Walter D. "Dissent in Eastern Europe: A New Coalition?" Problems of Communism 29 (1980):1-17.

Fallenbuchl, Zbigniew M. "Industrial Structure and the Intensive Pattern of Development in Poland." Jahrbach der Wirtschaft Osteuropas 4 (1973):233-254.

____. "The Polish Economy at the Beginning of the 1980's." In East European Economic Assessment, Part 1, Country Studies, 1980, pp. 33-71. Washington, D.C.: JEC, USGPO, 1980.

____. "Poland's Economic Crisis." Problems of Communism 31 (1982):1-21.

____. "The Polish Economy in the 1970s." In East European Economies Post-Helsinki. Washington, D.C.: JEC, USGPO, 1977.

____. "The Strategy of Development and Gierek's Economic Maneuvre." Canadian Slavonic Papers 15 (1973):55-70.

Feiwel, George R. Poland's Industrialization Policy: A Current Analysis. New York: Praeger, 1971.

____. Problems in Polish Economic Planning. New York: Praeger, 1971.

Feiwel, George R., and Wynncyczuk, Alexej. Recent Developments in the Polish Financial System. Washington, D.C.: U.S. Arms Control and Disarmament Agency, 1971.

Gamarnikow, Michael. "Poland Under Gierek: A New Economic Approach." Problems of Communism 21 (1972):20-30.

Gomulka, Stanislaw. "Poland's Economic Situation in the Second Half of the 1970s." Osteuropa-Wirtschaft 24 (1979):13-23.

Hohmann, Hans-Herman, et al., eds. The New Economic Systems of Eastern Europe. Berkeley and Los Angeles: University of California Press, 1975.

Kemme, David M. "The Foundation of Economic Reform in Poland: The Law on Self-Management of the Employees of the State-Owned Enterprise" UNC-G Working Paper Series, November 1981.

____. "The Foundation of Economic Reform in Poland: The Bill on State Enterprises." UNC-G Working Paper Series, December 1982.

Karpinski, Andrzej. Polityka uprzemy-slowienice Polski w latch, 1958-1968. Warsaw: Panstwowe Wydawnictiwo Gospodarcze, 1969.

Lipski, Witold. "Changes in Agriculture." Canadian Slavonic Papers 15 (1973):101-107.

Machowski, Heinrich. "Poland." In The New Economic Systems of Eastern Europe, edited by Hans-Herman Hohmann, et al., pp. 79-104. Berkeley and Los Angeles: University of California Press, 1975.

Montias, John M. "Inflation and Growth: The Experience of Eastern Europe." In Inflation and Growth in Latin America, edited by Werner Baer and Isaac Kerstenetzkj. New Haven, Conn.: Yale University Press, 1964.

____. Central Planning in Poland. New Haven, Conn.: Yale University Press, 1962.

____. "Price-Setting Problems in the Polish Economy." Journal of Political Economy 65 (1957):486-505.

____. "Producer Prices in a Centrally Planned Economy—The Polish Discussion." In Value and Plan, edited by Gregory Grossman, pp. 47-65. Berkeley and Los Angeles: University of California Press, 1960.

____. "Poland: Roots of the Economic Crisis." Association for Comparative Economic Studies Bulletin 24 (1982):1-19.

Mujzel, Jan. "Central Control of Income Flows in Planned Economies, A Case Study: Poland." In Internationale Wirtschaft: Venglerche und Interdependezen, edited by F. Levcik. Vienna: Springam, 1978.

Nuti, Domenico Mario. "Large Corporations and the Reform of Polish Industry." Jahrbuch der Wirtschaft Osteuropas Band 7, 1977:345-405.

Pelczynski, Zbigniew A. "The Downfall of Gomulka." Canadian Slavonic Papers 15 (1973):1-23.

Plowiec, Ursula. "Poland's Foreign Trade Control System in 1971." Problemy Handlu Zagranicynego (4), 1972.

Rzeczpospolita, various issues.

Smolinski, Leon. "Economics and Politics IV: Reforms in Poland." Problems of Communism 15 (1966):8-13.

Staniszkis, Jadwiga. "On Remodelling of the Polish Economic System." Soviet Studies 30 (1978):547-552.

____. "On Some Contradictions of Socialist Society: The Case of Poland." Soviet Studies 31 (April 1979):167-87.

Trybuna Ludu, various issues.

Tyminski, Andrzej. "Changes in the Price System for Producer Goods in Poland (1971-76)." Soviet Studies 29 (1977):429-448.

Wanless, P. T. "Economic Reform in Poland, 1973-79." Soviet Studies 32:1 (1980):28-57.

Zielinski, J. G. Economic Reforms in East European Industry: Poland. New York: Oxford University Press, 1973.

____. "New Polish Reform Proposals." Soviet Studies 32:1 (1980):5-27.

____. "On System Remodelling in Poland: A Pragmatic Approach." Soviet Studies 30 (1978):3-37.

Zoeter, Joan Parpart. "Eastern Europe: The Growing Hard Currency Debt." East-European Economies Post-Helsinki. Washington, D.C.: JEC, USGPO (1977):1350-1368.

Zycie Gospodarcze, various issues.

3

Economic and Political Interdependence
in Poland's Foreign Economic Policy

Marcin Sar

The interdependence of economics and politics in a socialist state has acquired a more intense character than in any other historically developed system. While Poland may not constitute the most representative example, because of the severity of the post-1980 crisis, an analysis of that country's problems may fulfill valuable functions by clearly pointing out, as in a magnifying glass, typical characteristics of the shotgun marriage of politics and economics in a socialist state.

FOREIGN ECONOMIC POLICY IN A SOCIALIST STATE

By Foreign Economic Policy (FEP) I refer broadly to a state's activity in the exchange of goods, services, and capital with foreign countries. As FEP is logically an integral part both of the state's foreign policy and of the economic policy, one may consider the dual subordination and effects of the FEP in reference to the above-mentioned activities. But consideration of the FEP apart from the system of state policy as a whole can also be supported both by analytical and substantive considerations. In a socialist state the making of the FEP is a highly specialized activity in which the state's flexibility of decision-making is substantially limited by international constraints. The degree of independence of the FEP from the nation's foreign and economic policies is relative. It depends first of all on the level of economic development and on the specific economic strategy of a country. Every country, with the possible exception of those with an economic potential comparable to that of the United States or the Soviet Union, faces in the course of its development barriers stemming from unsatisfactory participation in the world economy. The opening of a nation's economy to the international environment and a development strategy based on intensive factors usually requires relative subordination to the rules of world economy. In this way the FEP's subordination to national foreign and economic policies weakens, and the FEP gradually achieves a greater degree of independence.

Theoretically, FEP's main objective is the optimalization of material exchange with foreign countries in order to fulfill the needs and interests of the society. The process of setting FEP's objectives and choosing adequate ways of implementing the decisions takes place on various levels of the society's organization. I deal here only with determinants pertaining to the central (national) level.* This position is based on two premises: centralized state organs constituted the only comprehensive system of interest articulation in Poland of the 1970s, and in the 1970s Poland acted exclusively at the national level in her economic relations with socialist countries and to an overwhelming extent in her economic relations with other countries.

This analysis focuses intentionally on a limited part of the broader entity. First, the FEP of Poland is purposefully separated both from the country's domestic economic policy and from its foreign policy. Second, FEP is analyzed only in the period 1970-80. Third, FEP is analyzed as a factor leading to the post-1980 crisis, which logically means concentration on its detrimental effects on the economy and not on FEP's accomplishments. Fourth, analysis is focused on identifying political determinants of the FEP, with little attention paid to potentially existing feedback effects or to other (ideological, military) determinants.

The four limitations should help to avoid risky generalizations concerning the whole economy, while indicating specific regularities of the function of Poland's FEP in the last decade.

---

*For a more comprehensive discussion of the FEP determinants and problems with their operationalization, see Marcin Sar, Jerzy P. Gieorgica, "Determinanty Podejmowania Decyzji w Zagranicznej Polityce Ekonomicznej Socjalistycznego Panstwa (Decision-Making Determinants in the Foreign Economic Policy of a Socialist State)," in A. Bodnar, ed., Radom 1980 Political Science Papers, Warsaw, Warsaw University, 1981.

The FEP under Gierek's Rule

The new economic strategy of Edward Gierek was introduced in the early 1970s. Poland made a sharp turn from a
model of self-sufficiency (inefficient import substitution) to an
export-oriented economy, widely open toward the West. The
introduction of superior Western technology was to bring Poland
more rapidly into the family of developed nations. Simultaneously
an expansion of food consumption was planned. Western credits
were to pay for the initial growth acceleration; increased exports, products of modernized industries, were to allow for
debt repayment in due course. The FEP was to become the
major tool in implementing the new strategy. This was an obvious
upgrading of past activity traditionally limited to selling surplus
goods and buying necessities abroad. Construction and implementation of this new strategy involved a number of economic
policy errors in the choice of preferred industries, income and
pricing policies, and miscomprehension of Western economic
cycles. Many of these errors resulted from political intrusion
rather than from the ineptitude of Polish economists. This
ambitious new economic expansion strategy was imposed on old
institutional and political structures that were poorly prepared
to deal with any nonroutine tasks.

The following discussion attempts to identify the most
significant distortions in the functioning of the FEP that were
inflicted by internal and external political factors.

INTERNAL POLITICAL DETERMINANTS

Monopolization of Power

Without trying to put the phenomena in hierarchical order
according to their contribution to the crisis, the monopolization
of power seems to be the prime source of numerous deficiencies
in the system. There are some well-known attributes of a
monopower situation: those governing are not exposed to sufficient pressures from the governed; the quality of socially
accepted objectives deteriorates in their selection and implementation; channels of information and communication become
blocked. As a result, the governing elite live in an artificial
world of self-delusion that feeds back to the system increasingly
harmful decisions.

In Poland, monopolization of power affected legal and
political systems in three major ways. First, some institutions

were disbanded or changed beyond recognition. This was the
case with many advisory groups of the central decision makers,
critical newspapers, or radio-TV programs, youth organizations,
and the Supreme Chamber of Control. Second, some institutions
are maintained but in practice are deprived of constitutional or
real participation in policy making. This was the case with the
Sejm (Polish parliament), allied parties (United Peasants' Party,
Democratic Party), and the National Unity Front (FJN). The
third effect is a merger of political power and administration,
generally in the form of a personal union. The same people,
or their close collaborators, occupy the top positions in the
Communist Party, government, and other central institutions.

Monopolization of power did not mean special privileges
for the whole Communist Party. The influence of average party
members on decision making at the national level was no greater
than that of nonparty citizens. In fact, the influence of both
was nonexistent, since the phenomenon of power monopolization
was enforced and intertwined with power centralization and
alienation. Lack of social participation in decision making within
the Polish United Workers' Party was especially detrimental to
the economy. The decisions were made by a small group of
leaders. Rank-and-file members as well as the Central Committee
were deprived of a role in policy making. As was stated in
"Information on the Causes of Strikes" at the Sixth Plenum of
the Central Committee of the Polish United Workers' Party in
October 1980:

> One warned about the consequences of the excessive
> indebtedness of the country, the widening of the
> investment front and the danger of inflation stem-
> ming from the budget policies. . . . In practice
> these warnings were ignored, resolutions were
> passed but not implemented. All voices indicating
> the dangers of selected policies were disregarded.
> Voluntaristic tendencies were becoming stronger
> and stronger and gradually propaganda policy was
> subordinated to them. It strongly affected the
> style of party functioning. Intra-party discussion
> was substituted by commands. The fundamental
> principle of democratic centralism was applied in
> an unbalanced way with excessive accent on
> centralism. [1]

Overzealous centralization deprived not only individual
citizens but also, and more dangerously, the production enter-

prise of an impact on the center's decisions. The centralized bureaucracy acted as exclusive owner of the country. The economy was treated not as a profit-making mechanism, but as a means of attaining domestic and foreign policy objectives. Hence, steady depreciation of economic determinants in decision making occurred, while the role of administrative command increased. Resistance of the economy, stemming at least from common sense, was being countered with multiple legal regulations and political commands. In this sense a perpetuum mobile was created, which only a total collapse of the economy could stop. A similar phenomenon in a single private enterprise would lead shortly to bankruptcy. The whole state could survive much longer because of such practices as exploitation of natural deposits, poorly controlled pollution of the environment, relatively cheap labor, and, last but not least, unreasonable extensive borrowing from abroad. Opportunities of maneuvering and postponing the final collapse were quite substantial here. The basic contradiction was that the privileged central bureaucracy struggled for its survival by strengthening the counterproductive system, which was the primary reason for the state's decline.

Political-Administrative Unity

The significant phenomenon, which in the area of the division of power distinguishes the 1970s from former periods, was the merger of political power (Communist Party apparatus) with administration (organs of government). The new bureaucracy monopolized prestige, power, and material profits. Political power lost its control over administration and in fact identified with it. Criticism was treated as a hostile action, and any substantial reforms were virtually impossible. The problem was addressed by Stanislaw Kania at the Sixth Plenum:

> The relations between the party and the state have to be seriously reconsidered by the Central Committee. . . . Especially detrimental was the far advanced union between the centers of political and economic decision making which deformed the decision-making process and blurred responsibility. [2]

Political-administrative unity led to identifiable results. Usurping administrative competencies by the political apparatus accelerated the ever-present tendency toward bureaucratization, substitution of long-term ideological objectives in favor of incrementalism and instrumentalism, and proneness to leadership by administrative command rather than by action. The merger of political power and economic administration affected negatively the quality of decisions, hampered the functioning of the economy, and increased the public cost of management. Close symbiosis of administration and political power resulted also in the unity of their interests. Promotion of unprofitable and socially unacceptable production was made possible through granting privileges to a relatively broad group of economic managers. This created a mutual reliance. Although managers did not enjoy significant decision-making power themselves, they could form different coalitions and exert pressure through regional and branch lobbies. More important, they supported this specific system of power since ". . . in another system, which would socialize and not nationalize the economy, this bureaucracy would be unnecessary."[3]

Centralized Bureaucracy and Flow of Information

The centralized bureaucracy was unwilling to listen to outside advice and was unable to reform itself from inside. The best example was provided by the most significant economic reform effort of the 1970s—the so-called Large Economic Organization (WOG). The central apparatus did not agree to share even the modest amount of power envisaged for a limited number of big enterprises. Instead of creating a first step toward economic reform, the WOG program was quietly discontinued by the passive resistance of the central bureaucracy that was supposed to implement it.

The monopolistic bureaucracy affected the flow of information in many directions and dimensions. Probably the most detrimental for the national economy was the distortion of information given to the leaders, information on which basic economic decisions were made. As observed in Zycie Gospodarcze weekly:

We have seen the limited competency of central decision-makers' lack of demand for authentic advising, keeping independent opinions and evaluations from the public, and presumptuousness in its own infallibility strengthened by court economists. . . . Political and economic leadership, deprived of reliable channels of information and independent evaluation by specialists, listened in that period

> only to its own voice and demanded the public
> share in this same illusion. 4

The term court economists refers to a group of specialists
whose main tasks consisted of rubber stamping decisions already
made. This practice developed gradually throughout the 1970s.
In the beginning it looked as if Gierek's team favored broader
participation by scientists and experts in shaping major economic
and social programs. Various advisory committees and councils
flourished, some of them making plans up to the year 2000.
However, formalized attitudes toward professional advice soon
prevailed. Some recommendations were retained as window
dressing, while others less amenable to the established policy
were neglected and/or classified. Their authors were often
dismissed or, less often, submitted resignations. According
to Professor Pawel Bozyk, probably Gierek's most influential
economic advisor, authors of critical reports were accused at
random of incompetence, lack of information in context, or
unproductive pessimism. Some resolutions were held up to
ridicule. 5

The rigid organism of a centrally planned economy has
proven its inability to adopt even fairly safe technocratic modifi-
cation. This supports a more general thesis that specific,
organizational solutions from modern Western systems cannot
be successfully transplanted on an unprepared body of command
economics. In order for them to succeed, their new environment
must be first seasoned by deep reforms of basic economic and
political mechanisms.

The functioning of the centralized bureaucracy was specifically influenced by psychological characteristics of the
leaders. A new kind of personality cult was created around
First Secretary Gierek. Central Committee members raised this
problem at the Sixth Plenum in 1980, seeing the egregious error
of the 1970s in the identification with new leadership rather
than with socialism. Most substantive decisions were presented
to the public as initiatives of the first secretary; any criticism
was seen as a personal attack on Gierek. Therefore, censorship
extended not only to specific unfavorable mass media opinions
on new development strategy but also to publicly known, costly
errors like the purchase of the Berliet bus technology.

It may be difficult to understand why many experts continued in the leadership camp despite the harsh treatment they
received, but Professor Bozyk's opinion on Gierek shed light
on the issue. When asked in a press interview why First Secretary Gierek dismissed neither Prime Minister Jaroszewicz nor
himself, Bozyk replied:

> It seems to me that Gierek generally avoided deci-
> sions. He wanted to know the truth, but did not
> want to, or could not use it as a political weapon.
> On the other hand I have to admit that he defended
> me against my enemies. One wanted to send me on
> a permanent mission abroad or nominate me to the
> Vice Chairmanship of the Planning Commission,
> but Gierek did not agree to it. [6]

A technocratic style of managing the economy can theoretically be effective when the leadership is sufficiently well trained
or can absorb professional advice on a regular basis, since
other channels of information from the governed do not function.
Neither of these alternatives was available in Poland in the
1970s. Hence, quite naturally, economic decisions were made
on noneconomic (political) or quasieconomic premises. An obvious
characteristic of political criteria is that one can hardly measure
them, which rules out application of cost and profit analysis
and imposes subjective evaluation. Employment of vague and
enigmatic principles of social preferences opened doors wide
for arbitrary central bureaucracy control based on megalomania
or on private interests. The central bureaucracy tried to
counterbalance the obvious ineffectiveness of arbitrary and
voluntaristic decision making through intensified propaganda
efforts. The worse the economic situation became, the stronger
were the so-called success propaganda campaigns. Insignificant
achievements were inflated into striking successes. Critical
policy interpretations were suppressed. Pervasive insincerity
grew; admiration for loud words flourished; cliche phrases were
used, among them "building of the Second Poland," "catching
up with the most developed industrial democracies." Poland
was called the "tenth industrial nation in the world."
    The propaganda mechanism was supplemented by selective
censorship. Cultural life and the humanities could counter this
system through unofficial means of expression. Economic analysis, however, requires basic information. And statistics were
commonly falsified. Many apartment houses were built, much
livestock grown, many pigs raised, but only on paper. Public
access to data concerning foreign economic policy was guarded
in the extreme. There was no way to learn anything specific
about prices in Polish-Soviet trade or Poland's foreign indebtedness. Does it not sound interesting when the chairman of the
State Council and a full member of the Politburo complains that
this phenomenon encompassed the latter body to the extent
". . . where one could not, for example, obtain in spite of many

entreaties any information about the actual indebtedness of the country?"[7]

Personnel Policy

To blame Gierek's select decision-making team for all the shortcomings of the economy in the 1970s would be an over-simplification. The number of people responsible is much greater. Therefore, it would be fruitful to have a closer look at the principles of personnel policy implemented by the leadership of the period:

In electing cadres one preferred people prone to implement passively the decisions of their superiors. The promotion of nonconformist cadres was hampered. . . . Some were even dismissed from social, political and economic activity.[8]

Nomenklatura reserved all important positions for party members or people approved by the party apparatus. Nevertheless, neither the ideological views nor the professional qualifications were the basic criteria for selection; subjection to relevant superiors was. This negative selection process of leading cadres, based on subordination and forced compliance, led to wrong decisions and, consequently, to substantial economic and social losses.

The function of nomenklatura was clearly observable in the FEP. Executive positions within the Foreign Trade Ministry, foreign trade enterprises, and economic missions abroad were regarded as lucrative sinecures because they entailed, among other assets, frequent travel abroad and per diem allowances in hard currency. Rueful protests of economists could not stop the steady flow of appointments made often in return for political or personal loyalty and services. It may be worth stressing again that nomenklatura did not restrict executive positions to Polish United Workers' Party members. It meant consent by an adequate-level party committee to a certain nomination. According to Polityka, nomenklatura accounted for 15 percent of the positions in the economy.[9]

The high economic costs of nomenklatura, not to mention its social and psychological effects, did not deter these practices because of the blurred borders of accountability and decision-making discretion. This has not only enhanced voluntarism but also encouraged corrupt practices. Although this problem did not contribute significantly to the present economic difficulties of Poland, in that it was not luxurious villas and foreign travel at state expense that brought Poland to a crisis, it was a prominent social issue that affected the political situation.

Wlodzimierz Bojarski, a professor of the Polish Academy of Sciences, perceives the problems in terms of social justice:

> Anonymity in economic and social life and obscuring the accountability must be ended. If a cashier takes from the state 1,000 zlotys, this offence is prosecuted with the whole strictness of law . . . while the erroneous but perhaps not unselfish purchase of the manufacturing license and the waste of billions worth of equipment is only a "misjudgement which could happen to anybody."[10]

Impunity and corruption within the bureaucratic elite affected the public, which began to regard these phenomena as normal practices. Demoralization spread within the society. Respect for law and equality under law as well as work ethics suffered significantly. In regard to the FEP, specifically, a significant number of contracts with the West put the Polish side in an inferior position. Reasons varied from incompetency of foreign trade decision makers, who lacked adequate economic or legal training, to petty bribery, which was often out of proportion to the losses it caused. As a result many purchases, especially machinery, did not meet expected objectives, contractual fines had to be paid, or investments were not completed by foreign contractors. A perfect example of the latter is the infamous construction of the Polish Airlines hotel in Warsaw.

Western firms were quick to recognize opportunities in this state of affairs. In instructions for trading with Poland unconventional methods were emphasized often, bringing to mind, but on a smaller scale, the past Lockheed practices.[11]

Pressure Group Activities

The FEP also suffered from the activities of pressure groups. FEP institutions did not constitute a pressure group by themselves. This was the logical result of the auxiliary role of foreign trade in the national policy. Pressure groups developed alongside political power within the bureaucracy throughout regions and branches of the economy. This process was accelerated by the relative abundance and availability of foreign

credits in the early 1970s. The lack of a rational economic
strategy and of a functional interest articulation mechanism
allowed strong groups to become even stronger, and as a result
interregion and interbranch disparities substantially increased.
Lack of a comprehensive strategy allowed pressure groups to
shape investment policies in a voluntaristic way. In the absence
of economic indicators enterprise managers were often evaluated
according to their ability to generate investment. Needless to
say, only investments in Western products and technologies
were regarded as valuable.

Existence of competing pressure groups affected the political
system's effectiveness. Correct functioning of FEP demands
coordinated policies and legally determined relations between
relevant government agencies and party organs. In reality
there was a lack of adequate cooperation between the Ministry
of Foreign Trade and the Ministry of Foreign Affairs. One
even spoke at a certain period about the antieconomic attitude
of the latter. Even worse, similar rivalry took place at the
top level of decision making in the Communist Party:

> . . . evaluation and conclusions prepared in the
> Central Committee were neglected or treated as a
> challenge to the government or even personal
> intrigue. . . . In effect, Politbureau meetings
> devoted to economic issues were dominated by
> party leaders responsible for specific branches
> of the economy in the Government. . . .
> Participating in such meetings, one could not resist
> the feeling of complete isolation from the country's
> realities. It was like life in a different world.[12]

The functioning of special interest groups does not in itself
constitute pathology as shown by the experience of other countries. In Poland's case, however, pressure groups acting within
the organs of the government system merged with the upper
echelons of the economic managers. The ministries pursued
their own particular interests instead of promoting a process
of impartial moderation in which group interests would be democratically articulated and aggregated. Overgrown ambitions
and political-ideological inhibitions of the ruling elite made it
possible for pressure groups to thrive. This resulted, for
example, in preferential treatment of the automobile and steel
industries that condemned less impressive branches of the
economy—light industry, energy production, and agriculture—
to notorious underinvestment.

Planning System

Politics affected FEP indirectly through the planning system. Developed in the late 1970s, the idea of an open plan exposed the national budget to unending corrections stemming from pressure group activities. Whatever the merits of planning, as expressed in a national budget bill submitted to the Sejm, they were profoundly wasted during the following year. Long-term planning could not function in such a situation. The role of the Planning Commission evolved toward an ad hoc decision-making executive organ to the detriment of its strategy formulation tasks. According to the not-too-self-critical complaints of the former Planning Commission chairman:

> In spite of official adherence to the superiority of
> social objectives, our party did not have such a
> policy besides slogans. This substantially hampered
> five- and one-year planning. The supremacy of
> operative decisions of political authorities also
> detrimentally influenced planning.13

Frequent interventions of deputy premiers and telephone calls from the Central Committee surely did not make life easy for any planners, but the planning system also had its own deficiencies. The foreign trade enterprises had to fulfill plans for exports and imports that were expressed often in quantitative terms only, usually in dollars or tons. Eagerness to fulfill a plan often contradicted basic principles of economic effectiveness. Lack of a coherent system of Polish zloty exchange rates hampered financial incentives for export-producing enterprises. Offered profits were disproportionately small in comparison with necessary efforts to ensure, for example, satisfactory quality.

State monopoly of foreign trade added an extra step between domestic producers, foreign buyers, and foreign trade organizations (FTO). Coordination of various FTOs was inadequate and led to the duplication of efforts in developing foreign markets. Often similar goods were exported at cheaper prices and imported at more expensive prices because of the rigid division of competencies among the FTOs and because of pressures to fulfill the plan. Preoccupied with pursuing their own particular interests, relevant ministries did not control economic validity and effectiveness of investments from abroad.

The weakness of the financial control of global borrowing led to dangerously excessive indebtedness in comparison to export capacity. An instrumental attitude toward the FEP deprived it of a rationally constructed strategy. This can be best observed in Poland's international financial relations. Wrongly conceived attitudes toward the credit policy (in this case one should blame the court economists rather than the decision makers) argued for borrowing as much and as quickly as possible since credits "do not cost anything because of the steady depreciation of Western currencies."[14] The effects of this approach, described by a Central Committee member as "I never come back with empty hands,"[15] are clearly seen today.

An analogous situation existed in foreign trade. The basically correct idea of opening Poland's economy to the world market was realized incrementally and inconsistently; that is, it did not develop a necessary program of export-oriented branches of industry. As a result, new investments from the first half of the 1970s promoted increased imports instead of contributing to exports. Long-term vision was dominated by fascination with dynamics. Qualitative and structural aspects of economic progress were disregarded.

EXTERNAL POLITICAL DETERMINANTS

West Oriented Development Strategy

The Gierek team's foreign policy toward the West is probably the brightest aspect of its record. Normalization with the Federal Republic of Germany and intensification of political relations with other West European countries and the United States created a favorable atmosphere for the expansion of economic cooperation. Although the oil crisis and economic recession activated protectionist policies in the West, this factor can be disregarded as it is relatively insignificant in comparison with the domestic causes of the present economic situation. Similarly, arguments blaming the West's generosity in granting credits or negotiating proficiency and experience for Poland's crisis sound unconvincing. Excessive dependence on Western imports, an almost hopeless level of indebtedness, and clearly disadvantageous commercial contracts are direct results of internal determinants, often of a political character. For example, exploitation of foreign-policy-originated opportunities by internal forces can be well observed in the infamous Berliet bus transaction as described in Polityka:

In 1972 a top level visit to France was prepared. One could not go with empty hands. One had to have some serious proposals for Polish-French cooperation. The machine manufacturing lobby immediately took advantage of the situation and presented its own proposal to purchase the license from Berliet, although it was obvious from the beginning that this was not the bus we needed.16

The policies of Western governments and private banks in the 1970s created an environment for an economic acceleration strategy based on Western credits and technology. However, Western credits had no strings attached that would control their utilization. Hence, the responsibility for final results of this process belongs almost exclusively to the participants in the domestic system of power.

Ties with Soviet Union

The post-August 1980 crisis gave a new impetus to numerous opinions accusing the Soviet Union of economic exploitation of Poland. Such opinions are much more frequent in Poland than in the West; quite contrary views are held by the Soviet public. This phenomenon seems to be a logical reaction to a lack of reliable relevant information over many years. The problem was taboo in the mass media, which were almost never allowed to go beyond traditional propaganda-like cliche phrases. This reinforced prejudices and suspicions well justified in the Stalin era and before. Improved information in Poland in 1980-81 makes it possible to question the merits of such common views.

It seems that the Council for Mutual Economic Assistance (CMEA) system of raw materials pricing (so-called stepping prices) favors importers from the Soviet Union. According to First Deputy Minister of Foreign Trade Nestorowicz, Poland paid, for example, 8.5 zloty dewizowy billion (about $2.1 billion) for all raw materials imported from the Soviet Union in 1980. That would cost zloty dewizowy 19.5 billion (about $4.9 billion) on the world market. One ton of crude oil cost Poland about $100 less than the world price.17

This opinion seems to be generally shared by a number of Western specialists, especially by the Wharton Econometric Forecasting Associates.18 While their arguments may well be valid, they do not give a full answer to the basic, though usually more emotional than scientific, question—"who exploits whom?" For one should also take into account murky problems of transfer ruble regarding pricing of Polish machinery, ships, and consumer products exported to the Soviet Union. Thorough analysis should encompass mutual deliveries of military equipment as well. It is here that lack of any data is most evident. Many Polish economists suspect that the Soviet Union may use her monopolistic supplier position to set up prices that easily make up for price structures of nonmilitary products that favor Poland.

In the case of raw materials, products are standardized and the world market serves as a reliable frame of reference. In the case of individualized products, a number of factors difficult to quantify play an important role. The Soviet market accepts large amounts of Polish products that would be hardly competitive on Western markets; it allows long-term production planning based on a stable customer; it also serves as a cushion for internationally troubled industries like shipbuilding.

Industrial product trade between Poland and the Soviet Union suffers additionally from the absence of even primitive market-type price indicators. In other words, even in the absence of malice or systemic exploitation, prices of industrial goods must be distorted in many instances. One may well doubt if even those with unrestricted access to data in both countries have a clear picture of the overall situation.

If the Soviet Union were to be blamed for the problems of the Polish economy one should do it rather in historical terms of imposing a specific type of development strategy in the 1950s and specific international division of labor in the 1960s. Simple comparison with other East European countries in the 1970s does not indicate any special role played by the Soviet Union in Poland's FEP as compared with East Germany, Czechoslovakia, or Hungary. In this sense the finding of economic relations with the Soviet Union a major factor in Poland's financial and economic crisis of 1980-82 seems to point more to ideologically preconceived notions than to an objective scrutiny of reality.

Commitments toward Other CMEA Countries

Another popular opinion blames Poland's participation in CMEA, which in the so-called socialist division of labor imposes unprofitable tasks on Poland. The picture is, however, much more complicated as far, at least, as the last decade is concerned. Polish decision makers were so excited by the prospect of increased cooperation with the West that possibilities available within CMEA were often neglected. The information of the Sixth Plenum put this problem rather mildly:

> Imported know-how was not fully utilized . . .
> because the proportion of unsuccessful purchases
> was too large. . . . By industrial cooperation
> with socialist countries, one could advantageously
> solve many problems which one tried to solve by
> purchasing know-how from capitalist countries. [19]

This process was strengthened by the actual slower pace of
CMEA economic integration in the 1970s. Poland was not the
only country that developed commercial relations with the Western
countries faster than with CMEA partners. Nevertheless many
potential chances were wasted. Acting as pressure groups,
industrial sectors—mainly the electric and machine building
branches—convinced political leaders that valid projects could
be realized only through cooperation with Western firms. During
the last decade Poland purchased 428 technologies abroad.
Only 30 of them came from Poland's two primary trading partners,
the Soviet Union and the German Democratic Republic. [20]
    Some healthy industrial cooperation efforts between Poland
and neighboring countries were terminated, especially with
Czechoslovakia. Many interchangeable Western technologies
were purchased by CMEA countries on a strictly bilateral basis,
especially in the automobile and telecommunication industries.
Economic effects of concentration of capital and mass-scale
production were lost quite often because of particularistic
pressure group interests or nationalistic pretensions.
    On the other hand, one may observe that the highly sophis-
ticated structure of political cooperation within CMEA was, at
least in Poland, poorly translated into a motivational system
toward international integration on a branch and enterprise
level. According to my personal observations and interviews
in Poland, integrational decisions of single enterprises were
based usually on two premises. One, mostly they were under
pressure from administrative commands—"we were told to do it."
And two, in smaller part, from an effort to create a window-
dressing impression of doing something "integrational," "because
otherwise we would not get new investment funds."[21]

POLITICAL AND ECONOMIC INTERDEPENDENCE

    An analysis of Poland's FEP in the 1970s seems to make
possible some more general conclusions concerning interdependence of politics and economics in a socialist state. Poland's FEP

in the 1970s was exposed to an increasing predominance of political determinants over economic ones. This predominance, present primarily at the macroeconomic (national) level of decision making, subsequently expanded to the microeconomic (enterprise) level. It was realized both through institutionalized channels (central planning, foreign trade monopoly) and informal ways (nomenklatura, pressure groups, monopolization of power by bureaucracy).

The predominance of political determinants lowered the general effectiveness of the economy. This in turn affected negatively the political system by simultaneously increasing overall discontent and consolidating detrimental practices of political intrusion since the political system was unable to self-reform. Possible solutions to the worsening situation were perceived in multiplying orders rather than in limiting political influence on the economy.

Economic costs of maintaining this vicious circle were high and possibly could have been afforded for a longer period of time because of easy access to domestic resources—raw materials, cheap labor—and to external resources—foreign credits. But depletion of these resources proved the dysfunctionality of the system, and a crisis situation followed. Ways out of this situation lead through radical depoliticization of economics and through the establishment of a political system auxiliary to the reformed economy. One may observe that the maximal scope of economic reforms is delimited by political and ideological determinants of internal and external systems. At the same time, however, these determinants have to include the size of economic needs and psychological phenomena (work motivation, credibility of government) of people involved in this process.

Thorough analysis should address the scope of the political determinant's detrimental effects on FEP. This seems hardly possible in quantitative terms since, suffice it to say, the frame of reference in the form of a cohesive system of economic per-formance parameters in a centrally planned economy is lacking. In such a situation, the student of the problem has to limit his or her objectives to putting relevant determinants in order according to their weight assigned by decision makers and to reconstructing their causal relationship.

External political factors played a relatively passive role in Poland's FEP of the 1970s. They contributed to the creation of a favorable external environment but did not influence signifi-cantly the formulation and implementation of specific strategies. They may be treated as a constant since their role in causing the 1980s crisis was marginal when compared to internal deter-minants.

The main characteristics of Poland's political system in the 1970s, which detrimentally influenced the FEP, was the steadily diminishing social participation in decision making. Historically, the system of economic management in FEP existed prior to decreasing social participation or increasing alienation of power. Yet the system's inability to correct itself was due basically to the diminished social participation.

The quasitechnocratic rule introduced by Gierek's team interacted with inherited economic management systems, creating the most important phenomenon of the political-economic system of the 1970s—monolithic bureaucracy. Monopolization and centralization of power were primarily responsible for the entire sequence of effects in economic policy, including the FEP. These effects extended into the economic, political, and social life. Among the most prominent was the strategy of economic development that was rather well-intended but erroneously conceived, constructed, and implemented. In each of these stages one could find incrementalism, arbitrariness, and incompetence. The strategy and economic management system lacked self-correction mechanisms. The political-economic bureaucracy monopoly treated reformist proposals as hostile actions oriented directly against its interests. The survival of the monolithic bureaucracy depended directly on a distorted flow of information. Specifically tailored propaganda successfully cut off both the central decision makers and the public from the realities of the nation's economic situation.

Maintenance of power by the monolithic bureaucracy demanded a specifically shaped personnel policy. It was founded basically on loyalty to individuals at the expense of loyalty to ideology and/or professional qualifications. Monolithic bureaucracy rule effectively dismantled the institutional system of power from the party itself to the executive, legislative, and judicial branches of government, as well as to social organizations. The main characteristic of that system of decision making was the overlapping of competencies and blurring of borders of accountability.

In general, one may conclude that the FEP of Poland in the 1970s was clearly following the national economic policy. The influence of the international environment and of Poland's foreign policy was insignificant. For this reason FEP was subject to all the illnesses of the national economic policy.

THE FEP IN THE 1980s

Sixteen months of Solidarity did not impose significant changes on the FEP. As with the overall economy, more data became available to the public, more scandals were revealed, competent people were allowed more of a say, more corrupt officials were dismissed but the basic institutional and decision-making structure was left intact. The FEP was frequently discussed as part of radical economic reform proposals. These proposals were never close to implementation. The struggle for political power seemed to absorb the bulk of energy and basic economic issues did not generate much interest. However, the rapidly deteriorating financial situation reduced FEP's already questionable independence from politics when credit availability and rescheduling agreements became heavily dependent on non-economic considerations in Poland and abroad.

The imposition of martial law in December 1981 first paralyzed the FEP together with the rest of the economy and later raised vital questions as to its future role. It seems fairly clear that the state of limbo strategy of the Polish economy in 1982 cannot last much longer. Up-to-date efforts have been focused primarily on reducing losses and surviving at any price.

Warsaw will soon be compelled to make critical decisions concerning the scope of its cooperation and dependence on both the Soviet Union and the West. The choice is complicated by the existence of differing attitudes and interests within the ruling elite as well as by often contradictory interests of the Soviet Union, United States, and Western Europe in regard to Poland.

The principal distinction between conceivable options refers to availability of foreign (Western) credits. If credits become available, foreign trade may change in character from the major economic bottleneck to a leading factor in economic recovery. If credits are not available the only alternative is further integration within the Soviet economy, and, on a smaller scale, with other East European countries. Economic reasoning clearly favors the option based on cooperation with the West. Its implementation, however, depends on meeting a number of political conditions.

The first condition requires some level of accommodation between the rulers and the ruled in Poland as well as sensitivity to economic problems among the ruling elite, which would overcome its political and ideological imperatives and prejudices. The second calls for a concrete improvement in Soviet-U.S. relations, especially in the field of arms control. It is hard to expect both superpowers to treat Poland at her own merits while their bilateral relations deteriorate. The third condition asks for an international assistance program necessarily based on interbloc coordination and relative goodwill.

Fulfillment of these political conditions would mean a major breakthrough in the post-World War II patterns of East-West relations and therefore does not seem likely. Its absence will have grave consequences for the Polish economy and consequently for the political and economic conditions of life for the Polish people for the rest of this century.

NOTES

1. "Informacja o przebiegu i tle wydarzen strajkowych (Information on the Course and the Background of the Strike Events)," at the Sixth Plenum of the Central Committee of the Polish United Workers' Party (CC PUPW), Nowe Drogi, October/ November 1980, p. 47.

2. Stanislaw Kania at the Sixth Plenum of the CC PUWP, September 4-5, 1980, Nowe Drogi, October/November 1980, p. 28.

3. Ernest Skalski, "Dlaczego Nie Mozna Inaczej," Tygodnik Solidarnosc, August 1981.

4. Mieczyslaw Nasilowski, "Reorientacja Myslenia i Dzialania," Zycie Gospodarcze, November 19, 1980.

5. See Pawel Bozyk's pronouncement at the Sixth Plenum of CC PUWP, September 4-5, 1980; Nowe Drogi, October/ November 1980, pp. 294-296.

6. Pawel Bozyk, "Interview," Polityka, October 30, 1980.

7. Henryk Jablonski at the Sixth Plenum of the CC PUWP, Nowe Drogi, October/November 1980, p. 270.

8. "Informacja o przebiegu i tle wydarzen strajkowych," Nowe Drogi, October/November 1980, p. 55.

9. Piotr Moszczynski, "Dobry Fachowiec Alg," Polityka, October 17, 1981.

10. Wlodzimierz Bojarski, Przeglad Techniczny, December 21, 1980.

11. For more information see Jozef Kusimierek, Przeglad Techniczny, September 6, 1981.

12. Manfred Gorywoda at the Sixth Plenum of the CC PUWP, Nowe Drogi, October/November 1980, pp. 317-318.

13. Tadeusz Wrzaszczyk at the Sixth Plenum of the CC PUWP, Nowe Drogi, October/November 1980, p. 99.

14. Wieslaw Rydygier, "Zludzenia i Rzeczywistosc," Zycie Gospodarcze, October 12, 1980.

15. Eugenieusz Stawinski at the Sixth Plenum of the CC PUWP, Nowe Drogi, October/November 1980, p. 206.

16. Stanislaw Gruzewski, "Jak do Tego Doszlo?" Polityka, October 18, 1980.

17. Interview with Tadeusz Nestorowicz, Trybuna Ludu, September 21, 1981.

18. Wharton Econometric Associates estimates Soviet trade subsidies to Poland over the 1970s at a 1982 value of $13.6 billion, The Economist (London, February 13, 1982).

19. "Informacja o przebiegu i tle wydarzen strajkowych," Nowe Drogi, October/November 1980, p. 48.

20. "Licencje: Niewykorzystane Mozliwosci," interview with Deputy Minister of Science, Higher Education and Technology, Mieczyslaw Kazimierczuk, Zycie Partii, September 16, 1981.

21. Marcin Sar, "Zagraniczna Polityka Ekonomiczna PRL (Poland's Foreign Economic Policy)" in Jozef Kukulka, ed., Problemy i Kierunki Miedzynarodowej Aktywnosci Polski Ludowej, 1944-1979 (Warszawa, KAW, was to appear in 1981).

4.

Agriculture and the Polish Renewal

Andrzej Korbonski

INTRODUCTION

When the district court in Warsaw met on May 12, 1981 to consider granting legal recognition to an independent union of Polish peasants, Rural Solidarity, people outside the court building carried banners that read: "If you register us, you'll eat bread and butter with ham."[1] This single sentence, which called for the legalization of an independent union of Polish peasants, epitomized to a large extent the critical problems of Polish agriculture at the beginning of the 1980s, raising the question of whether the slogan reflected only wishful thinking or whether it truly represented a promise of things to come.

Seven months later—to the day—the imposition of martial law by General Jaruzelski, followed by the imprisonment of thousands of free trade unionists, including the leadership of Rural Solidarity, terminated, at least for the time being, the unprecedented experiment of an independent peasant trade unionism in a communist state.

Finally, at the end of June 1983, in the aftermath of Pope John Paul II's second visit to his native country, it became known that the Polish military regime agreed to the establishment of an endowment or a foundation, controlled by the Catholic church, which would provide financial aid to individual Polish peasants. The foundation was to channel initially a minimum of $2 billion in the form of grants, the funds for which have been raised by Catholic church agencies in West Germany, France, and Italy.[2]

These three events, occurring within roughly two years, provide a good illustration of the complex character of the Polish farm sector in the early 1980s. This means that anyone attempting to analyze the current situation in Polish agriculture is faced with a complicated and difficult task that stems largely from the nature of the beast itself. It would be fairly easy to discuss Polish agriculture as an economic sector. The literature on the subject is quite voluminous and so are the official statistical data. The same is true for rural sociology, which has long enjoyed a venerable tradition in Poland. One could even come up with an analysis of the politics of Polish agriculture. The problem is that none of these studies would be very satisfactory and all of them would provide only a partial explanation of the difficulties experienced by the farm sector and of the sharp dilemmas faced by the Polish military junta trying to find a solution to the various problems.

The peculiarity of Polish agriculture lay in the fact that in the past thirty years it has become an increasingly complex amalgam of closely intertwined political, economic, and social issues that have defied an easy solution. Moreover, as suggested by one of the most perceptive observers of the contemporary Polish scene, in no other socioeconomic sector in Poland could one find so many deeply rooted prejudices, conflicts, and myths that, although discredited in practice a long time ago, were still considered as dogmas by the ruling party.[3] As a result, the official policy toward agriculture since the mid-1950s has been characterized by a kind of schizophrenia, with pragmatic and rational thinking interspersed with dogmatic and irrational ideas. The conflict between them came to a head in the second half of the 1970s, contributing to the emergence of the current political and economic crisis.

The purpose of this chapter is to highlight some of the economic, social, and political issues confronting Polish agriculture during the critical three years from the signing of the social compact between the workers and the government in Gdansk in August 1980 to June 1983. Thus an attempt will be made to analyze the chain of events that linked these two dates and led directly to what appears to be a new chapter in the postwar history of Polish agriculture.

AGRICULTURE PRIOR TO 1980

The present crisis in the farm sector is an outcome of policies that began at the time of the communist seizure of power after World War II. The various developments have been analyzed in greater or lesser detail and there is no need to

restate the various arguments. [4] Only a brief summary will
suffice to provide the necessary background for the main narra-
tive.

There is no doubt that the various difficulties faced by
Polish agriculture since then were above all political rather than
economic. The generally unimpressive economic performance
of the farm sector was clearly the outcome of faulty, if not
perverse, political decisions made by the Polish ruling oligarchy.
The incontestable conclusion that emerges from looking at the
official policy toward agriculture in the 1960s and 1970s is that
the Polish leadership has essentially reverted to its traditional
stance of regarding agriculture as a marginal sector that had
to be barely tolerated as a necessary evil. To put it differently,
the private sector, which still accounted for a lion's share of
agriculture production, had in particular been perceived officially
as a cow that could be indefinitely milked without receiving much
in return. The attitude, of course, was hardly new. It had
strongly influenced the Polish party's collectivization policy in
the 1940s and 1950s and it clearly permeated the more benign
policy toward the private sector during the Gomulka rule. The
only real break in the adversary relationship vis-à-vis the
peasantry occurred in the early 1970s, but it proved to be
short lived.

There were so many mistakes committed by the Polish
regime in its farm policy in the second half of the 1970s that
it is difficult to single out the gravest one. Perhaps the most
erroneous one was its policy toward the private agricultural
sector. It was also the most puzzling one in view of its early
support of the individual peasants. Instead of maintaining the
policy favoring private agriculture, at some point in the mid-
1970s Gierek apparently decided to abandon it in favor of
providing strong support to the socialized sector. His addresses
at the Central Committee Plenary Meeting in October 1974,
devoted entirely to agriculture, as well as at the Seventh Party
Congress in December 1975 had little to say about helping the
individual peasants and much about aiding the state sector and
pushing socialization of agriculture. [5] The latter proclamation,
announcing the acceleration of the socialization process, represented a major watershed in the official farm policy.

The reasons for the decision to speed up socialization of
agriculture are obscure. There is no evidence of any pressure
in that direction on the part of the Soviet Union and other East
European countries and thus the initiative had to come from
inside, most likely from Gierek himself. It may be speculated
that having failed in his economic strategy, Gierek was worried

about Moscow's reaction and tried to ingratiate himself with the Kremlin by atoning for his sins via accelerated socialization.[6] There is also little doubt that both Gomulka and Gierek harbored a considerable inferiority complex toward the rest of the Soviet bloc because of their inability to eliminate private agriculture, and while Gomulka did little to remedy the situation, Gierek, whose subservience to Moscow was widely known, decided to please the Kremlin by putting an end to private farms.

Since collectivization was thoroughly discredited in Poland the method chosen by Gierek was to be that of etatization (pegeeryzacja), which consisted of forcing individual peasants to surrender their holdings to state farms rather than forming collective farms. While no terror or other forms of outright coercion were to be used against individual peasants, everything else was being done to make private farming as unattractive and unprofitable as possible, thus providing an incentive for the peasants to transfer their land to state ownership, in the name of the old and venerable Stalinist slogan, "the worse, the better."

The policies used against individual peasants were many and varied, with the result that the peasants were robbed of any incentive to expand their output. Thus, while the prices received by the peasants between 1976 and 1979 increased considerably, so did the prices of fertilizers, building materials, and farm implements, which meant that the real farm income has not risen much, if at all, during that period.[7] What was even worse was the growing shortage of farm inputs resulting either from a decline in their output or the refusal to allocate sufficient quantities to the farm sector. Thus, the 1979 production of fertilizers, pesticides, tractors, ploughs, threshers, potato diggers, and other farm machines, as well as many building materials, was below the output in 1975.[8] Although official statistics indicated that agriculture was receiving increased supplies of energy, especially coal and electricity, there was evidence of perennial shortages of both inputs.

Thus, at the time of growing demand for foodstuffs, the private sector, still the mainstay of Polish agriculture, was neither able nor willing to expand production. In fact, output of some key commodities has actually declined. To be sure, some of the decline was caused by unusually poor weather conditions, but most of it was due to faulty government policies. Thus, the decrease in average yields of major crops was obviously affected by the reduction in the availability of fertilizers and farm machinery, while mounting waste and harvest losses were the result of lack of storage space and transport equipment.

The irrational price policy, which greatly reduced the profitability of individual farming, had some interesting consequences, especially with respect to livestock production and meat supply. The increasing cost of production, mainly that of fodder, resulted in large numbers of individual peasants abandoning livestock production. This was particularly true for the so-called worker-peasants—individuals employed in nonfarm sectors who still owned small farms and commuted to work. Until the late 1970s the worker-peasants raised livestock, mostly hogs, primarily for their own consumption but also occasionally for sale. When it was no longer profitable for them to do it, the consequences were twofold. On the one hand there was an overall decline in animal output, and on the other, worker-peasants, no longer able to satisfy their needs out of their own output, put an additional pressure on the available meat and bread supply channeled through the socialized distribution network. [9]

One of the most telling examples of truly perverse governmental policies concerned the attitude toward the most productive private farms. Despite frequent official declarations promising support for the efficient peasants, little of it was implemented in practice. A good illustration of the far-reaching indifference and disregard of official promises was provided by the policy with regard to land acquisition. One of the perennial problems affecting the performance of Polish agriculture was the small average size of farms, and the government had been on record encouraging peasants to buy or lease additional land in order to increase the scale of their operations. The main source of available land was the so-called State Land Fund (Panstwowy Fundusz Ziemi), a kind of soil bank, which, among other things, included land surrendered to the state by retiring peasants. Yet, according to official statistics, only relatively small amounts of land were actually distributed among individual peasants. [10] Similarly, peasants interested in buying more land were either denied bank credit or refused permission by local apparatchiki. Despite frequent complaints about the small size of farms and progressive fragmentation of private holdings, there is little doubt that the local bureaucrats in fact welcomed it, since declining production and efficiency of the private sector could be used as a good excuse to allocate more resources to the socialized sector.

The role of the middle- and low-ranking party bureaucracy in hindering the development and growth of the private sector cannot be underestimated. It was one thing for the ruling oligarchy to declare its support of individual farming, and another to have it implemented in practice. It may be taken for granted that the rural apparat—both party and government—did not take the official pronouncements too seriously. They had heard it many times before and ignored it just as frequently with total impunity. In their view, highly productive individual farms were serious obstacles on the road to socialization. Although the notorious epithet of kulak was no longer used in public, the official hostile attitude toward efficient, market-oriented peasants remained essentially unchanged for more than a quarter of a century.

By the late 1970s it became obvious that the Gierek regime was quite weak and unable (or unwilling) to force the bureaucracy to execute the policies favorable to the peasants. Moreover, it may also be taken for granted that Warsaw was poorly informed about the true conditions in the countryside and that most of the information was badly distorted, glorifying the accomplishments of the socialized sector and denigrating the efforts of individual peasants. The crisis of June 1976 showed that the Polish leadership had little or no idea about growing popular dissatisfaction and ferment in the country. The channels of communication between the ruling elite and the masses were clogged up for some time and the traditional linkages—the party, the press, and the different transmission belts—were not working properly. This did not seem to bother the Gierek regime, whose attitude toward the various problems plaguing the country was that of arrogance of power that made any rational discussion of peasant problems virtually impossible.

The reverse of the official antagonism toward the individual peasants was the policy favoring the rapid expansion of the state farm sector. As mentioned earlier, the ruling party has never become fully reconciled with the indefinite survival of the private sector. Since collectivization had no future in Poland, the government had essentially two possible options: to increase the public ownership of land or to socialize through the back door by fostering the development of various types of agricultural cooperatives.

The attempt to accelerate the etatization of the farm sector took different forms. On the one hand, farm inputs and investment goods that were not available to individual peasants were in plentiful supply on state farms. The latter were viewed as future granaries and meat factories and despite poor economic results and mounting losses, they were being handsomely endowed with all necessary inputs. Space does not permit a longer discussion of many examples of mismanagement on state farms; suffice it to say that the policy favoring the state sector had little to do with rational economic calculations.[11]

Toward the end of the 1970s it became fairly obvious that the official policy toward agriculture was a complete failure and that on the eve of the 1980s the Gierek regime found itself in a very difficult situation. Its ambitious plans to raise agricultural production and increase food supply lay in shambles and its inept policy succeeded in antagonizing just about every segment of the population, but especially the workers and peasants.

Until then the dismal failure of the agricultural policy was to some extent offset by increasing the import of food products. There was, per se, nothing wrong with importing grain and fodder, especially when the value of Polish food export more than paid for the import. However, beginning in 1972, Poland ceased to be the net exporter of agricultural commodities and the growing cost of imported grain and fodder began to swell the already heavy burden of Poland's hard currency debt.

By the summer of 1980 the economic situation on all fronts was rapidly approaching a crisis and some drastic measures were necessary. In desperation, disregarding the lessons of 1970 and 1976, the regime turned once again to the old trick of raising food prices, which it was apparently viewing as a palliative for all seasons. The official announcement was followed by a series of strikes, which ultimately led to the signing of a "social compact" between the government and the strikers, and to the creation of an independent labor movement, Solidarity.

THE POLISH PEASANTS AND THE CRISIS OF 1980-81

It may be argued that one of the reasons for the highly discriminatory treatment of individual peasants by the successive Polish regimes was the absence of an authentic, institutionalized pressure group that would be able to articulate the peasants' interests.[12] The industrial workers had their unions, which, albeit ineffectively, tried to protect their interests, as had the farm laborers employed on state farms, agricultural circles, and other socialized farm enterprises. Yet despite their large number, the private peasants were deprived of a formal representation.

The peasants' representation in the ruling Communist Party has always been low and, in fact, their relative membership has been declining.[13] Officially, it was assumed that peasants' concerns would be represented by the satellite political party, the United Peasant Party (Zjednoczone Stronnictwo Ludowe), which, especially since the collapse of the collectivization campaign in 1956, had often been consulted with great fanfare by the ruling party. There is little evidence, however, that it has ever amounted to anything more than a traditional transmission belt used as a window dressing to make official policies more palatable to the peasant. As a result, its membership between 1970 and 1979 increased by barely 10 percent, which could be taken as a testimony of low peasant interest in the party.[14]

It also appears that the peasants have not been widely involved in dissident activities that arose in Poland in the wake of the June 1976 crisis. This in itself was not greatly surprising, since until the explosion of the summer of 1980 the political opposition was almost entirely monopolized by members of the urban intelligentsia, whose efforts to build bridges to the industrial workers and the peasants remained largely unsuccessful. Thus, except for a few spontaneously formed groups protesting the government policy of land transfers to the state sector, the peasants appeared largely uninvolved and outside the mainstream of the dissident movement.[15]

It may be assumed that the individual peasants were surprised by the July and August strikes as much as the other segments of Polish society. Little is known about formal and informal contacts between the worker and peasant activists, possibly because there were none. Despite frequent official declarations about the continuing importance of smychka—the worker-peasant alliance—whatever contacts have existed must have been few and far between. During the worker riots in December 1970 and June 1976, the peasants remained on the sidelines and the same appeared true for their behavior in the summer of 1980. The peasants' indifferent attitude did little to establish close linkages with the workers, some of whom were heard to complain that the peasants were being pampered and spoiled by the government and that they were only interested in squeezing the urban consumers by charging exorbitant prices for their products. Nonetheless, these must have been the views of the minority since, interestingly enough, one of the 21 points in the social compact signed in the city of Gdansk on August 31, 1980 included demands for creating favorable conditions for the development of family farming, which the workers viewed as the permanent core of Polish agriculture; for equal treatment of all farm sectors with regard to acquisition of land and means of production; and for the rebirth of a genuine peasant self-government.[16]

There is no doubt that the dynamic growth of the workers' Solidarity movement provided an impetus for the creation of

similar movements by the peasants. Less than a month after
the signing of the Gdansk agreement, three separate rural
Solidarity groups applied to a Warsaw court for a formal registration. After several legal maneuvers Poland's Supreme Court
ruled in February 1981 that, since the individual peasants were
not employees but owners, they could not form a labor union.
Following a merger of the three peasant groups into a single
Rural Solidarity union, the new organization continued its fight
for legalization. Finally, with the active help of the Catholic
church, the peasants won their battle with the government,
which in April agreed to allow the formation of the Rural Solidarity that became formally legalized in May 1981. [17]

The new union issued a programmatic declaration that
spelled out its aim and goals. Its main purpose was the same
as that stated in the Gdansk compact, namely the creation of
lasting conditions of development of private farming seen as
the basic element of Polish agriculture. In contrast to its
industrial sister organization, Rural Solidarity readily acknowledged the leading role of the Communist Party in the Polish
political system and denied harboring any political ambitions.
The declaration also urged equal treatment for all farm sectors,
the creation of conditions that would persuade the young
peasants to remain on land rather than migrate to cities, and
greater powers being given to institutions of rural self-
government. Rural Solidarity indicated its desire to collaborate
closely with the industrial Solidarity movement, while retaining
its own separate identity. [18]

It remained to be seen whether Rural Solidarity would
develop into an authentic spokesman and defender of peasants'
interests. According to its own estimates, within a few weeks
of its formation the new organizations managed to enroll 1.8
million members, representing about half of all individual peasants. [19] Its elected leader, Jan Kulaj, a 23-year-old peasant
from southeastern Poland, appeared to be highly popular with
the rank and file and the union also enjoyed strong support of
the Catholic church.

Agreeing to the legalization of Rural Solidarity must have
been a bitter pill for the Polish government, which resisted it
for a long time. In its opposition to the new union, the regime
was strongly supported by the leadership of the puppet United
Peasants' Party (UPP), which saw the rapid erosion of its traditional status and its own role as the representative of peasant
interests being taken over by the new organization. That
resistance, however, did not last very long as the rank and
file of the UPP supported Rural Solidarity, rebelled against the

conservative leadership, and elected a new one that appeared to be more sympathetic to the aims of the new union.

The government's tactics toward Rural Solidarity resembled that used against the industrial union. In both cases there were lengthy delays in the implementation of the respective agreements and also attempts to minimize the role of Solidarity by supporting the old official unions, which were thoroughly discredited yet were artificially maintained with the help of generous governmental funding. In the case of agriculture, the regime attempted to resurrect the agricultural circles as a form of peasant self-government in an attempt to disrupt the unity of individual peasants.[20]

At the same time, however, there were signs that the ruling party, headed since September 1980 by Stanislaw Kania, was going to pay increasing attention to agriculture. One illustration of this concern was a relatively large number of peasants elected via secret ballot as delegates to the Extraordinary Ninth Congress of the Polish Communist Party, which met in July to discuss and approve various reforms aimed at democratizing the party. As a result there was a striking increase in the number of individual peasants elected to the party's Central Committee. Whereas only a single peasant sat on the Central Committee nominated by the Eighth Party Congress in February 1980, there were 29 peasant members of the committee elected in July 1981, representing, after the industrial workers, the second largest socioeconomic group in that important body.[21]

The new concern for agriculture was also reflected in a programmatic resolution approved by the congress.[22] The resolution emphasized the permanent character of individual farming as an integral part of Poland's socialist economy and guaranteed equal treatment for all agricultural sectors. It promised a major increase in farm investment and a large expansion in industrial production earmarked for agriculture. Finally, it came out in favor of greater self-government in the countryside with the participation of Rural Solidarity. For once the program contained no references to socialist reconstruction of agriculture, which until then had been the main focus of all party declarations dealing with agriculture. It was, without a doubt, the strongest official endorsement of individual farming since the dissolution of the collective farms in 1956.

The rising apprehension resulting from the dismal performance of the farm sector gave rise to a series of measures taken in 1981 that were intended to remedy the errors of the past. To begin with, the regime substantially raised prices paid to peasants, claiming that the increase brought the peasant per

capita income for the first time close to that of the nonfarm
sector. [23] On July 1, 1981, the state farms, which until then
were heavily subsidized and received preferential treatment in
the allocation of investment funds and scarce farm inputs, were
put on a full khozrashchet system, which meant, at least de jure,
the end of their privileged status. The latter measure was in
keeping with the demands of Solidarity—both rural and industrial—
which urged the regime to ensure equal treatment for all agricultural subsectors—state, cooperative, and private. Similar
demands appeared also in the blueprints for economic reforms
submitted by both governmental and nongovernmental bodies. [24]

Following its legalization, Rural Solidarity started negotiations with the government that focused on three major issues
which apparently were given high priority by the peasants.
They were, first, the legal acknowledgment of the permanent
status of individual farming in People's Poland; second, the
final recognition of individual property titles, some of which
remained unsettled since the days of the land reform of 1944;
and third, the already mentioned question of equal treatment
for all agricultural sectors. Although the negotiations dragged
on, it appeared that for once the government was willing to
accede to the demands of the peasants and make a radical break
with the past.

In the meantime, however, the economic situation was
getting from bad to worse. The disastrous harvest of 1980
reduced further the available food supply and there was growing
fear of widespread famine. The latter was averted by emergency
food shipments from the United States, the Common Market
countries, and some of the East European countries, including
the Soviet Union, which, however, did not prevent the introduction of meat and butter rationing. Fortunately the weather
cooperated in 1981, and that year's harvest turned out to be
better than its predecessor. The improvement was particularly
visible in the case of potatoes and sugar beets, which augered
well for the production of meat and sugar, the two items traditionally in high demand. [25]

Nonetheless, the improved harvest did not result immediately
in larger market supplies. On the contrary, the government
reported that both grain and livestock deliveries in the second
half of 1981 lagged considerably behind those of the previous
year, despite higher output. [26] Individual peasants appeared
reluctant to part with their output because of the rapidly growing
inflationary pressure, declining value of money, and increasing
shortages of basic farm inputs. Paradoxically, instead of stimulating deliveries, the rise in farm prices managed to reduce

procurements, since the peasants were not interested in hoarding worthless currency and viewed both their crops and livestock as capital assets whose value appreciated daily.[27]

The peasants' demand for cash was largely satisfied through their direct food sales to urban consumers. For all practical purposes the socialized food distribution system ceased to perform its basic functions, which, to a large extent, were taken over by individual peasants. Prohibited from selling some of their products such as meat on the legal open market, the peasants engaged in widescale black market operations, charging prices well in excess of the official ones and frequently demanding payment in hard currencies.

Nothing better exemplified the depth of Poland's agricultural crisis than this process of primitivization of food distribution. The regime attempted to increase the volume of procurements by introducing the so-called tied sales, whereby the peasants delivering certain foodstuffs would be entitled to purchase scarce household durables and other manufactured goods. The campaign fizzled out when it turned out that the peasants were much more interested in acquiring farm implements than in buying color television sets and the urban consumers resented the preferential treatment given to the peasants.

The latter reaction reflected the growing conflict between the farm and nonfarm segments of the Polish population. Faced with progressive scarcity of basic foodstuffs, the blue-collar workers in particular began again accusing the peasants of withholding food on purpose and trying to enrich themselves at the cost of the urban working class. There were growing demands, even among Solidarity members, for the reintroduction of compulsory deliveries as the only means of ensuring a steady supply of basic foodstuffs. The regime did little to mollify the conflict although it refused to reimpose the quota system, presumably in the hope that various other measures would persuade the peasants to deliver the necessary amounts to the state procurement agencies.

PEASANTS UNDER MARTIAL LAW

The imposition of martial law on December 13, 1981, accompanied by the arrest of the leadership of Rural Solidarity, affected Polish agriculture and the peasants much less than their industrial counterparts. In fact, from the start the military junta began to flirt with the peasants, hoping to induce them to increase the deliveries of foodstuffs.[28]

Thus, a few weeks after the coup, the Polish Communist Party together with the puppet United Peasant Party issued a proclamation reaffirming their support for the continuous existence of the private farm sector. In a well-publicized press conference in January 1982, the Minister of Agriculture strongly defended the private sector against hostile criticism of other East Europeans who blamed private agriculture for Poland's food crisis.[29] In March 1982, when General Jaruzelski made his first visit to Moscow since the imposition of martial law, he was accompanied by Vice Premier Roman Malinowski, the head of the United Peasants' Party, which was clearly a bow in the direction of the peasants. Also in March, a Sejm (parliament) committee began drafting bills guaranteeing the permanence of the private farm sector and regulating, once and for all, the question of individual land titles. In April, Jan Kulaj, the leader of Rural Solidarity, was released from jail and appeared on television, praising the military government's agricultural policies and promising to cooperate with the authorities "for the good of my country and for the farmers."[30] Everything was being done to assuage peasants' fears and to convince them that the military regime was their friend and supporter.[31]

It soon became clear that the governmental campaign to gain peasants' confidence and thus to persuade them to sell grain in order to ensure an adequate supply of bread during the first half of 1982 met with little success. The regime put high hopes in the so-called grain loan announced in late January, which instead of cash offered the peasants selling grain to the state in excess of their contracted quotas bonds redeemable in 1983-1985 at the then current prices and carrying a 7 percent interest. While the grain loan might be viewed as a carrot offered to the peasants, the government also applied a stick in the form of a new grain procurement plan, under which peasants would be allowed to purchase seed from the state only if they have delivered grain to procurement agencies.[32]

Both programs failed to persuade the peasants to sell more grain and the U.S. sanctions announced by President Reagan on December 23, 1981 closed off a major source of grain, further contributing to the existing difficulties.

At this time it is obvious that the success or failure of Polish agriculture in satisfying the demands put on it by the military regime will ultimately depend on the following four closely intertwined factors and/or conditions:

● the final, unconditional recognition of the private farm sector as a permanent component of Polish agriculture and society as a whole

•the ability and willingness of individual peasants to raise their productivity and output

•the ability and willingness of the government to provide the farm sector with all the necessary inputs and capital goods

•the willingness of the consumers to accept higher food prices

Insofar as the sanctity of private ownership of land was concerned, the military government tried on several occasions to come up with legal provisions, short of constitutional amendments, guaranteeing the permanence of the private farm sector, which, although discussed in the media, have not been approved as of the summer of 1983.

Whether the absence of constitutional guarantees has a major impact on the economic performance of the private farm sector is not entirely clear, but available evidence suggests that the Polish peasants in the early 1980s were not particularly concerned with the threat of losing their land to a state or a collective farm. Thus, demand for agricultural land has been growing in recent years (as has the price) and between 1978 and 1981 close to a quarter of a million young peasants embarked on farming as a career.[33] The various discussions concerning future structural changes in Polish agriculture anticipate growing polarization of the private farm sector between small farms owned by worker-peasants and large family farms, oriented toward the market and well equipped with farm implements and other inputs.[34] It may be assumed that even if the Polish parliament were to amend the constitution in favor of individual peasants, the impact of the new legislation would not be significant, considering the fact that the peasants traditionally distrust the government and do not put much credence in the ironclad character of communist constitutional law.[35]

There is no doubt that individual peasants as well as the socialized farm sector are capable of increasing agricultural production. All that is needed is a rational farm policy that, on the one hand, would provide the necessary farm inputs and, on the other, proper economic incentives for the peasants. The potential of Polish agriculture is quite considerable and has not as yet been fully utilized. In this context it is worth citing a report on Polish agriculture prepared by American farm experts who visited the country in 1982:

Unlike many countries of the world, one cannot view Polish agriculture without being impressed with the long-term productive potential. Further, achievement of much of that potential does not pose an

overwhelmingly formidable task. The natural resource
base and climate are good, the state of scientific
and technical knowledge is relatively high, an adequate infrastructure exists, and the human resource
base is excellent. With these necessary conditions
already existing, one can conclude that government
policies, perhaps foremost, have stymied development in the past and that policies present the greatest impediment to developmental progress in the
future.[36]

Thus, it is clear that until and unless the Polish industry
can provide Polish agriculture with the necessary inputs, the
chances of a major expansion of farm output are slim. It remains
to be seen whether the contemplated economic reforms, intended
to reduce the extent of central planning, especially in industry,
will stimulate the output of farm implements, chemicals (fertilizers
and pesticides), and other agricultural inputs, or whether the
government will be forced to put pressure on the industrial
branches to supply agriculture with needed means of production.
The slow progress in implementing the reforms would suggest
that the latter option appears more likely, at least in the short
run, assuming, of course, that the military regime is serious
about enhancing agricultural potential.
    As was pointed out earlier, one of the factors contributing
to the current economic crisis in Poland was the inability and/or
unwillingness of successive Polish regimes to raise the level of
retail prices of foodstuffs, which remained largely unchanged
for fifteen years. The result was the sharp increase in food
subsidies that gradually distorted the price differentials between
food and nonfood items and also greatly stimulated demand for
some foodstuffs, particularly meat, which soon became a political
good. Consumption of meat became the chief determinant of the
standard of living and popular welfare. The Gierek regime was
especially eager to acquire a modicum of popularity and maintained a large import of feed, which enabled it to expand meat
consumption as well as to increase balance of payments deficits.
The military junta raised food prices sharply on February 1,
1982, for once without violent popular reaction, in the hope
that the price increase would reduce demand for such items as
meat, thus lessening pressure on livestock production, peren-
nially the critical sector within Polish agriculture. This did not
happen, mainly because the Jaruzelski regime, fearful of workers'
reaction, allowed major wage increases to be granted toward the
end of 1982, which largely offset the price rise and helped to
maintain popular demand for food.

While demand for foodstuffs remained high, their supply
stagnated. The harvest in 1982 was above that for 1981, except
for potatoes and sugar beets, but grain deliveries were sluggish
as the peasants in 1982-83 continued to withhold grain from state
purchasing agencies. The reasons for it were simple and resembled those that existed a few years earlier. State purchase
prices remained considerably below black market prices; high
inflationary pressure accompanied by a shortage of farm inputs
and consumer goods made hoarding of currency highly unprofitable; and absence of feed concentrates forced the peasants to
feed grain to livestock, the prices of which remained high.
Thus, once again the peasants behaved in a highly rational
fashion, frustrating the efforts of the government, which despite
declarations to the contrary continued to treat the peasants as
simpletons.[37]

This is clearly the crux of the matter. The military regime
can pass constitutional amendments, promise the peasants a new
deal, and declare its undying support of the private sector
without inducing much corresponding increase in farm output.
What is needed is a fundamental change in official attitude toward
the peasants, who for once must be treated not only as full-
fledged citizens together with the blue- and white-collar workers,
but also as producers whose output is of immense importance to
the state. The peasant must be treated as a homo economicus,
capable of making rational economic calculations. As such he
must be allowed to organize production in the most efficient
fashion that would guarantee a reasonable return on his effort
and investment.[38] Until this is done, Polish agriculture will
continue limping along despite its great potential. It remains
to be seen whether the military regime will be able to avoid the
mistakes committed by its predecessors and to treat agriculture
with the respect that it deserves.

NOTES

1. John Darnton, New York Times, May 12, 1981.
2. Dan Fisher, Los Angeles Times, June 29, 1983.
3. Wladyslaw Bienkowski, "Rolnictwo po raz trzeci,"
Kultura (Paris) 3 (March 1977):75.
4. For details, see Andrzej Korbonski, Politics of Socialist
Agriculture in Poland 1945-1960 (New York: Columbia University
Press, 1965); "Peasant Agriculture in Socialist Poland Since
1956: An Alternative to Collectivization," in Jerzy F. Karcz,
ed., Soviet and East European Agriculture (Berkeley and Los

Angeles: University of California Press, 1967), pp. 411-431; "Victim or Villain: Polish Agriculture Since 1970," in Maurice D. Simon and Roger E. Kanet, eds., Background to Crisis: Policy and Politics in Gierek's Poland (Boulder, Colorado: Westview Press, 1981), pp. 271-297; Zygmunt Kozlowski, "Rolnictwo PRL na slepym torze," Kultura (Paris) 9 (September 1980):64-75; "Plane und Engpasse der polnischen Ernahrungswirtschaft," Osteuropa 30 (December 1980):1285-1302; Waldemar Kuczynski, Po wielkim skoku (Warsaw: NOWA, 1979), pp. 24-47; William J. Newcomb, "Polish Agriculture: Policy and Performance," in East European Economic Assessment, Vol. I, Country Studies 1980, A Compendium of Papers Submitted to the Joint Economic Committee, 97th Congress, 1st Session (Washington, D.C.: U.S. Government Printing Office, 1981), pp. 96-120; Agrar-produktion und Nahrungsverbrauch in Polen (Munster-Hiltrup: Landwirtschaftsverlag, 1981); J. S. Zegar, "Problems of Polish Agriculture in the 1970s and Expected Development in the First Half of the 1980s," in Karl-Eugen Wadekin, ed., Current Trends in the Soviet and East European Food Economy (Berlin and Munich: Duncker and Humblot, 1982), pp. 95-116.

5. "O dalsza poprawe wyzywienia narodu i rozwoj rol-nictwa," Nowe Drogi (Warsaw), 11 (November 1974):19-54; "O dalszy dynamiczny rozwoj budownictwa socjalistycznego—wyzsza jakosc pracy i warunkow zycia narodu," Nowe Drogi (Warsaw), 1 (1976):65-67. In his address to the Seventh Party Congress, Prime Minister Jaroszewicz pledged to increase the share of the socialist sector in agriculture from 20 to 30 percent. Radio Free Europe Research, Situation Report Poland/40, December 10, 1975.

6. In addition to a speed-up in farm socialization, Gierek also announced a series of constitutional amendments intended to bring the Polish constitution closer in line with the other East European constitutions. This was also interpreted as an attempt to please the Soviet leadership.

7. Rocznik Statystyczny 1980 (Warsaw: GUS), pp. 353, 358.

8. Ibid., pp. 143-145.

9. A notorious example of the irrational price policy was the fact that it had paid individual peasants to sell grain to the state and then buy bread to feed it to their hogs, thus contribut-ing to the shortage of bread in retail stores.

10. While in 1975 about 359 thousand hectares of privately owned land was acquired by the State Land Fund, only 17 thousand hectares were sold back or leased to individual peas-ants, which represented roughly one-third of the 1970 figures.

The situation improved considerably in the late 1970s when more land was being allocated to private peasants, most of it, however, on short-term leases. Rocznik Statystyczny 1980, p. 223.

11. For an excellent comparative analysis of the economic performance of the socialized and private farm sectors showing the striking superiority of the latter, see Ryszard Manteuffel, "Sila w rozmaitosci," Polityka, no. 3, February 21, 1981.

12. This section is largely based on my "Polens Landwirtschaft in der Krise Von 1980/81," Osteuropa 32 (July 1982): 576-587.

13. Individual peasants accounted for 11.1 percent of Communist party membership in 1970 and for 8.7 percent in 1978. Rocznik Statystyczny 1980, p. 25.

14. Ibid., p. 23.

15. For a brief history of peasant dissident groups, see "Chronicle of Peasant Dissidence," Radio Free Europe Research, Situation Report Poland/8, October 3, 1980; Peter Raina, Independent Social Movements in Poland (London: London School of Economics and Political Science-Orbis Books, 1981), pp. 115-180.

16. See, "Protokol porozumienia," Polityka, no. 36, September 9, 1980.

17. For a detailed chronology of events leading to the formal establishment of Rural Solidarity, see Radio Free Europe Research, Situation Report Poland/7, April 24, 1981, pp. 2-5.

18. Ibid., pp. 5-6.

19. John Darnton, New York Times, March 10, 1981.

20. For an interesting discussion of the relationship between the government and the individual peasants since the summer of 1980, see Leon Bojko, "Czas chlopow," Polityka, no. 13, March 28, 1981.

21. Zygmunt Szeliga, "Naprawde nowa ekipa," Politika, no. 30, July 25, 1981.

22. Nowe Drogi 8 (August 1981):139-142.

23. "Jakich Pan uzywa argumentow?" Zycie Gospodarcze, no. 38, September 20, 1981.

24. For a good example, see "Propozycje zasadniczych rozwiazan reformy gospodarczej w Polsce," Supplement to Zycie Gospodarczw, no. 46, November 16, 1980, pp. 13-14.

25. "Gospodarka w 1981 roku," Zycie Gospodarcze, no. 3, February 7, 1982. Total farm output in 1981 was estimated at 4 percent above 1980 level with crop production 20 percent above and livestock output 14 percent below 1980. Trybuna Ludu, January 4, 1982.

26. For details, see Frederick Kempe, "Troublesome Farmers Present a Crucial Test for Warsaw Regime," Wall Street Journal, February 27, 1982.

27. For two interesting accounts of peasant attitudes, see Witold Pawlowski, "Swinia lubi wegiel, nie pieniadze," Polityka, no. 36, September 5, 1981; Krzysztof Lis, "Na chlopski rozum," Polityka, no. 41, October 10, 1981.

28. In his address on December 13, 1981 proclaiming the imposition of martial law, General Jaruzelski specifically urged "brother peasants" not to "allow [their] fellow countrymen to starve" and to "take care of the Polish soil so it can feed us all." New York Times, December 14, 1981.

29. Harry Trimborn, "U.S. Sanctions Hurt Poland's Food Output," Los Angeles Times, February 4, 1982.

30. Michael Dobbs in Washington Post, April 29, 1982.

31. According to one veteran Western observer of the Polish scene, in the spring of 1982 the peasants were the only group within Poland that was satisfied with the military regime. Marion Donhoff, "Nicht alle sind gegen die neue Ordnung," Die Zeit, April 9, 1982.

32. John Darnton, "Farmers in Poland Pressed on Grain," New York Times, January 21, 1982. The ratio was 100 kilograms of seed for each 120 kilograms of grain delivered to the state.

33. Report to the Rockefeller Foundation and Rockefeller Brothers Fund by the Agricultural Mission to Poland, December 1982, pp. 30-31.

34. For details, see Anna Szemberg, "Obraz przemian agrarnych," Zycie Gospodarcze, no. 18, May 23, 1982.

35. For an interesting discussion of this issue, see "Jakie gospodarstwa takie rolnictwo," Zycie Gospodarcze, no. 20, June 6, 1982.

36. Report to the Rockefeller Foundation, p. 175.

37. For a recent example of governmental attitude, see "Co mial na mysli minister?" Polityka, no. 16, April 16, 1983. See also, "Po deszczu slonce," Polityka, no. 27, July 2, 1983.

38. For an encouraging sign that the official attitude might be changing, see Zdzislaw Grochowski, "Rolnicy nie sa winni," Polityka, no. 4, January 22, 1983. The author is Deputy Minister of Agriculture.

5.

Bread and Freedom:
Workers' Self-Government Schemes in Poland

Christine M. Sadowski

The attempt on the part of Polish workers and polity to create a mutually agreeable mechanism through which workers could articulate their needs and grievances to the party and government is as old as the Polish People's Republic. This chapter examines the institutional options that have been proposed, formulated, and tested over the past four decades. It takes the goal of greater participation of workers in the economic affairs of their enterprises and in their own economic well-being—and outlines the fate of that goal in post-World War II Poland.

Although support for this goal has grown over time, the goal itself has remained a more or less permanent feature in contemporary Polish society. It has taken the forms of factory councils, workers' councils, strike committees, opposition groups, and finally an independent trade union. The strategies and tactics of Polish workers have changed and grown more sophisticated, while the persistence with which they have pursued this goal over generations makes it difficult to imagine that martial law could end their quest. Moreover, the response of the polity to worker demands has been virtually constant and can be characterized as a strategy of incorporation and cooptation, rooted in a general unwillingness to delegate any real power to the workers. This chapter outlines the evolution of that stalemate.

The question of power is an important one. The workers have not sought to topple the ruling elite. They have not demanded the type of power necessary to govern a nation-state. They have, on the other hand, asked to have a genuine say in their own economic well-being. To the extent that this power has been claimed exclusively by the party and government in

Poland, the polity has viewed such worker demands as an infringement on its jurisdiction. It is therefore a question of decentralization of authority and the granting of autonomy to organizations representing the interests of workers. In short, this would mean the creation of a separate power base in a society committed through historical circumstance to centralized authority. To understand this is to get at the crux of the dilemma. Time and again, Polish workers have been told that while they would be allowed to dabble in economics, they would not be allowed to cross the line into the political arena. Thus Walesa was often heard reassuring the Polish polity that "I am not a politician; I am a union man." But unions are formed in an effort to gain power, and power is politics—even if it is the power to have an input into the quality of one's own life. Since the working masses have no bargaining leverage other than their labor, the withholding of that labor is the major form of power intrinsic to this social class.

Furthermore, whereas in capitalist societies raising salaries or cutting taxes also means increasing the purchasing power of workers, in Poland similar gestures made by the political elite would reap no such societal payoff. Viewed as unimportant consumers, workers in Poland have been placed in an even more vulnerable position than their Western counterparts. Because of the use of soft currency domestically and the need for hard currency for Western trade, the Soviet Union and East European states have been forced to view consumerist tendencies among their own citizens not only with ideological disdain but also as economically menacing.

Thus there are two major dilemmas surrounding the attempt of Polish workers to have a greater say in their own economic well-being: first, the question of how power can be shared in a society operating entirely under the leading role of the Polish United Workers' Party; and second, the question of the economic importance of Polish workers as consumers. Both are based on rigidly defined structural components of Polish society.

The struggle to influence one's own economic life is common, of course, to all labor movements—in socialist as well as in capitalist societies. And so labor organizations and trade union militancy were part of the working class tradition in interwar Poland as well. Between 1918 and 1939, some 2000 labor organizations existed in Poland, dividing workers along lines of industry, enterprise, political preference, and ethnicity.[1] More than 300 trade unions existed during this period, and by the late 1930s the strike had become a very popular form of worker protest.[2] During the period 1926-36, only the United States

and France had more strikes and strikers than did Poland.
Such a situation of numerous, small trade unions was intolerable
to the new post-war sociopolitical order, and as early as December 1945 the unions were collapsed into eighteen massive organizations.[3] These organizations more closely resembled Lenin's
formula for socialist trade unions, which were to serve as schools
of communism, activating and mobilizing workers to build the
new order. In addition, they were to act as transmission belts,
transmitting policy from the polity to the masses. Clearly, this
means that power was to be concentrated at the top. The
working-class struggle in post-World War II Poland has been
an ongoing effort to transfer some of that power to the rank-
and-file workers.

FACTORY COUNCILS

Even before the end of the Second World War, Polish
factory councils had emerged out of necessity. The war had
caused many prewar factory owners to flee, others to disappear,
leaving behind work crews to continue the task of production.
Such councils existed in the Eastern territories, headed by
the Soviet-established Lublin Committee, as well as in the Nazi-
occupied territories where councils emerged and operated underground.[4] These factory councils were originally in competition
with the trade unions, as neither had been granted clear jurisdiction over specific factory matters. In the early struggle
for power between political parties, the Polish Socialist Party
clearly sided with issues concerning the rank-and-file worker,
while the Polish Workers' Party (communist) sided with the
Leninist formulation of the vanguard and hierarchical command,
thus supporting government policy and factory management.

As early as 1944, workers in the Communist-ruled Eastern
territories had become upset with management's unwillingness
to entrust workers with increased power in decision making.
The final decision concerning the extent of worker participation
in management was not made until the socialist vs. communist
struggle had been settled. Factions within the Polish Socialist
Party continued to work through factory councils and trade
unions in an attempt to gain worker support, blaming the government apparatus and communists for the material hardships
incurred by workers. While socialists were gaining support
among the workers, the Polish Workers' Party decided in May
1945 to make sovereign the authority of management. Thus,
in the interest of efficiency, power was handed over to manage-

ment and technical experts, while the authority of the trade unions and councils was all but eliminated.5 The councils were left with jurisdiction over matters of worker employment and cultural affairs of the labor force, while factory directors had complete control over matters of production and wages.

Following a series of victories by the Socialists in elections to executive trade union posts, the Communists proposed an agreement, signed by both parties in November 1946, that neither side would do anything to undermine the status of the trade unions. Two months later, the factory councils were incorporated into the trade union hierarchy, thus permanently diluting the power of the councils.6 Until 1947, the councils had existed as autonomous organs. Their incorporation into the trade union structure was a further step toward totalitarianism. By 1948, the Communist Party had achieved its leading role in Polish society, and a government decree of 1949 mandated that each of the then 36 massive national trade unions formed a hierarchical structure, with local union branches subordinate to all directives issued from above,7 that is, from the Central Council of Trade Unions (CCTU) and the Polish United Workers' Party (PUWP).

This had been the period of consolidation of power by the new ruling elite, and this consolidation was accompanied by successful efforts to centralize all authority (political, economic, and social)—a centralization that would be held accountable for years to come, for the economic woes of the nation. For example, the blatant failures and shortcomings of Poland's Six-Year Plan, ending in 1955, were attributed precisely to the overcentralized system of authority that had just been constructed so purposively. Trade unions had not acted in behalf of workers, but instead had become agents of management concerned primarily with mobilizing workers to fulfill enterprise plans. Thus, decentralization and greater, more genuine worker representation became the order of the day. Coupled with Khrushchev's denouncement of Stalin, a period of unrest and experimentation with new alternatives was set into motion.

WORKERS' COUNCILS

So clear were the shortcomings of Poland's first Six-Year Plan that in the fall of 1955, the Central Committee of the PUWP appealed to workers for suggestions and proposals on how to improve the economic situation. One of the major centers for generating such proposals was the automobile factory (FSO) in

Warsaw where the party cell, the trade union organization, and white- and blue-collar workers met to discuss these issues. The results of their discussions came, quite significantly, under the heading of "worker autonomy," and included experimental enterprises (set up in select plants for a limited amount of time to test new management techniques) and workers' councils.[8] From proposals such as these, many plants spontaneously organized workers' councils. The tension that was mounting in factories was evidenced by the quick decision to increase workers' wages in April 1956.[9] The newly established workers' councils, however, intended to increase wages beyond these concessions, based on a system of profit sharing. The April wage increases did not reduce tension and were followed by the well-known Poznan riots two months later, when workers gathered under the common banner of "Bread and Freedom."

When Wladyslaw Gomulka came to power in October 1956, his initial intention was to introduce some measure of decentralization. By the early 1960s, it was clear that this idea had been tabled. He did, however, grant the workers' councils official approval and thus a permanent place—though not a permanent status—within the Polish factory system. On November 19, 1956, the rules governing the workers' councils were established. Councils were to have jurisdiction over matters of norms and wages and, in conjunction with the director, in drawing up and evaluating the fulfillment of the production plan and in determining plant expansion.[10] Aiding in increasing productivity would raise the standard of living and this was to be the central concern of the workers' councils.

In addition, councils were given the right to hire and fire management. It was this latter power that proved troublesome in the months that followed. Incidents occurred in which factories outright refused to sign wage agreements with ministries and in which councils advertised vacant managerial posts in an effort to find personnel whose qualifications went beyond the earlier exclusive emphasis on political reliability.[11] Councils were to be composed of two-thirds manual workers, whenever possible, though such blue-collar representation was rarely the case, particularly within council presidiums.[12]

Several problems presented themselves even before official policies began whittling away at the scope of the councils' activities. First, despite the new emphasis on worker autonomy and economic decentralization, enterprise autonomy had not been significantly increased. Enterprise plans were still largely formulated in conjunction with an established grand central plan. In fact, Sturmthal reports only two powers with which enterprises were entrusted: to save raw materials and to engage in sideline activities, that is, beyond the scope of the enterprise plan with profits affecting employee earnings.[13] Such powers amount to nothing more than the right to work harder and more economically and the right to be rewarded for doing so. They were not, on the other hand, entrusted with engaging in broader entrepreneurial activities or experimentation.

Second, the establishment of some measure of worker autonomy meant little in the context of general inefficiency. Writing for Nowa Kultura in April 1957, Professor Edward Lipinski insisted that "As long as there are no changes independent from the Councils, in the supply of raw materials, in indispensable deliveries and in equipment, as long as cooperation is not organized in a rational fashion, it is impossible for the enterprise to function well."[14] Indeed, if workers, or even enterprises, are given total autonomy in a largely non-supportive environment, their independence does not translate well into power.

Third, the relationship between the councils and management was not clearly defined. In some cases, both were to work together, in others they were to operate independently, while the councils had the power to accept or dismiss management. This relationship, as we shall see, was more clearly defined by May 1957 in favor of management.

Fourth, within the councils themselves, there were ongoing debates concerning the distribution of bonuses. Manual workers supported an egalitarian distribution, making all bonuses of equal size, regardless of one's status in the enterprise. Professional economists and others within the factory intelligentsia argued that in order to create incentives bonuses should be calculated as a percentage of base pay.[15] In some factories, councils adopted a policy of distributing profits on the basis of seniority alone. "This meant that a cleaning lady with three years' service in the factory might receive a greater share in the division of profits than a director who had only been there for two years."[16]

Decisions made during the Ninth Plenum of the CC-PUWP in May 1957 left councils with some of their management functions intact, but turned policy-making functions over to the trade unions. A series of new laws stipulated that although councils had the right to make proposals concerning the hiring and firing of management, such appointments and dismissals were to be made by the proper state authorities, albeit in agreement with the workers' councils. Furthermore, urgent decisions could be made by the director alone and the director could veto council decisions that were regarded as contrary to the enterprise plan.[17]

Councils had been established at the enterprise level on a voluntary basis. In order to put the strength of the movement into perspective, within the first six months after their ratification only one-third of the enterprises (though three-quarters of the industrial enterprises) had established councils. There was some suspicion that after May 1957 administrative officials had made it more difficult for new councils to come into existence.[18]

By April 1958, Gomulka proposed the creation of the Conference of Workers' Self-Management, which was to serve as an umbrella organization, incorporating trade unions, party cells, workers' councils, the youth organization, and the Chief Technical Organization. True worker self-government could not be achieved, he argued, if the party and unions were prevented from having an input.[19] Furthermore, the presidiums of the workers' councils were to be expanded to include the plant director, the union shop committee chairman, as well as party representatives. The fate of the councils was clear. As a final blow, where no councils existed none could be established. Instead, union and party organizations were to elect a subcommittee to operate in its place.[20] Appropriate laws for the establishment of the Conference of Workers' Self-Management were enacted in December of that year.

How did the workers feel about the fate of their councils? There is no evidence of overt protest. In fact, worker enthusiasm for the councils had been diminishing over this entire, though short, period of time. J. Kulpinska and M. Rokacz studied these changing opinions between summer 1956 and spring 1958.[21] They surveyed the opinions of workers in three factories at three different points in time: October 1956, April 1957, and February 1958.* They found in 1956 that blue-collar workers clearly had higher hopes than the technical personnel for the success of the councils in general. Furthermore, in expressing the benefits they expected the councils to yield, 78.7 percent of the workers said they expected higher incomes, while only 35.3 percent of the engineer/technical personnel expressed such

---

*The December 1956 survey included one large-scale enterprise, while the April 1957 and February 1958 surveys included the original enterprise, plus two medium-scale industries. All three were metal factories.

expectations. Conversely, 37.8 percent of the workers expected better organization within the factory as an outcome, while 53.0 percent of the engineer/technical personnel shared this view.

By April 1957, expectations had changed. Hopes among the three factories surveyed were now placed in better work organization and a larger earning capacity for the factory, while hopes for higher incomes had diminished significantly. The idea of socialist worker as consumer—or perhaps socialist worker with an ever better standard of living—was to be left for another time. Furthermore, the expectation that the workers' councils would improve relations among factory personnel and between workers and management was astonishingly low.

Comments made by individual workers, technicians, and engineers indicate that in one factory, dissatisfaction was based on the lack of power afforded the councils in relation to management, and in another factory, on the lack of initiative among council members. Indeed, by February 1958, respondents were voicing the opinion that the councils were breaking away from the work crew and that the councils themselves were at fault for this situation. Furthermore, by 1958, profit was no longer considered the single most important task facing the councils. For workers, influence over management and administration took on primary importance, while for engineers/technicians, the improvement of interpersonal relations within the factory was viewed as most crucial. Workers, by this time, were complaining that their interests were not being taken into account, that the councils operated on the basis of favoritism, and one worker was not even certain if the council was still in existence in his factory. Engineers and technicians complained that the councils had become subordinate to management, that workers were not aware of the council activities, and that the councils were serving as a stepping stone for promotion.

The fate of worker organizations in Poland remained fairly stable throughout the 1960s. During this entire period, workers' councils were bound by the same ambiguous laws that had been enacted in the late 1950s. Social scientists continued to do research on the topic, and party ideologists continued to write on the problems faced by the self-government scheme, but indeed, over time, the results were merely variations on a theme. Through 1967, studies reflected a keen awareness of the discrepancy between theory and practice with regard to self-management, but after 1967 the discussions ended. The decrease in the amount of information available on the topic seemed to have gone hand in hand with an increase in arbitrary elements within the self-management—or by now comanagement—scheme.[22]

RIOTS AND STRIKES

By the end of the 1960s, the role of the workers' councils
had been reduced to one of agreement with the suggestions and
directives of management, the party cell, and trade union. It
was soon to be officially admitted anew that workers did not
have a regular, institutionalized mechanism through which to
voice their concerns.

Real wages had dropped by the late 1960s, and the decline
in the standard of living was becoming increasingly obvious.
De Weydenthal asserts that a latent tension, which existed in
Poland throughout the 1960s, explains in part the reluctance
on the part of the polity to introduce badly needed reforms.[23]
It was not until May 1970 that the CC-PUWP decided to revamp
the system of material incentives by making wages dependent
on productivity indexes and by establishing separate bonus
schemes for white- and blue-collar workers. Bonuses for white-
collar workers were to come out of funds saved through decreasing production costs and introducing blue-collar unemployment.[24]
Blue-collar workers' compensation was to be calculated as a
proportion of white-collar bonuses. Clearly, this was an anti-
egalitarian policy, unlikely to have been supported by blue-collar
workers. Nevertheless, the workers had not been consulted
on this reform, which was to go into effect in January 1971.[25]

An additional step to rejuvenate the failing economy came
in December 1970 with the long overdue attempt to rationalize
food prices in Poland. The announcement of a 15 to 30 percent
increase in the cost of food and fuels was made on December 12
and workers' protests quickly erupted throughout Poland. What
is of particular interest to us here is that in both Gdansk and
Szczecin, workers, having locked themselves behind the gates
of their shipyards, spontaneously formed democratically elected
strike committees. These strike committees not only communicated
with other factories, but also, by having party and government
officials come to their shipyard to negotiate with them, received
official recognition as organizations representing the workers.

The workers demanded that the prices of food and fuel be
rolled back to their pre-December levels. This was accomplished
on February 15, 1971, along with the promise to freeze prices
for the next five years. In addition, because of the outrage at
how the protests and strikes were being covered in the official
press, they called for an end to censorship. For a short period
of time and to only a minor extent, the media did accommodate
this demand by reporting the violence and casualties that resulted
from the rioting in Gdansk.

In addition, however, and central to our concerns, the workers called for a truly independent union and official recognition of the strike committee as a legal, permanent representative of the workers. The newly elected (December 20, 1970) first secretary of the PUWP, Edward Gierek, said during the Szczecin negotiations that the existing organizations (PUWP and trade unions) were good enough and should be sufficient for the workers.[26] As for the strike committees, de Weydenthal informs us that they were dissolved when other concessions were met and the strikers returned to work. The government went to great lengths to insure that future links between activists and the work crew would be severed once and for all. "The measures taken against them included dismissals from shop-floor jobs through transfers to other duties, cooptation into established agencies of workers' representation with a view toward political resocialization, and, in some cases, direct political persecution."[27] Gierek had another formula in mind for ensuring that he be informed of future worker grievances. He set up a consultation scheme through which representatives were sent by the Central Committee to meet on a regular basis with workers in 164 select, large-scale industries. These representatives were to report their discussions to the party leadership.

In addition, the CC-PUWP acted quickly to contact the chairmen of the Conference of Workers' Self-Management and the directors of key industries and to encourage them to attend to matters of social welfare, to monitor the distribution of bonuses and awards so that workers would be rewarded "according to their effort and results of their work," and to give attention to issues of job safety.[28] In February 1971, at the Eighth Plenum of the CC-PUWP, Gierek announced that the incentive system drawn up in May 1970, along with its intention to introduce blue-collar unemployment, would not be put into effect. Gierek went on to praise the virtues of the trade unions, emphasizing the role they play in working conditions, social and cultural affairs, mobilizing workers to fulfill plans and increase output, and in improving relations within the factory. "Our party," he said, "will always support the development of inner-union democracy."[29] Clearly, the institutions were to remain the same, though the "consultation scheme" had been added, along with the promise of using "other methods of testing public opinion on various issues."[30]

The fate of the consultation scheme is as ambiguous and confused as the scheme itself. Not only was this practice never clearly defined or regulated, but also, because of the status of

the consultants (lecturers sent by the CC-PUWP), they were
unable to initiate change. Participation in the decision-making
process, the initiation of contact with work crews, as well as
the selection of topics for discussion were all clearly left within
the sole jurisdiction of the CC-PUWP. Moreover, through
individualized consultation, the PUWP was able to ensure that
workers were addressed as employees of a particular factory
or enterprise, thus retarding the growth of class-based social
tension. [31]

By 1972, the Ministry of Labor, Wages, and Social Affairs
had been established as yet another, high-level institution,
encompassing the concerns of factories, unions, and workers'
councils, and was put in charge of "controlling matters pertaining
to employment, wages, work organization, and working conditions." [32] Furthermore, by 1975, a new Labor Code was enacted
delegating more power to management, which was now to enforce
labor discipline by fining or dismissing "insubordinate" workers. [33]
Along with an earlier decision that called for closer supervision
by the CC-PUWP of the party cells in some 200 large-scale industries, the scenario of tightened control and extended bureaucracy
and centralization is complete.

During the first years of Gierek's rule, the standard of
living increased sharply and for the first time Poles began to
have a sense of economic security and hope for the future.
But the sudden decline after 1973 was just as sharp, and amidst
a climate of deflated expectations the five-year price freeze had
ended. The decision to increase food prices was announced on
June 24, 1976. Strikes and work slowdowns occurred throughout
Poland, though demonstrations and riots were much more limited
in scope than they had been in 1970. This is undoubtedly due
to the fact that the party was frightened and rolled back the
prices within 24 hours of the announcement.

THE OPPOSITION

The outcome of the 1976 riots in Radom and Ursus, as it
relates to this chapter, is the emergence of a wide variety of
dissident organizations. Prominent among these organizations
was the Workers' Defense Committee (KOR), which was established by intellectuals in direct response to mistreatment by the
militia of workers involved in the Radom demonstrations. Their
goals were to gain amnesty for the workers who had been imprisoned for their participation in these demonstrations, to
provide financial and legal support for the families of imprisoned

workers, and to call for an investigation of police brutality.
KOR was established in September 1976 and by September 1977
had achieved its purpose and exhausted its original goals.
Instead of disbanding, the organization renamed itself the
Committee for Social Self-Defense—KOR (KSS "KOR") and
continued to work on issues of human rights and civil liberties.
The significance of KOR, however, rests on its having signaled
to others in Poland that such an organization could exist outside
the officially sponsored government structures and could successfully pursue its objectives.[34]

Thus, the period between 1976 and 1980 witnessed the
creation of many other dissident organizations among which the
Free Trade Union movement is most important to us here. The
first organization of this type was reported to have been established in the fall of 1977 by a group of workers in Radom,
around an underground journal called Robotnik (The Worker).
The group "pledged itself to fight for the rights of the working
man independently of the official trade unions, which it described
as 'dead' institutions, and to support the creation of other
independent bodies to represent the Polish workers."[35] The
next Free Trade Union cell was established in Katowice in February 1978, and then in Gdansk and Sopot in April of that year.
KSS "KOR" had contributed significantly to the formation of
this movement and remained its faithful ally until KSS "KOR"
itself disbanded after the establishment of Solidarity. The
number of free trade union cells continued to increase, while
the movement appealed to Western labor organizations and to
the ILO in Geneva for "world-wide solidarity."[36]

We must pause for a moment here to ask the crucial question:
Why in the late 1970s had a Free Trade Union movement emerged
underground? To begin, the movement emerged because other
schemes had failed. In 1956, the first step toward incorporating
the workers' councils into the established party and administrative machinery had been the official recognition of these bodies
as legitimate organizations (that is, their ratification in November
1956). The second and final step was the decision to change
the scope of the councils' policy-making function and to incor-
porate them into a larger organization—the Conference of Workers'
Self-Management—which was to coordinate its activities. Thus
the workers' councils became part of the corporation with the
CC-PUWP serving as its board of directors. The same was true
in Poland with the consultation scheme the party developed after
the December 1970 riots. The CC-PUWP, by acknowledging the
need for more effective communication between the workers and
the party and by proceeding to set up its own structure to

accommodate those needs, actually succeeded in temporarily reducing social tension without introducing real change. Regardless of the ultimate intention of these meetings between party and workers, appeasement diluted the strength of potential sources of opposition. In addition, communication in and of itself offers no guarantees of action if only one side holds all of the power and the other side holds none.

Thus, the establishment of an underground* Free Trade Union movement in Poland was important for structural reasons. Any further mobilization could not have occurred without making the first step of separation. While alienated groups may exist within a society aboveground, the decision to go under provides a better opportunity for the crystallization of nuclei of power.

That the movement itself was moderate in size could not be denied. In 1978, it was estimated that at least twenty samizdat papers existed with a monthly circulation of no less than 20,000 and a readership of about 100,000.[37] These figures include all dissident communications in Poland—not only those of the Free Trade Union movement. But in addition to an estimation of numerical strength, the significance of the structural aspects of this movement must be considered. Dissident organizations were known to have existed in all industrial areas of Poland. The fact that they were not directly linked with the mass of Polish workers was less important strategically than the fact that they were a diverse set of groups, scattered throughout the country, who had separated themselves totally from the establishment. At that point their horizontal integration was more important than their vertical integration. Furthermore, by August 1980, the free trade union movement had existed for about three years, longer than the workers' councils of 1956 were able to maintain any degree of autonomy and certainly longer than the short-lived strike committees.

Meanwhile, special attention was being paid to the role of official trade unions in Poland. At the Trade Union Plenum of February 25, 1980, Gierek's address included the following statement: "The trade unions' fundamental duties include the defense of the working people's interests and concern for the conditions under which they work and live. I ask you to regard that sphere of your activities as most important. You should

---

*While most of these organizations operated rather openly, the term underground is useful in underlining the fact that they were totally separate from the official, established order.

take resolute and determined action against cases of favoritism and nepotism, the unjust distribution of wages and bonus funds and against every injustice inflicted upon people." In addition, he appealed to the trade unions to "increase at all times their impact on state policy."[38] Again, in light of the still growing Free Trade Union movement, such a statement reflects the seeming incorporation of demands being made by the opposition—demands that would have lost their impact in normal, aboveground discourse.

THE FREE TRADE UNION

On July 2, 1980, Poland's government made a third attempt at rationalizing food prices. As expected, worker strikes followed the announcement. What was different, however, in 1980 was that the government attempted to settle each strike individually, as it erupted, by negotiating wage increases with individual enterprises. As the strikes were individually settled new strikes arose, and it soon became obvious that no end was in sight. The strikes spread throughout various enterprises and regions of Poland, and before long what was to have been gained through the increase of food prices was being given back in wages to strikers.

The strikes continued through July and were manageable according to the new decentralized method of negotiation. Nevertheless, it was clear that, if and when the strikes hit either the shipyards or the coal mines, negotiation and settlement would become as urgent as the manipulation of workers would become difficult.* This happened on August 2, when the strikes began to spread to the Gdansk seaport. Strikes spread through the city by August 14, reached Szczecin by August 18, and included the entire Baltic seacoast by August 19.

While the demands made on August 14 in the Gdansk Lenin Shipyard were negotiated and met by August 16, the workers—led by members of the local Free Trade Union cells (including Lech Walesa, Anna Walentynowicz, Alina Pienkowska, Bogdan Lis, Andrzej Gwiazda, and Joanna Duda-Gwiazda)—decided to

---

*The shipyard and coal mines represent two of Poland's largest, most vital industries. The workers there, while among the best paid in Poland, are militant, powerful, and conscious of their strength.

continue their strike in the name of smaller enterprises, until all strikes were settled. This was the crucial turning point. The Lenin Shipyard made it possible for workers throughout Poland to send delegates to the newly formed Interfactory Strike Committee and to participate in negotiating many demands, including the establishment of an independent trade union.*

The negotiations reflected an awareness among the workers of polity strategies that had proved detrimental to them in the past. For example, when the demand for an independent trade union first started to be taken seriously by the party and government, Gierek announced in a speech broadcast over the radio (August 18) that a multilateral commission was to be established for the purpose of investigating worker grievances and that since the official trade unions had failed to keep in touch with the needs of the workers attempts would be made to ensure that they met this challenge in the future. [39] This announcement was ignored by the striking workers, who had heard such empty promises many times before. Desperate, at times pathetic, efforts were immediately set into motion by the government to bring about reforms in the official trade unions. It was even proposed that a new union, established by the workers, could exist as a separate branch union under the jurisdiction of the Central Council of Trade Unions (CCTU). The workers categorically turned down this option.

Meanwhile, the presidium of the CCTU met on August 19 to start preparing two bills: one on reforming trade union legislation and the other on workers' self-management. [40] The official press was filled with editorials on meaningful reforms about to take place in the union structure. [41] In the midst of these discussions and pleas to the workers not to abandon the existing trade unions, Jan Szydlak was ousted first from the Politburo (August 24) and then from his position as head of the CCTU (August 25). [42] Romuald Jankowski took on the duties of the latter position and soon was appearing on television (August 28) promising more reforms. [43]

---

*The Lenin Shipyard was not, of course, the only enterprise to set up an Interfactory Strike Committee. Such committees existed elsewhere in Poland, but did not get the same coverage as the one in Gdansk, since it was the first and largest strike committee and also one which welcomed coverage by the domestic and foreign press. The Interfactory Strike Committee at the Warski Shipyard in Szczecin banned the press from entering the yard.

By now it was obvious that the striking workers were not going to relinquish their demand for an independent union. The government and party negotiators, however, placed a final card on the table—that no organization could exist in Poland without recognizing the "leading role of the Communist Party."[44] The agreement was signed on August 31, providing for the establishment of a free trade union, guaranteeing the right to strike, and promising access to the media. Many workers felt betrayed upon discovering that the final agreement stipulated that their union recognized the leading role of the party. "Couldn't it have said 'guiding' instead of 'leading?'" they argued.[45] Walesa promised to raise the issue again and the official Solidarity statute reads that the union "acknowledges that the PUWP plays the leading role in the state."[46]

Solidarity's membership quickly grew to close to ten million.* The pleading on the part of leaders for workers to remain in the old unions eventually died down, while establishing the relationship between the old and new unions became the new issue of the day. Furthermore, shortly after the establishment of Solidarity, a third type of union came into existence—the Confederation of Autonomous Unions. This was composed largely of white-collar professionals who feared that their particular needs would not be represented in the massive blue-collar movement that had emerged.

The first order of business upon the establishment of Solidarity was a revision of the Polish labor union laws. On August 30, 1980, Gierek appointed a commission for this purpose, attached to the Central Council of Trade Unions and headed by Franciszek Rusek, chairman of the Labor and Social Security Chamber of the Supreme Court. This commission met with heavy criticism, first for its exclusive association with the official unions, and later for its foot dragging. It was replaced on September 23 (by Kania, the new First Secretary of the PUWP) and was composed of seventeen lawyers and legal experts, twelve Solidarity representatives, and five representatives from the official unions.[47]

A draft of the basic tenets of the labor union law was published in March 1981, amidst pressure to indicate that progress was being made. The principles in this document underline the right to free association and the right to form unions, as well

---

*The official trade unions had had a membership of ten million just before the establishment of Solidarity.

as the importance of each union being granted full rights, without privileges or favoritism. In addition to outlining the rules of eligibility for union membership, the document states that union statutes "may stipulate that union officers shall not simultaneously hold office in state administrative and economic agencies and political and social organizations."[48] Such a clause, again, reflects a firm commitment to union independence and a keen awareness of the manner in which the polity was able to dilute the strength of worker organizations in the past.

Since trade unions were to be responsible for the supervision and control of working conditions and the livelihood of workers, they were to be granted full information necessary to assess the situation under which they operated. The document also stipulated that, for this purpose, unions would be allowed to conduct their own research.

While union and self-government organs were jointly responsible for the social affairs of the workers, the unions were to act in defense of worker interests, while the self-government organs were to focus attention on comanagement in the enterprise. Furthermore, unions were to assume all responsibilities previously assigned to the workers' councils. These included evaluation of workers; awards, recommendations, and bonuses; labor discipline; handling individual cases of termination of employment; work schedules; vacations; social and cultural affairs; and professional training. If no union existed in a particular enterprise, employees were to elect a council to handle these matters. Where more than one union existed, each union was to attend to the needs of its own members. Finally, the document stipulated that when conflict arose within an enterprise, negotiations were to begin immediately and strikes could be called only after negotiations have ended.[49]

Along with questions of trade union structure, the issue of self-management was of paramount importance between the time the Gdansk agreement was signed and martial law declared. Self-government units within Polish enterprise were to be granted a broader range of activities, while continuing to emphasize their support for central planning. Their activities were to include approving enterprise plans, overseeing the fulfillment of plans, approving balance sheets and reports, making decisions concerning the distribution of social funds, and influencing policy concerning employment and wages. These changes were to be implemented gradually and only after the economic crisis had been overcome.

In addition to the above areas of jurisdiction, the question of whether or not self-government organs would be granted the right to hire and fire management was raised and debated at great length. Wouldn't leaving this matter solely in the hands of the state administration result in the same stagnant bureaucracy that had provoked the original cries of protest? Wouldn't failing to give self-management units this jurisdiction result in the trade unions being the only organizations in a position to keep a check on management? Why broaden self-government's scope of activity without extending its real power?[50] Solidarity took the most radical position on this issue, arguing that self-government organs should be granted full rights in managing the enterprise and in administering its assets. The opposition argued that the latter could never be implemented, as the funds belong to the state and not to the enterprise.[51]

A compromise was finally reached and the final version of the bill reads: "A director is appointed and recalled by the founding organ or workers' council (self-government)." However, the government administration and the trade unions were to draw up a list of those enterprises that were most important to the national economy, and in those industries the state administration would have the right to hire and fire management.[52] In addition, such appointments to managerial positions were to be based on competition, and for the purpose of monitoring this process, a competition commission would be established, composed of three representatives from self-government units, and one from each of the administration, bank, trade unions, political and youth organizations, and the Chief Technical Organization. Last, the bill specified that funds were national property and that an enterprise was only a user of these funds. Many of these issues were the same ones raised in 1956, only this time they were argued with greater knowledge and sophistication by the workers. The bill was passed in the Sejm in late September 1981, while a bill on enterprise autonomy and another on trade unions had not been passed before all union activity was outlawed.[53]

POLISH WORKERS AND THE FUTURE

Martial law restrictions imposed in Poland by Jaruzelski on December 13, 1981 suspended the Solidarity Independent Trade Union. Originally, the martial law government promised to reinstate free trade unions in Poland once restrictions were lifted, adding in February 1982 that past Solidarity union activists would be prohibited from taking part in all future union activity. Furthermore, unions would be allowed to reemerge only if they remained apolitical.[54]

Yet a union with purely economic and social goals cannot function in any meaningful way without being granted a measure of power. Since the acquisition of power by an independent group in Poland is viewed as political, authentic worker self-government and independent trade unions will not be allowed to reemerge. Solidarity was officially banned by the military government on October 8, 1982. Immediately after it was banned, new trade union legislation was enacted, without any form of consultation with Polish workers. The new trade union laws closely resemble those of the pre-August 1980 official unions in their intention. They are to be organized by branch rather than by region; they are to concern themselves exclusively with issues of worker welfare; and they are to remain virtually powerless. Solidarity's strength was founded on its right to strike. The new unions have this right only theoretically. So complicated is the procedure to get permission to strike and so involved are the steps of negotiation and arbitration that precede the request to strike, that the act of striking cannot, under current legislation, be utilized as an act of worker power or as a meaningful means of demanding concessions. And so Polish workers are back to square one with their cries for an organization that would truly represent them and their particular interests.

Some 2,500 individual unions were established in Poland during the first week of January 1983, with another 1,500 applications awaiting approval. They are, for the most part, being established without memberships, and the process of waiting to see if each is able to attract more than a handful of willing members has begun. (Incidentally, the notion of empty-shell trade unions has never before appeared quite so literal.) Nevertheless, the game of luring Poles back into officially sponsored unions is not yet over and the military government and party may still construct a situation in which it would be positively detrimental for Poles to remain outside the union structure (for example, by linking union membership with pension benefits, employment possibilities, increased opportunities for oneself or for one's children in gaining acceptance into institutions of higher education, etc.). After all, it matters little to the current rulers of Poland if union members be willing or unwilling—so long as they are members. If and when memberships are increased, the polity will consider this a successful return to the status quo and will once again ignore the fact that nothing has been settled.

The rulers of Poland are now facing the long, complicated, and painful task of settling the nation's economic crisis and trying to attain some measure of legitimacy in the eyes of the Polish population. Ironically, these crises might not have occurred had Polish workers been granted greater participation in the economic affairs of their enterprises and a greater voice in their own economic well-being. To ignore these needs may well amount to overlooking or sidestepping the possible solution to other problems. After all, repression is costly to orchestrate; efficient, dedicated work cannot be demanded; love of the party cannot be legislated; and solutions to the economic and political crises of Poland cannot be found if workers are ostracized from the decision-making processes.

When martial law was declared in Poland, the Western press described it as a return to Stalinism. But more than the repressive atmosphere associated with Stalinism, martial law was declared so that the rulers could consolidate their power and rebuild the economy. Such goals and purposes are indeed reminiscent of Polish society in the late 1940s. What is different is that the workers have defined their needs more clearly, more unanimously, and with more conviction. Furthermore, through lessons learned from the past, they have grown more sophisticated in their strategies. While issues of workers' self-management and truly independent trade unions may have been tabled temporarily, they will emerge again and again in Poland until they are settled to the satisfaction of the workers themselves.

ACKNOWLEDGMENTS

I gratefully acknowledge the research assistance of Ms. Ann Baumann.

NOTES

1. Leszek Gilejko, Zwiazki zawodowe w procesie przemian spolecznych w PRL. (Warsaw: Instytut Wydawniczy CRZZ, 1972), pp. 16-17.

2. Krzysztof Ostrowski, Rola zwiazkow zawodowych w polskim systemie politycznym. (Wroclaw: PAN, 1970), pp. 56-57.

3. Wladyslaw Ratynski, Partia i zwiazki zawodowe w Polsce Ludowej. (Warsaw: Ksiazka i Wiedza, 1977), p. 145.

4. Jamie Reynolds, "Communists, Socialists, and Workers: Poland 1944-48," Soviet Studies 30 (1978):519.

5. Adolf Sturmthal, "The Workers' Councils in Poland," Industrial and Labor Relations Review 14 (1961):381.

6. Reynolds, "Communists, Socialists," pp. 527-8.

7. Jan B. de Weydenthal, "The Workers' Dilemma of Polish Politics: A Case Study," East European Quarterly 13, no. 1 (1979):99.

8. Sturmthal, "The Workers' Councils," pp. 382-3.

9. Ibid., p. 385.

10. George Kolankiewicz, "The Working Class," in Social Groups in Polish Society, David Lane and George Kolankiewicz, eds. (New York: Columbia University Press, 1973), p. 104.

11. Ibid., p. 106.

12. Sturmthal, "The Workers' Councils, p. 391.

13. Ibid., p. 386.

14. Cited in ibid., pp. 392-3.

15. Ibid., p. 390.

16. Kolankiewicz, "The Working Class," p. 107.

17. Sturmthal, "The Workers' Councils," p. 391.

18. Ibid., pp. 391-4.

19. Ibid., pp. 393-4.

20. Ibid., p. 394.

21. J. Kulpinska and M. Rokacz, "Rada robotnicza w opinii zalogi," Nowe Drogi 8 (1958):64-86.

22. Zbigniew Maciag, "Funkcjonowanie organizacji spoleczno-politycznych w przedsiebiorstwie (samorzad robotniczy)," 4 Zeszyt Naukowy UJ (Krakow, 1972), p. 148.

23. de Weydenthal, "The Workers' Dilemma," p. 102.

24. Ibid., pp. 102-3.

25. Ibid., p. 103.

26. Marek Tarniewski, "The New Regime," Survey 25 (1980):133.

27. de Weydenthal, "The Workers' Dilemma," p. 108.

28. "Important Decisions and Intentions in the Interests of Working People," Contemporary Poland 2 (1971):11.

29. "E. Gierek's Speech at Eighth Plenum of the Central Committee of the Polish United Workers' Party" (unofficial translation), Contemporary Poland, February (1971), special edition: 31.

30. Ibid.

31. Jadwiga Staniszkis, "The Evolution of Working-Class Protest in Poland: Sociological Reflections on the Gdansk-Szczecin Case, August 1980," Soviet Studies 2 (1981):205.

32. de Weydenthal, "The Workers' Dilemma," pp. 108-9.

33. Ibid., p. 108.

34. Adam Bromke, "The Opposition in Poland," Problems of Communism, Sept/Oct (1978):42.

35. Radio Free Europe Research, Poland/23 (October 30, 1979):4.

36. Ibid.

37. Bromke, "The Opposition," p. 49.

38. Zolnierz Wolnosci, February 26, 1980, p. 2.

39. August 1980: The Strikes in Poland. Radio Free Europe Research, October 1980, p. 12.

40. Ibid., p. 14.

41. Ibid., pp. 11-13.

42. Ibid., p. 18.

43. Ibid., p. 20.

44. Staniszkis, "The Evolution of Working-Class Protest," p. 217.

45. August 1980, p. 22.

46. "The Statutes of the Independent Self-Governing Solidarity Labor Unions," Radio Free Europe Research, Polish Background Report/91, March 31, 1981 (emphasis added).

47. Anna Sabbat, "The 'Basic' Tenets of the Polish Labor Union Law are Published," Radio Free Europe Research, Polish Background Report/76, March 17, 1981, p. 2.

48. Ibid., p. 3.

49. Ibid., p. 6.

50. Karol Rzemieniecki, "Worker Self-Government in Poland: How a Compromise was Reached," Contemporary Poland 19 (October 1981):2-3.

51. Ibid.

52. Ibid., p. 4.

53. Ibid., pp. 1-4.

54. Los Angeles Times, February 22, 1982.

6.

Solidarity and Socialism

David S. Mason

Poland's independent labor union, Solidarity, was working
to create a society that was both freer and more genuinely
socialist. In pursuing the former goal, the workers stressed
the process by which policy was made in Poland. They called
for independently formed and governed labor unions and other
groups, for increased participation in policy making for nonparty groups, and for a relaxation of censorship. These process
issues were the major source of dispute between Solidarity and
the Polish United Workers' Party (PUWP) and finally led the
regime to declare martial law and rid itself of the union. These
issues and disputes have attracted the most attention in the
West.

But the issue of egalitarianism was also an important element
in the catalogue of workers' demands from the port city strikes
in August 1980 to Solidarity's first congress in October 1981.
These demands took two forms: for greater social and economic
equality through adjustments in wage and social policies; and
for restrictions on political and economic privilege that derive
from positions of political power. However, the content of these
demands during Solidarity's sixteen months was not unchanging.
Solidarity's conception of egalitarianism and its relationship to
socialism underwent substantial revisions. In part this was due
to the process of working through these complex issues, which
are central to a socialist society. But the changes also reflected
changes in the political and economic environment during 1981
and an increasing sensitivity to public opinion, which became
easier to gauge as research institutes attached to the universities,
the media, and Solidarity itself conducted remarkably revealing
polls of popular attitudes on social and economic issues.

This chapter examines the development of Solidarity's program on the issues of egalitarianism and privilege, how the regime reacted to these demands, and how they were related to the attitudes of the public. These issues are important for several reasons. First, these demands concerning equality were an important counterweight to Solidarity's program of increased participation. To ignore this side of Solidarity's program is to distort the meaning of the workers' movement. It was the combination of demands for greater pluralism and for a deepening of egalitarianism that made Solidarity's program unique and gave hope for the creation of a very new type of society—one that was within the socialist commonwealth, but more open and free than Yugoslavia or Hungary and more genuinely egalitarian than the Soviet Union or East Germany.

Second, in this realm of policy there was potentially much more room for agreement between Solidarity and the party than there was on the process issues affecting political participation. While the process issues directly threatened the authority and supremacy of the party, the issue of egalitarianism did not, even though it may have jeopardized the positions or privileges of particular people within the party apparatus. These issues posed some embarrassment to the party because Solidarity was asking the party to go further than it had along its own ideological line. But there was considerable support for Solidarity's social policies even from within the party. The imposition of martial law, however, ended any hope of compromise even on these issues.

SOCIAL AND ECONOMIC EQUALITY

The interest of the workers in an extension of social welfare and concern for the poor was evident from the very beginning of the strikes in the summer of 1980. Among the twenty-one demands submitted to the authorities by the Gdansk Interfactory Strike Committee (MKS), there were basically four categories. The first called for an expanded scope and degree of political participation and included the demands for free trade unions, freedom of speech and publications, and a freer flow of information.[1] The second set of demands called for improvements in the economic situation and included basic wage increases, improved meat supplies, and rationing of scarce products. The third set argued for elimination of privileges afforded to party and government officials, for appointments based on qualifications, and for restrictions on those stores that cater to those with hard currency. The fourth set of demands, the most numerous, related to the needs of the poorer workers and families in Polish society and to an expansion of nonmonetary state benefits. These demands included an increase in old age pensions, improvements in medical services, an expansion of state housing and nursery school facilities, and an extension in paid maternity leaves.

As numerous as these social welfare demands were, they did not occupy a prominent position in the list of twenty-one and were obviously less important than the other sets. In the course of the bargaining between the MKS and the government, however, these social welfare demands became both more extensive and more important. The best example of this is in the demand for increased wages. In the initial twenty-one demands, point number eight called for an across-the-board wage increase of 2000 zlotys monthly for all workers to offset recent price increases. One of the academic advisors to MKS asserts, however, that during the negotiations, the workers wanted a larger wage increase for the more poorly paid workers.[2] The final agreement between the workers and the government called for increased wages for all workers, but "especially to the lowest paid groups."[3] In other respects as well, the agreements reflected a greater sensitivity to the needs of the poorer workers than the original demands had. In several places in the agreement, there is reference to the need to establish a social minimum of earnings below which no family should fall. The agreements signed between the workers and the government commission in Szczecin also contained special provisions for increases of the lowest wages, of family and maternity allowances, and of the so-called social minimum.[4]

The differences in the texts of the Gdansk demands and the final agreements might be explained in two ways: by changes within the workers' movement; or by pressure for change from the government's side of the table. On the first point, it is quite clear that the composition of the MKS changed dramatically during the last two weeks of August, as the strike movement itself spread and expanded. The movement started among the skilled dockworkers, among the most highly paid workers in Poland. As the movement expanded it increasingly incorporated younger, less skilled, and less well paid workers. While the better paid workers were primarily interested in a general wage increase and in consolidating their gains and power with an independent trade union, the poorer workers may well have been more concerned with the basics of wages and nonwage benefits.[5] The interests of the newcomers were, therefore, more adequately reflected in the final agreement than in the initial demands.

During the 1970s there were also increasingly strong perceptions among Poles that wage differences had become excessive
and inequitable. Indeed, there had been a marked increase in
the wage spread during the first half of the decade as part of
Gierek's program to stimulate incentive.[6] Several polls conducted
in 1980 and the beginning of 1981 indicate that this had become
an issue of substantial concern to the population. In a poll
conducted by the Polish Academy of Sciences entitled Polacy '80,
89.6 percent agreed that there should be limits on the wages
of the highest wage earners and 70 percent supported more or
less equal incomes for every citizen.[7] Consequently, when the
strike did spread outside the shipyards, these concerns were
expressed and were incorporated in the eventual agreements.

The other factor that may have led to the more egalitarian
provisions of the final agreements was the government itself.
On August 15, two days before the release of the twenty-one
demands, Prime Minister Babiuch asserted that wage increases
had to be tied to productivity except for low income and retired
people and large families.[8] He also pledged to reduce the gap
between minimum and maximum wages. In the Gdansk negotiations themselves, government negotiator Jagielski made a similar
point, arguing that the poorer workers were in greater need
of a wage increase than the better-off ones.[9]

Indeed, the regime had expressed a firm commitment to
reducing social and economic inequalities for some years before
1980 and had experienced some success in this regard, contrary
to popular perceptions. There had been a substantial reduction
in the wage differences between white- and blue-collar workers
during the 1970s and after 1976 a narrowing of the gap between
the best and worst paid workers.[10] After 1976 there were also
substantial improvements in the average pension, even as a
percent of average wages.[11]

The party affirmed its commitment to reducing these differences at the Eighth Party Congress in February 1980 when it
pledged that "the government is taking steps toward reducing
differences in incomes and wages by means of increases in minimum individual wages, on the one hand, and on the other hand,
by proper management of the collective welfare fund which
includes annuities and pensions, family allowances, etc." There
was recognition by the leadership, even at the Eighth Congress,
that there was "discord concerning the unjustified disparity in
the material conditions of families" and a pledge to resolve such
problems.[12] It does seem from the limited poll data that exists
that party members were even more aware of these social inequalities than was the general population. While 84 percent of

nonparty members perceived that great or very great social inequalities existed in Poland, fully 92 percent of party members felt that way.[13] So it seems likely, then, that once the striking workers and the government commission sat down to negotiate in Gdansk there was a considerable area of agreement on some issues between the workers, especially the less well-paid ones, and the representatives of the regime.

In the months following the Szczecin and Gdansk accords, the government did make some efforts to fulfill the agreements though not always within the time limits specified in the agreements.[14] The independent labor union Solidarity was allowed to be formed and was eventually sanctioned by the courts. Censorship was eased somewhat and the liberalized regulations were incorporated in a new law on censorship in July 1981. The church was allowed to broadcast masses, and Solidarity was given access to the media and ultimately their own publication. All of these gains were not achieved without continued pressure from the workers.

On the egalitarian issues of wages and benefits, however, the government apparently needed little prodding. In a remarkable document published in the party newspaper Trybuna Ludu on January 30, 1981, there appeared the list of twenty-nine points from the Szczecin accords with a statement concerning the realization of each. On the issue of wage increases, the government pointed out that there had been unprecedented increases in the wage fund during 1980. The average wage in the socialist economy in December 1980 was 24 percent higher than in December 1979, and increases of another 17 percent were planned for 1981. (In fact, average wages increased by 25 percent in 1981, though cost of living increases neutralized this gain.) In accord with the Gdansk and Szczecin agreements, special attention had been paid to the poorest workers. In September 1980 the Council of Ministers raised the minimum wage from 1800 to 2400 zlotys monthly. The government also moved to increase pensions and payments for single parents with children, students in higher education, young married couples, retired people, invalids, veterans, and families. Effective in January 1981, the minimum pension was raised from 1800 to 2300 zlotys monthly and other pensions were raised 300 to 500 zlotys. Furthermore, the government pledged, in accordance with a resolution of the Central Committee's Seventh Plenum, to continue special efforts to improve the standard of living of those with the lowest incomes.

While these gains were important for Solidarity in a symbolic sense and important for the workers in an economic one, they

were not by any means the result of a comprehensive social
and economic program of the workers' movement. Such a program was eventually developed in the early months of 1981 by
the Center for Social and Labor Tasks, a think tank attached
to the National Consultation Commission of Solidarity. The
preliminary report on "The Directions of the Operation of
Solidarity" was published in both the official press and in
Solidarity's own newly inaugurated Tygodnik Solidarnosc in
April 1981.[15] This document was even more egalitarian in tone
than the Gdansk agreements. In fact, the issues of social
justice and social and economic equality were the dominant
themes of the program.

The draft program identified "the four main sources of
our inspiration" as "the nation's best traditions, Christianity's
ethical principles, democracy's political mandate, and socialist
social thought." The latter two principles, and particularly
the last, received the most attention in the subsequent pages.
The program asserted that "in their most essential nature, all
people are equal. That is why we will seek social equality."
Perhaps the most dramatic demonstration of the program's egalitarian bent appeared in the following passage:

> We recognize the principle that one should be paid
> according to the quality, quantity, difficulty and
> risk of one's work ("to each according to his work"),
> and we will seek to level off unjustified dispropor-
> tions in that regard. However, the principle of
> meeting the social minimum has precedence over
> the aforementioned principle.[16]

This, of course, is a reference to the Marxist formulation
that socialism, as a transitional stage to full communism, may
be characterized by the principle of "to each according to his
work." When full communism is achieved, the applicable formula
will be "to each according to his needs." The passage above
implies that this communist formula should have precedence over
the socialist one. In this respect, Solidarity seemed to be out-
flanking the party even on the left.

In seeking to apply these principles, the draft program
had a number of specific proposals for social and economic
change. Solidarity called for the development of a "social minimum in the sphere of wages, pensions and disability payments
to be introduced as soon as possible into the practice of structuring incomes." It appealed for increases in family allowances
and maternity leaves, but not for new wage regulations. Thus,

Solidarity was explicitly renouncing claims for general wage increases that would benefit all workers in favor of programs that "give priority to the economically weaker groups." The draft program also demanded that the costs of the economic crisis and programs for reform be borne primarily by the prosperous groups in society. This "should be appropriately taken into account in the system of increasing wages and taxes." There should be compensation to offset rising prices, but only to those earning the least and "those earning the most should obtain no compensation at all."[17]

As with many of the social welfare demands in the Gdansk and Szczecin agreements, the regime was sympathetic to these issues in the Solidarity draft program. In Jaruzelski's June 1981 speech to the Sejm on price reforms, he promised that the burden of the reforms would fall on middle- and upper-income groups and that low-income groups would be fully compensated for increases in the price of necessities. Such a system would at the same time, he said, "contribute to a reduction in the excessive disproportion between the lowest and highest incomes, something that has been universally criticized."[18] Later in the summer, the compensation formulas were announced, and there were indeed disproportionate benefits for the less well-paid and for those with families. Persons earning 3000 zlotys monthly would receive compensation of 1350 zlotys monthly, while someone earning 10,000 would receive only 1100. There were also to be substantial increases in family allowances, from 100 to 200 zlotys per month per child to 1200 to 1500 zlotys.[19]

The strongly egalitarian nature of the draft program for Solidarity was probably a reflection both of the vastly increased size of the organization, particularly after its formal acceptance by the Supreme Court in November 1980, and of the tide of public opinion against excessive disproportions in wages and incomes. Interestingly though, the final program adopted by the Solidarity congress in October 1981 exhibited far less of this egalitarianism. In this document, in stating the basic principles of Solidarity, there was no mention of socialist social thought as there had been in the draft version. In fact, the term socialism appeared nowhere in the eleven pages of the program.[20] This time, Solidarity is based on "the Christian ethic, our national tradition and the workers' and democratic traditions of the world of labor." The program explicitly acknowledged the importance for the movement of the Pope's most recent encyclical on human labor (Laborem Exercens). This is an important statement and may help explain the lack of a positive and explicit commitment to socialism.

In his encyclical, Pope John Paul II criticized both capital-
ism and Marxism. But the Pope did assert that labor has priority
over capital, that private property is subject to the demands
of the common good, and that social welfare benefits such as
unemployment benefits, pensions, and health care are a matter
of justice, not just of charity.[21] This commitment to the individual, and particularly to the poor and disadvantaged, was
prominent in the Solidarity Program. In several of the thirty-
six theses of the Program, Solidarity recognized its special
commitment to protect and support "the weakest groups of
people," "the poorest," and "those for whom life is hardest."
The program backed up this philosophy with specific proposals
to aid the poorest. Thesis six called for the establishment of
a "social minimum as the guiding principle of incomes policy"
and for efforts to protect the real incomes of "the least powerful
parts of society." The union opposed wage and social inequalities between places of work and regions and called for more
equitable administration of enterprise social funds.

But the Solidarity program did not adopt the language of
Marxism or socialism, as the draft document had, and instead
outlined a new type of society that supported both the individual
and the collective, much as John Paul's encyclical did. Solidarity
recognized the importance and imperative of protecting the poor,
but also called for greater involvement by the worker in the
determination of his or her living and working conditions and
environment. In many respects, the Solidarity program was
very similar to Laborem Exercens.

The partial retreat from egalitarianism between the spring
draft program and the fall final one may have been due in part
to the publication of the encyclical in the interim. But there
were other factors at work, too: the changed political and economic environment between the spring and fall of 1981; changes
in public opinion on the issue of equality; and the difference
in the groups who drafted the preliminary program and the
final one.

Probably the most important of these was the changes in
the economic environment. Contrary to the hopes and expectations of most Poles, the constitution of an independent trade
union and widespread changes in political leadership had not
brought an end to the economic crisis. Indeed, the crisis
deepened as production declined, the foreign debt grew, and
shortages spread throughout the economy. This increasingly
desperate situation had two main effects on the population's
values and their support for egalitarianism: it created a rising
demand for law and order; and it caused people increasingly

to be concerned with their own welfare, rather than that of others. The need for a return to normalcy is evident from the polling data as early as the end of 1980 and increased dramatically during 1981. At the end of 1980, the top priorities listed by the respondents were the standard of living (30 percent) and stability (19 percent), including calm, political stability and order. Both of these were ranked far higher, in fact, than democratization of life, a freer flow of information, limitations on censorship, and so on. By the end of 1981, stability was the top-ranked priority by 35 percent of the sample.[22] Thus, it is likely that in these increasingly difficult circumstances, the loftier goals of egalitarianism were left behind in the struggle for survival.

There were also during 1981 changes in the ways Poles viewed the concept of equality. While it is true, as discussed above, that most Poles strongly favored an equitable socio-economic system that paid particular attention to the poor, this did not always translate into a Marxian form of egalitarianism. In the Polacy '80 study, for example, the researchers tested attitudes on two sets of questions, characterized as the egalitarian model and the nonegalitarian-effectiveness model. While there was strong support for the former model there was even stronger support for the latter. For example, 70 percent of the respondents agreed that there should be more or less equal incomes for every citizen. Yet 96.9 percent agreed that compensation should be based strictly according to output and quality of work rather than on qualifications and position (53.9 percent). While 77.4 percent agreed that the state should pursue a policy of full employment, 85.1 percent agreed that unprofitable enterprises should be closed, and 90.3 percent agreed that inefficient workers should be released from their jobs.

Furthermore, by the end of 1981, as the Polacy '81 survey shows, the population had significantly reduced its support for the egalitarian principles, and increased its support for the effectiveness model. Support for limitation of the highest wages, for example, was down from 90 to 79 percent and for a policy of full employment from 78 to 54 percent.

These changes during 1981 were to a large extent due to the growing realization that egalitarianism might have to be postponed until the economy could be revitalized and the standard of living stabilized. This might require a greater role for incentives in production and a consequent widening of income differentials. As an analyst of yet another set of poll data put it, a "broadly interpreted egalitarianism" is the basic value

desired by most Poles for their sociopolitical system. But the
desire for equality is qualified, since "the majority demands
a fair distribution of material and other goods according to
the principle of 'to each according to his work.'"[23] This is
not the thoroughgoing egalitarianism that appeared in the draft
program of Solidarity in the spring. But it probably more
accurately reflected the attitudes of the majority of Poles, as
did the more moderate tone of the final Solidarity Program
adopted in October.

The final factor that affected the differences in the two
Solidarity programs was the different makeup of the drafting
groups for each. The spring preliminary program was drafted
by a think tank of intellectuals who tend to have a more social
democratic and theoretical orientation than the workers. The
draft program reflects this constituency. The final Program,
on the other hand, was hammered out by delegates to Solidarity's
Congress, and reflected the more concrete and pragmatic interests of the workers. The apparently deliberate omission of the
word socialism from the Program seems to be a symbolic rejection
of political ideology, or at least its language, even though the
Program supported many of the essential features of socialism.

THE ISSUE OF PRIVILEGE

The other aspect of egalitarianism in Poland was the resentment toward those with very high incomes and privilege derived
from positions of power. The demand for social and economic
equality was not so much for an absolute leveling as for restrictions on the richest and supplements for the poorest. Equality
and justice were the most desired values by Poles (90 percent),
taking precedence over law and order (82 percent), freedom of
expression (71 percent) and the ability to influence governmental
decisions (61 percent).[24] As noted above, there is a widespread
perception among Poles that there are very great social inequalities in Poland. But as Jacek Kurczewski notes of these polls,
"the inequalities principally are in the existence of privileged
social categories, distinguished by high incomes and state
position." The resentment about the position of the political
and economic elite is multifaceted, as indicated by Kurczewski's
prescription for remedying the problem:

It is essential that the leadership's living conditions
be made public, that the leadership be rotated, that
it be held responsible for mistakes and violations of

the law, and the principles of selection and promotion be democratized.[25]

Thus, in the eyes of the public, the elites were guilty on a number of counts: an unnecessary and undemocratic centralization of power and privilege; inequitably high incomes; and excessive perquisites and fringe benefits. The first of these, of course, was the most sensitive, and was not directly addressed in the public opinion polls. One poll, however, found that "bringing to justice those who abused their positions of authority" was the second most frequently voiced demand, behind only that for an improved supply situation in the economy.[26]

The complaints about the high incomes and extensive benefits for those in authority were, on the other hand, frequently aired and discussed. Even before August 1980 the issue of elite privilege was a grating one for many Poles. In the 1970 Gdansk and Szczecin strikes, and in subsequent discussions between the workers and party leaders, the workers frequently complained about the high salaries for directors and managers, unequal bonuses favoring management, and the excessive perquisites afforded such people.[27] In Szczecin there was a demand that the earnings of party and government officials should be limited to the average industrial wage.[28]

Wage and fringe benefits, especially for white-collar workers, were an important issue in arousing the anger of the workers during the summer of 1980.[29] The polls published in 1980 and 1981 vividly demonstrate the extent of resentment about high wages and privileges. In the Polacy '80 questions connected with the egalitarian model the statement with the most support was that there should be limits on the wages of the highest wage earners (89.6 percent). And as Kurczewski notes of the Polish Radio and Television data:

> the present egalitarianism is not directed against the differences in earning as such; neither is it directed against "private initiative," which usually attempts in these cases to play the role of "scapegoat", but it is mainly against the economic position and life style of the leadership apparatus.

Thus, a majority believes that:

> it is unfair that high positions are linked with privileges and demand that incomes be reduced, and that availability of goods in short supply,

such as housing and automobiles, access to special
shops, private clubs, clinics, etc., to persons in
high positions, be restricted.[30]

The complaints about elite privilege were reflected in the
demands of the workers from the very beginning of the strikes
in the summer of 1980. The workers of the Lublin FSC truck
factory, striking in early July, presaged the actions of the
dockworkers a month later with a list of thirty-five demands.
These demands did not include free trade unions but did attack
the higher family allowances and pensions for the police and
the army and demanded the abolition of commercial food prices
and the hard currency Pewex stores.[31] Both of these demands
were to appear in the Gdansk and Szczecin lists. The twenty-
one demands issued from Gdansk also included an appeal to
base the selection of leadership positions "on qualifications, and
not on party membership" and to eliminate privileges of the
police, the secret police, and the party apparatus through
equalizing family allowances, liquidating special stores, and so
on. As one of the expert advisers to the Gdansk MKS points
out, it was not so much a "liberal political culture" that dictated
these demands, but "the deeply egalitarian and anti-hierarchical
character of the workers' movement."[32]

It is significant that these demands for restriction of
privilege were aimed primarily at the fringe benefits available
to those in authority, rather than their basic salaries (although
this was also to become an issue). This reflects the popular
perception that fringe benefits and bonuses were increasingly
becoming a large proportion of the incomes and standard of
living of the managerial and party apparatus.[33] As a Solidarity
leader in Wroclaw pointed out:

Regular wages should occupy the dominant position;
bonuses and awards should not exceed a dozen or
so (kilkanascie) percent of overall wages, because
it becomes much more difficult to measure wages
and equity.[34]

The issue of privilege and abuse of authority was much
more prevalent in the April Draft Program of Solidarity than
it had been in the twenty-one demands. This was due to a
growing awareness on the part of the Solidarity leadership that
this was an important issue for the workers, as was increasingly
reflected in the public opinion polls. But it was also a result
of the increasing openness with which these previously sensitive

issues were being treated by both Solidarity and the regime in open forums and in the media.

In addressing the "basic reasons for the crisis," the Draft Program bluntly stated that "the disappearance of democratic institutions and the resulting profound division between society and the apparatus of power within the present system of public life are at the bottom of that crisis." To remedy this, the Draft called for a more open and democratic political system, but also for severe restrictions on the privileges of the economic, social, and political elites. These demands included a progressive income tax, taxes on luxury items (such as luxury automobiles and vacation homes), restrictions on "unjustified privileges for the power apparatus" (such as apartments, office cars, special health services, pensions, and allowances), the definition of a maximum income level, and the revelation of "the income and properties of persons with standing in the power apparatus." The draft program also called for the establishment of a constitutional court to judge those who had abused their offices. Finally, since those in authority had caused the crisis, the costs of the reform should be borne primarily by the most prosperous groups, "particularly by people enjoying privileges linked with the exertion of power."[35]

Just as the October Solidarity program backed off somewhat from the egalitarianism of the Draft Program, it was also much less specific and demanding on the issue of privilege. The program did repeat the Draft's condemnation of central party and state institutions for bringing the country to ruin. It specifically called for the trial and punishment of those who were responsible for the brutality against workers and students in 1956, 1970, and 1976 and for those who were responsible for the economic collapse between 1970 and 1980. The program also appealed for the establishment of self-government and autonomous political institutions throughout society.

But the program did not specifically call for restrictions on the privileges of the elites, for special taxes on the rich, for revelation of the incomes of party and state officials, or for these people to bear the burden of the economic reforms, as the draft program did. There are several factors that can help explain this change: the different purpose and tone of the October Program compared to the April Draft, and accomplishments of the regime in meeting some of the criticisms raised in the earlier draft.

While the April Draft spent a good deal of time dwelling on the reasons and responsibility for the crisis and assumed an almost vindictive tone at times, the October program had none of these qualities. The October program was forward looking, positive, and conciliatory. Its stated purpose was to help the country get through the difficult months of the approaching winter through economic and political reform. It called on all people of goodwill to participate in these reforms. While it did appeal for some people to be brought to justice for their actions, its criticisms focused largely on the system rather than on any political groups. The changes needed to be made in the organization of society, the economy, and the political system by introducing the principles of democracy, pluralism, and self-government. The privileged elites were not treated as the scapegoats.

The other factor that may have caused Solidarity to back off somewhat on the issue of elite privileges was that the regime had made some real headway in meeting the criticisms and answering the demands of the workers expressed in the summer and following spring. These actions included publishing the salaries of party and state officials, restricting the privileges of the elites, insuring more turnover in party leadership positions, and investigating those guilty of abuse of office.

The regime was fairly quick to take action on the issue of special privileges for government and party officials. In Trybuna Ludu's publication of the twenty-nine demands of the Szczecin protocol and the realization of each five months after the agreement, it is clear that the regime took seriously the complaints about privileges. Thus the regime claimed to have raised family allowances (presumably nearer to the levels in the military and the militia), equalized the distribution of food to enterprises, removed deficit goods from the Pewex stores, pledged to apply stricter standards to the appointment and retention of leading cadres, and to consult the labor unions on which workers should be sent to schools and factory courses.[36]

In response to continuing concerns and rumors about the salaries of managers and government and party officials, there was an apparent campaign in March and April 1981 to publish salary figures and quash the most extreme rumors. It was revealed, for example, that in Siedlce the city chief earned just 10,500 zlotys monthly compared to the average industrial wage of 7,000. In Krakow, the head of a production department earned 15,000. Even more to the point, Deputy Minister of Labor, Wages, and Social Affairs Karpiuk directly tackled the question of the salaries of the elite in an interview on Radio Warsaw.[37] Karpiuk revealed that the prime minister received 28,100 zlotys monthly, that a deputy prime minister receives 25,900, a minister 23,700, and a deputy minister 19,800. He

also addressed the question of pensions, claiming that the top
pensions for state and party officials were 26,700 zlotys monthly
(compared to a national average of 2,681) and that the very
highest pensions in Poland were 37,000 for a stage performer
and 35,000 for a journalist. The next month, the party monthly
Zycie Partii reported the salaries of top party officials: 25,930
for a member of the Politburo and a secretary of the Central
Committee; 23,700 for a secretary of the Central Committee;
and 19,800 for the head of a division of the Central Committee
or for a wojewod committee. As the article took pains to point
out, these salaries were not high compared to equivalent positions
in the state or the economy. And in addressing the question
of nonwage benefits, it claimed that "workers in the apparatus
may not have other sources of income and are not receiving
any other bonuses or periodic awards."[38] Whether or not this
was true in the past, it seems that the party was making an
effort to restore some degree of credibility and legitimacy by
cracking down on the privileges of the elite, especially in the
party.

The party had also apparently gotten the message that
the public wanted the organization to clean up its own act and
to take action against those who had abused their privileges.
This was done both at the top, where a number of important
and visible bureaucrats were dismissed and publicly condemned
(including Director of Polish Radio and Television Maciej Szczepanski) and also throughout the party apparatus. In a resolution
adopted by the party's Central Committee on March 30, 1981,
the committee instructed the appropriate bodies in both the
party and the state apparatus to accelerate work in "defining
political responsibility of party members guilty of violations of
law and of moral principles" and "determining the extent of the
criminal responsibility of persons guilty of exploiting their functions for personal gains and of violation of legal standards."[39]

The party also made efforts to adopt more democratic
principles in its operation and allow more rotation in positions
of authority. In preparation for the Ninth Extraordinary Party
Congress in July 1981, the Central Committee twice revised
the rules under which delegates for the congress (and lower
level bodies) are nominated. Under the previous rules, special
electoral commissions nominated the delegates for the party
conferences at the primary, provincial, and national levels;
only 15 percent of the available seats could be nominated from
the floor by party members attending the lower level conferences.
The provisional rules adopted by the Central Committee in December 1980 allowed for 50 percent of the nominations to come from

the floor.[40] But even this higher limit was criticized and some local and provincial party organizations had already raised the limit unilaterally. Reflecting these events, the April Plenum of the Central Committee, in adopting the final rules, allowed an unlimited number of nominations to come from the floor.[41] Elections were also to be held by secret ballot.

The result of these rule changes was an unprecedented level of turnover in party leadership at all levels of the party organization. In the elections leading up to the party congress, it was reported that 50 percent of the first secretaries and 40 percent of the executive committees of the primary party organizations had been replaced, and that fully 75 percent of the leadership of village, town, and urban district party committees was new.[42] These changes were sufficient to lead Soviet Party Leader Brezhnev, in an open letter to the Polish leadership, to complain that the PUWP leadership was failing to defend its "experienced cadre" and that many "revisionists" and "opportunists" were being elected in the preparatory conference elections.[43] It is not surprising, given these changes at the lower levels, that there was also unprecedented turnover at the top. At the party congress elections of the Central Committee in July 1981, there were 279 candidates for 200 seats. Of the 200 elected, 182 were new; this was a 91 percent turnover (compared to 32 percent in the February 1980 election),[44] an unprecedented figure for Central Committee elections in Poland and indeed for the entire Soviet bloc. In the elections for the top party organs, there was also extensive turnover. Seven of the eleven full members of the Politburo lost their seats on that body, as well as all five candidate members and five of the eight Central Committee secretaries. Furthermore, several of the new Politburo members were ordinary workers, with no prior administrative experience. In a contested and secret election for the party first secretary, Stanislaw Kania was re-elected with 1311 votes to 568 for Kazimierz Barcikowski.[45]

All of these changes indicate that the party was sensitive to the charges of privilege, unrepresentativeness, and stagnation and was making moves to correct these deficiencies. Indeed, since the party was now competing for legitimacy and support with Solidarity and the church, the party had to take such measures to try to salvage some of its battered credibility. The party's moves in this direction may have been one of the factors accounting for the softened tone on the issue of privilege in Solidarity's October program.

CONCLUSIONS

There are strong egalitarian and antihierarchical beliefs
among the Polish population, and these were reflected in the
demands of the workers and formalized in the written programs
of Solidarity. The vigor with which these demands were expressed, however, varied over time. After the initial strikes
in August 1980, the strike movement grew and became more
egalitarian. By the next spring, the Draft Program of Solidarity
was radical in its demands for a more egalitarian social system
and for the elimination of privileges for the elite. By the time
of Solidarity's congress the next fall, this radicalism had been
tempered somewhat. This was due partly to a deepening of
the economic crisis and its effects on public opinion, and partly
in recognition of the efforts the regime had made in the intervening year to meet the workers' demands.

On the issue of egalitarianism, at least, there seems to
have been some genuine possibility of agreement and accord
between Solidarity and the regime. While there were deep
divisions between these two forces on the process issues of
power sharing, on the social policy issues, at least, there was
room for compromise. The party was at least formally committed
to the principle of egalitarianism and the elimination of privilege
from society, as was Solidarity. The party had made some real
efforts to meet the criticisms that Solidarity had raised in this
area. The possibility of cooperation was also enhanced by the
high degree of overlapping membership between Solidarity and
the Polish United Workers' Party. It was estimated in January
1981 that every sixth member of Solidarity was also a member
of the PUWP. If this were true, that meant that almost half
(46 percent) of all party members were also in Solidarity.[46]
Even among the party leadership there were split affinities.
During the July party congress, it was estimated that 20 percent
of the congress delegates were Solidarity members.[47] As one
of Solidarity's expert advisers noted, there were strong common
interests between the renewal movement in the party and Solidarity's rank and file.[48] There was another interesting overlapping
membership issue with regards to the third pillar of contemporary
Polish society, the Catholic church. Over two-thirds of all
party members are also believers.[49]

Both in terms of membership and orientation, then, there
were strong common interests among Solidarity, the party, and
the church. But the possibility of compromise was suddenly
ended with the imposition of martial law in December 1981.
While there were some common interests in policy issues, and

in particular on the issue of equality, the issues of political
participation and political control continued to divide Solidarity
and the party. These issues, of course, directly threatened
the supremacy of the party, which was consequently reluctant
to grant concessions. As the stalemate continued, tensions
increased, and the economy stagnated, the authority and
membership of the party declined even further. Jaruzelski
and the military stepped in to reestablish control and to prevent
further gains for Solidarity.

In its efforts to discredit Solidarity, the martial law regime
contended that Solidarity had become dominated by antisocialist
forces. It pointed to Solidarity's Program as an example of this,
with frequent references to the Program's omission of the term
socialism. But it is clear from the discussion above that there
were strong socialist elements in the Solidarity movement and
in the Program. The real problem from the regime's point of
view was that Solidarity had become antiparty and that the
supremacy of the party was being undercut. This was of greater
concern to the regime than the policy issues that Solidarity
raised.

ACKNOWLEDGMENTS

The author would like to thank the International Research
and Exchanges Board for sponsoring research in Poland in early
1982 and the Summer Slavic Research Laboratory of the University
of Illinois for supporting research in Urbana in 1981.

NOTES

1. The twenty-one demands are listed in "Program NSZZ
Solidarnosc," Tygodnik Solidarnosc, October 16, 1981; a trans-
lation of the demands appears in Jadwiga Staniszkis, "The
Evolution of Forms of Working-Class Protest in Poland: Socio-
logical Reflections on the Gdansk-Szczecin Case, August 1980,"
Soviet Studies 33 (April 1981):222-3.

2. Staniszkis, pp. 217-18.

3. The Gdansk agreements appeared in Glos Pracy and
Zycie Warszawy on September 2, 1980, and are translated in
William F. Robinson, ed., August 1980: The Strikes in Poland
(Munich: Radio Free Europe Research, 1980), pp. 423-34.

4. Ibid., pp. 416-19.

5. Evidence for this hypothesis is strong, though circum-
stantial. Public opinion polls conducted at the end of 1980, for

example, showed that poorer workers were much less likely to
have perceived an improvement in their standard of living during
the 1970s; that they more strongly favored wage increases bene-
fiting the poor; and that they more frequently identified the
standard of living as the major problem in the country than did
wealthier workers.

6. See David Mason, "Policy Dilemmas and Political Unrest
in Poland," Journal of Politics 45 (May 1983):397-421.

7. Polacy '80: Wyniki Badan Ankietowych (Warsaw:
Polska Akademia Nauk, 1981), pp. 106-7.

8. Radio Warsaw, August 15, 1980, 2005 hours; summarized
in Robinson, August 1980, p. 106.

9. Robinson, August 1980, p. 355.

10. Mason, "Policy Dilemmas," Table 3; Wieslaw Krencik,
"Tempo wzrostu a rozpietosc plac w latach 1970-1979," Gospodarka
Planowa, April 1980, p. 208; Rocznik Statystyczny 1981 (Warsaw:
Glowny Urzad Statystyczny, 1982), p. 169.

11. Mason, "Policy Dilemmas," Table 1; Polityka, November 3, 1979, p. 4.

12. Trybuna Ludu, July 19-20, 1980, p. 3.

13. Jacek Kurczewski, "W Oczach Opinii Publicznej,"
Kultura, March 1, 1981, p. 9. This article is based on data
collected by the Center for Public Opinion Research (OBOP) of
Polish Radio and Television.

14. On governmental delays in implementing the wage
increases, see Neal Ascherson, The Polish August (London:
Penguin, 1981), pp. 188 ff.

15. "The Directions of the Operations of Solidarity, the
Independent, Self-Governing Labor Union, in the Current
Situation of the Country," Glos Pracy, April 14, 1981 and
Tygodnik Solidarnosc, April 17, 1981; translated in Radio Free
Europe Research, Background Report no. 210, July 22, 1981.

16. Ibid., p. 4. Stress in original.

17. Ibid., pp. 13 and 16.

18. Trybuna Ludu, June 13-14, 1981.

19. Trybuna Ludu, July 22, 1981.

20. "Program NSZZ Solidarnosc."

21. New York Times, September 16, 1981.

22. Polacy '80, p. 70; and Polacy '81. Polacy '81 (Warsaw:
Instytut Filozofii i Socjologil, PAN, n.d.).

23. Kurczewski, p. 9.

24. Ibid.

25. These are all suggestions made by the "Experience
and the Future" group as well. See Poland Today: The State
of the Republic, comp. by the "Experience and the Future"

discussion group with a preface by Jack Bielasiak (Armonk, New York: M. E. Sharpe, 1981), especially pp. 173-82.

26. Jacek Maziarski, "Do We Want Strong Authority?" Kultura, January 25, 1981, pp. 1, 8; translated in Joint Publication Research Service, East Europe Report (no. 77612), March 18, 1981, p. 9.

27. See "Poznan 1956-Grudzien 1970," Dokumenty, no. 35 (Paris: Instytut Literacki, 1971); Daniel Singer, The Road to Gdansk: Poland and the USSR (New York: Monthly Review Press, 1981), pp. 176-7.

28. Cited in J. M. Montias, "Economic Conditions and Political Instability in Communist Countries: Observations on Strikes, Riots, and Other Disturbances," Studies in Comparative Communism 13 (Winter 1980):291-2.

29. See Jean Woodall, "New Social Factors in the Unrest in Poland," Government and Opposition 16 (Winter 1981):44; and Staniszkis, p. 227.

30. Kurczewski, p. 9.

31. Singer, pp. 214-5; and Montias, p. 297.

32. Staniszkis, p. 212.

33. Woodall, pp. 39-40.

34. Odra, no. 10 (1980), p. 9.

35. "Directions," pp. 5-18.

36. Trybuna Ludu, January 30, 1981.

37. Radio Free Europe Research, Polish Situation Report no. 15, March 20, 1981, pp. 24-26.

38. Zycie Partii, February 1981, p. 40.

39. Radio Free Europe Research, Polish Situation Report, April 13, 1981, p. 15.

40. Zycie Partii, February 1981, pp. 9-12.

41. Trybuna Ludu, April 30, 1981; and J. B. de Weydenthal, "Polish CC Plenum Sets the Stage for Party Congress," Radio Free Europe Research, Background Report no. 131, May 11, 1981, pp. 2-4.

42. Radio Free Europe Research, Polish Situation Report no. 12, July 3, 1981, p. 2.

43. Ibid., no. 11.

44. Washington Post, July 18, 1981 and New York Times, July 18, 1981.

45. New York Times, July 20, 1981, p. 5.

46. Kurczewski, p. 9.

47. New York Times, July 20, 1981, p. 5.

48. Staniszkis, p. 229.

49. Zycie Warszawy, January 12, 1980 and January 8, 1981; and Polacy '81.

7.

Public Opinion
and Political Disruption

T. Anthony Jones, David Bealmear, and
Michael D. Kennedy

As in Czechoslovakia in 1968, the political disruptions in
Poland between July 1980 and December 1981 were accompanied
by a dramatic change in public opinion polling. Questions that
were not asked in normal times began to be routine, and results
that previously would have been kept secret were published
openly in the mass media. Although most of the surveys have
yet to be made available, there are a number already published
that provide detailed information on a wide variety of issues,
and it is to these that this analysis will give attention. We will
concentrate mainly on the results of four major surveys taken
during mid-to-late 1980 and early in 1981 and will briefly compare the results with those available from other surveys done
both inside Poland and by Radio Free Europe-Radio Liberty in
Western Europe.

In addition to their interest as sources of information about
Polish society, however, these surveys also are of interest for
the insight they give into the changing status of public opinion
research in Eastern Europe. While the Polish situation is clearly
unusual, the quick resort to opinion polling by both the official
agencies and by Solidarity showed just how far in its evolution
the status of public opinion research had come.

Public opinion research, in the sense that the West under-
stands it, was not practiced during the Stalinist era in Soviet-
type societies. A researchable public opinion was considered
an anomaly, in that public opinion was not something that was
to be discovered through research, but something that was to
be created and guided. This approach derived from the Leninist
perspective on socialist revolution. It was Lenin's position that

the proletariat could not by itself come to a level of revolutionary class consciousness sufficient to achieve revolution. It was necessary to have an enlightened vanguard party to lead the working class to a successful socialist revolution. This position was used and extended by Stalinist policy to grant the party a superior consciousness over the people and their more immediate wishes. In that sense, public opinion had no position under socialism comparable to that in the West; if public opinion was not supportive of the party position, it was either backward or counterrevolutionary and contrary to the goals of building social- ism. Public opinion polling, consequently, remained undeveloped.

With Khrushchev's assumption of power and his denuncia- tion of Stalinist policy, the way was opened for the development of social science research in the Soviet Union.[1] Similarly, in other countries of the Soviet bloc, leadership style was an important determinant of the role public opinion research was to play. In Czechoslovakia, Antonin Novotny's strict Stalinist style of leadership inhibited the development of public opinion research, in the name of suppressing bourgeois sociology and fostering the scientific approach of Marxism-Leninism. The Institute of Public Opinion Research, dissolved in 1948 at the time of the communist takeover, was reestablished in 1967 under pressure from internal elements and from the Soviet party leader- ship.[2] The ascension of Alexander Dubcek to leadership a year later not only opened the door to further research, but actively encouraged it; since polls were generally supportive of his reformist policies, they could be used by Dubcek in the political arena.[3]

In the post-Stalinist era, then, public opinion has come to play a different and extended role in socialist society. At the same time, however, the development of survey and public opinion research has not occurred in a unilinear manner, nor has it progressed similarly in all countries. In a recent survey of these developments, Gitelman has discerned two major schools of thought among socialist researchers as to what socialist public opinion means. These two scholars are mainly distinguished by their views on the homogeneity of public opinion. The traditional, monist position holds that public opinion is essentially homogeneous and nonantagonistic under conditions of socialism, and is best observed through such traditional avenues as letters to the editor, institutional decisions, and so forth. Public opinion research is to play only an ancillary role, providing supplementary information to make more efficient central decisions and in that way enhance the development of socialism. The pluralist position, on the other hand, emphasizes the utility

of public opinion research as a means for discovering the contradictions of society within and between groups. Social groups
are assumed to differ on all but the most fundamental issues,
and survey research into these differences is seen as a means
for increasing the sense of citizen participation and of extending
socialist democracy. [4]

Most European societies do not have firmly entrenched
political cultures that foster the use and development of public
opinion research, since in general, "the pre-Communist political
cultures of Eastern Europe did not highly value participation
and consultation with mass public opinion."[5] In addition, the
strength of the social science tradition in a country appears
to be an important factor in the development of opinion polling.
This is especially true in the case of Poland, whose tradition
of social research dates back at least to the late nineteenth
century. Correspondingly, Poland today has one of the most
vigorous and consistent public opinion research activities in
Eastern Europe, Yugoslavia being the only other country of
which this may be said.

The extent to which either conception of public opinion
and its research predominates in a country depends, of course,
on many factors, including "leadership style, political culture,
and general level of societal development and the social science
traditions of each country."[6] Public opinion research is also
intimately connected with the political stability of the country
in question, a factor that should not only affect the frequency
of polling, but also the control of the surveys and the importance
they are accorded by the central government. Awareness of
the public mood is crucial in periods of public upheaval, as is
shown by the reestablishment of the Czechoslovak Institute of
Public Opinion Research and the recent increase in polling in
Poland. Public opinion research in socialist society may be an
aid to democratization, since it makes the demands of that society
better known to the government. Moreover, by publicizing
results, indirect pressure can be put upon the government to
fulfill those demands. At the same time, polls may also be used
by political leaders to gauge and manipulate the situation. [7]

THE POLISH CRISIS AND PUBLIC OPINION

The speed with which strikes occurred and spread following
the changes in meat prices on July 1, 1980 and the course of
events that led to the signing of the agreement of August 31
are by now well known. In addition to their dramatic form and

consequences, however, these events brought about some equally dramatic changes in the gathering and dissemination of information on public opinion. The carrying out of opinion surveys became something of a minor industry in 1981-82, and they quickly became a part of the political struggle itself, as newspapers prominently published the results. As a consequence, Poles were able to learn in some detail how the general population was reacting to events as they occurred and, more important, the extent to which there was a consensus on these events and on the structure and organization of Polish society. The results of these surveys are of interest, therefore, not only for the information they provide on public opinions of current events, but also for the insight they afford into Poles' views of the nature of their society.

In what follows, we will focus mainly on the results of four major polls taken between September and December 1980. Rather than examining each poll separately, we have organized the data from these polls around a number of general issues, so that the form and dynamics of public opinion in the fall and winter of 1980 can be more easily appraised.

Attitudes toward the Strikes

On September 4 and 5, almost exactly two months following the first strikes, a poll was conducted in which respondents were asked their opinions on recent events.[8] The responses, according to level of education, are shown in Table 7.1. The most frequently given opinion is that the strikes and unrest were "an unavoidable consequence of existing policies." Among those respondents with an elementary education, 38.1 percent expressed this opinion, as compared to 63.4 percent of those with higher education. The second most frequently chosen response was that events were a justified protest of the working class, although how this differs precisely from the earlier response we are not told. However, in this case, those with higher education were somewhat less likely to choose this response than were those with less education. While a small percentage thought the protests were justified but unacceptable in the form that they took (from 2.1 to 8.5 percent), virtually no one saw them as the result of antisocialist forces. Moreover, although few people were surprised at the events, there were differences by educational level, with 10.6 percent of those with elementary education being surprised, compared to 0 to 4.2 percent of the other groups.

TABLE 7.1

Opinions of August 1980 Developments
(Question: "In your opinion, what were the latest developments?")

Evaluation	Respondent's Education: Elementary	Basic Technical and Incomplete Secondary	Secondary	Higher
A surprise	10.6	1.7	4.2	0
Basically a result of the activities of antisocialist and anarchist forces	0	1.7	0	0
An unavoidable consequence of existing policies	38.1	50.4	58.0	63.4
A healthy shock for the whole of society	14.2	11.1	10.9	10.4
A justified protest of the working people, but unacceptable in its form	7.1	8.5	2.1	5.2
A justified protest of the working people, acceptable in its form	28.3	35.9	24.9	18.2
Something else	0.9	0	0	2.6
Total*	99.2	109.3	100.1	99.8

*No explanation is given for totals other than 100 percent.
Source: *Polityka*, September 4, 1980.

These results confirm what participants and reporters had been claiming, that the strikes had strong popular support. In a poll taken a few days earlier, 89 percent of the respondents had said that they thought the strikes were justified.[9] This support was subsequently to erode, however, as seen by responses following the warning strike of October 3, when general support fell to 67 percent, with 17 percent saying the strike was unjustified. Among workers, support was slightly higher (72 percent), but white-collar employees and farmers gave only 65 and 56 percent positive responses, respectively.[10]

Further erosion of support occurred during 1981, falling from 62 percent support for the strikes of January, to 46 percent support for the work stoppage of October 28 (the last stoppage before the imposition of martial law).[11] Surveys conducted by Solidarity's own opinion research organization also found declining support for strikes during this period, and this may have been a factor in the argument advanced by Walesa that the indiscriminate use of strikes was counterproductive.[12]

Opinion on the Agreements of August 31

The agreement between strikers and the government, in which Solidarity was legalized and various political and economic changes were promised, was greeted with what may best be described as cautious optimism. Knowledge of the content of the agreement was very high, with 90 percent of those claiming to know it very well. Although only 28 percent thought that the agreements would be carried out fully, the majority (52 percent) thought that they would be partially carried out, with only 9 percent saying that they would not be adhered to at all.[13] Doubts were further evidenced by the fact that 65 percent thought that the agreements were being put into effect too slowly, and that 71 percent thought that the workers were doing more to implement them than was the government. By November 18, 68 percent were saying that implementation of the agreement was going too slowly.[14]

The most detailed data yet available on attitudes to the agreements were provided in a poll undertaken in December 1980.[15] This is an especially interesting poll in that it breaks down the responses by social category. In response to the question "What is your attitude toward the August agreements?" 60.1 percent said that they were very much in favor, 31.6 percent were somewhat in favor, 1.5 percent were somewhat against, and 0.5 percent were strongly against. The remainder responded

that it was either hard to say (4.6 percent) or they did not
know or lacked enough data to have an opinion (1.7 percent).
Men were rather more in favor of the agreements (66.6 percent)
than were women (53.6 percent), and members of the United
Peasants' Party (UPP) and the Democratic Party (DP) were
rather more in favor (68.4 percent) than either Polish United
Workers' Party (PUWP) members (58.4 percent) or nonparty
people (60 percent).

This poll also found that the feelings expressed in earlier
polls that things were progressing too slowly were still in evidence. Thus, 67.4 percent of the respondents thought that
the agreements were being "unduly delayed," compared to
17.2 percent who thought they were not, and 15.3 percent who
found it "hard to say." Among workers, there was even greater
feeling that there were undue delays, with 75.4 and 74.6 percent
of qualified and unqualified workers saying this, respectively,
and 76.4 percent of Solidarity members saying this. As one
might expect, managerial personnel (both higher and middle
level) gave lower responses (56.9 percent saying too slow,
28.1 percent saying not too slow), as did members of the other
trade unions (59.5 and 24.1 percent). Less dissatisfaction was
also found among those with higher education (56.9 and 27.2
percent), but members of political parties were closer to the
general population; thus, 61.1 percent of the UPP and DP members considered the implementation of the agreements to be too
slow. An analysis of the subsample of those who were dissatis-
fied with the pace of implementation shows that the government
was seen to be the main cause of this, 61.6 percent of the
respondents laying the blame there. Solidarity was not seen
as the cause of this slowness, only 1.1 percent saying it was
the union's fault, although 27.3 percent said that both sides
were responsible. Of the remaining respondents, 5.1 percent
said it was difficult to say and a further 5.0 percent said it
was due to "someone else" (an oblique reference, no doubt,
to the Soviet Union). Blaming the government was highest
among workers, Solidarity members, and farmers (68.2, 66.8,
and 64.7 percent, respectively), and among those having or
practicing a religion (64.1 percent). Members of other unions
and nonbelievers were less likely to blame the government, the
figures being 51.6 and 49.6 percent, respectively.

Support for the agreements was found to be highest among
workers, 62.6 percent of whom declared themselves to be strongly
in favor. Other groups were significantly less enthusiastic,
with farmers, scientists, specialists, white-collar employees,
and civil servants, being from 31.8 to 44 percent strongly in

favor, while officials and administrators in industrial, party, and state organizations were only from 3.6 to 10.5 percent in favor. Of the latter group, from 6.1 to 22.8 percent expressed themselves strongly against the agreements. (Unfortunately, no separate figures are available for these multiple categories.)

Given the close association between educational and occupational levels, we would expect on the basis of the above data that support for Solidarity would be negatively related to educational level, and this is what the December poll shows. While 57.9 percent of the sample were strongly supportive of Solidarity's activities up to that time (and 31.2 percent were somewhat supportive), the figures for strong support were 47.1 to 49.2 percent among those with higher education, 54.2 percent among those with complete high school education, and 66.9 percent among the workers in general. Farmers were at an intermediate level, with 54.9 percent expressing strong support. Not surprisingly, 75 percent of Solidarity members unconditionally supported their leadership's activities, only 1.6 percent expressing antagonism. Support was lowest, again not surprisingly, among PUWP members, 44.9 percent of whom were strongly in favor of Solidarity's activities, and 9.8 percent of whom were against them to some degree.

Finally, responses to the question "Is the emergence of an independent union, embodied in Solidarity, connected with society's hope that it will protect labor interests better than the old unions?" showed a markedly similar pattern. Thus, 57.9 percent said definitely, 31.2 percent to some extent, 2.4 percent not, 0.6 percent said definitely not, and 7.9 percent found it difficult to say. Strongest agreement was found among Solidarity members (71.8 percent) and workers (66.2 percent), with lower responses among those with higher education (56.6 to 59.5 percent), farmers (54.6 percent), and clerical workers (51.2 percent). Groups being least supportive were PUWP members (47.3 percent) and members of the other unions (45.4 percent).

Attitudes toward Social Changes

At the beginning of September, 80 to 90 percent of those being polled were clearly in favor of changes being introduced in Polish society, only 5 percent expressing strong opposition to change. At the same time, only 60 percent said that they expected social, economic, and political improvements to result from the agreements. This caution is also evidenced by results of the November 18 poll in which 40 percent of the respondents said that they did not think that any significant changes had taken place, a further 19 percent saying that the situation was worse than it had been earlier with regard to food supplies, consumer goods, and coal supplies. Only 12 percent said that there had been changes for the better, with reference being made to wage increases, retirement pensions, improvements, democratic liberties, and changes in the party and government; among factory workers, 32 percent said that management attitudes toward workers were better, while 56 percent saw no change.[16]

In general, support for the changes introduced during the summer was very high. Thus, by mid-September, 86 percent were expressing approval of the increase in pensions, 76 percent approved of the increase in the minimum wage, and 84 percent approved of the elimination of Saturday work and the extension of weekday hours.[17]

While expectations for an improvement in living conditions were relatively low in July (22 percent expecting improvements in the near future), they increased to a high of 70 percent by September 2, and then fell to 59 percent in mid-September, 48 percent in October, and 38 percent by the end of November. Early December saw a slight rise to 48 percent. These changes were related to perceived changes in the economic situation; while 46 percent had said that the economic situation was bad in February 1980, 65 percent said so in July, 86 percent in September, 96 percent in October, and 92 percent in November.[18]

The major gain perceived by the population was clearly that of the development of new trade unions. As the results of the September 4-5 poll show (Table 7.2), this is especially true of those with most and with least education. It is likely that this is the result of the former considering the likely general political and social consequences of this, and the latter seeing it as a gain in power by workers to pursue their own interests. Governmental commitment to improve the standard of living was also seen as a significant gain, but less so by those with elementary and higher education than among those with technical and secondary education.

More detailed information on the expected effects of the changes being introduced was provided by the same poll, in which people were asked, "What do you think the effects of the latest developments will be on the following matters during the next three years?" Table 7.3 shows the pattern of responses, grouped by educational level and by "degree of optimism" within educational levels. Those respondents with less than higher education were more optimistic regarding the time it takes to

TABLE 7.2

Opinions of the Results of August 1980 Developments
(Question: "What, in your opinion, is the most important result
of the latest developments?")

| | Respondent's Education | | | |
	Ele-mentary	Basic Technical and Incomplete Secondary	Second-ary	Higher
Commitment to im-prove the material standard of living of working people	36.3	47.9	44.6	22.1
Announcement of the emergence of new trade unions	51.3	41.9	41.5	57.1
Major increase in the potential of the existing trade unions' activities	6.2	15.4	7.3	3.9
Clear delineation of the scope of censor-ship by the Depart-ment of Media Control	1.8	3.4	4.2	5.2
Something else	2.7	0	2.1	11.7
Total*	98.3	108.6	99.7	100.0

*No explanation given for totals other than 100 percent.
Source: Polityka, September 4, 1980.

TABLE 7.3

Opinions of Future Effects of August 1980 Developments
(Question: "What will be the effects of the latest developments on the following matters during the next 3 years?")

Issues Affected	Complete and Incomplete Elementary			Basic Technical			Secondary			Higher		
	0	P_1	P_2	0	P_1	P_2	0	P_1	P_2	0	P_1	P_2
Time waiting for an apartment	58.4	39.9	1.8	62.4	35.6	6.8	62.7	36.2	1.0	41.5	58.5	9.2
Food supplies	70.8	27.4	3.5	70.0	30.0	7.7	73.2	26.9	3.1	67.5	31.2	6.5
Supply of consumer durables	62.0	34.5	0.9	66.4	33.6	4.3	66.3	33.1	1.0	49.4	50.6	9.1
Level of awareness in society	84.1	14.2	0	92.4	7.6	0.9	85.0	13.0	1.6	83.2	15.6	2.6
Social relations at the workplace	63.8	35.4	12.4	63.7	27.3	8.5	49.2	38.4	7.3	45.5	54.5	15.6
Workers' self-government	69.9	26.2	0.9	76.1	23.9	3.5	77.2	20.3	1.6	75.4	22.1	2.6
Openness of political life	64.7	29.2	4.4	72.0	28.7	5.1	73.1	25.4	2.1	53.3	44.2	10.4
Participation by the public in important decision making	72.5	23.9	1.8	81.0	19.0	3.4	70.4	24.3	1.0	46.8	50.7	6.5
Relations between authorities and the general public	62.9	35.5	9.8	70.7	29.3	7.7	68.9	36.0	4.7	54.6	45.4	15.9
Credibility of information	61.1	39.8	6.2	68.5	31.6	5.1	69.4	29.5	0.5	55.9	42.9	9.1
Relations between church and state	74.3	21.3	1.8	78.9	21.1	1.8	79.3	20.7	1.0	65.0	33.8	6.5
Purchasing power of money	14.2	82.4	44.3	23.5	46.2	36.8	19.1	78.8	37.9	6.5	93.5	73.5
Elimination of overemployment	46.9	47.9	9.8	54.6	45.4	6.0	43.6	54.4	6.7	35.1	64.9	7.8
External security of the state	41.6	52.2	17.7	29.3	69.7	22.3	24.4	66.9	14.0	13.0	84.4	16.9
Political unity of society	65.5	28.3	6.2	58.6	41.4	14.5	60.1	37.3	15.0	36.4	61.1	40.3
Performance of the health service	61.9	34.5	3.5	70.5	29.5	7.7	73.1	26.9	0.5	46.8	53.3	6.5
	N=113			N=117			N=93			N=77		

0 = those saying effects will be positive; P_1 = those saying effects will be negative; P_2 = pessimists minus those thinking there will be no change.

Source: Polityka, September 4, 1980.

148

obtain an apartment (59.4 to 62.7 percent) than were those with higher education (41.5 percent). The same is true for expectations about food supplies, although the overall level of optimism is higher. Expectations for an increase in consumer goods are slightly lower than those for food, with greatest pessimism in evidence among those with higher education. Among the standard of living questions, respondents gave the most pessimistic answers regarding the likely effects of the changes on the purchasing power of money, optimistic responses ranging from 6.5 percent among the college educated to 23.5 percent among those with basic technical education. Respondents with middle-levels of education were least pessimistic relative to the other groups, but even they were strongly pessimistic.

Respondents in general were fairly optimistic about the effects on such sociopolitical issues as public awareness, social relations at the workplace, workers' self-government, openness of political life and access to decision making, relations with authorities, and so on. As in other cases, however, those with the most education were the least optimistic, although even among this group responses of optimism were typically between 40 and 65 percent. The various groups are similar in their feelings about the effects of events on national security, responses being almost equally split among pessimistic and optimistic, save in the case of those with higher education, who split approximately 75 and 35 percent, respectively.

Finally, we also have some fragmentary data on attitudes to inequalities in Polish society and on changes thought desirable. In the September 1980 survey, 82 percent perceived the existence of "significant or even dramatic social inequalities," with party members having an even higher number (92 percent). Further, 86 percent saw wage differences as "blatant," 67 percent thought that the not-so-well-off were wronged in relations with the well-to-do, and 61 percent thought that it was unjust for those in high office to have the privileges they did. The same poll found that inequality and justice were the issues most frequently defined as very important, with 90 percent choosing this response. Securing law and order was seen as very important by 82 percent, freedom of expression by 71 percent, and having society influence state policies and decision making by 61 percent.[19] Similar findings were reported by other surveys, including one undertaken in December 1980 in which 90 percent of the respondents were in favor of limiting the incomes of highly paid workers, and as many as 70 percent were apparently in favor of equal incomes for all citizens.[20] While these figures may be inordinately high, another survey in late 1980 did find

61 percent of those polled saying that those in high office should have a reduction in income and in access to material privileges, and a further survey in May 1981 found 81 percent of respondents in favor of a heavy tax on luxury items typically enjoyed by the most privileged groups.[21] These findings, however, need to be tempered by other findings by sociologists and pollsters that show support for linking income to quality of work. The issue, it seems, is that of unearned privilege rather than the differentiation of living standards as such.

Attitudes toward Leaders and Institutions

Information on this is at present limited, but what little we do have indicates a low level of support for both the old leadership and for some of the new leaders who emerged following the fourth plenum of the Central Committee of the PUWP in late August. A poll following this plenum found only 43 percent of respondents accepting Gierek's speech in which he admitted that mistakes had been made, apologized for them, and took personal responsibility. The new premier, Pinkowski, who replaced Babiuch, had a much higher acceptance level, with 75 percent of those polled approving of his speech. Almost two weeks later, on September 5, Gierek was replaced as first secretary of the party by Kania, a move welcomed by only 55 percent of those polled, 30 percent saying that they were indifferent to changes in leadership.[22]

What these surveys illustrate is the low and declining faith in party leaders, and increasing support for leaders in government, especially those related to parliament (Sejm) positions. By May 1981, the party was the least-trusted institution in Poland, according to a survey conducted by the Center for Public Opinion Studies of Polish Radio and Television. Asked to evaluate fifteen organizations and institutions according to the amount of confidence and trust they had in each, respondents produced the rank order shown in Table 7.4. Thus, the Catholic church was given the highest ranking (81 percent giving an unqualified vote of confidence), with the Army and Solidarity coming in somewhat behind at 64 and 62 percent, respectively. In last place was the PUWP with a mere 10 percent giving it a vote of unqualified confidence, and 60 percent giving it a negative rating. In less than a year following the first series of strikes, therefore, the party inspired the least confidence of all the major institutions and organizations. In addition, support was apparently lowest among those under 40 years of age and among

TABLE 7.4

Public Confidence in Institutions and Organizations
(Question: "Do you have confidence in the following institutions
or organizations?")

Institution or Organization	Percentage Responses to "Do you have confidence . . ."				
	Yes	To Some Extent Yes	To Some Extent No	No	Difficult to Say
The Catholic church	81	13	1	2	3
The Army	64	25	2	1	8
Solidarity	62	29	3	2	4
Parliament	39	43	8	3	7
Chief Board of Control	35	34	12	8	11
Council of State	29	44	11	6	10
The government	28	41	19	7	5
Public prosecutor's office	24	36	16	13	11
The courts	23	36	18	12	11
Branch trade unions	21	35	19	11	14
Front of National Unity	21	29	12	10	28
People's Militia (police)	17	25	25	26	7
The Democratic party	16	37	13	5	29
The United Peasants' party	14	32	15	10	29
Polish United Workers' Party (Communist)	10	22	30	30	8

Sample: Representative sample of the population above 15 years of age.

Source: Unpublished Research Report, Komitet Do Spraw Radia I Telewizji "Polskie Radio I Telewizja," Osrodek Badania Opinii Publicznej I Studiow Programowych, Nr. 16/207, May 1981.

unskilled workers, although precise figures on this are not available.[23]

The same pattern was found in a separate poll conducted in Krakow in late May-early June 1981. Asked to rate the performance of various groups and institutions in helping to alleviate the crisis, 96.2 percent said the performance of party leaders was bad or very bad, with 75.7 percent giving the same rating to the central government and 59 percent to the television and radio. On the other hand, ratings of good or very good were given to the Catholic church by 85.6 percent and to Solidarity by 77.5 percent; coming in a distant third was the Sejm with 49.7 percent.[24]

In a poll conducted about a month later by the Solidarity Center for Social Research, the sample consisting of only Solidarity members in the Warsaw area, very low estimations of the political system were (unsurprisingly) also very prevalent. Thus, only 2 percent of the respondents were satisfied with the way authorities were governing, seeing no need for reforms. Fully 40 percent, however, felt that the system required a fundamental overhaul; another 31 percent wanted partial but nevertheless far-reaching changes.[25] In the same poll, those favoring changes were asked what specific changes were necessary, the most frequent responses being more influence for the people, increased openness of public life, elimination or reduction of special political privileges for the Communist Party, democratic changes in the election process, enhancement of the role of representative groups, and the introduction of a system of rotation for people occupying positions of authority in government. In short, Solidarity members wanted "democratization, liberalization, and departyization of their state."[26]

These results, together with the results of Solidarity-sponsored polls in April following the Bydgoszcz affair,[27] show that there is evidence of strong support among the membership for Solidarity's political demands, casting doubt on the regime's contention that the increasingly radical political demands were the work of a small, unrepresentative group within Solidarity.

Rural Public Opinion

One of the more surprising consequences of the free trade union movement was the emergence and legalization of Rural Solidarity, a union of private farmers. Some light is shed on the attitudes of farmers during late 1980 by the results of a poll undertaken in November and December.[28] Although only

TABLE 7.5

Farmers' Opinions about Effects of State Policy on Farmers

	State Policy Most Favorable for Farmers	State Policy Least Favorable for Farmers
1944-48	4.0	8.0
1949-55	2.3	27.9
1956-63	17.0	1.5
1964-70	6.6	3.5
1971-75	45.2	1.5
1976-80	7.1	39.4

Source: Compiled from Polityka, March 7, 1981 (other answers and no opinion responses not included).

preliminary results of this survey are available, they are still of great interest.

As Table 7.5 illustrates, the period of 1971-75 was perceived by farmers as the time when official policies were the most favorable of any since World War II. The low rating given to 1976-80, with 39.4 percent seeing it as the period least favorable for farmers, is an indication of the level of frustration among private farmers in the period leading up to the development of Rural Solidarity. The only other period that comes close to this rating is 1949-55, a time when private farming was being eliminated in favor of the creation of Soviet-style collective farms. This policy was reversed following the 1956 revolt that brought Gomulka to power. The restoration of private farming following this event accounts for the 17 percent favorable rating given to the period 1956-63.

As we would expect, the blame for farmers' problems is laid mainly at the doors of the party and the government. Asked who, in their opinion, was responsible for the formulation of farming policy, 36.8 percent of the farmers said the PUWP and 23.2 percent said the government. Parliament was mentioned by 9.2 percent, the UPP by 2.5 percent, and PUWP and UPP jointly by 5.2 percent; a further 10 percent mentioned other sources, and 13.2 percent had no opinion on the matter.

Policies being pursued in 1980 were seen by most respondents as having a harmful effect on agricultural production, with

16.7 percent saying these policies would result in a substantial
decrease in productivity, and a further 32.7 percent saying
they would decrease productivity to some extent. Less than
a quarter of those interviewed thought that the policies would
improve matters, 21.6 percent saying some increase in productivity would result, and 2.9 percent saying productivity would
improve substantially; other answers and don't know responses
accounted for the remaining 12.9 percent. Clearly, the situation
of individual farmers would differ according to size of holding,
degree of capitalization, and so forth, and hence policies would
affect them differently. This would account for the lack of
consensus in the above figures, a conclusion strengthened by
the fact that 34.4 percent saw policies as favorable for them
personally, and that 53.1 percent saw them as affecting them
unfavorably. Surprisingly, farmers aged 60 years and above
are reported to be most optimistic, although no figures are given
to support this.

Finally, the survey has provided us with some insight into
farmers' perceptions of social and economic inequalities in Polish
society. Asked if, as rural residents, they felt they had rights
equal to those enjoyed by people living in cities, respondents
gave a picture of relative deprivation. Although 61.8 percent
said they received equal health services, only 33.9 percent
said they were equally able to fulfill basic daily needs. In the
case of pensions of all kinds, only 34.4 percent said they were
equal to city dwellers. Educational opportunities for children
were perceived as more nearly equal (44.9 percent equal, 53.1
percent unequal), but participation in cultural activities in
general was seen as equal by only 12.6 percent (83.3 percent
unequal). The greatest inequality, as we might expect, was
perceived in participation in holidays and vacations, with 91.9
percent saying they were worse off than those living in cities.

It is not surprising, therefore, that marked economic
inequalities between urban and rural areas are perceived, some
indication of which may be seen in Table 7.6. Although 28.3
percent of the rural population are seen as being rather wealthy
(and, indeed, some private farmers are doing quite well economically), the rural areas are seen as more heavily weighted to
lower economic levels than are urban areas.

While perceiving themselves as relatively worse off than
urban dwellers, farmers evaluate their work more highly than
that of other occupational groups, as shown by the data in
Table 7.7. While manual workers are rated as falling just under
farmers in terms of occupational status, white-collar, managerial,
and official occupations are rated poorly, from one-third to almost

TABLE 7.6

Opinions about Levels of Affluence
(Question: "If we accept that people in our country may be
divided into four groups according to their degree of affluence,
then what percentage of the population belong to these groups?")

	Population	
Level of Affluence	Urban	Rural
Very rich	22.2	12.1
Rather wealthy	32.5	28.3
Rather limited means	28.1	37.2
Of limited means	17.1	22.5

Source: Polityka, March 7, 1981.

TABLE 7.7

Evaluation of the Work of Various Workers' Categories
(Question: "How would you evaluate the work of various categories of workers in the national economy?")

	Evaluation		
	Good	Average	Bad
Farmers	58.4	28.2	13.4
Workers	46.0	31.0	23.0
White-collar employees	29.4	34.8	34.8
Middle management	29.2	35.2	35.4
High management, officials	21.6	29.5	48.6

Source: Polityka, March 7, 1981.

half of these categories receiving the lowest rating. Clearly, this shows a relatively high level of antagonism toward higher social strata, which, together with farmers' perceptions of social and economic inequities, may be seen as indicating a rift between rural and nonrural strata in Poland. At the same time, differentiation within the rural community meant that farmers' support for Rural Solidarity was less (at least according to this poll) than that of urban workers for Solidarity. Thus, whereas support for Solidarity reached as high as 90 percent, only 55.1 percent of the farmers were in favor of an entirely new organization to represent their interests, 17.8 percent saying that existing agricultural cooperatives could perform the functions of a farmers' union quite adequately. At the same time, 81.7 percent thought that farmers should have their own union, even if there was disagreement about the form it should take. Survey results such as these show evidence of a relatively high degree of class consciousness among private farmers. Indeed, the strength of this is remarkable given their internal differences and their position as self-employed owners of productive property.

PREFACE AND POSTSCRIPT TO THE POLISH AUGUST

The polls we have considered so far were carried out in Poland during the period immediately prior to and after the creation of Solidarity. There are also, however, a number of surveys undertaken by the Radio Free Europe-Radio Liberty (RFE-RL) Opinion Research Center during the 1970s and in the period leading up to the imposition of martial law in December 1981, which provide a wider context of opinion within which the Polish surveys may be evaluated. While it is not possible to cover all of these, we will briefly look at a number of the more interesting surveys.

In a series of surveys of Polish visitors to Western Europe between 1974 and 1979-80, RFE-RL polled 10,000 or so people on how they would vote in hypothetical free elections. As can be seen from Table 7.8, although hypothetical support for the Communist Party remained relatively stable between 1975 and 1980, support for a Democratic Socialist Party steadily eroded (from 52 percent in 1974 to 32 percent in 1979-80). Support for right-of-center parties, however, increased during the same period, with the Christian Democrats gaining 5 percent, the Peasant Party 10 percent, and the Conservative Party 5 percent. The extent to which problems were creating changes

TABLE 7.8

Party Preferences in Hypothetical Elections

Party	Percent of Respondents Choosing				
	1974	1975	1976	1978	1979/80
Communist Party	2	5	4	5	6
Democratic Socialist Party	52	49	38	39	32
Christian Democratic Party	27	26	30	31	32
Peasant Party	8	11	14	13	18
Conservative Party	4	2	5	5	9
Don't know, other	7	7	9	7	3

Source: RFE-RL, Trends in Hypothetical Party Preference . . ., Nov. 1981, p. 13.

in political orientation in Poland not found in other parts of Eastern Europe is illustrated by the results of surveys given to Hungarian and Czechoslovakian visitors to Western Europe during the same period. In these other two societies, there were no discernible changes in hypothetical party choice, and certainly no consistent movement away from left-of-center parties.

Aside from the question of people's hypothetical party preferences, we have some information on the more realistic issue of the public evaluation of socialism's ability to perform adequately as a socioeconomic system. As can be seen from RFE-RL polls from the mid to late 1970s, public attitudes became decidedly more negative. In response to the question, "How does socialism work out in practice in Poland—very well, well, badly, or very badly?" the percentage given a positive evaluation fell from 22 to 15 percent, while negative evaluation increased from 58 to 72 percent (see Table 7.9). This decline, moreover, was found among all age groups, although it is clear that the older a respondent was, the more likely it was that a negative evaluation would be given (see Table 7.10).

These results show that changes in the economy were being reflected in people's consciousness and in their evaluation of and support for the system as a whole. In addition, they demonstrate that public opinion research can provide a reliable

TABLE 7.9

Opinions on How Socialism Works in Poland
(Question: "How does socialism work out in practice in Poland?")

	Percent of Respondents Choosing	
	1975-76	1979-80
Very well	3	2
Well	19	13
Badly	43	44
Very badly	15	28
Undecided	18	11
No answer	2	2

Source: RFE-RL, Eastern Socialism-Western Democracy . . . ,
Nov. 1981, p. 20.

measure of popular awareness of societal problems, their nature, and consequences. One of the more interesting findings of a comparison of internal (Polish) and external (RFE-RL) polls is the extent to which their results are compatible. Further evidence for this contention comes from surveys conducted by RFE-RL from late October 1981 to the declaration of martial law on December 13 of the same year. In early December, figures published by the Polish Press Agency were being used to demonstrate a purported erosion of support for Solidarity. Thus, confidence ratings had allegedly fallen from 74 percent in September 1981 to 58 percent in November of that year.[29] Since, in retrospect, this period was a prelude to martial law, it is possible that the Polish leadership may have been trying to prepare the ground for a movement against Solidarity by pointing to its (alleged) declining level of support among the population. The external RFE-RL polls, however, show no sign of any discernible erosion. Asked if Solidarity was more or less popular in late 1981 than at its inception, 47 percent of those polled said it was more popular, 30 percent said there had been no change, and only 18 percent said it was less popular; the remaining 5 percent were no answer and other responses. When asked "How many Poles fully support Solidarity today?" 2 percent said all do, 47 percent said 90 percent do, and 32 percent said

70 percent do; only 16 percent said 50 percent or less of the population supported Solidarity fully, with 3 percent giving no answer.[30] Finally, in response to the question, "Do you think that Solidarity has gone too far in its demands?" 77 percent said no, 18 percent said yes, and only 5 percent had no opinion or some other response. Thus, as late as the last few weeks before martial law, these external polls were showing continued high levels of support for, and confidence in, Solidarity. This is consistent with the earlier internal polls and cannot but call into question the validity of official claims of a sharp decline in popular support for Solidarity.

External surveys have also found a relatively high level of support for open opposition in Poland. In surveys conducted by RFE-RL from April to December 1981, Poles were asked if they were in favor of opposition by dissidents (defined as those

TABLE 7.10

Opinions by Age on How Socialism Works in Poland
(Question: "How does socialism work out in practice in Poland?")

	Evaluation		
	Positive	Negative	Difference
Percent of respondents choosing by age			
Up to 25			
1975-76	36	41	5
1979-80	25	58	33
26-35			
1975-76	28	55	27
1979-80	16	72	56
36-50			
1975-76	17	62	45
1979-80	15	77	62
Over 50			
1975-76	11	72	61
1979-80	7	81	74

Source: RFE-RL, Eastern Socialism-Western Democracy . . . , Nov. 1981, p. 21.

openly opposing the government).[31] Of those surveyed, 63
percent were in favor, with 16 percent against, 10 percent
undecided, and 11 percent giving no answer. Men were somewhat more in favor than women (66 to 61 percent), and those
with higher education were more in favor than those with
secondary or elementary education (81, 71, and 60 percent,
respectively). Responses also varied by occupation, with 53
percent of farmers being in favor, compared to 62 percent of
workers, 74 percent of white-collar workers, and 80 percent
of those in higher occupations.[32]

Finally, there is ample evidence from both internal and
external polls that public opinion reflected a strong consciousness of the deteriorating economic situation. Thus, surveys
conducted from 1975 through 1980 (Table 7.11) showed an
increasing concern about the decline in living standards. Moreover, and more significantly, survey results arranged according
to occupational status and income showed an increasing polarization between the better- and worse-off sections of Polish society.
As we can see from Table 7.12, the higher the occupation and
income, the more likely it was that real improvements in respondents' standard of living would be reported. Among those at the
lowest levels, however, considerable deterioration was more
likely to be reported. These findings take on added significance
in the light of evidence showing relatively widespread acceptance
of egalitarian values in Polish society, with even those who are

TABLE 7.11

Public Assessment of Recent Developments in Material
Conditions/Living Standards

Recently Mate-rials Have:	Mid-1975	Mid-1979	Feb. 1980	July 1980	Sept. 2, 1980
Improved	77	56	52	35	29
Remained unchanged	15	25	27	29	17
Deteriorated	33	16	18	32	50
No opinion	5	3	3	4	4

Source: Reported in Pravda, p. 168. Polls conducted by
Public Opinion Research Center of Polish Radio and Television,
based on a national representative sample of the adult population.

TABLE 7.12

Subjective Assessment of Family Living Conditions in the 1970s
(Question: "Taken overall, did your family's living conditions improve over the years 1970-1978?")

Social Category	Improved		Remained Unchanged	Deteriorated		Other
	Considerably	Somewhat		Considerably	Somewhat	
Economically active	11.2	52.3	22.1	9.2	3.1	2.1
Including						
Workers	6.6	51.6	26.5	9.2	3.4	2.7
Intelligentsia	16.8	50.3	18.3	7.8	4.0	2.8
Peasants	11.7	56.7	17.2	10.3	2.7	1.4
Peasant workers	11.2	52.7	25.4	8.3	1.8	0.6
Pensioners	9.0	37.4	27.0	18.4	6.0	2.2
Economically active by per capita monthly family income:						
Up to 1000 zlotys	8.0	50.6	21.3	12.9	6.1	1.1
1001 to 1500 zlotys	5.4	54.6	26.2	9.6	2.3	1.9
1501 to 2500 zlotys	11.4	51.1	22.7	8.9	3.2	2.7
2501 to 3500 zlotys	13.9	60.9	15.3	6.7	1.9	1.3
3501 to 5000 zlotys	23.7	46.2	20.4	6.5	1.1	2.1
5001 zlotys and above	27.3	27.3	36.4	3.0	—	6.0

Source: Reported in Pravda, p. 170, from L. Beskid in Nowe Drogi, No. 6, 1980, p. 142.

in favor of continued inequality in incomes setting fairly low limits to the amount of inequality desirable.[33] It is possible that this egalitarianism has important effects upon public opinion formation. For example, in a recent report of surveys of self-perceived standards of living in comparison with actual (that is, official) income levels, Sufin found a marked tendency for people to underestimate their income's ability to provide for the require-ments of life.[34] It may well be that this results from an individ-ual's comparison of his or her personal income with that of those who are doing considerably better, which, from an egalitarian standpoint, makes matters seem much worse than they are. This, in turn, would be expected to exacerbate public percep-tions of economic trends over time, and hence public opinion about the overall performance of the system. Whatever the mechanisms of the process may eventually turn out to be, how-ever, these and similar findings lend further support to Alex Pravda's argument that the Polish events of 1980-81 are to a large extent due to perceptions of relative deprivation, which he terms the result of the development of premature consumerism in Poland.[35]

CONCLUSION

Periods of political disruption are of interest to students of public opinion in socialist societies because they create a climate in which surveys on sensitive issues are possible to an extent not found in normal times. As we have seen, in Poland (as in Czechoslovakia twelve years earlier), rapid political changes provided conditions in which public opinion on the political system, on political leaders, on social and economic inequality, and on basic sociopolitical institutions could be measured. In the Polish case, as shown above, some tentative conclusions can be drawn based on the public opinion polls administered and published prior to the imposition of martial law. First, it is clear that during a period of social and political instability, public opinion polling constitutes a significant source of information for political leaders. Issues are raised and polls are directed toward gathering information on politically relevant (and sensitive) topics. While the Polish case does not directly resolve the monist/pluralist debate about public opinion in socialist societies, it does show how public opinion polls can be used to uncover the extent and strength of political dissensus during a period of liberalization and instability. As the poll data reveal, political disaffection was widespread and deep, and this has implications for our second concern.

If the political leadership of a Communist Party is out of touch with public opinion due to the lack of meaningful elections, if a party is more concerned with controlling public opinion than with reflecting it, and if there is a history of little (or poor or irrelevant) public opinion polling, then surveys may be an invaluable source of information for leaders once liberalization or instability begin and the leadership tries to adjust to the situation. In the Polish case, the combined scope of the strikes, along with the development of widespread support for Solidarity, were indictments of the policies and program of Gierek. And, as the poll data reveal, the Polish people felt that the regime and party could not command their trust and had failed to improve the quality of life.

Moreover, the results of these polls were openly published and widely disseminated, themselves becoming a part of the process of debate and transformation. In normal times, the public has only a fragmentary knowledge of public attitudes on issues, having access only to the opinions of those with whom they come into daily contact. Access to information via the media is necessarily limited even when censorship is relatively mild, and aggregate data on opinion (particularly on sensitive topics) are not generally available. The impact of opinion polls in times of change, therefore, must be even greater than it would otherwise be, and as we learn more about these situations it may become clear that polls have a significant influence on social and political actions. Unambiguous indications of how and to what extent poll data actually affected people during the Polish August are not yet on hand. Our brief survey of surveys indicates that this issue is in dire need of further study.

Public opinion surveys during the Polish August focused on many politically sensitive issues, and their results reveal that political dissatisfaction was both far ranging and of long standing. This raises the question of whether public opinion during normal times is distorted, and if so, to what extent it is distorted. Data gathered during periods of change provide a useful basis for the evaluation of surveys conducted in normal times. While the methodological problems are no doubt severe, such a comparison may give some indication of the extent to which the political system imposes a suppressor effect on responses. It has long been obvious that often the highly positive responses on politically sensitive issues are an artifact of the political climate, but we have never been able to assess how much distortion (either by respondents or those reporting the results) is occurring. As more data collected in times of change become available, we may be in a position to address better the question of response distortion in socialist societies. To the extent that this becomes possible, then the study of public opinion in socialist countries may finally be firmly integrated into the general discipline of public opinion studies. The result of this is likely to be as beneficial for the latter as it would be for a better understanding of socialist societies themselves.

What, if anything, can we say about future developments? In spite of the current setbacks, it is likely that the evolution of the status of public opinion will continue. Given the complexity of Polish society, and the regime's need to anticipate (at least minimally) public reaction to programs and policies, there can be no return to the earlier, simpleminded conception of public opinion polling. The regime is as well aware as anyone that public opinion on various issues is differentiated by status and social group, and this gives them an opportunity to use this diversity in a rational, calculated way. Even if the results are not disseminated, therefore, we may anticipate continued support for opinion research and the development of increasingly sophisticated methods of measurement. At the same time, civil society has also learned the value of such research, as evidenced by the development by Solidarity of its own public opinion research group. This trend is likely to continue, and indications are that it is doing so at present. As a result, we may look forward not only to the continuation of public opinion research in Poland, but to its fragmentation as various groups (official and unofficial) engage in opinion research as both a way of finding out how people are responding to events and general conditions and as a way of generating information for use in political struggle. If this prediction proves accurate, then we shall have entered a new stage in the development of Polish society, for opinion research will have become a resource for broad social groups and strata and a mechanism for shaping (as well as gauging) the social consciousness. Once the links between private attitudes and public opinions have been forged, the costs of trying to return to the status quo ante may be very high indeed. It remains to be seen if the political leadership is willing or able to pay the price of trying.

NOTES

1. Walter D. Connor, "Opinion, Reality and the Communist Political Process," in Public Opinion in European Socialist Systems, eds. Walter D. Connor and Zvi Gitelman (New York: Praeger, 1977), pp. 167-187.

2. Zvi Gitelman, "Public Opinion in Czechoslovakia," in Public Opinion in European Socialist Systems, eds. Walter D. Connor and Zvi Gitelman (New York: Praeger, 1977), pp. 83-103.

3. Ithiel de Sola Pool, "Public Opinion in Czechoslovakia," Public Opinion Quarterly 34 (1970):10-25.

4. Zvi Gitelman, "Public Opinion in Communist Political Systems," in Public Opinion in European Socialist Systems, eds. Walter D. Connor and Zvi Gitelman (New York: Praeger, 1977), pp. 1-40.

5. Ibid., p. 7.

6. Ibid.

7. Georges Mink, "Polls, Pollsters, Public Opinion and Political Power in Poland in the Late 1970's," Telos 47 (1981): 125-132.

8. Polityka, September 13, 1980. The poll was taken on September 4-5, including those employed in larger industrial plants and institutions in the state-controlled part of the economy. Pensioners, the retired, the unemployed, and farmers were not included.

9. Kultura, March 1, 1981. Conducted on September 1-2 by the Center for Public Opinion Surveys and Program Studies of the Polish Radio and Television. This survey was of 1,000 people over the age of 15 years, but no information is available on sampling or the characteristics of those polled.

10. Ibid.

11. Polish Press Agency English wire, November 18, 1981. Quoted in James P. McGregor, "Polish Public Moods in a Time of Crisis," paper presented at the 23rd Annual Convention of the International Studies Association, Cincinnati, Ohio, March 24-27, 1982, p. 14.

12. Ibid.

13. Kultura, March 1, 1982.

14. Ibid.

15. Kultura, March 22, 1981. The survey was taken in December, and conducted by the Institute of Philosophy and Sociology of the Polish Academy of Sciences. The population surveyed and the size of the sample are not given.

16. Kultura, March 1, 1981.

17. Ibid.

18. Ibid.

19. Ibid.

20. Zycie Gospodarcze, May 10, 1981. Quoted in McGregor, p. 9.

21. Ibid.

22. Kultura, March 1, 1981.
23. Polityka, June 17, 1981.
24. Press Research Center, Spoleczenstvo polskie przed IX zjazdem PZPR, Krakow, 1981. Quoted in McGregor, p. 18.
25. Ludwik Dorn, "Polling the Poles: A Report from Solidarity HQ," Public Opinion 4 (August-September 1981):5-7.
26. Ibid., p. 6.
27. Ibid.
28. Polityka, March 7, 1981. Taken in November-December and conducted by the Institute for Rural Development and Agriculture of the Polish Academy of Sciences, this poll included only farmers. Sample size is not given.
29. Zycie Warszawy, December 4-5, 1981. Quoted in McGregor, p. 17.
30. Polish Attitudes Toward Solidarity Prior to the Military Takeover, Radio Free Europe-Radio Liberty, East European Area Audience and Opinion Research, December 1981, p. 3.
31. Attitudes to Open Opposition by Dissidents in Pre-Martial-Law Poland, Radio Free Europe-Radio Liberty, East European Area Audience and Opinion Research, March 1983, p. 3.
32. Ibid., pp. 4-5.
33. Stefan Nowak, "Values and Attitudes of the Polish People," Scientific American 245:1 (1981):45-53.
34. Zbigniew Sufin, "Spoleczne uwarunkowania i konsekwencje kryzysu," Nowe Drogi (December 1980):69-80.
35. Alex Pravda, "Poland 1980: From 'Premature Consumerism' to Labour Solidarity," Soviet Studies 34 (1982):167-199.

BIBLIOGRAPHY

Attitudes to Open Opposition by Dissidents in Pre-Martial-Law Poland. Radio Free Europe-Radio Liberty, East European Area Audience and Opinion Research, March 1983.

Connor, Walter D. "Opinion, Reality and the Communist Political Process." In Public Opinion in European Socialist Systems, edited by Walter D. Connor and Zvi Gitelman, pp. 167-187. New York: Praeger, 1977.

Dorn, Ludwik. "Polling the Poles: A Report from Solidarity HQ." Public Opinion (September 1981):5-7.

Eastern Socialism-Western Democracy and the Functioning of the Two Systems. Radio Free Europe-Radio Liberty, East European Audience and Opinion Research, November 1981.

Gitelman, Zvi. "Public Opinion in Communist Political Systems." In Public Opinion in European Socialist Systems, edited by Walter D. Connor and Zvi Gitelman, pp. 1-40. New York: Praeger, 1977.

Gitelman, Zvi. "Public Opinion in Czechoslovakia." In Public Opinion in European Socialist Systems, edited by Walter D. Connor and Zvi Gitelman, pp. 83-103. New York: Praeger, 1977.

McGregor, James P. "Polish Public Moods in a Time of Crisis." Paper presented at the 23rd Annual Convention of the International Studies Association, Cincinnati, Ohio, March 24-27, 1982.

Mink, Georges. "Polls, Pollsters, Public Opinion and Political Power in Poland in the Late 1970s." Telos 47 (Spring 1981): 125-132.

Nowak, Stefan. "Values and Attitudes of the Polish People." Scientific American 245 (1981):45-53.

Piekalkiewicz, Jaroslav A. Public Opinion Polling in Czechoslovakia, 1968-69: Results and Analysis of Surveys Conducted During the Dubcek Era. New York: Praeger, 1972.

Pool, Ithiel de Sola. "Public Opinion in Czechoslovakia." Public Opinion Quarterly 34 (1970):10-25.

Pravda, Alex. "Poland 1980: From 'Premature Consumerism' to Labour Solidarity." Soviet Studies 34 (1982):167-199.

Polish Attitudes Toward Solidarity Prior To The Military Takeover. Radio Free Europe-Radio Europe, East European Area Audience and Opinion Research, December 1981.

Sufin, Zbigniew. "Spoleczne uwarunkowania i konsekwencje kryzysu." Nowe Drogi (December 1980):69-80.

Trends in Hypothetical Party Preference Among Respondents From Czechoslovakia, Hungary and Poland. Radio Free

Europe-Radio Liberty, East European Area Audience and
Opinion Research, November 1981.

8.

The Transformation
of Political Elites

Barbara A. Misztal and Bronislaw Misztal

The Polish crisis of 1980-81 made questionable the accuracy of many predictions concerning the political system of communism. Three aspects of the crisis are particularly relevant. First, the Communist Party (PUWP) faced a situation where it was no longer the primary institution for mediating social and economic initiatives. For the first time since 1944, forces other than party elites introduced ideas of social transformation. Moreover, these ideas were brought forth without the party's approval. Second, the 1980-81 transformation gave birth to new social and political elites, breaking the party's monopoly over the formation of elites. Third, the response of the party to this qualitatively new situation was the militarization of the political elite.

POLISH POLITICAL ELITES BEFORE AUGUST 1980

Western observers have viewed the position of elites in communist systems—including Poland—primarily through the new class, convergence, and pressure group perspectives. All three approaches agree in classifying the early development of the Eastern European political system as being marked by a revolutionary movement regime.[1] The situation in Poland, however, was different. The higher echelons of the first PUWP Central Committee were composed of relatively few personnel firmly committed to communist ideology.[2] In fact it was not until 1948 that there was "a movement towards a more Party-centered elite."[3] In subsequent years this tendency was to become more prominent. By 1954 <u>apparatchiki</u> made up 30 percent of the Central Committee, and 51 percent by 1964. Paradoxically, the proportion of state bureaucrats in the same body decreased from 48 percent in 1954 to 17 percent in 1975.[4]

The first generation of the ruling elite in Poland was composed of communists who, although living in exile in the Soviet Union, had managed to avoid the early periods of Stalinist purges, and a second group of former resistance activists, who had survived the German occupation in Poland. In the 1960s this group was gradually replaced by a new "generation that had no links with the international Stalinist mentality of the leaders of previous years."[5] As a result, the ideology of communism was weakened as it was no longer required to legitimate the system, and since "a stress on ideology and its role may threaten the existence of the system."[6] Ideological legitimization was replaced by bureaucratic, technical criteria of competence. The proportion of professionals in the Central Committee thus increased from 2.8 percent in 1948 to 12.9 percent in 1959. By 1968 it totaled 15.3 percent.[7] This elite attempted to subordinate all social groups to the control of the party.

The result was a growth in social tensions in the late 1960s, in turn producing deepening conflicts at the top level of the party leadership. The lack of normal mechanism for the circulation of the political elites, however, led to situations where regroupings of the elite resulted primarily from political crises. Gierek's replacement of Gomulka in the aftermath of the workers' upheaval in December 1970 marked the end of an era. From then on nobody believed "that the path of democratization [could be realized] through the party."[8]

Throughout the 1970s Poland was governed by a sort of social contract where both sides, the ruling group and society, agreed to give something up.[9] The authorities let go their ambition to control the entire sphere of public life, allowing some level of autonomous self-organization in the civil community. Society, on the other hand, diffused its constant challenge and defiance of the regime.

The curtailment of the party's sphere of control weakened its authority and promoted a bureaucratic struggle for power.[10] In the early 1970s, Gierek's team decided to remove the conditions for the potential reappearance of alternative, locally based political leaders. The state administrative system was restructured, and numerous locally based organizational levels were dissolved. A new centralist system of administration replaced the confederation of local governments that were perceived as a threat to the authorities. Further, to avoid the reemergence of alternative structures, the party penetrated and identified itself with the state administration.[11] The reform thus deprived local officials of their power by subordinating them to the central bureaucratic elite. This led to a situation where there was "almost no real devolution of power, no area in which a subordinate state or Party body [had] complete authority."[12]

Instead the loyalty of the elites in the 1970s was based primarily upon patron-client relationships between the central leadership and the local elite. These relationships served to define membership in the power apparatus but were not governed by any rules and instead depended entirely on the influence of a given patron.[13] The system favored one particular mechanism of elite recruitment: cooptation. Classically, the way to "work one's way up was to become a very committed regional or branch organizer and . . . then . . . to take part in vital Party courses and schools."[14] During Gierek's tenure, the route to power took this form. The consequence was the gradual petrification of the communist political elite.

The privileged position of the party's elite was strengthened in the mid-1970s by the development of the national economy through revitalized policies of intensive industrial growth and increased efficiency. Paradoxically, these policies were advantageous to foreign capital, which embarked upon a policy of loaning money to Poland. The import of foreign capital had the effect of not only restructuring Polish industry, but also the political elite. Even as the economic boom turned into a bust during the second half of the decade, it did not limit the power of the new elite. For the threat of economic deterioration only reinforced the elites' tendency to secure its own access to economic and social privileges. The inevitable result was a deepening of the gap between society and the ruling elite.

The lack of openness in political life ruled out interest group participation in the political system. Only one of these interest groups remained on the scene: the power elite itself. Its policy was based on the expansion of consumer goods for private consumption throughout society. Not surprisingly the most conspicuous drives in this direction were exhibited by the elite members themselves. Indeed, the process of the disproportionate acquisition of material wealth by the elite was to be finally sanctioned by the passing of a new law concerning the positions of nomenklatura. Passed by parliament in 1973, it granted special allowances and tax exemptions to all party and governmental officials.

The social understanding of 1970 was finally brought to an end by the outburst of workers' protest over price increases in June 1976 and by the wave of repressions that followed. Out of this failure the authorities allowed the emergence of new forms of interest representation. These formations met "all the criteria of corporatist type of politicization of society and structuring of interest articulation. The corporatist structure was organized on functional rather than a horizontal class basis."[15]

After 1976, Gierek's government attempted to bring about stability through the segmentation of society. Payoffs were selectively applied to pacify different groups of the working class and the intelligentsia, and rewards were adjusted to the aspirations of different layers of society. Some groups received coupons for material goods (cars, color television, etc.) that were not available on the open market. Others were granted concessions in the form of limited freedoms. The consequence was the establishment of a feudal differentiation of privileges and the segmentation of problems throughout the entire society. In this system "corporatist groups, owing to their semi-legal participation in politics, did not have any specialized political apparatus and their impact on politics was more a result of the style of the particular ruling team than of lasting institutional arrangements."[16]

Overall, Gierek's era was marked by a gap between the slightly expanded elite's structural boundaries and its visibly narrow policy-making boundaries.[17] The credibility of the party was constantly reduced by such factors as centralization of the economy and political management, the failure of developmental programs, expanded corruption, pressure group lobbying, and deepening social differences. And it was finally shattered by the increased privileged position of the party elite.[18]

THE RULING ELITE IN THE 1980s

Elements of participatory democracy were brought about by the creation of Solidarity as an independent trade union, an event that strongly affected the existing political elite. If the guarantees given to the striking workers in August 1980 were to be maintained, the whole idea of the leading role of the Communist Party had to be redefined. The situation was influenced by several facts—first, the sociopolitical mobilization of Polish society that overnight created a ten-million member movement, and second, by at least one-third of the PUWP rank and file signing up with Solidarity. Furthermore, for the official party elite the surrogate source of legitimacy was based on propagating the idea that economic and social success was achieved in unison by the entire society. The events of August 1980 and the ensuing political polarization revealed the illusionary nature of these claims.

After August the party faced the possibility of losing its leading role in many spheres of socioeconomic life. The resultant identity crisis could be solved either by successfully stabilizing the party's old role in a reduced form or by destroying Solidarity as an autonomous institution.[19] The developments in the first months of the new trade union's existence revealed that the authorities were attempting to settle on the latter course. Their strategy of dealing with Solidarity in this initial period was to separate the party from the government, at least in the eyes of the population. This reversed ten years of effort to consolidate the party with the state administration during Gierek's tenure.

The idea of the new leadership was to depict the government in a positive light and to elicit public approval, sympathy, and support for the state administration. The latter's dealings with Solidarity were depicted by the controlled press as peaceful and conciliatory. The party elite, on the other hand, took the role of challenging and opposing Solidarity by setting limits for concessions and compromises. According to this strategy "the government would be able to negotiate with the unions uncompromised by responsibility for the much tougher attitudes struck by the Party."[20]

In other words, the strategy adopted by the communist regime resembled a good cop-bad cop scenario. The attempt failed in the short term, however, for the political forces in Poland were not well balanced at the time. Solidarity gained much more authority than expected. When the provocative attempts to curb the growing power of the union failed in the Bydgoszcz incident of March 1981, it became clear that the party was threatened by internal factionalism and external isolation. According to Arato, "such a paradoxical outcome exposed the top leadership to a double attack. On the one hand, the apparatus and the security forces were mobilized with Soviet support, against a policy of weakness and retreat. . . . On the other hand, there was an open attempt on the part of rank and file organizations, the horizontal links movement to force a democratization of the party. . . ."[21]

The leadership watched with fear the extensive political mobilization of the party's rank and file that preceded the Extraordinary PUWP Congress of July 1981. During the course of the pre-congress campaign and at the meeting itself, the elite managed to eliminate the most radical, reform-minded candidates. At the same time, it had to sacrifice elements from the hardline faction as well. The consequence was that the newly elected Central Committee consisted of a significantly small proportion of the professional party apparatus (1.5 percent in 1981 compared to 16.3 percent in 1980 and 29.4 percent in 1964) and of central government members (2.5 percent in 1981 compared to 18.8 percent in 1980, and 36.4 percent in 1959). At the same time, the proportion of military men doubled in comparison to 1968, both in the Central Committee and in the government. The percentage of brand new members of the Central Committee increased from 16.0 percent in 1980 to 90.5 percent in 1981.[22]

This entirely new method of recruitment to the political elite culminated in disorientation among party members. They were unable to distinguish between formal membership in the central administrative or executive bodies and real power. Although elected, the new people in the Central Committee were not able to influence the party bureaucratic apparatus, which remained unrelenting in its opposition to the processes of change. In fact, the real victor of the 1981 party congress was the bureaucracy. From then on, the "leadership adopted their 'policy' of no retreat."[23]

As a result there was a widespread disappointment among the population in the effects of the emergency PUWP Congress. The nondefined character of the elected elite, the petrification of the apparatus, and the lack of a consistent party program were the reasons for this disillusionment. Moreover, the political leadership avoided discussions of genuine economic and social reforms during the congress. As one journalist noticed, "the governmental reform program was—in some way—a method of defense against the reform itself."[24] In reality, reforms prepared by social strata threatened by change are rarely reforms. Large-scale economic innovations were not only dangerous to the apparatus, but also to a significant part of the planning and managerial elite. They feared the suggestions for the dissolution of the centralized state administration and the transformation of ministries into small staffs of experts, as well as the elimination of parallel departmental structures within the party and government executive bodies. Altogether about 200,000 entrenched bureaucrats were threatened by the possible loss of their posts. This army of people was obviously not interested in the idea of reform. Since the executive power of the party leadership was based completely on the apparatus, no reform was possible against the will of the apparatchiki, for the ruling elite was unable to challenge the only source of its own power. Reform, then, although it could have been the platform for reconciliation between the political elite and society, was not implemented in the crucial period of August 1980-December 1981.

The last, and perhaps the most important, sphere of domestic politics that could have helped the ruling elite to avoid further isolation from society was its relationship with the new collective actor on the scene, Solidarity. Until the PUWP Congress in July 1981 the idea of a dialogue with Solidarity was officially approved as the policy of the party. This program had negligible results. Although the party appointed dozens of negotiators to discuss issues and bargain with trade union activists and different partial agreements were reached and signed, the political elite made no moves to introduce real structural changes. Behind the scene, hundreds of obstacles were created against Solidarity's claim to existence as the legitimate representative of the working class. It became clear in the first year of confrontations that the official program of loose dualism could not provide a solution to the social impasse in Poland.[25]

The congress made evident the inertia of the regime, and the party's determination to maintain the whole institutional framework of its rule. This attitude was rapidly reinforced by the appointment on October 18, 1981 of General Jaruzelski to the position of the PUWP's first secretary, in addition to his leading government and military posts. The move signified not only the consolidation of authority but the abandonment of the strategy of dividing responsibility for the crisis between the party and the government. Paradoxically, many Solidarity activists perceived this shift as indicative of a softening in the regime's position, and many hoped that Jaruzelski would bring peace by controlling the extreme wing of the political elite. His centralist leadership, however, started to compete with Solidarity not about political programs (these were never a matter of question for top party officials), but for initiative, control, and power over the processes of production and participatory politics. Among the state and party bureaucratic organizations the demand for old-style cadres and for obedience and discipline reemerged with great force.

THE SOLIDARITY ELITE

Nonetheless, during the initial period of renewal, the rapid development of the Solidarity movement introduced elements of

pluralism into Polish society. The emergence of independent
trade unionism radically transformed the existing arrangement
of social and political forces. This first truly authentic organization of broad social masses voiced the aspirations and articulated the demands of the entire society. Therefore the union
immediately became a counterbalance to centralistic and bureaucratic tendencies and emerged as a social force that had to be
taken into consideration by the communist power holders.

The most general feature of the new union was that it had
to cope with a wide range of problems while acting within a
hostile social and political environment. The party's major response to Solidarity's actions was an attempt to curb the renewal
tendencies, to impose a program of retreat from the Gdansk
agreements of August 1980, and to implement a return of the
ancien regime. As a result the majority of steps taken by
Solidarity, and most of its internal processes, were determined
by the responses of its antagonist—the Communist Party.

Solidarity emerged as a movement of dissent, anger, and
revolt originating primarily in the industrial working class.
In its later development this movement embraced the entire
society but its leaders and militants belonged mostly to a generation that matured in the 1970s: Gierek's political era. They
experienced the deteriorating economy and tightened opportunities characteristic of the second half of the 1970s. At the same
time this generation inherited political expectations expressed
during the October 1956 uprising and the March 1968 students'
revolt, as well as the wave of strikes and protests in 1970 and
1976. While their values were those of social justice, democracy,
and freedom, they entered the job market and the social system
during a politically orchestrated rise in consumer expectations.
They were, however, latecomers to the political scene. Major
economic and political positions remained firmly in the hands of
an earlier generation of people in their 40s and 50s. Reduced
professional and economic opportunities excluded the younger
generation from the network of interdependency within the
establishment. Deprived of material assets, access to privileges,
and positions of power, they had little to lose by defying the
status quo.

From this group of people emerged the initial leadership
of the newly formed trade union. The leaders of the working
class were formed primarily by the spontaneous experiences
and actions during the strikes in the summer of 1980. The
predominant position of Lech Walesa as the head of the workers'
movement was established during this initial phase of labor
activism, supporting the thesis that a climate of uncertainty

and unpredictability is breeding ground for the emergence of
charismatic leadership. Walesa's role was shaped by the organizing and negotiating skills he demonstrated during the decisive
phase of the August 1980 negotiations with the government. His
position was further strengthened during the period of wildcat
strikes and social conflicts in 1980-81, when he played the role
of a fire extinguisher. He managed to maintain his leadership
during the ensuing period of bargaining and compromise due
to his charismatic appeal, even in the face of overt criticism
at the Solidarity congress in September 1981.

Similarly, the selection to the Interfactory Strike Committees (MKS) during the first wave of strikes in the summer
of 1980 was based mostly on voluntary access and spontaneous
participation in the organization of work stoppages. Later on
the MKS became the founding and steering bodies for the
formation of the new trade union, and its members were joined
by other volunteers in creating the union's organizational network. The emerging national leadership of Solidarity consisted
of about 40 semiprofessional activists who served as Walesa's
executive staff. Following a discussion on internal union
democracy—that critically evaluated Walesa's authoritarian
tendencies—the composition of this leading elite was partially
transformed. Democratically elected leaders of the regional
chapters were included in Solidarity's National Consultative
Commission (KKP). This body had formerly consisted solely
of delegates from the biggest industrial plants and had not
gone through a far-ranging process of selection.

The final shape of the union's elite was thus a compromise
between the ideas of charismatic leadership and of democratic
representation. It was a national leadership based on vertical
subordination and regional representation through horizontal
links that resembled a body of revolutionaries more than a body
of functionaries. The 1981 congress of Solidarity, for example,
gathered 849 delegates representing mostly local and regional
elites. Available information shows that 50 percent of the delegates were workers, 32 percent were from the intelligentsia,
and 18 percent were of peasant origin. Only 5.7 percent of
delegates were simultaneously Communist Party members.[26]
There was, however, an overrepresentation of several categories
among the convention delegates, namely representatives from
large industrial plants and the university educated.

At the time of the congress, three currents of political
activism were crucial for the movement. The differences in
activism closely reflected the different levels that formed Solidarity. The lowest level, the rank-and-file members, acted in local

units through their direct representatives. Perceiving the sociopolitical system from below and being immediately linked with the labor process, these people were highly politicized and radicalized. In contrast, the highest level, the national elite of Solidarity, perceived the system in terms similar to moderate party officials. Characteristically, their language referred to the limits presented by external factors (e.g., Soviet interests) and the necessity of evolutionary reform. This Solidarity elite sought to impose limitations on the revolutionary movement by enforcing negotiations and bargaining and by avoiding at all costs direct involvement in politics.

The situation of elites at the intermediate level was different. The leaders of the regional chapters had to face the different tendencies of the rank and file and the national elite. They were exposed to the radical demands of the masses and to countervailing pressures for moderation on the part of the leadership. While mid-level leaders were supposed to transmit the policies of Solidarity's national elite to the masses, these policies, especially following deterioration of the relationship between the party and the union in the first quarter of 1981, were not radical enough for the rank and file. The communication pattern involved the reciprocal transmission of messages, but did not absorb sufficiently the concerns of the masses. The consequence was an increasing gap between the demands for change emanating from the rank and file and the involvement of the union's leadership in the politics of compromise.

This contradiction could have been solved either by pressures from below to promote new leaders to the national level or by the creation of a more representative system of intermediate communication to bring more rank-and-file support for the national elite's policies. In other words, one option required Solidarity to acquire a more sophisticated leadership capable of dealing with the authorities at a time of increasing tensions between the party and the union. The other option required the existing elite to give more attention and to meet the broad demands of union members. Since neither of these happened, the centralist tendencies of Solidarity's top leadership collided with the democratic drive of rank-and-file activists.

The issue emerged into the forefront of Solidarity's problems. It took the form of growing differences among the Solidarity elite in regard to the sociopolitical role of the union, embodied by in the dispute between the fundamentalists and pragmatists. The former, represented primarily by a few regional leaders within the KKP, expected the program to be radical in order to meet the demands of the masses. The latter, centered around Walesa and his advisors, proposed compromises on questions of workers' control and self-government, as well as on the model of accommodation between the state and society. These strains made the union vulnerable to two potential dangers: first, the possibility of an uncontrolled uprising of the whole society, where Solidarity as an organization would not be able to direct the course of events; second, internal divisions within the union increased the likelihood of a governmental attempt to repress by force the independent social organization. The paradox of the situation was that any attempt by the leadership of Solidarity to defuse the situation through compromises with the authorities made the union vulnerable. Such forms of reconciliation were perceived by the power elite as expressions of weakness and tended to foster hardline attitudes and coercive measures on the part of the communist regime. These steps in turn provoked greater discontent of the masses and led to more radical political demands. The consequence was a rapid deterioration of the political conditions in Poland in the fall of 1981, culminating in the use of force by the political establishment.

What was a problem from the very beginning becomes increasingly clear. Solidarity could not be both a "union without a legal sphere of operation" and a revolutionary movement unable to engage in real revolution.[27] The criterion for the former was genuine party recognition of the union's role in society, while only the proclamation of an open revolution could satisfy the latter. Solidarity could be neither and therefore suffered a permanent identity crisis.

THE MILITARY AND POST-MARTIAL LAW ELITES

Observations of Western analysts that in Poland "the military is not likely to develop into an effective interest group" proved to be incorrect in 1981.[28] After the appointment of General Jaruzelski to leading government and party positions (in February and October 1981, respectively), several other military officers were appointed as new ministers and Central Committee members. At the time of the martial law declaration there were already six uniformed members of the cabinet and four in the top party administration. These facts are ample evidence that even before December 13, 1981, Jaruzelski held a conglomeration of power that was unprecedented in the countries of Eastern Europe. In addition to the changes among the political elite, several other attempts were made throughout 1981 to build up the prestige of the military. For example, military officials were assigned to review the civilian administration, with the clear idea of revealing the inefficiency of former bureaucrats. This was then translated into assignments of top military officers to the posts of civilian administrators, a process accelerated after the imposition of martial law.

The military takeover in effect moved the party elite into the shadows. While declaring the state of war to the nation, General Jaruzelski was not introduced as the head of the party, but only as chief of the newly established Military Council of National Salvation (WRON) and as Chairman of the Council of Ministers. The first few months of martial law also consolidated the position of the military elite throughout the system. This was accomplished by the displacement of the administrative elite and the subsequent militarization of industrial plants, ministries, and enterprises. Altogether about 300 plant managers were reportedly dismissed and replaced with military commissars with unlimited executive powers.

At the same time during the first part of 1982, unprecedented restrictions were imposed on the party's political life. All the principles of democracy won by the party's rank and file as a side effect of Solidarity's existence disappeared. Within the party elite a stalemate developed between the old, hard-line party leadership and the military officials. The leading generals regarded themselves as free agents, while the hard-liners hoped for the reestablishment of their earlier authority. In effect neither was the old party elite able to impose repressive measures against society, nor was the military allowed to make major concessions. The party leadership, however, did use the opportunity presented by the military action to introduce crucial changes within its own group. The leadership crushed both the moderate and the radical opposition, withdrew from the practice of internal democracy, and took over the initiative in the economic sector from the state administration.

In the second half of 1982 it became evident that the military turned out to be an efficient administrator. The officers' former experience in policy implementation facilitated the process of exerting power.[29] They were unable to increase productivity in the plants, but were able to protect the communist stronghold through the umbrella of coercive threats. This threat was directed not only against defiant Solidarity leaders but also against high-ranking civilian administrators who formerly held positions in the power elite. In the summer of 1982, for instance, military control led to a complete reshuffling of the state administrative apparatus in the province of Torun.[30]

The effectiveness of the military takeover is also reflected by the creation of countless controlling agencies that report directly to the military authorities. These agencies widen the functions of military, as compared to their pretended original tasks at the moment of the imposition of martial law. The official justification for the state of war was to restore the social order that was supposedly threatened by the development of pluralistic political structures. The military elite did not, of course, bring order or peace. Polish cities immediately became the scenes of riots and organized opposition that was, and remains, unprecedented in any communist-ruled country. It did bring, however, very deep changes in civilian political life. All those suspected of pro-Solidarity sympathies were removed from the state apparatus. The issues of social order, legality, and restoration of party legitimacy became meaningless. Instead, the new target was the creation of a loyal, pro-Soviet power network. Simply, the major function of the military was to engineer a more orthodox and more conservative state system that would eliminate any future Solidarity-like dangers to the existing form of socialism.

Within the communist organization itself, almost all key positions in the provincial apparatus have been taken over by new personnel. The social characteristics of these new appointees consist of a conspicuous antielitism, a low level of education, and a modest level of consumption—in an open attempt to be identified as part of the rank and file. Simultaneously, the new party officials also believe in social and political differences, in the class struggle, and in the need for the dictatorship of the party. The ambiguity of the current situation, the uncertainty of the power hierarchy, and the unprecedented competitiveness of the military elite have given rise to inter-class aggression and the fostering of a vision of society in conflict. Martial law, therefore, brought violence and political struggle to the language and consciousness of the power elite, something that has been absent a long time in the formal sphere of Polish political life. While accepting the force of the military and its efficiency in imposing measures of normalization, the Polish people do not believe in the good intentions of the current power holders. From the good cop-bad cop scenario only the second element remains in Polish politics, and in any case one has to acknowledge the existence of the policeman. The cynicism of the political language has gone so far that recently one of the leading columnists compared the relationships between the authorities and society to those of an old marriage: they hate each other but there is no way to resolve the alliance.[31]

The lifting of the martial law in July 1983 did not alter the situation. Rather it only moved the conflict deeper within the consciousness of the people who denounce the ideology, justification, and policies of the power elite, but nevertheless have to acknowledge its political and coercive strength.

The 18 months of martial law revealed the structural inability of the current leadership to offer any reasonable solution to the conflict of values in Polish society. Society remained unified in its nonviolent resistance to the coercive forces. It also displayed its moral support for the suspended Solidarity trade union. Under the circumstances, while the political authorities can administer the state, they cannot effectively govern society: "General Jaruzelski's regime, in a stalemate with the sullen hostility of public opinion, knows that it must somehow buy at least acceptance, if not endorsement from the Church, if it is to have a chance of building the 'national reconciliation' it must have to survive."[32]

For this reason the role of the clergy and the Catholic episcopate has rapidly increased. Paralyzed in its political role, the ruling elite obviously considered allowing the politicization of the Catholic hierarchy. While Poles are unwilling to listen to the regime, they might follow the line imposed by the church. This, of course, would mean an even greater paradox in the political life of Poland. The country would be administered by a relatively insignificant number of disorganized Communist apparatchiki with very weak executive power. At the same time, society would be governed and morally led by a well-educated and organized clergy, experienced in contacts with the people.

The immediate consequence of such a trend would be corporatization of political life in Poland. It is possible that some Catholic-political organization, resembling the Spanish Opus Dei would emerge to handle both the pressure from the communist administration and the expectations of the mobilized society.

CONCLUSION

The events of the Polish crisis contribute to the verification of various hypotheses about the possible transformation of communist systems and the role of political elites in this process. Two such attempts have already failed: the reform from above (Czechoslovakia, 1968) and the revolution from below (Hungary, 1956). The third option was created by the events in Poland: pressures to democratize the system through a slow but persistent

process steered from below. This method of reform has also
failed. The manner of its failure indicates the reason for the
inefficiency of the third strategy. What Solidarity really failed
to achieve was the self-organization of civil society. Solidarity
did produce the emotions, motivations, and values that were
an alternative to the existing political order. What it did not
bring, however, had much more of a strategic meaning, for
the movement lacked both an elite and a network of organization
and communication that could have challenged the existing
communist system. Solidarity undoubtedly contributed to the
split in the power structure and to the loosening of state controls over society, but it did not create a counterpower—in this
sense the elite of Solidarity missed its political destiny.

The developments of 1980-82 brought about a deep inner
corrosion of the Marxist ideology of the state, revealing the
corruption of the entire system and depriving the masses of
any illusions about state power. The only lesson that society
eventually drew from these events was that the party (or any
other communist authority) was not a credible partner for society
in its struggle for democracy and reform. Both the way power
is exerted by the regime and the way it is challenged by society
lead to further and deeper political crises.

The developments in Poland have also abolished several
myths concerning the possibility of social movements in communist
systems. The most significant delusion was the enthusiastic
belief of the masses that the power elite could be brought to
their knees and that this would be enough to change the political
structure. In light of the bitter experience of Solidarity, it
is now clear that structural reform requires other strategies.
A minimal condition seems to be that a faction of the existing
power elite must be interested in the objective of reform and
must be able to cooperate with the movement's leadership in
order to institutionalize reform.

Other barriers to change within the sociopolitical system
of communism are also evident. First, the party's vulnerability
to political innovation is determined by the degree of threat to
the political interests of the party itself. The more the communist organization is threatened by an alternative elite and
its ideology, the more likely is it to accept reform. Second,
the political elite is interested in maintaining routine methods
of administration and not in the realization of far-reaching
political objectives. Therefore, the eventual coalition between
the alternative elite and the old one is not possible on the
grounds of political and economic development. Third, since
the ruling elite is self-perpetuating, it identifies with the

administrative and executive apparatus of the party. Subsequently, the apparatus cannot be an ally or a bargaining
partner in the coalition with the alternative elites. This imposes
very limited possibilities of action for alternative elites in communist systems. They have to be strong enough to threaten
the power elite, and yet sophisticated enough to recognize the
degree of compromise necessary to succeed. Given the military
strength of the regime, and its ultratotalitarian character, it
seems very unlikely that under current conditions in Poland
the remnants of the alternative elite will achieve their reformist
objectives without the immediate coercive response of the regime.
The political process of the emergence of social movements and
the production of alternative elites has to begin anew to affect
the transformation of the political system in Poland.

NOTES

1. Samuel P. Huntington, "Social and Institutional
Dynamics of One-Party Systems," in Authoritarian Politics in
Modern Society, eds. Samuel P. Huntington and Clement H.
Moore (New York: Basic Books, 1970), pp. 23-26.
2. Carl Beck, "Leadership Attributes in Eastern Europe:
The Effect of Country and Time," in Comparative Communist
Leadership, ed. Carl Beck (New York: David McKay, 1973),
p. 103.
3. David S. Lane, "The Role of Social Groups," in Social
Groups in Polish Society, eds. George Kolankiewicz and David S.
Lane (New York: Columbia University Press, 1973), pp. 302-
326.
4. Jack Bielasiak, "Recruitment Policy, Elite Integration
and Political Stability in People's Poland," in Background to
Crisis Policy and Politics in Gierek's Poland, eds. Maurice D.
Simon and Roger E. Kanet (Boulder: Westview, 1981), p. 107.
5. Adam Michnik, "What We Want To Do and What We
Can Do?," Telos 47 (1981):69.
6. Huntington, "Social and Institutional Dynamics," p.
27.
7. Beck, "Leadership Attributes," p. 104.
8. Michnik, "What We Want," p. 68.
9. Ibid., p. 71.
10. For a general discussion on this issue see Huntington,
"Social and Institutional Dynamics," pp. 5-9.
11. Jaroslaw Piekalkiewicz, "Polish Local Politics in Flux,"
in Local Politics in Communist Countries, ed. Daniel Nelson
(Kansas: Kansas University Press, 1980), pp. 178-186.

12. Neal Ascherson, The Polish August: The Self-Limiting Revolution (New York: The Viking Press, 1982), p. 111.

13. Jack Bielasiak, ed., Poland Today (Armonk, N.Y.: M. E. Sharpe, 1981), pp. 33-56.

14. Stanislaw Starski, Class Struggle in Classless Poland (Boston: South End Press, 1982), p. 43.

15. Jadwiga Staniszkis, "The Evolution of Forms of Working Class Protest in Poland: Sociological Reflection of Gdansk-Szczecin Case," Soviet Studies 23 (1981):204.

16. Ibid., p. 205.

17. Bielasiak, "Recruitment Policy," p. 127.

18. Starski, Class Struggle, p. 48.

19. Andrew Arato, "Empire Versus Civil Society: Poland 1981-82," Telos 50 (1981-82):33.

20. Ascherson, The Polish August, p. 263.

21. Arato, "Empire Versus Civil Society," p. 34.

22. Zygmunt Szeliga, "O ruchu w gabinetach rzadowych," Polityka 1330, October 30, 1982, pp. 4-5.

23. Arato, "Empire Versus Civil Society," p. 34.

24. Ernest Skalski, "Kto Przeciw," Polityka 1251 (September 1981):5-6.

25. Ascherson, The Polish August, Chapter 8.

26. Calculated by the authors from Tygodnik Solidarnosc, October 16, 1981.

27. Arato, "Empire Versus Civil Society," pp. 35-40.

28. Dale Herspring, "The Polish Military and the Policy Process," in Background to Crisis: Policy and Politics in Gierek's Poland, eds. Maurice D. Simon and Roger E. Kanet (Boulder: Westview, 1981), p. 226.

29. Ibid., p. 228.

30. Witold Pawlowski, "Ten rok jest na przezycie," Polityka 1308 (May 1982):3.

31. K.T.T., "Co ja tu robie," Polityka 1338 (December 1982):16.

32. Neal Ascherson, "The King of Poland Comes Home," The Observer (London), June 19, 1983, p. 9.

9.

Polish Intellectuals in Crisis

Jane Leftwich Curry and Joanna Preibisz ————————————

This chapter began as an attempt to understand why the agreements that signaled the start of the short-lived Solidarity era in Poland were made between worker representatives and government representatives while intellectuals and the rest of the intelligentsia essentially sat on the sidelines. The evidence of the intellectuals' and intelligentsia's weakness and isolation from events came in their failure to predict the rise and success of Solidarity, much less to encourage or help organize the actions of the workers.

Although groups of intellectuals in the establishment and the opposition were highly critical of the Gierek regime and its policies throughout the latter half of the seventies, the vast majority simply did not see a possibility of forcing change in the system or its leadership. They also did not see workers as capable of organizing themselves to force change, even though a number saw workers as the only group with the power to bring about that change. So, depending on their relationship to the authorities and their personal ideology, they were enemies, onlookers, go-betweens, or uninvited advisors as the negotiations for the initial agreements between workers and government went on. After the August 1980 agreements were signed, intellectuals did not gain a lead. They continued to follow the workers and react to their successes. Workers organized themselves to solve what both groups had seen as Poland's problems. Professional groups organized to solve their own problems. Intellectual dissidents eventually dissolved their organizations in face of the workers' victories. Some, who had been leaders in parts of the intellectual community, took leading

roles in the government and party factions, and others tried
to serve as links between the new unions and the authorities.
In large part, they reacted to events instead of putting forth
any program defining the developments of the Solidarity period.

Following the declaration of martial law, however, the
battle for control of the intellectuals was waged as though
they were major enemies and obstacles to the regime. Large
numbers of intellectuals as well as workers identified with the
Solidarity movement were arrested. Sharp attacks were made
in the mass media on the treachery of the intellectual class.
And, in what appears to have been an attempt to break the
bonds that had developed between intellectuals and workers,
the two groups were put in separate detention camps with many
of the intellectual detainees kept in far better conditions than
worker detainees. On the other hand, repression of Solidarity
by force was seen as a real possibility more among the intelligentsia than among workers or peasants during the entire
period of Solidarity's strength. Once martial law was imposed,
however, many intellectuals who had accepted the Gierek
regime refused to accept the martial law regime. So nearly
one-third of the Polish journalists simply did not return to
their jobs or did not bend enough to pass ideological verification
tests. Actors, artists, academics, and others established codes
of professional ethics to govern their behavior under martial law.
Both white- and blue-collar workers returned to work peacefully
in all but a few cases.

Explaining the function of intellectuals in Polish politics
is complicated by the variety of social and occupational roles
which they perform and by the limits of materials which are
available on them and their actions. The definition and identification of the "intellectuals" in Polish society is difficult. First
of all, while statistical data has been generated sporadically on
specific professional groups, most of that data deals with low
level professions and were collected in the sixties and not in
the Gierek era. Second, in scholarship from both the West
and the East, the nature of an "intellectual" has not been
precisely defined. The definitions range from the Marxist notion
of "mental worker" which includes all those whose labor is not
directly productive and so includes those individuals who work
in bureaucracies whatever their educational background and
independence to the Western philosophical approach to intellectuals as society's critical thinkers, a characteristic that excludes
those who remain in the establishment. Furthermore, in a communist society where virtually all occupations are bureaucratized
into positions in the state and where the distinction between

the roles and views of individuals' public and private selves is increased by state domination of earning possibilities, the identification of intellectuals is even more complex. For simplicity's sake, I have primarily used the term "intellectuals" for individuals and groups that identify themselves as such in their own self-definitions. Because of the restrictions imposed by the state, some of these individuals, by their own choice or because they are excluded from other usual intellectual occupations, do perform manual labor. Others are a part of the broader intelligentsia in their work lives. As such, they are and were a part of the broader grouping of "white collar workers." This group, some of whom see themselves as intellectuals and others who do not, was particularly significant in the Gierek era and the Solidarity and martial law periods. Contact with it was the main contact that the broader population had with the "intellectual class." Many intellectuals were in it and functioned with their bureaucratic interests in mind in their work world while acting independently in their private lives. And, finally, the actions of the class of white collar workers, whatever the critiques of intellectuals, were a deciding force in the events in the late seventies and early eighties in Poland. As a result, although this is primarily about the thinking and blocks to intellectual leadership in the traditional sense, I have also used the term intelligentsia where it seemed relevant to the issue at hand.

The data which I have used comes, of necessity, primarily from the writings of intellectuals about Poland's problems and options—a set of writings which is more prolific than any other in Eastern Europe. This is supplemented by data from interviews and discussions in Poland itself and with individuals who had come to the United States. More exact statistical and attitudinal data are not basically available on "intellectuals" per se. What does exist, particularly from the Solidarity period, focuses richly on the attitudes of individuals divided by the educational levels but does not focus specifically on intellectuals. Therefore, as with much in this field, many of the conclusions are based on impressionistic data.

The inability of intellectuals to lead the workers and their position as targets of attack after the declaration of martial law raise theoretical questions about the role of intellectuals in political life and in social change. After all, under normal circumstances, Western theories of political participation link education, high job status, and social and economic position to efficacy and high political position. Intellectuals and white-collar workers thus should have been the most active and

effective political actors.[1] Theorists of revolution from Crane
Brinton to Samuel Huntington pictured revolutions (as opposed
to the temporary anomic violence of worker and peasant revolts)
as growing out of a link between the intellectuals and workers
or peasants. According to these theories of revolution, it should
also have been the intellectuals who stimulated and organized
other classes to act.[2]

Clearly, Polish intellectuals did not fill these roles in the
1980s. Their failure to lead was a product of the environment
in which they had to survive, an environment that allowed
critical discussion within groups, but kept it from being made
widely available; enlarged divisions between groups, and created
irresolvable problems made more insoluble by the massive growth
of the bureaucracy under Gierek. This paralyzing environment
contributed to intellectuals' thinking about Poland and its problems and led to their emphasis on restraint and the impossibility
of real change. This view was held strongly enough to discour-
age the preparation of comprehensive tactical plans for triggering
real change. Rather, alternatives were posed in terms of being
ready when the opportunity was made by gradual social transformation or external changes. And, that same Gierek-era
environment created a large grouping in the intelligentsia whose
life was tied up in the strength and survival of the bureaucracy.
It also made it impossible for intellectuals committed to reform
within the party to see change and reform as possible or to act
to moderate policy even on an individual level because they
were caught by bureaucratic barriers. Finally, the environment
and restrictions of the 1970s and the lack of comprehensive
plans made it impossible for intellectuals to take over once the
workers liberated Poland. This failure, in turn, may have
been one of the reasons that Solidarity lasted so long and went
in the direction it did only to find itself unable to survive and
that martial law was an option to stop the transformation of
Poland.

THE ENVIRONMENT FOR FAILURE

The failure of the intelligentsia to play its traditional role
as a predictor and leader of social revolution was not a sign of
the weakheartedness of the Polish intelligentsia. Far more of
them were involved with underground publications, human
rights groups, and open discussions than anywhere else in
Eastern Europe, in spite of the sanctions that the Gierek
leadership imposed for these activities. Records of professional

discussions and groups such as the Experience and the Future
of Poland, an independent group of intellectuals from various
fields and political leanings; Poland 2000, an Academy of Science
consortium organized to bring outstanding scholars together to
predict future options, and "the Red Sofa" group, an informed
discussion club of party intellectuals and those they invited to
join; provide real evidence of the existence of critical views
and dissatisfaction within the establishment in the 1970s. The
censors' documents and information from private conversations
also indicate that many tried pressure from within.[3] At the
same time, it cannot be denied that there were many intellectuals
who participated and benefitted in the Gierek regime, however
real their personal commitment.

The reasons for the lack of leadership by the intelligentsia
and its lack of a full understanding of the potential of the working class were imbedded in the political system and the barriers
that were developed between the intelligentsia and workers and
peasants. A premium was put on moving out of the working or
peasant class and staying out of it. The cutbacks in social
services under Gierek put education (the traditional road to
social mobility) beyond the reach of most working- and peasant-
class youths. So intelligentsia and the working class were
divorced from each other because working-class youths could
no longer move up and link their parents' class with the class
of their fellows in the university.[4]

The intellectuals were also not from a homogeneous class.
Those who entered the intelligentsia from the 1940s to the 1960s
came from widely different backgrounds. Even within the
declared opposition, there were Catholics and former Communists;
prewar intellectuals and young, upwardly mobile technocrats
from the working class; as well as individuals from various
professional groups.[5] These differences in background, although not directly correlated, were reflected in differences
in personal ties and political positions. These splits were
amplified in the intelligentsia as a whole. And they were
worsened by the differences in the experiential base of different
age groups—for some memories of prewar Poland and, for others,
World War II, Stalinism, or only Gierek's promises. As a result,
although there were personal ties between the opposition and
the establishment, the intelligentsia and every group within it
were socially and politically divided from within.

The centralized information and decision-making system
imposed by the Gierek leadership on what had traditionally
been fairly loose structures of control made communication
through public channels nearly impossible.[6] While these con-

trols were in place, intellectuals had no way to notify others of their discontent or their thinking about alternatives. Nor did they have access to the kind of information they had gathered before about all segments of the population. Even the establishment of an active opposition press did not solve this problem. It was published in what, for Eastern Europe and the Soviet Union, were large numbers of copies. But it still reached only a small fragment of the population, basically the fragment already in the intellectual centers (Warsaw, Lublin, and Krakow). These publications did not circulate easily or widely among other groups elsewhere in the society. Therefore, the intellectual leadership was seen by the public as collaborating with the Gierek regime. Their other views and actions were basically unknown to the working class.[7]

Beyond the differences in personal background and ideology within the intelligentsia, the industrialization and bureaucratization of the Gierek era created a class of technocrats and an ever-expanding class of bureaucrats. Both of these groups had strong interests in maintaining the Gierek regime and its policies of increased industrialization and centralization of administration. In spite of the inadequacies individuals in these groups saw in the system around them,[8] they shared the general perception that industrialization itself was valuable. It was the composite decisions of these two groups that dissident and establishment critics attacked. Their criticism also raised objections to the dramatic increase in the size and social and material wealth of this group. As they saw it, it was these bureaucrats and technocrats who kept them from reaching the Gierek leadership. In fact, from the information now available it appears that bureaucrats and technocrats, along with the military and police, were threatened by the possibilities of economic and political reform that appeared to be the ultimate results of Solidarity's gains and demands.

The failure of the intelligentsia as a class to lead in 1980 as they had in 1956 and their counterparts had in Hungary in 1956 and Czechoslovakia in 1968 was also a product of the strength of the party leadership. For the first time in Polish history, there was a united party leadership of individuals all closely tied to the top party leader. As a result, the splits in the party leadership that normally encouraged discussion and allowed intellectual criticism to be published did not exist. Intellectuals simply could not find allies in the leadership nor were the controls on public discussion reduced as economic and social problems grew.

Finally, the Polish intelligentsia failed to lead because it focused on the necessary compromises, the historical lessons of past uprisings, and the possibility of Soviet invasions like those in Hungary and Czechoslovakia. Virtually no one imagined that workers would organize or the Soviets would be as tolerant as they were, simply because there was nothing comparable to this year of miracles.

This reaction of shock was paralyzing. Events took such a surprising and rapid course after the formation of Solidarity that there was no time to create solid programmatic solutions. Plus, the torrent of information released after Gierek's fall and the collapse of the economy created a situation where no solution seems viable and applicable to the crisis Gierek's policy created.

OPPOSITION CRITICS

The declared opposition's assessment of the social and political situation in the late 1970s, reflected in its activities and limited appeal, precluded its assuming a leading role in August 1980. This, even though these opposition critics tried both to voice the concerns of a diverse group of intellectuals and to speak for the needs of other social groups: workers, peasants, and the Catholic church. In time, some workers and peasants had openly joined this opposition. The church, however, did not participate directly in or encourage dissent officially. It nevertheless gave tacit support to dissident causes and spoke on behalf of some harassed dissidents far more actively than it had in the pre-1976 era.[9]

The programs of dissident intellectual groups did not aim at bringing about rapid sociopolitical change by violent or peaceful means, in spite of the fact that all groups understood and stressed the desperate need for a fundamental transformation of the system. They, like intellectuals in past years,[10] expected violent attempts at change to be made by the society but they did not expect these to lead to real effective and ordered change. This was most clearly stated by the anonymous members of the PPN (Polish League for Independence) in their Program of 1976: "The countries of the socialist bloc, . . . are in a state of continuing, although concealed crisis. . . . The crisis is bound to come into the open, both internally and internationally."[11]

At the same time, dissident critics underestimated the revolutionary changes in the Polish working class and its readiness to be an active force in the society. They did not anticipate the workers' high degree of self-discipline and capacity for self-organization in the summer of 1980. In part, the workers owed this newly realized strength to the efforts of the Free Trade

Unions founded on the Baltic coast and in Silesia in 1978. The leaders of these unions had already begun organizing a grass roots workers' movement shortly after the unsuccessful 1970 strikes on the Baltic coast. Espousing the goals of that movement, the Free Trade Unions orchestrated occasional local strikes, intervened on behalf of individual workers, organized events to commemorate the bloody December 1970 strikes, and published pamphlets in conjunction with the uncensored fortnightly Robotnik (The Worker), which contained articles on the labor movement in Poland and abroad. In spite of the fact that some of the contributors to Robotnik were workers, the publication was actually produced by intellectuals through KOR (Committee for the Defense of Workers).[12]

The cooperation that existed between KOR and Robotnik represented one of the few successful alliances between dissidents and workers. The theoretical importance of the working class as a vehicle for change was not grasped by many members of the intellectuals. This, even though Jacek Kuron, one of the founders of KOR, pointed out in 1978 that workers' movements had a much better chance of succeeding than those sponsored by the intellectuals. Although poorly organized and badly informed, the workers, in his opinion, wielded real political influence since the economic survival of the system depended on them. Any united action by the workers could paralyze the country, while the intellectuals, in spite of their superior network of information and communications, would never have real political power.[13] For this reason, while KOR members sought to achieve their goals by encouraging active self-government in the society as a whole, they gave special attention to the problems of workers' self-organization.[14]

The immediate stimulus for KOR's foundation was the need to provide financial help and legal assistance to the families of workers arrested in Ursus and Radom during the food riots of June 1976. Over time, its program also came to include demands for such basic democratic rights as freedom of speech and belief, and the right to strike. These objectives, expressed formally in the Declaration of the Democratic Movement of October 1977, were accompanied by specific criticism of the existing political institutions.[15] As a platform for action, KOR attracted both the exponents of the so-called Lay Left ideology and some Catholic intellectuals, who took part in publishing such regular journals as Biuletyn Informacyjny (Information Bulletin), Glos (The Voice), and Robotnik. KOR's attempt at a lasting alliance with the workers represented the first time in postwar Polish history that such a liaison had been sought by either workers or intellectuals.

Another prominent dissident group, ROPCiO (Movement for the Defense of Human and Civil Rights), was formed in March 1977. It focused primarily on violations of human and civil rights. But just as KOR attempted to establish links with the workers, ROPCiO, in addition to its basic activity of exposing human rights abuses, tried to forge an alliance with Polish farmers. It played a role in the creation of the Independent Peasant Movement, the Provisional Committee for the Independent Farmers' Trade Unions, and the independent periodicals Placowka (The Post) and Gospodarz (The Farmer), concerned chiefly with the problems of organizing individual farmers and with the agricultural policy of the state.[16] Both KOR and ROPCiO offered to provide active support for the formation of Believers' Self-Defense Committees and Peasant Self-Defense Committees, which organized various effective grass roots actions in the interests of the local religious and farming communities.[17]

In general, the liaisons between the intellectuals and other social groups were loose and intellectuals were limited to serving as invited speakers. The two major opposition forces also tried to provide services that would give workers and peasants a sense of their own strength and convince them of the usefulness of the opposition. ROPCiO opened consultation-information centers in various cities, while KOR set up an intervention bureau. This was done in an effort to create public access to information on citizens' rights, offer free legal assistance, intervene on behalf of victims of official harassment, and maintain a continuous flow of information to the Western media as a means of checking the repressive policies of the regime. As of 1979, however, neither group found these services to be very well used.[18]

The dissident intellectuals also expended a considerable effort articulating the formal structures within which they would operate so that a variety of sociopolitical views could be accommodated. This was no small feat, as the intellectual dissidents were divided into two separate camps. The Lay Left, comprising intellectuals previously associated with the regime but disillusioned with that experience (for example, former Marxist revisionists such as J. Kuron) and searching for a system closer to the ideas of democratic socialism, was primarily affiliated with KOR.[19] Those members of the intelligentsia, among them several Catholic intellectuals, who professed views closer to the political Right, tended to join ROPCiO or other similar but smaller organizations.[20] Thus, ROPCiO, which was established to defend human rights in Poland as its main goal, attracted mostly proponents of the nationalistic tradition and of Polish independence from the Soviet Union. The two camps, Left and Right, harbored a deep mutual distrust and, as a result, often found themselves locked in struggles with one another. Only under attack from the authorities did KOR and ROPCiO back each other with public support, financial assistance, and an exchange of ideas. Around them sprang up dozens of fragmentary groups: Free Trade Unions, an Independent Peasant Movement, an Independent Student Movement, PKOZRiN (Polish Committee for the Defense of Life, Family and Nation), and KPN (Confederation for an Independent Poland). The most militant of them, KPN was an anti-Soviet organization lobbying for the overthrow of the PUWP as a prerequisite for a completely independent Poland; it organized separately—spurred on, but hardly supported, by either of the two major groups or the Catholic church.[21]

There was, therefore, in the opposition, a significant division of political views with regard to questions such as the sovereignty of Poland, the optimal political system, and the interpretation of history. On the kind of economic reform necessary or the need for the democratization of basic social institutions, however, there was some measure of agreement between the groups. All saw decentralization of the economy and open access to policy making as necessary. To aid in this process, the opposition forces put out journals and policy studies providing information and encouragement for individual action, hoping thereby to compensate for the information missing from the Gierek media. On the whole then, the internal divisions among the intellectuals were not articulated in such a way as to make them the sole cause for any lack of intellectual leadership in 1980.

Rather, it was the very forces that had brought the opposition to life that later undercut its mass appeal by making contact with the bulk of the population almost impossible. The obstacles to freedom of speech, religion, and association that the democratic opposition organized to fight, such as rigid censorship and suppression of open debate by the police, Internal Security Service, and the courts, kept intellectuals from finding out what the broader public thought about important issues and from being seen airing their views. Thus, the wide range of dissident activities—individual interventions, consultation-information centers, occasional strikes and public demonstrations, lectures and courses offered by the TKN (Society for Academic Courses), and the publication of a variety of journals, studies, and novels by several independent publishing houses—did not produce the desired effect. The opposition managed to capture audiences only in large cities with intellectual communities like Warsaw, Krakow, and Lublin, around some large industrial enterprises, and in a few isolated villages, mostly in the Lublin district.[22] The rigid state controls imposed on the official media kept the media out of the dissidents' and even critical intellectuals' reach.[23] Hence, the opposition forces were left to their own devices in disseminating their views: laborious retyping of materials, stealing state-owned duplicators, or smuggling in new ones from abroad. Most of the work had to be done secretly by volunteer workers during their free time. Even more important, by their own admission, the dissidents had to combat patterns of socialization that had for years encouraged Poles to be completely passive. This perception of hopeless and unshakeable apathy in the population was held by both Catholic and Lay Left activists.[24]

Besides the problems of scope, access, and choice of issues, the dissident circles were reined in by a fear of a Soviet invasion. For the opposition, four options existed for Poland's future: gaining complete sovereignty; acquiring the same status as Finland (neutral but not entirely sovereign); maintaining the status quo; or being incorporated into the Soviet Union. Most believed that the last option was most likely to occur as a reprisal for attempts at democratic change.[25] A minority group within the opposition argued with this view, criticizing fellow intellectuals for a lack of insight.[26] However, the criticism that rejected the almost mythic fear of Soviet action had little resonance. It demonstrated, however, some awareness among opposition intellectuals of unorthodox approaches to the question of the Soviet Union.

Operating under the constraint of necessary compromises, such as the recognition of Poland's geopolitical location, and under the assumption that any change would require years of patient work, the intelligentsia did not feel ready to assume the demanding task of politicizing workers or any other social group. The effect of this restraint was to make it seem fruitless, if not counterproductive to the dissidents, to push for a real coherent program of change. The extent to which this was true is clear from the program of the PPN, the most underground of the dissident groups and the only one not to reveal the identity of its members:

> It is an integrated programme implying a complete
> reconstruction of the economic or political system.
> It would be possible, however, to put its separate
> elements into practice independently, without en-

dangering the whole, by using existing opportunities. In this sense, ours is an evolutionary program.[27]

On the balance, the alliance of KOR, an intellectual organization, with the workers, or ROPCiO and KOR with the farmers,
in spite of its formidable successes, marked an isolated, though
important, trend in dissident organizations. Most of dissident
activities aimed at organizing their own ranks and publishing
periodicals and other literature explored the new political
awakening and sought to combat social apathy. The awareness
of the limitations resulting from worker apathy and Soviet
intolerance seemed to most of the opposition to put any possible
change years away. The best they allowed themselves to hope
for was a gradual evolution and reeducation process for which
they would provide information and encouragement. Workers,
in their perception, were usable and crucial weapons, but
hardly self-starters. As a result, general critiques seemed
far more appropriate than specific proposals in solving Poland's
daily economic problems. Because their analysis was limited
to such general observations, it was highly unlikely that dissidents would emerge as revolutionary leaders in a specific situation.

ESTABLISHMENT CRITICS

Disaffection and criticism of the political, economic, and
social situation in Poland was not done solely by the opposition
in the latter half of the 1970s. Unpublished surveys and re-
views of letters to newspapers showed a broad agreement among
the intelligentsia on Poland's problems and their rank ordering.
And, although the tactics used were different, their critiques
were not unlike those of the declared opposition. This was
also a result of the similarity and interconnections between the
opposition and establishment intellectuals by virtue of their
common backgrounds and their long-term patterns of friendship.[28]
The vocalization of this discontent took place in two intellectual circles that remained within the establishment: the Catholic,
humanist intellectual circles and the intellectual community of
academics, journalists, and writers, many of whom were or had
been involved with the Communist Party, in major cultural centers. Until after the Gdansk settlements were completed and
the academic year was underway in 1980, most of the participants
in these discussions were from the prewar generation and not
the postwar baby-boom generation. Later, with the advent of

Solidarity's renewal, young adults did get involved. But they tended to form their own circles and were inpatient with the conservatism of their elders.[29]

The hub of Catholic intellectual discourse throughout the entire postwar period was the ZNAK group. After 1956, it had parliamentary delegates, a number of journals, and discussion clubs. Its position had (since the mid-1950s) been a humanist alternative to the so-called party line. But its views were not necessarily representative of those of the church hierarchy. Their concerns were to support the cultural pluralism that existed in Poland because of the strength of Catholic culture and to encourage individuals to maintain Poland's democratic traditions at least in their individual ideologies. In doing this, they accepted the "geopolitical" necessity of a communist regime in Poland but rejected it as a permanent and natural system for Poland.[30]

More secular critics viewed with alarm the situation that had developed under communist rule in these same areas. The intellectuals, even those involved with the arts, initially saw Gierek as a positive force for Poland: They were concerned with modernization of Poland. Gierek was a modernizer. They looked to the West culturally, so did he. And, he openly cultivated them by promising increased investment in those areas that affected professional lives of those in both the technical and the humanistic professions.[31]

Behind the scenes in the late 1960s, Polityka journalists, under the leadership of their editor-in-chief, Central Committee liberal Mieczyslaw Rakowski (who later served as deputy prime minister under General Wojciech Jaruzelski) took the lead in lobbying for modernization and encouraging Gierek to take power. They drew up a plan for 1969 that was an undeclared platform for change from the low-growth, stagnation policies of the 1960s and circulated it to a few top men like Gierek who they thought might put it into effect. Their plan reflected the concerns of many intellectuals. The basic argument was that communist rule in the 1970s had to be changed dramatically from what it had been in the 1960s because there was a new, highly educated, urban population. This would require, in their view, a complete shift from the long investment cycle, increased costs, and poor living standards. On the political front, they stressed the necessity of providing greater opportunities for discussion and participation in order to give the population a greater sense of responsibility for its actions.[32]

Their program in the area of investment was largely enacted in the early 1970s even though the concerns that they voiced about a reasonable restructuring of prices, investment based on overall planning of Poland's economic future, and the long-term primacy of a consumer industry over an export industry were ignored. In the areas of information and cultural growth, only a facade of liberalism was put up by the Gierek regime. What this meant in the long run was that intellectuals, like those whose views were more or less reflected in this Polityka document did not initially see the pitfalls in Gierek's strategy of importing modernization. Therefore, they were trapped by their own initial support of him and his programs and found it hard to attack the conceptualization as opposed to the implementation of the Gierek program.

The Polityka critique, with its emphasis on dealing with the new generation of educated Poles by allowing them to participate and help move the country forward, was the forebearer of the themes that appeared in the critiques of Gierek's rule made by academics, professionals, journalists, and writers throughout the 1970s. As the system grew more bureaucratized, the critiques of these groups were more and more sharply focused on political degeneration, caused by the deformations of Gierek's centralized mobilizing system, as the root of Poland's problems. Economic reforms were treated throughout this period as far lesser issues.

The frustrations and the paralysis of these groups grew as did their criticisms. They were not only no longer courted but they were also excluded from policy making and ordered about by bureaucrats in the party apparatus even if they were established party politicians.[33] Their criticisms and recommendations had no effect. And, in the middle to late 1970s, as their criticism grew, the control of the mass media by the Gierek Press Department and the censors also grew.[34] Therefore, their criticism, even on minor issues, never appeared in the mass media. This created the impression among those who only saw them through the mass media that they were collaborators and not critics. It gave no forum to those who were blacklisted, a group that included a number of individuals who remained in the Communist Party and were reluctant to join the declared opposition. And, it eliminated the basic forum for intercommunication among the Polish intelligentsia. What this lead to was the fragmentation of the intelligentsia into formal groups brought together by professional or personal ties. This, in large part, occurred in Warsaw circles. Ties to the larger population were limited since even those who had come from worker or peasant backgrounds had long since ceased to have regular contacts with those from their past. As a result, links between individuals without personal contacts were weakened and any interclass communication that had existed before was destroyed.

The first priority of the intelligentsia was, therefore, to reestablish contacts within their class. In February 1979, an attempt was made, for example, by intellectuals in Warsaw to generate some intergroup communication and press a reevaluation of the direction of the policy coming from outside the declared opposition. Initially, one hundred invited participants representing liberal party members, Catholics, and other intellectuals were summoned to a formal session of what was to be an ongoing public discussion group called Experience and the Future of Poland. Presentations were given on social conditions in Poland and their deterioration by two experts who had served as policy advisors to Gierek. Their criticisms and those of the questioners were too strong for the group to be allowed to continue formal meetings.

So a steering committee of journalists and academics started a series of reports based on answers to broad questions solicited by them from prominent intellectuals. In the two reports that preceded the August 1980 events, stress was placed on the need to arrest the process of political decay by recognizing workers and the rest of society as partners in a dialogue on the situation in Poland. To do this, much of the machinery for rule that Gierek had built up and the intelligentsia resented would have had to be torn down. Heavy emphasis was laid on the need for open access to information for the population. Coupled with this, the establishment critics in this group pressed for the development of structures for participation by all groups in the society and for making the participation of these groups truly meaningful. One of the basic organizations that these critics said would have to be either restructured or begun afresh were real free trade unions.

They went further and advocated economic and political reforms involving a full-scale decentralization of authority and responsibility and budgetary reallocations that would provide for consumer goods and public services. And although they perceived corruption and the irrationally unequal distribution of social services and consumer goods that became a full-blown epidemic in the Gierek system as a disease pervading the entire society, they assumed it was feasible to stem the epidemic if workers were given full access to information and some level of responsibility for decisions affecting their lives. Then, they felt, dramatic cutbacks the economic policy of the 1970s had made necessary, as well as higher prices and greater pressure on workers to be productive, would be acceptable.

In foreign affairs, this group and the general intelligentsia sensed that Gierek had not seriously explored the limits of Soviet tolerance and moved to these limits. At the same time, it was made clear that the West was as implicated in the problems of Poland and the maintenance of the status quo as the Soviet Union was. So, they felt, it could not be counted on to press Gierek to facilitate reform or change.[35]

This analysis was characteristic of a plethora of analyses and discussions that were being carried out in Poland in the late seventies as the failure of the Gierek regime became more and more evident. Formal and informal groups formed in major intellectual centers in Poland ranging from an elite group in the Polish Academy of Sciences formally charged with long-term prognostication (Poland 2000) and the legally recognized Catholic Intellectual Clubs as well as groups formed spontaneously or organized for instructional purposes which became seats of discussion in various professional organizations (the Writers' Union, Journalists Association, Economists' Association, Polish Sociological Association, and others) to informal meetings held in individual apartments like the "Red Sofa" group of Party members and their invitees from groupings of other persuasions which sponsored discussions of what they considered key issues. Many of these groups intersected and were cross-fertilizing, according to those involved. And, most of their discussions and conclusions were outgrowths of debates that occurred in family and friendship groups throughout Poland.

Before the strikes, many intellectuals silently circulated their critiques and hoped that the party leadership would notice. They had no real hope that change could be forced or that the workers would act and create their own organization to take power. In fact, as many connected with this group pointed out, "What To Do?", the title of the second report, was a misnomer and implied far more of a programmatic statement than it represented.[36]

In the poststrike period, these groups, like the intelligentsia as a whole, fragmented. Some supported reforms in the party and acted as advisors and negotiators for the government side. Others took on activist roles in their own professional organizations. Still others became active in Solidarity. And, a large middle segment of the intelligentsia, especially the technocrats and bureaucrats, simply coped with the changes as they occurred. A survey done between the strike settlements and the ouster of Gierek showed that this group, more than any other, was nervous about the potential outcome of the eruption of Solidarity and the changes that resulted. While only 8 percent of those counted in the entire survey group thought that the events had put the country only one step from disaster, 12 percent of those with higher education who were interviewed thought this was the case, and only 5 percent of this group altogether excluded this as a possibility. The division between intellectuals, the intelligentsia, and workers was even more dramatically evidenced in a series of in-depth interviews with workers, intellectuals, and bureaucrats in the fall of 1981. [37]

THE INTELLECTUALS UNDER SOLIDARITY

As Solidarity grew stronger and the party became weaker, the positions of intellectuals became even more complex. Many younger members of the intelligentsia from all kinds of occupational groups became active in Solidarity and pushed for radical reforms and for the Solidarity organization to begin putting forth reform proposals. Former members of the intellectual opposition joined Solidarity as individuals or acted in conjunction with it. Eventually these groups felt their raison d'etre had ceased to exist and disbanded or essentially disappeared in the onslaught of Solidarity. [38] Other professionals who had been on the fringe of the opposition during the Gierek years pushed to take over in the void of power.

On the other hand, it was workers more often than members of the intelligentsia who spontaneously turned in their party cards. So few workers involved themselves in party activities and the elections for the Extraordinary Party Congress that white-collar representatives dominated that congress: 66.7 percent of the delegates were from the intelligentsia. [39] More intellectuals than workers were pessimistic about the possibility for maintaining the level of change that had been carried out in the year after the August strikes. [40] Finally, it was, after all, members of the intelligentsia who continued to sit in bureaucratic positions and often appeared to have at least aided in the pressure against Solidarity that maintained the tension in 1980-81.

Repeatedly, during the eighteen months after the formation of Solidarity, the intelligentsia appeared to look for a solution and found none. The Experience and Future group reconstituted itself in the post-August period and put out two more analyses (one before the extraordinary congress and one after the declaration of martial law). It posited scenarios ranging from an open bloodbath as a result of conservatives leading an attack on the workers to a continued standoff leading the country to, at best, evolutionary change. [41] The delegates to the party congress failed to come up with enough of a consensus in their committees to provide any proposals for change. And many were calling for a government of experts by the summer of 1981. None of these groups, however, generated a platform that got real popular visibility and support.

In response to the formation of Solidarity, a Committee of Cultural Associations was organized. It originally was led by individuals from academic and professional groups with the writers' union, the philosophical and historical associations, and the journalists' and artists' associations playing primary roles. Eventually, some thirty-three intellectual organizations fit under its umbrella. This group came to speak for Polish intellectuals as a whole. Responsibility was ceded to it by Solidarity for the drafting of a censorship law to fulfill the Gdansk agreements, since this was an area in which Solidarity was interested only in the final outcome and not the mechanism itself.[42] This group and other intellectual organizations did research and took stands on the other problems and policies as well.

In effect, this group, like the intellectuals it represented, lobbied for its own interests and concentrated on making itself independent of both the government and the workers.[43] Characteristic of this desire for autonomy was the organization of the First Congress of Polish Culture, planned for December 12 and 13, 1981. Intellectual groups each contributed to printing invitations, got a donation of theater space and speakers' time, and held the congress with only its selected member-delegates in attendance. The congress was intended to present the concerns and proposals of each of the intellectual groups. It was actually telecast on December 12, 1981, but that night many of that day's leaders were interned and the congress, and the umbrella organization itself, was dissolved.[44]

In part, the reaction of the intelligentsia to the changes after August was a rational response. What they saw around them in Poland and in the world situation did not seem to offer any realistic promise of a solution. It was also a situation in which they were the most powerless group. Without any operational programs that would also be acceptable to both the workers and the party, the intelligentsia could not take the lead, especially since they had been relatively invisible in the Gierek years. At best, they could provide a coherent analysis of the problems and try to protect their own interests against worker gains and government pressure. But this did not ensure them either contact or full credibility with the workers. Ultimately, their inability to see options further fragmented the intelligentsia by leaving them to search for scapegoats and putting them in a position where they did not perform their traditional role of leadership either as the prewar intelligentsia or as the postwar intelligentsia had done through their positions in the party or in the cultural and technical elite.

INTELLECTUALS UNDER MARTIAL LAW AND BEYOND

Ironically, given the lack of intellectual power in the Solidarity period, the intellectual community has been the most devastated by the declaration of martial law and the policies that were imposed. For all Poles who had hopes for Solidarity and peaceful change in Poland, the imposition of martial law was a tragedy. For the intellectual community in Poland, it marked the end of their community and, for many, their professional lives as well. The changes that occurred in the fabric of intellectual life as a result of the policies of the martial law and postmartial law regime as well as the intellectuals' reaction to those policies have changed intellectual life in Poland more than anything since World War II. They have fragmented the intellectual community into bitterly divided units, something no event before was able to do.

In the initial period of martial law, large numbers of intellectuals were detained or sought for detention because of their work with Solidarity, their roles as spokesmen for professional groups, or their earlier involvement in opposition groups. Coupled with that, professional associations and journals were suspended. Journalists, actors, and academics had their workplaces closed down. They themselves were under attack. Yet the conditions for most intellectuals who were detained were far better than those for worker-activists. This, at least inadvertently, was an attempt to divide intellectuals and workers. And although many intellectuals could not return to work because their workplaces had been closed, even those who worked for Solidarity institutions and journals were paid throughout the suspension period. Other members of the intelligentsia who in their private lives may have supported Solidarity were untouched. Bureaucracies continued to function with only what appears to have been token intervention by military officers assigned as overseers. Finally, a comparatively tiny group from the intelligentsia joined the martial law regime.

Half a year after martial law was declared, most of the detained intellectuals were released. Some prominent journalists remained out of work or had less visible positions because they

no longer wanted to be identified as "regime" journalists or
refused to take or failed to pass political verification examinations
given by boards of the military, the party, and editorial personnel.[45] Actors and actresses and many other intellectuals
refused to appear on television as a sign of their opposition to
martial law. And the concession on academic autonomy won by
the now former rector of Warsaw University in the initial months
after martial law was lost; an initial verification of the academic
community was carried out in the summer of 1982.[46] For those
in major intellectual centers, this verification did not result in
a wholesale purge. In fact, many continued to teach what they
had taught in the period of freedom of Solidarity. For those
in less visible and protected institutions, there were political
purges in the verification process. And for all, the verifications
left a sword of Damocles hanging over their heads. The Association of Polish Journalists was formally disbanded and replaced
by a proregime rump organization, which still cannot draw
members.[47] Other intellectual organizations that had taken
the lead in moves for change under Solidarity were suspended.[48]

Intellectual discussion and writing began again in spite
of martial law. The initial intellectual protests over the declaration of martial law were supplemented by prognoses and recommendations for the future. The small minority of intellectuals,
like former opposition leader Jacek Kuron, began by pressing
for a national uprising to force the government's collapse.[49]
It appears only young students from universities and high
schools involved themselves in such violent actions. Instead,
large numbers openly expressed their disgust by symbolic
peaceful gestures like leaving their professions in the pursuit
of honest work, aiding those interned or out of work, and
turning in their party cards and creating an alternative cultural
life. Groups like Experience and the Future of Poland and others
writing in the reemerging underground press advocated peaceful
protest and the avoidance of violent action.[50] The tragedy in
their eyes and for the future of their role in Poland is that,
with the imposition of martial law and the continued control,
they are even less able to see a chartable course for Poland.
Their conclusion, based on the documents available in the West,
is that the possibility of reconciliation and reform is less likely
now than before. Again they find themselves observing,
criticizing, and recording events. For ultimately, in their
minds, they and their country are, as Jan Jozef Lipski said at
the First Congress of Polish Culture "like the Titanic preparing
to sink."[51]

Even with the suspension of martial law, the situation for
Polish intellectuals did not improve. Those who refused to be

coopted into working in their professions under the constraints of martial law did not return to their old posts. The restrictions governing intellectual life were not reduced. Many were even strengthened when martial law ended. Detainees were encouraged to leave Poland, but many intellectuals found they did not have the skills to get visas or employment in the West. And while workers who were Solidarity's top leaders were freed, KOR members and leaders were held for trial.

The most dramatic change, however, was the increased isolation of intellectuals from others in their own community and in the society. Before, childhood and personal ties had been strong enough to keep the intellectual community integrated across generational lines, political divisions, and professional affiliations. The defeat of Solidarity and the hopes of intellectuals left younger generations much more embittered than their elders. Close personal friendships were broken by disagreements over individual decisions to collaborate, opt out, or go into the opposition; and professionals were caught under different pressures—some able to function relatively normally and others under continued interference. Furthermore, while before there had been contact between some of the political elite, the intellectual establishment, and those who opposed the regime, the declaration of martial law severed most of these ties. Where before there had at least been political and personal interaction, the lines were now sharply and bitterly drawn, with both sides feeling themselves betrayed. And in spite of the fact that some intellectuals elected to take honest jobs in private industry or working-class occupations, the strict control of the regime over the media and the refusal of the regime to let dissenters operate freely redivided workers and intellectuals—especially since little was known about intellectual protests and boycotts outside of the major centers of Warsaw, Krakow, and Lublin.

The bureaucratic structures, on the other hand, were unchanged and even strengthened after martial law. But although many in the intelligentsia had their jobs protected by martial law, large numbers elected to leave their posts if they qualified for early retirement. This opened up positions that had been sought by those in the postwar baby-boom generation of university graduates—people who were both unreconciled to the defeat of Solidarity and in need of jobs to survive, establish themselves, and support their families. After all, whatever their personal beliefs, these young adults had little to fall back on and little hope for the future. As a result, the bureaucratic structures of the new regime will be peopled with those who work not out of support or even toleration of the regime but out of a sense of having no other option and little hope for a better future.

The behavior of Poland's intellectuals from the late 1970s on does not, on the surface, fit into traditional patterns of intellectual leadership of movements for change. The reasons for Polish intellectuals' inability to lead are not, however, related to their acceptance of the system. Instead, they are products of the structures inherent in communist systems which divide intellectuals from the rest of the society and increasingly set up bureaucratic commitments and controls. Finally, the emergence of spontaneous organizations in August 1980 and the rapid string of gains that followed were so fast that intellectuals were never able to formulate coherent and achievable platforms to guide popular actions. This was one of the causes of the radicalization of Solidarity. At the same time, the movement toward links between intellectuals and workers that was attempted by KOR and achieved in at least a limited degree under Solidarity was clearly seen by the political rulers as a major threat. The victories and defeats of what was initially a workers' movement also clearly triggered strong enough feelings among intellectuals that they were unwilling to "forgive and forget" as many had after earlier reform movements were defeated. So, while the regime sought to isolate those most identified with Solidarity and appeal to the rest of the intelligentsia, large numbers elected not to give their support at some personal cost to the martial law regime. In doing this, they erected clear and strong barriers between those who tolerate or support the regime and those who do not. Each group had begun to develop its own political and cultural milieu. And, ironically, given their failure to lead in 1980-81, the development of these individual worlds makes it increasingly unlikely that intellectuals will be able to lead change either from within or without the government establishment and Solidarity's membership in the future although clearly Poland's problems are not resolved.

NOTES

1. Sidney Verba and Norman Nye, Participation in America (New York: Harper & Row, 1972), Chapter 6; Gabriel Almond and Sidney Verba, Civic Culture (Princeton, New Jersey: Princeton University Press, 1963); Alex Inkles and David H. Smith, Becoming Modern (Cambridge, Massachusetts: Harvard University Press, 1974).

2. There is a mass of literature on the causes of revolution. Whether the focus is on ideology, leadership, social disharmony, or the failure of the existing government, the leadership of the intellectuals is a basic element in the models of revolutionary bases. No attempt here will, therefore, be made to list all of the relevant literature. Instead, readers are referred to William Overholt's comprehensive survey and critique of the literature on revolution, Revolution (Croton-on-Hudson: Hudson Institute, 1975) and to the classic references: Crane Brinton, The Anatomy of Revolution (New York: Random House, 1965); Samuel Huntington, Political Order in Changing Societies (New Haven: Yale University Press, 1968); and Chalmers Johnson, Revolutionary Change (Boston: Little Brown, 1966).

3. Jane L. Curry, The Black Book of Polish Censorship (New York: Random House, 1984).

4. Walter Connor, Socialism, Revolution and Mobility (New York: Columbia University Press, 1979), p. 121 and Poland Today (Armonk, New York: M. E. Sharpe, 1981), p. 94.

5. Interview data, 1979.

6. For a comparison of the Gomulka and Gierek methods and extent of control, see Jane L. Curry, The Media and Intra-Elite Communication: Organization and Control of the Media (Santa Monica, California: Rand Corporation, 1981).

7. Interview data, and unpublished survey data, 1979.

8. Given the lack of survey data for this group, more impressionistic evidence must be relied on. This group was unrepresented in the democratic opposition and its members did not support the Solidarity movement or disband in response to the liberalization around them (although in many factories, managers worked with Solidarity members and leaders to solve problems on a local level). Under Gierek, according to interviewees in Poland, the party and state bureaucracy were enlarged and given far greater control than ever before over regional affairs. Finally, the decentralization plans of Solidarity economists and nonaffiliated economic specialists would have been highly disadvantageous to this class.

9. Abraham Brumberg, "The Open Political Struggle in Poland," The New York Review of Books, Feb. 8, 1979, p. 32; see also annotations of Bratniak, No. 12-13 (September-October 1978) and of "A Pastoral Letter from the Polish Bishops on the Subject of Children's Rights" and of Rev. St. Malkowski, "The Church as a Place for Meetings of the Members of the Self-Defense Movement," Spotkania, No. 9 (October 1978), in Joanna Preibisz, Polish Dissident Thinking: An Annotated Bibliography (New York: Praeger, 1982).

10. Jacek Kuron and Karol Modzelewski, "An Open Letter to The Party," Revolutionary Marxist Students in Poland Speak Out (New York: 1968); Mieczyslaw Rakowski, "December 1970: The Turning Point," Canadian Slavonic Papers 15 (1973), especially p. 30.

11. The original text first appeared in Tydzien Polski (London), May 15, 1976, and was reprinted in P. Raina, Political Opposition in Poland, 1954-1977 (London: Poets and Painters Press, 1978), p. 469.

12. "'Robotnik' Editor on Unofficial Workers Movement," Labor Focus on Eastern Europe, Vol. 3, No. 5 (November 1979-January 1980):11-12.

13. See annotation of Jacek Kuron, "Towards Democracy," Krytyka, No. 3 (Winter 1978), in Preibisz, op. cit.

14. Ibid.

15. Brumberg, op. cit., p. 30.

16. See annotations of Gospodarz and ROPCiO documents on the Fourth National Conference of ROPCiO (December 9-10, 1978) in Preibisz, op. cit.

17. See annotations of Placowka, No. 5/1 (April 1979) and of ROPCiO documents on the Fourth National Conference of ROPCiO in Preibisz, op. cit.

18. Brumberg, op. cit., p. 33.

19. For more information see Adam Michnik, Kosciol, Lewica, Dialog (The Church and the Left—a Dialogue) (Paris: Instytut Literacki, 1977).

20. Association of Polish Students and Graduates in Exile, Dissent in Poland (London: Veritas Foundation Press, 1977), p. 181.

21. See annotations of KPN documents in Preibisz, op. cit.

22. See annotations of the Peasant Self-Defense Committees' documents in Preibisz, op. cit.

23. See annotation of Stanislaw Baranczak, "The Facade and Rear," Puls, No. 2 (March 1978), and of "The History of a Certain Preface," Puls, No. 6 (Spring 1979), in Preibisz, op. cit.

24. See annotations of Maria Bogusz, "Why Are We Together?" Bratniak, No. 12-13 (September-October 1978) and of "Experience and the Future" Report (1979), in Preibisz, op. cit.

25. For more information see Bogdan Madej, Polska w orbicie Zwiazku Radzieckiego (Poland in the Orbit of the Soviet Union) (Lublin: Biblioteka Spotkan, 1978).

26. Ibid.

27. See Raina, op. cit., p. 471.

28. Interview data, 1979. In Poland during this period, establishment intellectuals were quite familiar with the writings of their colleagues in the democratic opposition and often reported seeing them socially because of their common personal background, previous work, schooling, or family ties. In addition, there was an entire gray sector of individuals who had not declared themselves part of the opposition but who were blacklisted for their critical views. These individuals often served as further links between the two groups. A number of individuals involved in the Solidarity-government negotiations also reported that workers were concerned when their advisors were on personal terms with government negotiators.

29. See, for example, the Independent Students' Movement, which established itself autonomously from professors' groups and from Solidarity. In addition, one exemplary case was the splitting off of Wektory (a journal edited by young journalists and economists who in their advertising referred to themselves as the newest and most radical journalists) and Problemy Ekonomiczne (the regular journal of the Society of Polish Economists).

30. Interview data. See also, Andrzej Micewski, Wspolrzadzic Czy Nie Klamac? (Paris: Libella, 1978).

31. Interview data, 1975. (It is also clear from a survey of the literature of professional groups in the early 1970s that Gierek carefully courted them, increased investment initially in these areas, and played on their perception of him as a miracle worker from Silesia. It was also the case that in the 1960s Silesia had been far more prosperous than other areas in Poland and also more closed off so that, while these groups saw that their fellows were doing far better in Silesia than they were in other areas, they had no idea at what political cost.)

32. "Polityka Plan Rok 1969."

33. Interview data, 1979. For a full and strong critique of this period, see Miecayslaw Rakowski, Rzecspospolita na progu lat osiemdziesiatych (Warsaw: Panstwowy Instytut Wydawniczy, 1981), p. 234-53.

34. Curry, The Media and Intra-Elite and the Black Book.

35. Poland Today, p. 113.

36. Interview data, 1980.

37. Polityka, September 4, 1980, and Polacy 1981, manuscript, Institute of Sociology, University of Warsaw, 1982.

38. See Edward Lipinski's opening speech at the Solidarity Congress when he announced that, with the development of Solidarity, there was no longer any need for the Committee for Social Self-Defense (KSS "KOR") to continue to exist.

39. Report of Mandate Commission, Stenogram z obrad planarnych IX Nadzwyczajny Zjazd Polskiej Zjednoczonej Partii Robotniczej (Warsaw: Ksiazka i Wiedza, 1983), p. 144.

40. Polacy 1981 (Polish Academy of Sciences: Institute of Sociology, 1982).

41. Doswiadczenie i Przyszlosc, "Spoleczenstwo wobec kryzysu" (February 1981), reprinted in Kultura 5/404 (1981): 109-173.

42. "Censorship: Issues and Documents," Radio Free Europe, Situation Report 23 (December 20, 1980):35-48.

43. Interview data, 1982.

44. Interview data, 1983.

45. Current estimates from within the Polish journalism community are that approximately 2,000 of Poland's 6,000 journalists are out of work. Dokumenty SDP (underground compilation of SDP statements put out in the late spring, 1982).

46. Interview data, 1983.

47. Interview data, 1983.

48. These included the film makers, artists and writers' unions in the months preceding the lifting of martial law.

49. Jacek Kuron, "Open Letter," The Nation.

50. Doswiadczenie i Przyszlosc, "Polska Wobec Stanu Wojennego" (February-March 1982).

51. Transcript, First Congress of Polish Culture (December 1981).

10.

The Catholic Church
as a Political Actor

Dieter Bingen

BACKGROUND: CHURCH-STATE RELATIONS, 1944-80

The first government under the leadership of the Polish Workers' Party (PPR) guaranteed in the Lublin Manifesto of July 1944 freedom of conscience and the rights of the church.[1] On September 12, 1945, however, the Government of National Unity withdrew from the Concordat of 1925, thereby abolishing a number of longstanding privileges of the Catholic bishops. In the future the state's referent was the Constitution of 1952 (amended in 1976), which established a complete separation of church and state (Article 82.2) while guaranteeing freedom of religion and conscience (Articles 67.2, 81.1, and 82.1). According to the Catholic community state-church relations were thus not regulated by agreement. Many future conflicts arose as the Communist party and the church engaged in a struggle for the soul of Poland, both seeking historical legitimization as authentic representatives of the nation.

In 1946-47 the restriction of church life began with the nationalization of the Catholic press and the barring of Catholic publications from public libraries. The Seventh and Eighth Plenums of the Communist Party worsened relations between Communists and Catholics by providing for the censorship of church publications, the disbanding of youth and caritas associations, the elimination of church radio broadcasts, the nationalization of hospitals, and the confiscation of large amounts of church property.[2] The Communists sought an organizational monopoly in society through restrictions over the activities of all competing social groupings. The Catholic church, by its very mission and manner of operation, opposed such totalitarian claims and had the overwhelming support of the population. Still the party aimed at reducing the role of the church by restricting it to the performance of religious rituals and by artificially isolating it from the community.

The objective of dividing the clergy from the people proved unsuccessful. While on April 14, 1950, a compromise agreement between the government and the bishops was concluded,[3] it did not prevent further restrictions on the operations of the church. On February 9, 1953, a decree gave the state considerable supervisory rights over matters traditionally under church jurisdiction. This critical situation was symbolized by the arrest of the primate of Poland, Stefan Cardinal Wyszynski, on September 26, 1953 and his subsequent internment. Further measures endangered the mission of the church, including a ban on religious instruction in primary schools in January 1955.[4] In addition, there was an attempt to weaken the Catholic church from within. Patriotic priests acceptable to the state were pushed into key church positions, and the PAX movement of progressive Catholics was supported by the authorities.[5]

Destalinization and the rise of Wladyslaw Gomulka to the top of the Polish United Workers' Party (PUWP) altered in a favorable way the situation of the Catholic church. Cardinal Wyszynski was permitted to return to Warsaw on October 28, 1956. The agreement of December 8, 1956 restored religious instruction to the educational curriculum. The Catholic laity emerged as a domestic political influence, and the Catholic political group, ZNAK, was represented in the Sejm.[6]

In May 1957, Gomulka explained that he saw a need for coexistence between believers and nonbelievers and between the church and socialism.[7] The church used this situation to make itself heard again. However, after a brief period of relative openness, the authorities responded to the perceived Catholic challenge by calling on supporters of Polish atheism to struggle with the Catholic hierarchy for the domination of the national souls.[8] Soon thereafter, religious instruction in the schools was eliminated by the law of July 15, 1961. In response, the church built its own strong network of religious instruction, decisively contributing to Catholic education.[9]

Tensions between the state and the church mounted over the novena (1957-66) prepared by Primate Wyszynski to celebrate Poland's millennium.[10] Although the founding of the state and the Christianization of Poland coincided in 1966, ideological considerations prompted the state to try to separate official celebra-

tion of the millennium from the religious commemoration. The
church in turn charged that the government was engaged in
the falsification of history. In 1965, the state media had unleashed a propaganda campaign to discredit the Polish episcopate
on the pretext of a previous reconciliation letter of the Polish
bishops to the German episcopate.[12] Despite these efforts,
the millennium celebration of the church proved to be more
successful than the government-sponsored events. Thus, state
and church relations worsened and direct contact between the
state and the church was curbed.

The unrest of December 1970 prompted the new first secretary of the PUWP, Edward Gierek, to seek support from the
Catholic church to overcome political and economic difficulties.
On March 3, 1971, in a meeting between Cardinal Wyszynski
and the new premier, Piotr Jaroszewicz, the government chief
emphasized the need for a normalization of relations.[13] As a
sign of changing policy, in July 1971 the government announced
the transfer of previously confiscated German church property
to the Polish church. On June 28, 1972, the Vatican, in a
gesture of goodwill, permitted the establishment of Polish dioceses
in the formerly German western territories of Poland.[14]

Despite these developments, there were still outstanding
issues between the state and the church. Controversies arose
over the construction of churches, the state-planned introduction
of full-day schooling, and divergent stands on birth control.
The church increasingly stood up for human rights, legitimized
in its actions by the authorities' adherence to the Helsinki agreement. At the beginning of 1976, the church aligned itself with
the opposition by sending to the government two memorandums
that challenged controversial passages in the draft of a new
constitution.[15] This pressure forced the passage of weakened
amendments in regard to the leading role of the PUWP and to
the nature of Polish ties with the Soviet Union.[16] In the summer,
the church lent its public support to workers who were arrested,
released, and then harassed for their participation in disturbances
in Radom and Ursus.[17] At the same time, the church cautioned
moderation to the working class—as it had done in 1956 and 1970.

As symptoms of an economic, social, and moral crisis became more threatening after 1976, the authorities attempted to
strengthen the frequently announced, but minimally implemented,
dialogue with the Catholic church. In September 1976, party
chief Gierek called on the church to offer its cooperation with
the state.[18] On October 29, 1977, the first meeting between
Cardinal Wyszynski and Gierek occurred, with the primate raising
the possibility of closer collaboration in matters concerning the

welfare of the Polish people.[19] The short communique on the
meeting confirmed a common concern about the "unity of the
Poles" and "the well-being of the country."[20]

The price demanded by the church in exchange for normalization was outlined in countless pastoral letters and communiques of the bishops' conferences. The church hierarchy
cited a number of features that adversely affected the situation
and would have to be gradually eliminated, including the bellicose
atheism of the mass media, which endangered youth; state educational practices that contradicted national culture and Christian
morals; censorship of church news and Catholic magazines;
insufficient provision of goods; increasing corruption; a moral
and ethical crisis evident in falling work morale, alcoholism,
and disregard for the truth; and state family policy.[21]

Confronting a situation that seemed hopeless, the authorities
tried to bring the church to a more cooperative stance. The
leaders knew that in the event of a major social conflict, the
church would not hesitate to stand up for the rights of the
population. What the party wanted to prevent, under all circumstances, was the direct cooperation between the church
and the opposition. Thus, the episcopate, while supporting
the demands of the Committee for the Defense of Workers (KOR)
for ending repression, never explicitly identified itself with
their political ideas.[22] There can be little doubt that the church
sought to avoid the reputation of being a political opposition.
Its mission as a disseminator of holy writ forbade it from playing
the role of a political party.

The situation for the party and the state became more
confusing after the October 16, 1978 election of a Polish pope.
The choice of Karol Wojtyla as pope led to a genuine explosion
of national pride and self-confidence. The equation, Papiez-
Polak, had a fascinating attraction even for those social strata
that formerly had a detached attitude to the church. The election of a Polish pope was even more a national than a religious
event.[23]

The Polish leadership channeled national enthusiasm as
much as possible in a direction serviceable to the stabilization
of the system, to be crowned by a papal visit to Poland.[24] The
first official and semiofficial explanations indicated the essential
party viewpoints, with ideological emphasis upon the ways in
which improved state-church relations could assure social peace.[25]
Nonetheless, the party was on the defensive politically, given
Poland's membership in the Warsaw Pact, the dominant position
of the church, the economic crisis, and the strengthening of
the opposition. The selection of a Polish pope had added another

burden for the party leadership, complicating its already delicate situation.[26]

In domestic political discussions after October 1978, the party continued to emphasize the possibilities for cooperation and normalization in state-church relations. In the opinion of the Catholic hierarchy, however, a few more essentials were required for an authentic normalization: legal status for the Catholic church; elimination of censorship; the provision of church broadcast time on radio and television; religious instruction in the schools; and the abandonment of atheistic propaganda in school instruction.[27] For the party, the cooperation was to extend to respect for work, the fight against social-moral pathologies, cultivation of patriotism and national traditions, and fostering of the Polish ideals of tolerance.[28] As a result, an area of conflict developed between the state and the church, as well as the Vatican, over the timing of a papal visit to Poland. It took several months to produce a reasonable compromise, and in March 1979, it was agreed that the pope would visit in June.[29]

After the official announcement, the Polish media emphasized that the visit of the pope would not alter the principle of the leading role of the Communist Party and the lay character of the People's Republic. They cautioned against such illusions and suggested to the church that it refrain from interfering in sensitive social, economic, and political areas.[30] On the other hand, the Catholic forces hoped for improvements in the position of the church with respect to its societal and political demands.[31]

On a triumphant tour in Poland on June 2-10, 1979, the pope set new vistas for the domestic development of the country. The main themes in the speeches of John Paul II were the indestructible link between the Roman Catholic church and the Polish nation, respect for basic individual human and civil rights on the basis of the universal recognition of such ideals, and the strengthening of the spiritual unity of Europe on the basis of Christian values.[32] Through this emphasis on the human character of Catholic teachings, the pope internationalized the national and religious demands of the Polish church. The church thus became less assailable in a domestic political sense. Moreover, Christian humanism had more of a stimulating, rather than a quieting, effect in Poland. In addition, the papal messages communicated a Christian-Slavic messianism, which implied the need for uniting all of Europe despite the existing bloc structure.[33] Cardinal Wyszynski had already expressed such European-Christian sentiments during the visit of a delegation of the Polish bishops to West Germany in September 1978.[34] With these messages, the Polish pope raised the self-confidence of his countrymen, inspiring a new will for assertion and courage.[35] The communist authorities were in a weakened position and were ill-prepared to deal with a more demanding and self-confident society. The papal election and visit were milestones that accelerated the erosion of the domestic political power base of the PUWP, which had clearly lost the struggle for the Polish soul.

Under existing conditions (membership of Poland in the socialist bloc), however, the destruction of the PUWP or its incapability to act were never satisfactory objectives for the church. The church consistently acted in circumspect ways while supporting calls for universal human and civil rights, democratization, and personal freedom.[36] It certainly sympathized with the emerging opposition movement, but necessarily disassociated itself from direct political challenges to state power that could imperil its own future status in the socialist order. The strike movement in August 1980 was a challenge for the church as well. A new, independent, sociopolitical actor was born.

Despite the self-defined limitations for the large majority of the population, the church had become the sole, independent, large organization that could oppose the power of the PUWP—or at least act as a lobbyist for the interests of that majority. The various discussion groups and opposition movements actually affected only those citizens who were actively engaged in politics. However in the late 1970s, perceptions of mutual interest developed among the autonomous societal groups on the basis of humanistic, moralistic, and patriotic values propagated by the opposition and the church.[37] This was a consequence of the party leadership's failure to integrate society into the desired pattern. Thus while the church did not see itself as a political power, it became de facto a political force that asserted its influence in a moderate way. In a sense, the church and its symbols provided a repository for collective resistance against an incapable party leadership and government, offering moral strength in the period prior to the renewal (odnowa). For example, on the ninth anniversary of the bloody workers' unrest in Gdansk (December 17, 1979), the Polish episcopate expressed its support for opposition demonstrators who were arrested. The church emphasized that its position was based on the principle that freedom of speech should be guaranteed for all citizens, whatever their beliefs.[38]

THE CHURCH AND THE POLISH SUMMER OF 1980

When the massive strikes broke out on the Baltic coast in August 1980, the episcopate was surprised by the strength of

the workers' protests. In the first days of the strikes in Gdansk
and Szczecin, the episcopate avoided taking a clear stand on
the side of the strike committees (MKS) and all of their demands.
The church generally refrained from making official statements
during the first week of the strike on the Baltic coast. The
primate himself took no direct position on the strikes while
attending religious festivities in Czestochowa (August 15).[39]
On the other hand, he commented explicitly and favorably on
the August 1920 victory of Pilsudski's Polish Army over the
Red Army, stating that God had helped the fatherland when
its freedom had been threatened.[40] A sermon with such content
at that sensitive moment exemplified the raison d'état philosophy
of the Polish church. The church was manifesting its concern
for the independence and sovereignty of the Polish nation and
state at the precise moment when Polish workers carrying the
cross were devotedly demanding concrete freedoms for themselves, society, and the church. The Catholic church, viewing
itself as the guarantor of the independence of the Polish nation,
was highly sensitive to the decay of state authority and seemed
more fearful of outside interference than perhaps was justified
in those August days. Cardinal Wyszynski's conduct revealed
the complicated relationship of the church with the state and
exposed in addition a patriarchal attitude toward society.

While church behavior may not have been homogeneous in
the perceptions of the strikers, there is little doubt that they
considered the church and their Catholic beliefs as the strongest
bulwarks of support in their confrontation with state power.[41]
Many displayed their absolute faith in the church, the pope,
and the nation by hanging pictures of the pope and the madonna
on factory doors, by regularly holding masses and engaging in
confessions, by singing church songs, and by calling for spiritual
assistance. The strikers awaited a principled explanation from
the primate. This came in the primate's sober sermon of
August 17, when he spoke out for freedom of speech in Poland
and emphasized that the state could not remain indifferent to
the workers' demands for societal, moral, economic, and cultural
rights. At the same time, he argued that in order for quiet
and balance to prevail, diligent work and thrift would be necessary.[42] The address could not be understood as unqualified
support for and solidarity with the workers. In any case, it
was not broadcast in Poland, but was transmitted by Radio
Vatican. On August 20, the pope spoke for the first time, re-
emphasizing the primate's position.[43] Bishop Kaczmarek of
Gdansk, however, expressed his solidarity with the goals of
the MKS during a visit to striking workers at the Lenin Shipyard.

He stated that, contrary to the statements of the government, the MKS was the authentic representative of the striking workers--a position intended to calm the apparently suspicious primate. [44] On the basis of these statements, and considering the pastoral solidarity of the priests who were present at the shipyards, one can assume that there were differences of opinion within the Polish Bishops' Conference over conduct toward the strike movement. According to some observers, the primate did not fully perceive the realities of the situation, which became even more evident in his sermon of August 26.

The workers had high expectations that the primate would offer explicit support for their cause in his August 26 sermon at Czestochowa. However, while the primate spoke at great length in his fifty-minute address about the value of the family and work in Polish society, he linked his sympathy with the goals of the workers with a warning appeal for moderation. [45] In many Catholic circles disappointment was expressed toward the cardinal who normally was so brave, but who here seemed hesitant and wavering. Since the sermon could be interpreted by many Poles as a call for the workers to return to work, the strikers were let down, but did not retreat from their challenge. [46] Perceiving a negative reaction to the sermon, the Polish Bishops' Conference felt compelled to point out on August 28 that they had expressly confirmed their support for the workers' demands in their own communique of August 26. [47] The state mass media were accused of having disguised critical aspects of the primate's statements. They reproduced Cardinal Wyszynski's speech in a shortened form and concealed the church's condemnations of the state's atheist propaganda and its insistence upon Poland's sovereignty. [48]

Considering the well-known heterogeneous composition of the MKS, one positive effect of the church's call for moderation was the internal strengthening of the wing that was ready to compromise with the state and wanted to avoid a total confrontation based on accusations of antisocialist behavior. On August 27-28, Cardinal Wyszynski sent Professor Romuald Kukolowicz as his personal representative to the Politburo. The emissary offered to mediate between the government commission and the Gdansk strike committee. Having achieved the consent of the party leadership, Kukolowicz flew to Gdansk with the Catholic lawyers Andrzej Wielowiejski and Andrzej Swiecicki to seek to influence the responsible actors. [49] Catholic intellectuals also exercised a constructive influence as expert advisors to the Gdansk strike committee (especially Tadeusz Mazowiecki, the chief editor of the Catholic monthly magazine,

Wiez, and later chief editor of the first national union newspaper, Tygodnik Solidarnosc, who served as a legal advisor to the MKS).

The results confirmed the value of the patience and the prudence of both the strikers and the state. In the Gdansk and Szczecin agreements, two demands were achieved that were especially important to the church: access to the state mass media and a limitation on censorship. In the Gdansk agreement, point three stated that an administrative law would be adopted delineating what items could be published and what subjects would be subject to censorship.[50] The point guaranteeing church access to the mass media conveyed a commitment to fair state regulation of administrative and organizational matters affecting religious communities. The government assured that there would be radio broadcasts of the Sunday mass within the framework of an agreement that would be concluded with the episcopate at a later date.[51] In the Szczecin agreement, wider access of the Catholic church to the mass media was talked about only in a general vein.[52]

The position and attitude of the primate and the episcopate demonstrated that the church had remained a calculating opponent of the party and government during the revolutionary situation of summer 1980. This description applies mainly to the rather socially and politically conservative majority of the episcopate. Many younger priests, however, put themselves unconditionally in solidarity with the demands of the independent social forces without fully recognizing the elements of raison d'état taken into account by the primate-led episcopate. The measured position of the primate brought him the thanks of the new first secretary of the PUWP, Stanislaw Kania, who had been responsible for years for relations between the church and the state and party.[53] Thus, the events of August 1980 had considerably strengthened the position of the church in its relations with the state.

On the other hand, the church (especially the primate) had not definitely gained in its relations with workers. For a short time, the danger existed that the moral authority of the church as an institution would suffer a substantial loss. Cardinal Wyszynski had certainly underestimated the limits of party maneuverability, as well as the authority of a unified, authentically representative organization of the working class in its dealings with the Communist Party. At the spiritual breakfast of the primate and the strike leadership held on September 7, Wyszynski demonstrated some interest in clarifying the situation and in clearing up misunderstandings.[54] Underlying this

development was the fact that, for the first time, the church
had not come forward as the sole representative of the interests
of the entire nation toward the party. Rather, for the first
time, the working class had stood up in the interest of the
nation, while retaining a full consciousness and appreciation of
national sentiments toward Catholicism and the rights of the
church. It is worth mentioning here that despite certain doubts
that arose over the concrete positions of church officials, the
Catholic church, with its idolized pope reflecting the values of
the nation, remained a central symbol and source of working-
class unity and of the justness of the workers' cause.

After the summer events of 1980, it seemed that in the
long-run developments could lead to a weakening of the role
of the church, which had found a competitor in the unified,
well-organized, disciplined, and mature working class. If this
novel Polish state of affairs had persisted, the influence of the
church over the working class might have diminished. After
all, the philosophy of the church and its patriarchal role—at
least under the leadership of the primate—did not place it
unconditionally on the side of an organized working class with
respect to concrete societal and political questions affecting a
modern industrial society. However, after December 1981 the
party's renewed policy of repression in the work place and in
society served to forge new links between the population and
the church.

THE CHURCH IN THE POST-AUGUST 1980 CRISIS

Developments in Poland after August 1980, including
mounting criticism and self-accusations within the PUWP and
party-controlled mass organizations, confirmed the warning
words of the bishops that had been ignored for years by party
and state officials. The church did offer to cooperate in solving
basic national questions, especially the catastrophic economic
situation. Its contribution was primarily that of a fire brigade
in situations that threatened dangerous confrontations. When
the tests of power between the new independent union Solidarnosc
and the government seemed to lock into a stalemate, or when
one of the two competing organizations intended to marshall its
forces, the Catholic church intervened. It served as a mediating
third actor in the new three-cornered party/state-Solidarity-
church maneuverings. In doing so, the church was always
concerned with the fate of the nation. It tried to represent
community and transcendental values and to avoid the pursuit

of direct political power, thus freeing itself from the specific
political machinations in which both the PUWP and the new union
engaged. The church knew what it could lose if it became too
directly and deeply involved in the existent political game.

The weekly Sunday radio broadcasts of religious services,
beginning on September 21, 1980, represented the first major
success of the church in the post-August 1980 period.[55] The
workers had cleared the way for the Catholic church in this
area by including in their catalogue of demands in Gdansk and
Szczecin the objective of widened church access to the mass
media.

The Polish Bishops' Conference expressly thanked the
workers for their efforts in opening up the mass media at their
October 15-16 meeting. The conference promised its continued
moral support for the working class, but warned Solidarity
that the limits of party/state tolerance were unknown and that
a moderate approach should be followed given outside pressures
by other socialist states.[56]

On September 24, 1980, following a long period of inactivity,
the episcopate and the government met in a common commission
under the chairmanship of Krakow Cardinal Macharski and Vice-
Premier Barcikowski to discuss questions of mutual interest.[57]
In the following months their negotiations led to the realization
of important church demands: the improved position of diocese
seminaries, the freeing of members of seminaries from military
service obligations, increased circulation of the church press,
permission to import and distribute an uncensored Polish edition
of Osservatore Romano (120,000 copies), new consideration of
an assured legal status for the church, and discussion of the
nature of religious care and control in youth camps.[58]

After the founding of Solidarity, the Polish party leadership considered it important for the Catholic church to maintain
a definite influence over union policy. The party, perceiving
its own weakened position in society, saw the Church as a
counterbalance to the non-Leninist socialist opposition it feared
would dominate Solidarity (particularly the activists of KSS
"KOR"). Since the party itself had lost direct influence over
the masses, it needed an intermediary. The explicit influence
of the church was considered a lesser evil than the danger
that Solidarity might become a socialist or Christian opposition.
The damage that might be incurred by a growing political role
for the church was considered to be limited and calculable,
whereas KSS "KOR" activists within Solidarity were seen as
posing major risks. As a result of this complicated situation,
on October 21, 1980 the new party chief, Kania, held his first

meeting with Cardinal Wyszynski.[59] Kania, it appears, requested that the primate exercise a moderating influence on the unions and raised the possibility of further church cooperation with the state. The discussions also surely concerned whether the pope could assist in achieving a settlement in Poland. The official communique underscored that the talks dealt with important matters affecting domestic peace and development. It was stressed that cooperation between the church and the state would serve national interests, furthering the welfare and the security of the country.[60] Immediately following the meeting, Wyszynski flew to Rome for a visit that lasted more than two weeks. He and numerous Polish bishops engaged in detailed discussions with the pope about the events in Poland.[61]

Following the delayed registration of Solidarity on November 10, 1980, Lech Walesa and key leaders of the union were received by Cardinal Wyszynski. In keeping with church policies adhered to by the primate and the episcopate since the Poznan workers' revolt of 1956, Wyszynski warned the unionists to maintain a proper hierarchy of values in their activities: the nation should be thought of as the first priority, then society, then the state, and finally the broad sphere of human labor.[62]

The unveiling of the memorial for the victims of the 1970 workers' unrest in Gdansk on December 16, 1980 constituted one symbol of the political role of the Catholic church during the process of renewal. At the commemorative ceremonies, a holy mass was held with Cardinal Macharski officiating (representing the ill primate), assisted by Bishops Dabrowski (Warsaw), Kaczmarek (Gdansk), and Glemp (Olsztyn). The Polish head of state, Professor Henryk Jablonski, as well as leading representatives of the PUWP were present. The hundreds of thousands attending the ceremonies listened to a message from the primate and a telegram from the pope.[63] The religious content of the celebration guaranteed a quiet and dignified atmosphere on the emotional occasion. Such a religious-patriotic channeling of the feelings of the masses was surely in the interests of the party and state organs, which lived in fear of hostile political demonstrations. The momentous day of commemoration could have offered a situation of confrontation. Instead, the mediating church, the new independent unions, and the governing party realized the necessity for controlling emotional eruptions and avoiding politically disruptive force. During the course of 1981 there were several more occasions when religious rites were utilized to discipline the masses at nationally and politically significant memorial celebrations (for example, June 28, 1981 in Poznan and July 10, 1981 in Lublin). In these cases, the

party considered the political influence of the Catholic church
a lesser evil than the potential danger of opposition political
demonstrations.

Shortly before the emotional commemoration on the Baltic
coast, the Bishops' Conference had warned against activities
that could expose Poland to threats to its freedom. After this
conference, a representative of the episcopate, Alojzy Orszulik,
directly criticized the KSS "KOR" activist Jacek Kuron.
Orszulik's utterances certainly reflected concern on the part
of the episcopate over socialist tendencies in the union. At
the same time, his remarks were disapprovingly received by
leading figures of Catholic lay organizations. The incident
surely gave evidence of tensions within the church over the
political influence of KSS "KOR" activists in the Solidarity
union.[64]

In the following months, the Catholic church acted repeatedly as a fire brigade in order to prevent threatening
confrontations between the independent societal forces led by
Solidarity and the officials. The intervention of the church in
the winter of 1981 brought the cessation of some prolonged
local strikes and new agreements (e.g., those in Ustrzyki
Dolne and Jelenia Gora). The prevention of an announced
nationwide general strike following the events in Bydgoszcz
(March 19, 1981) was achieved largely due to the direct intervention of Primate Wyszynski. In that case, Premier Wojciech
Jaruzelski met with the critically ill cardinal at the primate's
residence.[65] Credit can also be assigned to the primate for
the official recognition of the independent union of private
farmers in April 1981.[66] In the first months of 1981, it must
also be noted that Lech Walesa (the then undisputed leader of
Solidarity) was very receptive to the moderate counsel of
Cardinal Wyszynski. The independent trade union movement
maintained a basically positive stance toward the church and
the influence of the church on Solidarity was substantial—
a situation that changed dramatically during the summer of 1981
when political opposition to the regime intensified.

As the opposition mounted, the state and party became
increasingly concerned with the episcopate's authority over
society, viewing it as a moderating influence. The church did
seek to calm tensions, as was indicated in an April 1981 commentary by the chief editor of the influential Catholic newspaper
Tygodnik Powszechny: "Collectively, Polish society is fully
engaged on the side of Solidarity in the struggle for a better
republic. However, the overwhelming majority of society
expects Solidarity to maintain moderation and judgment, as it
had done up to now."[67] By taking such positions, the Catholic

church consciously exposed itself to the danger of being both used by the authorities and misunderstood by the population. The course of events in spring 1981, however, documented that the church could still temporarily count on youth and the working class. During the first six months of 1981, the church was at the high mark of its political influence and held the most significant national and moral authority. Cardinal Wyszynski and Pope John Paul II were the symbols of its enormous emanation.

The acknowledged societal role of the Catholic church during the period of renewal became clear, for example, on May 3, 1981, when the historic Constitution of 1791 was officially commemorated for the first time since World War II. Since this occasion coincided with the religious holiday for Mary, Queen of the Poles, church services took place throughout the country. Thus, the borders between the religious and political roles of the church were blurred. For example, religious, national, and political symbols intermingled in the celebration of the May 3 Constitution held in the Holy Cross Church in the center of Warsaw.[68] The 190th anniversary of the first constitution of Poland was commemorated with a concert of spiritual music. Attentive observers noted that the walls and columns of the baroque church contained memorials for Wladyslaw Reymont, the honored writer of national epics and winner of the Nobel Prize, as well as the poet Juliusz Slowacki, a leading Polish romanticist who hailed the triumphal march of Slavic Catholicism. At the entrance of the Holy Cross Church, Solidarity members distributed the text of the May Constitution of 1791,[69] which guaranteed essential citizens' freedoms and provided for a constitutional order designed to lead the country out of domestic decay and dependence on its neighbors. At the beginning of the celebration in the overcrowded church, well-known personalities read out the most important articles of the constitution. Thus, in a house of God, the major concepts of the renewal process (truth, dignity, equality, and justice) were emphasized. The blending of political, social, and spiritual values so evident since August 1980 were once again evident.

SHOCKS IN POLAND: THE ASSASSINATION
ATTEMPT AGAINST THE POPE AND THE
DEATH OF THE PRIMATE

Just a few days later, an assassination attempt against John Paul II took place in Rome. The May 13, 1981 assault on his life released a spontaneous and widespread outcry among believers and nonbelievers in Poland. Throughout the population a sudden, common depression was noticeable—a symptom of the psychologically unstable situation in the country that had developed during the spring. The delirium of the renewal had by no means passed, but the euphoria was becoming uncertain. Solidarity was certainly completely integrated in the societal organism and had become a permanent (or so it seemed) factor in sociopolitical life, but the government and party seemed paralyzed in the face of the heavy pressure emanating from all sides—both domestic and external. The government employed tactics that postponed the basic decisions required for economic improvement. The party licked its own wounds, and contended with the union unnecessarily over many secondary issues. No one knew how the situation would unfold. "Power lies in the streets, but no one picks it up" was a common saying in Warsaw during the spring of 1981.

In this unstable atmosphere, the pope provided spiritual strength. For many, he was the sole helper for a needy Poland. Only the pope could still extend his protective hand over the country—or so thought many common people. Even among some of the intelligentsia, a belief in miracles promised the only exit out of the seemingly hopeless situation. Hadn't the pope aroused his country from resignation and lack of courage and renewed perspectives with his June 2, 1979 speech in Warsaw? "May your spirit descend and renew the face of the earth—of this earth!" Wouldn't he also help Poland in this extremely difficult situation of renewal? There were many irrational yet powerful reflections that moved the people of Poland at this time. People believed Rome could still help Poland, but the assassination attempt constituted a tremendous shock. Would all hope fade away with the deliverer of this hope near death? The disgust and terror generated by the assassination attempt on the champion of universal values, the personification of good and humanity, and the dedicated servant of Poland and people universally evoked a true unity within the nation. Polish state television had to adapt to this mood and immediately reported authentic and uncensored news surrounding the assassination attempt, including direct broadcasts from Rome and responses throughout Poland. The coverage emanated from overcrowded churches as well as interviews from the streets of Warsaw giving citizens' reactions to the events in Rome. There was even a broadcast of a previously censored film report about the pope's spiritual background and his work in Poland.[70]

Two weeks later on May 28, 1981, the primate died. Wyszynski, who had for over three decades held the fate of

the Catholic church in his hands, had already become a myth.
In the obituaries of the Polish press, he was called a "great
statesman"[71]—a belated appreciation of the political role of the
church in socialist Poland. On Warsaw's Victory Place, on
May 31, 1981, a gigantic wooden cross and a crowd of some
hundred thousand accompanied Cardinal Wyszynski on his final
journey. His coffin stood on a catafalque at the foot of an altar
visible to all bystanders. Never before had Poland seen so
many cardinals publicly assembled. On the way to St. John's
Cathedral where he found his final resting place, he was accompanied by Chairman of the Council of State Jablonski, Deputy
Premiers Rakowski and Ozdowski, Foreign Minister Czyrek, and
other Central Committee members of the PUWP. The Solidarity
union delegation composed of Walesa, Anna Walentynowicz,
Andrzej Gwiazda, Bogdan Lis, and other union leaders followed
the state leadership. At the crypt, the head of state took his
leave with a bow before the coffin, while the Deputy Premier
Ozdowski, member of the Catholic deputies' group PZKS, which
grew out of the neo-Znak group, kissed the primate's coffin
and knelt before it. The scenes were broadcast by Polish television to millions of Polish households. Even the Communist
Party newspapers hailed Stefan Wyszynski as the great Polish
statesman of the post-World War II period.

THE CHURCH FAILS TO PREVENT CONFRONTATION

In the period immediately following the death of the primate,
it became increasingly evident that conflict over the road to
renewal remained undiminished despite the recent manifestations
of national unanimity. With the passage of time, it became
clearer that the crisis was not solely a Polish matter, but that
developments were being observed by the socialist neighbors,
especially the Soviet Union, with ever-growing mistrust and
impatience. Moscow expected that the Polish comrades would
undertake strong measures to retain the power of the party
and liquidate the dual leadership (party-Solidarity). A struggle
for power of a basic nature was in progress in Poland. The
primate had been able to temper the intensity of this struggle
for a short time, but he could not prevent the confrontation.
Despite the diminishing means of the church to moderate
conflict, it remained a highly sought counselor in difficult
situations concerning the party and the unions. This was
certainly the case on June 5, 1981, when the Central Committee
of the PUWP received a critical letter from the Communist Party

of the Soviet Union, in which Party Chief Kania and Premier Jaruzelski were reproached for failing to keep the situation under control.[72] The Soviets called for radical change, even suggesting the appointment of new people at the top of party and governmental ranks. On this same day, a delegate of the episcopate was invited to consult members of the Central Committee. One member informed him of the content of the letter from Moscow, conveyed a sense of helplessness on the part of the party leadership, and requested advice.[73] The complicated developments in Poland are forcefully documented by this party request for assistance addressed to the Polish episcopate. Of course, the Catholic church itself had no surefire solution to the existing situation, but that is a different matter.

Still, at the end of May, the pope had made a gesture intended to ease tensions by appealing to the government and to Solidarity for thirty days of mourning and national meditation.[74] This did not produce substantial effects. Given the critical situation in Poland, the vacancy in the seat of the primate seemed to last a long time. These were dangerous weeks, especially because the pope, the most influential advocate of renewal in Poland, was handicapped after the assassination attempt. The new primate, Jozef Glemp, decided to continue to pursue a course of mediation. He was conscious that the temporary political role of the church stemmed from a situation in the country in which state power failed to find any common language with society.[75]

The state immediately indicated that it sought and needed the cooperation of the new primate. Just one day after his installation in office (July 10, 1981), a discussion between Glemp and Jaruzelski took place.[76] The episcopate became more active in issuing calls for moderation on all sides. On August 13, 1981, it warned about attempts "to use growing tensions for political fights" and about "hate and revenge."[77] On August 26, in a sermon at Czestochowa, Primate Glemp complained directly about the increasing polarization in the nation and attributed responsibility for the strained situation to both sides, while indicating the state positions were somewhat more blameworthy.[78] His critical estimation of the political situation caused Glemp to travel personally to the Solidarity congress in Gdansk. From the Cathedral of Oliwa on September 5, 1981, he called on the union people to make sacrifices and to show their readiness to promote peace.[79] However, the tone of the congress, including the demand for free elections, the "Appeal to the People of Eastern Europe," and the political stridency of the Solidarity program signaled that church influ-

ence over the union movement was diminishing.[80] Nevertheless,
the party leadership sought the support of the Catholic church
in moderating or disciplining the union. The changing substance
of the party approach since September was indicated by the
call for a front of national understanding—as a great coalition
of Communists and Catholics. Was this to be in terms of actual
governing or just greater consultation—or in terms of a three-
sided alliance of party, church, and Solidarity that would involve
the direct participation of the church in politics? Or the establishment of a Christian Democratic Party, in which the political
ambitions of Solidarity could also be incorporated and moderated?

Primate Glemp, who spent the period of October 16-21 in
Rome, agreed with the pope that the church, whatever its
political role, was not permitted to engage in politics directly
and permanently.[81] At a meeting with Premier Jaruzelski on
October 21, he agreed, therefore, only to a very general common
announcement that the "growing difficulties make the formation
of a wide platform of national understanding absolutely necessary."[82] The first mutual meeting of Glemp, Walesa, and
Jaruzelski on November 4, however, brought no reconciliation
of viewpoints.[83] The radicalization of both sides proceeded
further in November. On November 28, the Sixth Plenum of
the Central Committee of the PUWP decided to authorize the
PUWP deputies' group in the Sejm to introduce a law regarding
extraordinary measures (among other things, forbidding strikes).
On the strength of that, the presidium of Solidarity threatened
a general strike on December 3. Against the objections of its
church advisors, on December 12, 1981 the union announced
the scheduling of December 17 as a day of national protests and
demanded a referendum about confidence in the government
and the possibility of holding free elections.[84]

Primate Glemp had decided on December 7 to intervene
directly in the emerging political crisis—an unprecedented event.
In a letter, he warned the parties, the Sejm, and Premier
Jaruzelski that providing special authority to the government
through an emergency law "would poison the atmosphere" and
would provoke Solidarity "to a general strike."[85] Glemp's intervention produced no effects. On December 13, 1981, martial
law was imposed on the Polish nation.

THE CATHOLIC CHURCH AND THE STATE OF WAR

On the morning of December 13, a member of the PUWP
leadership informed Primate Glemp of the state of war. He pro-

tested against the decision. On the same day, Glemp delivered
a sermon in Warsaw in which he warned the government and
society about the dangers of a bloodletting.[86] His appeal to
moderation apparently contributed to the avoidance of major
violence.

The Main Council of the Polish Bishops' Conference decided
on December 15, 1981 to issue a message to the nation to be
read in all parishes.[87] The message had a condemnatory tone
toward the state measures, including its use of force. When
miners were subsequently killed in the Wujek mine during a
police action against a protest strike, the primate curtailed
the reading of this message, hoping that it would prevent
further bloodshed. This decision was criticized by elements
of the population who hoped for a strong antigovernment stand
by the church.[88]

Misunderstandings by the public also arose over the radio
sermon Primate Glemp delivered on January 24, 1982.[89] In the
sermon, he spoke out against the participation of priests in the
Committees for National Salvation supported by the ruling
military council. At the same time, however, he confirmed
that there were possibilities for laymen to participate in an
authentic public life. The primate's reservations toward the
committees were expressed rather hazily, providing an opportunity for exploitation by the state propaganda organs.[90]
Many segments of the public were furious, knowing that the
church was on the side of Solidarity, not the committees initiated
by the leadership.

On the very day after the imposition of martial law, the
church pleaded for Solidarity officials and representatives.
For example, the church proposed that the interned Lech Walesa
be freed, at which time he would be lodged in a domicile belong-
ing to the church. In that setting, he could meet with the legal
advisors of Solidarity who were still not interned, as well as
with members of the union's presidium and regional commissions
whose freedom was being energetically sought by the church.
The leadership organs of Solidarity would then be in a position
to work out proposals for discussions with the government and
to consider the future of the union. The government initially
showed some interest in this proposal and did permit the church
to provide for the spiritual care of Walesa and of other internees.[91]

Yet weeks passed and Walesa was not freed. First a rumor
campaign began, followed by a full-fledged press effort, to
claim that Walesa was inflexible and arrogant. He was charged
with making unreasonable demands. Seeking to counteract that

image, Walesa presented a written explanation to a representative of the church on January 17, 1982, in which he said: "I am ready to take up discussions without any previous conditions on the basis which has been agreed upon by representatives of the church and state."[92]

In subsequent weeks, the authorities started a press campaign against Solidarity. It was obvious that they wanted no revival of Solidarity. The interventions by the church had had no success other than bringing some humanitarian compromises. Nonetheless, the church did not give up its efforts for Solidarity. The bishops once again demanded the reactivation of the independent union in a communique following the February 25-26 meeting of the Polish episcopate.[93] At the same time, the church sought to overcome the deep split in the Polish nation and to build a bridge of understanding. This was the purpose of a new thrust by the primate that was undertaken in the form of theses for the building of a new dialogue. The proposals certainly did not come directly from the primate, but emanated from the Social Council of Catholic Laymen. This council was formed after December 13 at the initiative of Glemp and was initially considered an organization of voluntary assistance for the persecuted workers, farmers, and intellectuals. Somewhat later, it evolved into a consultative organ for the primate. The chairman of the council, the senior figure among independent Catholics and professor of law emeritus, Stanislaw Stomma, was a long-time leader of the Catholic group ZNAK in the Polish Sejm. Former Catholic expert advisors of Solidarity such as Kukolowicz, Wielowiejski, and Micewski also were leading members of the council.

On April 5, 1982, they issued their theses composed of programmatic principles designed to guide Poland out of its dead end.[94] They adopted the position that the Catholic church was, under existing conditions, the sole institution capable of viewing the situation objectively. They stressed that great hopes for the renewal of political and social life had been awakened in Poland since August 1980, but that the tragedy of martial law threatened a national decline. Therefore, it would be unquestionably necessary to seek new perspectives and motivating forces for the nation. A new search for understanding would be essential, but one that would assure the validity and the fulfillment of all agreements concluded from August 1980 on.

The authors emphasized that Jaruzelski himself, in his explanation of martial law on December 13, 1981 and in his address to the Sejm on January 25, 1982, conceded an appropriate aware-

ness of the need for fulfillment of such existing agreements.
Such a step, the council emphasized, would also strengthen
the credibility of state power. The people of Poland would
have to be assured that they would be integrally involved in
policymaking. The fulfillment of the interrupted or abandoned
reforms would, of course, have to take into consideration the
geopolitical situation of the Polish state and its existing alliances.
But social peace among citizens could only be established in
the form of cooperation between the leading state powers and
the representatives of relevant societal groupings. The representation of the workers and their organizations, the farmer's
union, scientific and cultural associations, and of youth and
student organizations would be essential.

The council further emphasized that domestic peace could
only be maintained if the internees were freed, an amnesty
granted, and the suspended organizations permitted to operate
once again. Media policy would have to be fundamentally
changed. Almost three chapters of the theses were devoted
to the union question. The authors emphasized that union
pluralism should once again be established and demanded that
Solidarity be given back its rights in accordance with signed
agreements. They recognized that a Solidarity of the future
would certainly have to be nonpolitical and to act in line with
the papal encyclical Laborem exercens. The proposals of the
government about the role of the unions could create a certain
sense of helplessness. Certainly the problem of the role of
unions would have to be solved quickly and constructively.
Thus, Solidarity also would have to scrutinize its previous role
and activities in a self-critical manner. The council held that
the readiness to do so was already present in many unions.
Solidarity would have to understand that despite provocations
from the authorities and the worsening economic conditions, it
also had made mistakes that led to the weakening of state power
and to the development of mistrust on the side of members of
Poland's alliance. In the conclusion, the hope was expressed
that these theses would be discussed with good intentions by
all of those to whom they were addressed and by all who could
make a constructive contribution to overcoming the tragic
situation.

Contrary to the hopes of the social council and of the
episcopate, the theses were not directly discussed in the media
and there was no forthcoming official reaction to the proposals.
On the other hand, the military government refrained from
mounting a frontal attack on the church. On April 25, 1982,
Jaruzelski and Glemp met to discuss the "continuing, compli-

cated situation."[95] At this time, the government stressed that
it desired to continue a constructive dialogue between the state
and the church.

Just a few days earlier, Deputy Prime Minister Ozdowski
received the chief editors of Catholic daily newspapers and
magazines that were still cooperating with the government in
order to underline the strong desire of the government to
cooperate with the church to overcome the crisis, especially
with regard to questions concerning "the moral renewal of
society and the family."[96] On April 27, Minister Jerzy Kuberski,
the head of the office for religious affairs, met with representatives of the committees for national salvation, the PUWP, the
noncommunist political parties, and PAX to outline the government's perspectives on further collaboration with the Catholic
church.[97] Kuberski did not dwell on Solidarity, but on the
committees whose support he was seeking to gain from the
church. He emphasized the constitutional principles of freedom
of belief, separation of church and state, and emphasized that
both the church and the state share a common task: to secure
social peace in the country. He called on the church to support
efforts aimed at normalization in accordance with its own moral
authority and educational tasks. Kuberski's message stressed
the necessity for mutual respect of national unity by the state
and church.

In the meantime, a continuous struggle for power was
being waged within Jaruzelski's leadership between hard-liners
and centrists over the relationship to the Catholic church and
to the suspended Solidarity movement. This was evidenced by
a series of provocative party attacks that began in May. In
certain publications, the Catholic church was attacked in
threatening tones as the ostensible point of origination of
demonstrations that had been mounted against martial law.
On July 12, the Soviet newspaper Izvestiia charged that most
antiregime demonstrations in martial law Poland had begun
after masses in the churches. These growing efforts to impli-
cate the church in actions inimical to the government sounded
the alarm among the religious authorities.

In the face of this situation, the Polish episcopate demonstrated a more noticeable tendency to view the Jaruzelski regime
as the lesser of evils, the possibility of Soviet intervention being
the greatest of evils. Thus, the Polish episcopate did not exert
considerable pressure regarding a papal visit to Poland—a
possibility that was discussed with increasing frequency since
June 1982. Although the church had clearly insisted that Pope
John Paul II be permitted to visit the six hundredth anniversary

of the shrine of the Madonna of Czestochowa, it was no longer urging, as it had before, that this take place in August 1982. The church had noted the condemnation of the proposed papal visit by the Soviet news agency TASS,[98] and had decided to refrain from putting Jaruzelski in an even more delicate position. Informed Catholic circles felt that insistence on an August visit would only strengthen the position of the hard-liners in the Polish Communist Party.

Discussions between the Catholic church and the government continued without interruption. While the government avoided public rejection of the theses of the Catholic Social Council for the reestablishment of social peace, it also had not expressed its opinions about the proposals for a societal settlement. Silence on this latter matter was seen in the Catholic camp as an indication that the hard-line faction would not accept the crucial demands and the relegalization of the unions. On the other hand, it became increasingly evident that neither the Polish episcopate nor the moderates around Jaruzelski wanted to close the doors on discussion promoting social peace.

As the political events of 1982 unfolded, it became clear that neither a papal visit or a full normalization would take place. The pope's journey to his homeland would not occur until the summer of 1983. Both Primate Glemp and General Jaruzelski were seeking a common formula for compromise in which neither the church nor the Polish leadership would lose face. That meant that the church might see itself compelled to face the facts created by martial law that it had previously refused to acknowledge. Since the Catholic church thinks in terms of time frames other than those of communist politicians or even independent union activists, Solidarity might come to be viewed as an ephemeral work of man—one of the many forms of life in Polish history that come and go. As a transcendental association of believers, the church joins with no worldly power. Thus, the repeated statement of the dead Primate Wyszynski retains significance: the church is not a party and cannot be incorporated by a party. The church demonstratively showed its positive feelings for renewal of 1980-81 and for Solidarity. At the same time, while sympathetic toward Solidarity, it was never fully integrated into the renewal movement.

It is within this context of the church's position that the spectacular meeting between Glemp and Jaruzelski took place on November 8, 1982, one month after the banning of Solidarity. The ensuing contacts between the church and the state led to an agreement in the first week of March about the period of the second papal pilgrimage to Poland, and the visit by Pope

John Paul II to his homeland was announced for June 1983.
The episcopate sought to present the visit as an effort at moral
renewal to which the entire nation would subscribe. To defuse
the controversy surrounding the primate's moderate political,
but ethically well-founded, course, Glemp obtained the cardinal's
hat on February 2, 1983. The hope was to strengthen the
spiritual authority of Glemp with the clergy and society.

The pope's pilgrimage on June 16-23, 1983 had some positive
consequences for all forces in Poland—the government, the
Catholic church, and society. The Jaruzelski group in control
of the government appraised the visit as confirmation of its
stabilization course for the country. Through a forceful presentation of this view in official statements and the state-
controlled media, in the short term at least the papal visit
proved profitable for the leadership. Politically, despite the
pope's desire, the opening of a real dialogue with social forces,
especially the working class, is unlikely. Instead the government is bound to offer in the future a one-sided dialogue with
appointed partners.

The Polish nation's expectations for the pope's visit were
fulfilled, as John Paul II made clear in his statements that the
church stood for the moral and social values of society. The
pope spoke the language of the nation as he confirmed that
the ideals of society had deep roots in the universal Christian
message and that the Polish struggle of 1980-81 was legitimate.
While strengthening the moral tone of society, the pope also
prepared it for future political hardships. He made clear that
the battle had ended with defeat and that the nation had to be
patient to preserve its values and renounce its hatred. The
pope was in solidarity with the people; he was simultaneously
able to articulate their thirst for justice and achieve a psychological decompression of society.

Through this remarkable mixture of challenge and caution
the pope demonstrated that his approach was different from
that of Primate Glemp. There was thus no demonstrative sign
of support for Glemp on the part of John Paul II. The difference
between the two men, however, is essentially one of style, for
both agree on the fundamental question of the church's position
in Poland. The pope and the primate are realists in their
assessments of the political situation and have no illusions
about future developments in the country.

Since the meeting of Jaruzelski and Glemp on April 25,
1982, it was clear to the church that there was no place for
Solidarity in the social and political structures of normalized
Poland. Furthermore it was evident that within a measurable

period of time there would be no public role for Lech Walesa
as a leader of the trade union. The pope had no power to undo
the principal decisions of the Polish leadership, and it is thus
false to speak about the sacrifice of Walesa by the pope.[99]
He neither appointed him, nor cast him aside for an alleged
new Catholic trade union. Such a development would not fit
the theological stand of the Catholic church in Poland and would
contradict the political position of the communist leadership in
Warsaw. On the contrary, John Paul II underscored the inces-
sant validity of Solidarity's and the nation's moral values
throughout his visit.

In conclusion it is worth emphasizing that John Paul II
refused to fulfill the hope of the Jaruzelski leadership and
grant the Polish government legitimacy. But the pope respected
the political realities in the sense that he admonished the nation
to think of the church's mission to prevent violent resistance
and not to preach hate. Instead the focus of the papal remarks
throughout his pilgrimage across Poland was respect for the
values of truth, justice and confidence. On the one hand,
through his public statements the pope underscored impressively
the importance of the Catholic church for the Polish leadership
and revealed once again the church's role as the stable anchor
of Poland's political system. On the other hand, the pope's
visit made clear that the church has deep roots among all
generations and all social strata of the Polish population—
deeper than ever before in the history of socialist Poland.

NOTES

1. "Manifest Polskiego Komitetu Wyzwolenia Narodowego,"
in Manifest PKWN (Warszawa: KiW, 1974), pp. 11-25.
2. M. K. Dziewanowski, The Communist Party of Poland:
An Outline of History (Cambridge, Mass.: Harvard University
Press, 1976), pp. 241-51.
3. Ibid.
4. Bernhard Stasiewski, "Die Kirchenpolitik der polnischen
Regierung nach 1945," in Osteuropa-Handbuch Polen, ed. Werner
Markert (Köln-Graz: Bohlau Verlag, 1959), pp. 356-66.
5. See Andrzej Micewski, Katholische Gruppierungen in
Polen: PAX und ZNAK 1945-1976 (München: Kaiser-Verlag,
1978).
6. Stasiewski, op. cit., pp. 363-64.
7. Ibid., p. 365.

8. See materials concerning the political-ideological preparation of the Sejm election campaign during the Seventh Plenum of the CC of the PUWP (January 20-21, 1961) found in Nowe Drogi, No. 2 (1961).

9. See Historia kosciola w Polsce, Vol. II (Poznan-Warszawa: Pallotinum, 1979), p. 221.

10. Stefan Wyszynski, Wszystko postawilem Mary (Paris: Editions du Dialogue, 1980), pp. 115-67.

11. See Hansjakob Stehle, Nachbar Polen. Erweiterte Neuausgabe (Frankfurt a. Main: S. Fischer Verlag, 1968), pp. 139-68.

12. Listy Pasterskie Episkopatu Polski 1945-1974 (Paris: Editions du Dialogue, 1975), pp. 829-36.

13. Karl Hartmann, "Staat und Kirche nach dem Macht-wechsel in Polen," Osteuropa 2 (1972):123.

14. Historia kosciola w Polsce, op. cit., p. 244.

15. KNA (Katholische Nachrichen Agentur) Informations-dienst, No. 18 (April 29, 1976).

16. Micewski, op. cit., pp. 323-32.

17. George Blazynski, Flashpoint Poland (Elmsford, NY: 1979), pp. 272-73.

18. Wielaw Myslek, "Panstwo i kosciol," Nowe Drogi 5 (1979):70.

19. Blazynski, op. cit., pp. 338-39.

20. PAP (Polish Press Agency), October 29, 1977.

21. Dieter Bingen, "Die katholische Kirche im polnischen Sozialismus," in Polen-Das Ende der Erneuerung? Gesellschaft, Wirtschaft und Kultur im Wandel, ed. Alexander Uschakow (München: Beck 1982), p. 159; dpa (German Press Agency), November 7, 1978.

22. Blazynski, op. cit., pp. 272-73.

23. Dieter Bingen, Papst Johannes Paul II. in der pol-nischen Publizistik. Zum Verhältnis zwischen Staat und Kirche (Köln: Berichte des Bundesinstituts für ostwissenschaftliche und internationale Studien, No. 44, 1979).

24. Ibid., pp. 2-8.

25. PAP, October 17, 1978; Zycie Warszawy, October 18, and 21-11, 1978.

26. Bingen, Papst Johannes Paul II, op. cit., pp. 9-10.

27. See Pastoral letters of September 27, 1978 and June 5, 1979.

28. Myslek, op. cit.

29. PAP, March 2, 1979; Zycie Warszawy, March 7, 1979.

30. Mieczyslaw Rakowski in Polityka, March 8, 1979.

31. dpa, March 12, 1979.

32. Pielgrzymka do ojczyzny. Przemowienia i homilie ojca swietego Jana Pawla II (Warszawa: Instytut Wydawniczy PAX, 1979).

33. Bingen, Papst Johannes Paul II, op. cit., p. 35.

34. See Begegnungen der Konferenz des Polnischen Episkopats mit der Deutschen Bischofskonferenz in Deutschland im September 1978 (Bonn: Sekretariat der Deutschen Bischofskonferenz, 1978).

35. Jerzy Turowicz in L'Avvenire (Milano), October 16, 1980; Jerzy Urban in Zycie Literackie (Krakow), November 1, 1981.

36. See the Gdansk Agreement of August 31, 1980 in Denis MacShane, Solidarity: Poland's Independent Trade Union (Nottingham: Spokesman, 1981), pp. 151-60.

37. See Adam Michnik, Kosciol, lewica, dialog (Paris: Instytut Literacki, 1977).

38. Frankfurter Allgemeine Zeitung, December 18, 1979.

39. Frankfurter Allgemeine Zeitung, August 18, 1980.

40. Ibid.

41. See Gdansk 1980: Oczyma swiadkow, selections and translation by Barbara Torunczyk (London: Polonia Book Fund Ltd., 1981).

42. KNA, No. 194, August 21, 1980.

43. Frankfurter Allgemeine Zeitung, August 21, 1980.

44. Ibid., August 23, 1980.

45. KNA-Dokumentation, No. 24, August 28, 1980.

46. Frankfurter Allgemeine Zeitung, August 30, 1980.

47. Ibid., August 29, 1980.

48. Trybuna Ludu, August 27, 1980.

49. Hansjakob Stehle, "Kirche und Papst in der polnischen Krise," Europa Archiv 6 (March 25, 1982):163.

50. MacShane, op. cit., p. 153.

51. Ibid.

52. Zycie Warszawy, September 2, 1980.

53. Speech of Stanislaw Kania closing the Sixth Plenum of the Central Committee of the PUWP, September 6, 1980, Nowe Drogi 10/11 (1980):41.

54. Frankfurter Allgemeine Zeitung, September 10, 1980.

55. Karl Hartmann, "Die Erneuerungsbewegung in Polen," Osteuropa, No. 1 (1982), p. 11.

56. Tygodnik Powszechny, October 26, 1980.

57. Frankfurter Allgemeine Zeitung, September 26, 1980.

58. See Stehle, op. cit., p. 164.

59. Radio Warsaw, October 22, 1980.

60. Trybuna Ludu, October 23, 1980.

61. Hartmann, op. cit., p. 13.

62. Slowo Powszechne, November 21, 1980.

63. Zycie Warszawy, December 17, 1980.

64. Stehle, op. cit., p. 166.

65. Zycie Warszawy, March 27, 1981.

66. Hartmann, op. cit., p. 14.

67. Tygodnik Powszechny, April 12, 1981.

68. See Bingen, "Die katholische Kirche," op. cit., pp. 149-50.

69. W rocznice-uchwalenia Konstytucji 3 Maja (Ustawa Rzadowa prawo uchwalone dnia 3 Maja 1791) (Warszawa: Instytut Wydawniczy Zwiazkow Zawodowych, 1981).

70. Polish Television, Program 1, May 13, 1981.

71. Zycie Warszawy, May 29, 1981.

72. Letter of the CC of the CPSU to the CC of the PUWP, Frankfurter Allgemeine Zeitung, June 11, 1981; Pravda, June 12, 1981; Trybuna Ludu, June 11, 1981.

73. Information provided to the author.

74. Homily of Pope John Paul II, read by Cardinal Macharski of Krakow during the ceremony on the Plac Zwyciestwa, May 31, 1981, Zycie Warszawy, June 1, 1981.

75. See the interview with Primate Glemp in Polityka, August 31, 1981.

76. Trybuna Ludu, July 13, 1981.

77. Frankfurter Allgemeine Zeitung, August 15, 1981.

78. Ibid., August 28, 1981.

79. Frankfurter Allgemeine Zeitung, September 7, 1981.

80. See Dieter Bingen, "Solidarnosc—eine polnische Gewerkschaft und gesellschaftliche Bewegung," Aus Politik und Zeitgeschichte, Belage Tür Wodnpeitung Das Parlament, B 29-30, 1982 (July 24, 1982), pp. 20-22.

81. Stehle, op. cit., p. 168.

82. Frankfurter Allgemeine Zeitung, October 23, 1981.

83. "Political Summit in Warsaw," Radio Free Europe-Radio Liberty Background Report 314 (Poland), November 13, 1981.

84. See Erik-Michael Bader, "Der Staatsstreich gegen den polnischen 'Gesellschaftsvertrag': Die Verfassungswirklichkeit 1980-1981 und der Coup des 13. Dezember 1981," Europa Archiv 9 (May 10, 1982):285-286; Tygodnik Solidarnosc, December 11, 1981.

85. Full text reported by AFP, December 8, 1981.

86. Radio Warsaw, December 13, 1981.

87. Full text published in Le Monde, December 18, 1981.

88. See the New York Times, January 6, 1982.

89. Radio Warsaw, January 24, 1982.

90. Trybuna Ludu, January 25, 1982.

91. Paul Roth, Die katholische Kirche in Polen und ihr Verhältnis zur Gewerkschaft "Solidaritat", Informationsdienst des Katholischen Arbeitskreises für zeitgeschichtliche Fragen e. V., No. 115 (1982), p. 8.

92. Ibid., p. 9.

93. "Polish Bishops' Conference Appeals for a Social Accord," RFE-RL, Radio Free Europe Research, Poland 4 (March 3, 1982):9-10.

94. Full text published in Informationsdienst, op. cit., pp. 13-25.

95. Trybuna Ludu, April 26, 1982.

96. PAP (English), April 19, 1982; see Jerzy Ozdowski, "Udzial katolikow w odrodzeniu Polski," Kierunki 4 (May 2, 1982).

97. Radio Warsaw, April 27, 1982.

98. TASS, July 10, 1982.

99. See Virgilio Levi, Onore al sacrificio, in Osservatore Romano, June 25, 1983.

11.

The Communist Party during the
1980–81 Democratization of Poland

Z. Anthony Kruszewski

BACKGROUND: SOCIOECONOMIC DISLOCATIONS
AND THE PARTY

One cannot begin to chart the full impact of the historical events of 1980-81 without understanding the momentous transformation of the decision-making authorities of the Polish United Workers' Party during those years. That transformation began initially as a shift of party personnel. When such cosmetic changes proved inappropriate, given the vastness of the cleavage between the ruling Communist Party and the working class, the party undertook a large-scale attempt at revitalization of its leadership, structures, and performance. That experiment ended in failure and imposition of martial law.

The roots of that cleavage stretch, however, not only to the June 1976 price riots in Radom (and elsewhere), but even further to the bloody confrontation between authorities and workers in Gdansk in 1970 and even to the Polish October of 1956. Significantly, of the five major confrontations since 1956, all but the university-centered and intelligentsia-based events of March 1968 were working-class clashes with communist authorities. The working class became the spokesman of the social, political, religious, and national aspirations of the Polish people. Since 1976, an alliance was forged between the workers, the Catholic church, and the intellectuals, the latter in an advisory capacity. Thus, we have witnessed a new phenomenon on the stage of Polish history, whereby the moral authority and leadership of the country passed for the first time into the hands of the workers (although the power structure supposedly had been under their control since 1944).

The party was furthermore confronted unexpectedly with a new element—the election in 1978 of the Polish pope. That element, simultaneously religious, nationalist, and political, occurred in the thirty-fourth year of communist ascension to power in Poland. Its impact was aptly summarized in The Guardian (London): "One of the newest slogans of the Polish Communist Party hanging on many buildings proclaims 'the party is with the people' but on at least one such banner someone unknown has added 'but the people are with the Pope'."[1]

The election of a pope from Poland, a churchman considered by many Communists to be a potentially more dangerous opponent than Stefan Cardinal Wyszynski,[2] only compounded the perennial state of socioeconomic and political crisis the party had been confronting since at least 1956. John Paul II's triumphant return to Poland in the summer of 1979 made an enormous psychological impact on the Polish people and electrified the working class in particular, giving them renewed strength and hope for a better life in the future.

While noncommunist citizens of Poland reinforced their resilience in anticipation of their struggle for a renewal, encompassing all areas of Polish public life, the communist hierarchy of the Polish United Workers' Party (PUWP) had visibly run out of steam long before the challenge of 1980-81. They could not afford to ignore that challenge, especially one so unique in the context of Soviet-type societies.

Thus one has to explore the underlying causes of the vicissitudes of the Polish party in the past. In October 1956 most important aspects of the communist system in Poland nearly collapsed. Only after drastic reforms of Stalinist practices and acceptance of compromises with noncommunist segments of the population (e.g., pressures that resulted in decollectivization of agriculture,[3] relative freedom of worship,[4] including temporary reintroduction of religious instruction into the state school curriculum, and relative freedom of informal expression), was the party able to contain the dangerous situation arising partly from the self-inflicted misdeeds of the Stalinists.

But soon after the little stabilization of the late 1950s and early 1960s, the party again encountered serious internal problems that resulted first in the student riots of 1968 and then in the bloody workers' riots of December 1970. In that instance, price increases, economically justified but callously implemented just before Christmas, cost Gomulka his leadership. Whether the power struggle within the ranks of the party leadership contributed to that situation is now academic. The result was the first change of government caused by mass discontent. Riots and subsequent recognition of errors in tactics brought about the new leadership of Edward Gierek.

A new surge of optimism and a considerable measure of public, not only party, support was triggered by those changes. New economic incentives and a considerable opening to the West, especially toward the Federal Republic of Germany and the United States, enabled Poland to obtain enormous credit (resulting in indebtedness of over $27 billion) to pursue modernization of industry, but initially positive results were stymied again by the riots of June 1976.

Incredibly, the party almost repeated the pricing error of 1970, and after the riots of 1976 again had to rescind its decision. The events of both 1970 and 1976 had ominous implications for the PUWP. Unlike the student riots of 1968 or the Polish October of 1956, these events destroyed the myth of working-class support for the leadership's policies.

Furthermore, confrontations over the government's economic policy after 1976 brought responses not only from dissident intellectuals (like those in March 1968), but from workers who were then supported by the intellectuals and the church.[5] Hence, these 1976 confrontations had potentially dangerous significance for the government, affecting the system's future stability. For the first time since 1947, a semilegal, however small, opposition and press came into existence in Poland, creating a modicum of pluralism that the government continued to harass, but did not feel safe to suppress totally.

Suppression obviously was in its power, but such action was avoided until December 13, 1981, for fear that it would jeopardize Poland's budding economic relations with the West. Hence that political dilemma in the highly strained economic situation, compounded by natural disasters and poor harvests, increased the immobility of the leadership, and the underlying mood of general uncertainty regarding future trends was stressed openly in the press.[6]

Although some reforms were implemented and largely retained after 1956 and again after 1970 (e.g., decollectivization, relative freedom of informal expression since the Polish October, and broadening of economic contacts and trade patterns with the West since Gierek's ascent to power), the dominant fear within the party was that these reforms might get out of hand. This restrictive paradigm caused the party to watch constantly over the proper balance between permissiveness and authority within the communist system.

The need to secure and safely perpetuate the leading role of the party de facto paralyzed any possibility for free experimentation with new models, approaches, and ideas, and thus destroyed any potential socioeconomic benefits to the system and the society. These constraints caused the containment of reforms, especially economic, that were long overdue given the pressures generated in the system by the status quo of perpetual shortages.[7]

The restrictive limits of socioeconomic experimentation that the system allowed by design hampered the social participation which the reform was aiming to increase. The example of agricultural difficulties is a case in point since the party was unable and unwilling, due to ideological restraints, to move toward remedying food shortages through drastic, but necessary, reforms, for fear of jeopardizing the socialist model it had upheld in the past. This in turn caused growing social dissatisfaction with the system's performance and promoted instability.

The regime, caught in this dilemma, relied increasingly on grain imports from the West, resulting in ever-growing indebtedness. A streak of bad harvests, due to climatic reasons, did not improve the situation. The impact of these food shortages on the political stability of Poland, which could and should be agriculturally self-sufficient, should not have been underestimated by the party.[8]

A revolution of rising expectations was the biggest potential enemy of the party. These expectations were unleashed in part by the relative freedom of foreign travel and contact with the capitalist world (e.g., in 1979 some 602,000 Poles visited the West, and 1,016,000 Westerners, including 59,000 Americans, visited Poland).[9] The opening of emigration after 1956 (not a common phenomenon in the socialist countries, except in Hungary and Yugoslavia) resulted in the arrival of 595,000 people to the Federal Republic of Germany alone and more than 250,000 to the United States, Great Britain, France, and Israel.[10] Many of these people permanently established abroad visited their old homeland. In addition to these officially approved movements, some 140,000 people chose to remain abroad while visiting the West between the population censuses of 1970 and 1978.[11]

The paradox was that after the events of 1970, in its eagerness to appease disgruntled young men, especially students, the government made it very easy for them to travel abroad. Thereafter, thousands of Polish students worked during their vacations in Sweden, Norway, France, Great Britain, and Austria, with many earning more during those few months than their parents earned in years back home.

Instead of easing tensions, this policy, which the party was unwilling to discontinue due to the personal involvement of its members' own families, increased income disparities while raising the level of aspirations of homecoming students, who were now able to compare the standard of living of Western countries with that of their own homeland. Furthermore, eager to encourage the inflow of hard currency (e.g., 600,000 Poles now have $0.5 billion in dollars on deposit in the Polish State Bank in interest-bearing accounts!),[12] the government pretended not to notice the ideological aspects of the situation.

These contacts created a relatively free flow of ideas and people (except printed materials) and promoted the lively state of the arts, drama, and literature in Poland, not only in step with the West but often far ahead. This was in direct contrast to the socialist realism of the pre-1955 period, which was still largely a rule in most other socialist countries.

The events of 1976-77 also led to the appearance of the unofficial (if not really underground) press and organizations,[13] including a private university lecture series (the Flying University, whose distinguished namesake started in 1885-1905, in the then tsarist-ruled Poland). In early autumn of 1979, the first illegal opposition party was created (the Coalition for Polish Independence), and other semilegal groups organized several large-scale (3,000 to 5,000 participants) open air meetings to commemorate events officially frowned upon by the Communist Party.

The above phenomenon only added to the non-Marxist characteristics of the Polish situation, in which deviations from the norms flourished after 35 years of communism. Although the contrived revolution of 1944-45 largely eliminated the aristocracy, landed gentry, industrialists, and businessmen as separate classes, a well-defined class structure did exist and was visible even to the uninitiated observer. Almost all old class usages, traditions, titles, and prerogatives of leisure were fostered, appreciated, and avidly sought (e.g., organized hunts became the most prestigious leisure occupation of the affluent strata in that socialist society; horse races also were flourishing and elaborately described in the press).

The party's monopoly of power in a society suffering from all sorts of economic shortages also resulted in rampant corruption (or, as it is delicately called, influence peddling). If anything, this author, after observing the scene directly for 25 years, became convinced of the rapid increase of this phenomenon. Other negative social aspects included sluggish productivity, absenteeism, alcoholism, and poor work discipline. All these problems coexisting in a social context marked by the increasingly visible revolution of rising expectations indicated troubled times ahead for the party and the society.

It is also interesting to note the changing composition and levels of education and aspirations of the party during 1945-80. One of the major achievements of the party in the postwar years was the urbanization and industrialization of the country, which directly transformed the life styles and level of aspirations of the whole nation.[14] These goals had been achieved at high social cost but were real achievements (see Tables 11.1 and 11.2).

However, the pressure of modernization forced the party to increase education levels within it. Since the party did not want to share power with nonparty experts, except in subservient roles, it had to reeducate its members to provide them with a modicum of preparation for the increasingly complex tasks the party was called upon to handle.

As the party doubled its university-trained members in eighteen years (1960-78) and achieved a ratio three times that of the population at large, its composition became increasingly white-collar and bureaucratic.[15] Workers in 1978 composed only 45.7 percent of its membership and peasants only 9.4 percent (or 2.4 percent less than in 1960),[16] a paradoxical profile for a party ostensibly speaking for the proletariat (see Table 11.3).

This increase in recruitment of intellectuals and professionals did not generally improve the party's decision-making efficiency, at least in public perceptions. Many new members were indeed proforma members largely deprived of promotion and/or leadership possibilities. Mindful of these structural problems, but largely afraid to remedy them through experimental and nondoctrinal approaches, the party experimented in the 1970s with one remaining option—structural reorganization and decentralization. Results of that reform did not prevent catastrophe. There even exists doubt whether these reforms had been motivated by the quest for efficiency and modernization. For example, by dividing large provinces into smaller units,[17] the administrative reform of 1975 primarily destroyed any power blocs threatening the Politburo and the Central Committee. It prevented, if anything, the formation of new mechanisms potentially challenging the status quo.

Moreover, the pre-1980 attempts at party revitalization were generally a failure. These efforts were engineered by younger members of the party, who aimed at instituting reforms within a framework of controlled change that also had techno-

TABLE 11.1. Educational Level of Population[a]

Level of Education	1960[b]			1970			1976			1978		
	Total	Men	Women	Total	Men	Women	Total	Men	Women	Total	Men	Women
Total (in thousands)	20004	9260	10744	24015	11445	12570	26294	12586	13708	26694	12800	13894
Higher	415	285	130	655	426	229	959	580	379	1202	698	504
Secondary[c]	2046	989	1057	3198	1440	1758	4709	2008	2701	5288	2208	3080
Basic vocational	630	471	159	2531	1711	820	3870	2536	1334	4628	3048	1580
Elementary[d]	7838	3556	4282	11620	5378	6242	12379	5691	6688	12163	5542	6621
Total (in percentages)	100.0	100.0	100.0	100.0	100.0	100.0	100.0	100.0	100.0	100.0	100.0	100.0
Higher	2.1	3.1	1.2	2.7	3.7	1.8	3.6	4.6	2.8	4.5	5.5	3.6
Secondary[c]	10.3	10.7	9.9	13.4	12.7	14.1	17.9	16.0	19.7	19.8	17.2	22.2
Basic vocational	3.1	5.1	1.5	10.6	15.1	6.6	14.7	20.1	9.7	17.3	23.8	11.4
Elementary[d]	39.3	38.5	40.0	48.8	47.3	50.1	47.1	45.2	48.8	45.6	43.3	47.6

[a]For years 1960 and 1970 data of national censuses; for 1976 estimate as of December 31.
[b]14 years and over.
[c]Including postsecondary and incomplete higher education.
[d]Including incomplete secondary.

Source: Rocznik Statystyczny 1978. Glowny Urzad Statystyczny, 38, Warszawa, Table 10 (55), page 34, and Rocznik Statystyczny 1980 40, Table 11 (61), page 37, GUS, Warszaw, 1980.

TABLE 11.2. Population According to National Censuses

Census Data	Total	In Thousands				Women per 100 Men	Percentages		Sq. Km.
		Men	Women	Cities	Villages		Cities	Villages	
December 9, 1931	32107[a]	15619	16488	8731	23185	106	27.4	72.6	82
February 14, 1946	23930[b]	10954	12976	7517	16109	118	31.8	68.2	77
December 3, 1950	25008[c]	11928	13080	9605	15009	110	39.0	61.0	80
December 6, 1960	29776[d]	14404	15372	14205	15200	107	48.3	51.7	95
December 8, 1970	32642	15854	16788	17064	15578	106	52.3	47.7	104
March 30, 1974	33636	16313	17323	18213	15423	106	54.1	45.9	108
December 7, 1978	35061	17079	17982	20150	14911	105	57.5	42.5	112

a-d In the division between cities and villages were not included: a—192,000; b—304,000; c—394,000; d—370,000.

Source: Rocznik Statystyczny 1980. Glowny Urzad Statystyczny, 40, Warszawa, Table 1 (51), page 29 and the data from Maly Rocznik Statystyczny 1939, GUS, 50, Warszawa, Tables 4-11, pages 10-18.

cratic overtones. The structure of the party, however, did
not permit very sweeping changes since there was a large degree
of commitment to past administrative usages, despite some efforts
aimed at decentralization connected largely with the administrative
reform of 1975.[18]

What was evident and quite visible even then was the fatigue
of the leadership, which no amount of old-style exhortations
could cover up or remedy. Even among high-ranking members
of the party elite, the prevalent frame of mind was one of dis-
illusion with both the implementation of party goals and their
reception by the people at large. The party machinery, and
indeed the whole system, was increasingly afflicted by excessive
bureaucratization and noninnovative rule application, which
served as the only standard of performance. Furthermore,
the party members reflected, in their private individual aspirations, the general attitudes and values of the society, which
were generally traditional. Thus the propounded theory and
implemented reality had very little in common, but the party
members aspired to and eschewed the non-Marxist life-style
and privileges.

The leadership of the party was relatively younger than
in some other socialist countries, largely due to the upheavals
of 1956, 1970, and 1980-81. Hence the past experiences of the
old elite were no longer commonly shared,[19] but there was a
lack of attempt made to recruit new leadership from outside the
circle of people partaking in privileges. This served to reinforce
the status quo and preserve the party monopoly. In this respect,
not much divided the old leader Gomulka from Gierek or Gierek
from the new leader Kania. Commitment and loyalty were
cherished and ultimately rewarded, rather than competence
and problem-solving ability.

Trends within the PUWP did not portend any great modifi-
cations of leadership style, even with ascendancy of relatively
young leaders installed after the Polish August of 1980, because
prevalent styles of cooptation predetermined most of the future
styles and rules. More than anything else, these rules and
usages prevented any significant innovation within the party
and have been the major stumbling block on the path of innovation.

Who, then, were the revitalizers of the party? They were
both within and outside the party. The latter either were
dropped from the party for too vehement criticism of some
aspects of theory or practice or were dropouts who, although
considering themselves Marxist, could not reconcile day-to-day
party practices with the theory propounded by the very same

TABLE 11.3.   Members and Candidates of the Polish United Workers' Party (as of December 31)

Description	Totals 1960	1965	1970	1976	1978	Percentages 1960	1965	1970	1976	1978
Total	1,154,672	1,775,049	2,319,963	2,568,366	2,930,448[c]	100.0	100.0	100.0	100.0	100.0
of which candidates	176,683	203,931	189,211	258,634	348,509[d]	15.3	11.5	8.2	10.1	11.9
Cities[a]	797,086	1,228,904	1,629,291	1,888,520	2,165,601	69.0	69.2	70.2	73.5	73.9
Villages[a]	357,586	546,145	690,672	679,846	764,847	31.0	30.8	29.8	26.5	26.1
Women	177,242	322,490	521,797	625,140	766,242	15.3	18.2	22.5	24.3	26.1
Total	1,154,672	1,775,049	2,319,963	2,568,366	2,930,448	100.0	100.0	100.0	100.0	100.0
18-24 years	99,159	160,038	257,001	146,397	227,848	8.6	9.0	11.1	5.7	7.8
25-29 years	201,010	282,351	328,652	394,344	460,254	17.4	15.9	14.2	15.4	15.7
30-39 years	390,202	597,277	726,974	705,273	810,668	33.8	33.7	31.3	27.4	27.6
40-49 years	215,649	383,151	583,691	707,328	746,693	18.7	21.6	25.2	27.5	25.5
50-59 years	248,652	231,349	255,760	407,086	465,995	21.5	13.0	11.0	15.9	15.9
60 and over		120,883	167,885	208,038	218,990		6.8	7.2	8.1	7.5
Total	1,154,672	1,775,049	2,319,963	2,568,366	2,930,448	100.0	100.0	100.0	100.0	100.0
Education										
Higher	60,891	114,804	182,185	279,182	351,087	5.3	6.5	7.9	10.9	12.0
Incomplete higher	14,934	47,495	90,117	104,019	98,283	1.3	2.7	3.9	4.1	3.4
Secondary: vocational	113,258	245,066	376,914	484,650	598,219	9.8	13.8	16.2	18.9	20.4
general education	97,475	119,125	160,667	211,633	254,880	8.4	6.7	6.9	8.2	8.7
Incomplete secondary	134,299	150,685	163,415	127,648	129,043	11.6	8.5	7.0	5.0	4.4
Basic vocational		130,758	255,786	413,250	520,116		7.4	11.0	16.1	17.9
Elementary	432,114	681,483	870,011	817,511	863,871	37.5	38.3	37.6	31.7	29.5
Incomplete elementary	301,701	285,633	220,868	130,473	114,949	26.1	16.1	9.5	5.1	3.9
Total	1,154,672	1,775,049	2,319,963	2,568,366	2,930,448	100.0	100.0	100.0	100.0	100.0
Workers	465,225	712,151	934,425	1,154,481	1,339,547	40.3	40.1	40.3	44.9	45.7
Agricultural workers	49,437	52,744	61,062	63,196	70,624	4.3	3.0	2.6	2.5	2.4
Peasants	136,133	207,034	265,708	238,344	274,617	11.8	11.7	11.5	9.3	9.4

Engineers, technicians, technical supervisors[b]	89,837	169,266	246,346	228,585	265,206	7.7	9.5	10.6	8.9	9.1
Agronomists and other agricultural and forestry specialists[b]	12,733	19,924	28,628	32,618	37,217	1.1	1.1	1.2	1.03	1.3
Teachers	43,803	97,362	141,485	140,490	148,574	3.8	5.5	6.1	5.5	5.1
Physicians[b]	3,228	8,113	11,904	14,383	15,531	0.3	0.5	0.5	0.6	0.5
Paramedical personnel	5,211	12,571	18,784	–	–	0.5	0.7	0.8	–	–
University faculty members	3,514	6,269	11,397	20,532	18,120	0.3	0.4	0.5	0.8	0.6
Journalists, artists, writers	3,029	4,434	5,066	–	–	0.3	0.2	0.2	–	–
Lawyers and judiciary personnel	3,744	5,916	7,580	–	–	0.3	0.3	0.3	–	–
Economists, planners, accountants	45,802	79,289	117,300	112,957	123,372	4.0	4.5	5.1	4.4	4.2
Retired and pensioners		62,463	102,483	179,503	208,648	–	3.5	4.4	7.0	7.1

aClassified according to the basic party organizations.
bAccording to profession practiced.
c3,091,900 in 1980.
d291,600 in 1980.

Source: Data from the Organization Department of the Central Committee PUWP as quoted in Rocznik Statystyczny 1978, Urzad Glowny Statystyczny, 37, Warszawa, Table 6 (41), page 22, and Maly Rocznik Statystyczny 1981 24, Table 3 (24), page 20, GUS: Warszawa, 1981.

party. Both categories were usually younger and better educated than the party rank and file.

In the events of October 1956,[20] March 1968, December
1970, June 1976, and especially since August 1980, the revitalizers boldly exposed (in spoken word and print) the misdeeds of the party and its members, as well as its hypocrisy.
In this quest, the leaders of the various dissent groups were
strangely parallel to the Western youth of the 1960s, who exposed
the hypocrisy of their societies and demanded adjustment of
deeds and words.[21]

In their quest for reforms and reformation of the party,
they espoused a more libertarian orientation. Being wholly
socialized under the system, they often aspired only to reform
of the reforms, advocated increased participation, and condemned party elitism. In the chain of events beginning in 1956
and still in progress, these elements adhered to the idea of
party revitalization. Prior to August 1980 some of these semi-
legal or illegal groups had passed the point of no return in
their criticism of the party. After being forced out of the
ideological community by counterreform forces in the PUWP,
they were partly restored to their previous status only after
September 6, 1980.

A unique additional problem faced by the party since the
beginning of its rule but especially since 1956 is the role and
strength, recently further enhanced, of the Roman Catholic
church, which de facto has a hold on the overwhelming proportion of the Polish people. The party has long since tacitly
admitted its inability to curtail the church, short of the introduction of terror. Governmental harassment of the church was
largely counterproductive and only increased the latter's
strength. Hence, the danger to the party, either in the status
quo or in formal accommodation (such as permission to broadcast
mass every Sunday on the Polish radio, granted soon after
August 1980), has further weakened the Marxist tenets of the
Polish United Workers' Party.

Additional difficulties for the party stemmed from a lack
of any mechanism for succession, since such a mechanism would
inherently threaten the political and organizational continuity
of the party. Hence, only major breakdowns and rebellions
remained as a means for overhauling the party elite and bureaucracy.

Furthermore, although the Party in the past had rejected
polyarchic developments in the sense of political competition
and established social pluralism, it could not avoid bargaining
with the society about some of its rules and values in the early

1970s.[22] Renewed alienation of the intellectuals from the party soon thereafter resulted in a decrease in their membership in the party. Otherwise, why suddenly were no figures given in 1978 for party affiliation of these groups? They were always scrupulously listed in statistics published in the past.[23]

Alienation of that stratum, however, was not a new phenomenon in view of its self-perceived sociopolitical role in Polish history. However, attempts by the intellectuals to reform the reforms instituted by the Communists did not achieve the desired results. It was only after 1976, with the formation of the Committee for the Defense of the Workers (KOR), that intellectuals started playing an entirely new role[24]—that of advisors to the workers who were about to reassert themselves in the Polish August of 1980, but on a new vast scale, which the party now was unable to cope with and check by use of old conventional methods.

THE PARTY'S ROLE DURING RENEWAL

The basic and very serious errors committed by the Gierek team in planning, investment, and management resulted in an overall economic breakdown. Although not visible at first, the stage was set for a new confrontation between the party and the emerging worker-intellectual-church alignment. The elections of 1980 afforded the party a pretext to change its team slightly by removing the unpopular Prime Minister Piotr Jaroszewicz and replacing him with Edward Babiuch. It was too little and too late, especially since party central authorities were affected only minimally. Hence no substantial changes were made in the real decision-making authorities.

When the cause for a workers' rebellion was created by the party in the form of price increases of meat products July 1, 1980, a series of wildcat strikes spread across the country in the face of the increasing inability of the party to check this challenge to its rule. When the Lenin Shipyards in Gdansk (third-largest in the world) were paralyzed in August 14, 1980, it resulted in an entirely new and explosive confrontation between the party and the working class all across Poland. The resulting Gdansk agreement of August 31, 1980, and similar ones signed at Szczecin and Jastrzebie, created an absolute anomaly in the communist world—the autonomous Free Trade Union Solidarity within a hegemonic political system. Strikes or threats of strikes by practically all sectors of the economy led to the party's de facto capitulation or at least a paper agreement to a new political compact--a supposed partnership of the party and Solidarity.

Whereas as late as spring 1980 the party did not yet feel it was necessary to make any drastic changes either in the Politburo or other decision-making organs, such restructuring took place within barely one week after the Gdansk agreement. Stanislaw Kania replaced Gierek, and there were changes made in the Politburo and the government. Attempts were made to give the appearance that the party was making an effort to confront the new and vastly changed power relations within the Polish political system. The new front men, like Kania, appeared to be pursuing moderate policies toward Solidarity and the church.

The then new Polish Prime Minister Jozef Pinkowski said, "Society expects from the government a guarantee that we will keep our word and faithfully implement publicly undertaken obligations of both an economic and social nature," and, "The realization of the principles of socialist democracy requires in public life its corollary--systematic and open information about the status of the state and national economy. We will take care of that. . . ."[25] Furthermore, he tried hard to appease the people by saying, "I want to state with appropriate reverence that the last days gave us proof of deliberate and patriotic concern of the leadership of the church and the overwhelming part of the clergy."

The then new Politburo member, Andrzej Zabinski, representing the party, expressed even more interesting thoughts in response to the prime minister's speech: "The working class which is and will be the principal creator and defender of the socialist Poland reminded us sharply and angrily that in the general developmental activities many human aspects were lost and that we did not adequately fulfill basic human needs and not enough did we listen to their voices and opinions."[26]

After some additional shattering admissions, Zabinski said something ominous: "We are supporting the democratic process of renovation of the Trade Unions but not an individualistically imposed decision of each worker and working establishment about joining the Union." Today, after delegalization of Solidarity, these words are worth remembering.

Was that not a harbinger of future reneging on the agreement to allow a free labor union? Was that not contradictory to what Prime Minister Pinkowski said about "faithful implementation of publicly undertaken obligations?" But a great deal more time had to lapse before the party and Solidarity were set on an ultimate collision course. The dramatic events of 1980-81 had yet to produce the establishment of a 9.5 million-strong unified free labor union (26 percent of the total population of Poland or 46 percent of the adult cohorts 20-65 years old)[27] and the mounting pressure for democratization of structures and policies within the PUWP, culminating in the Ninth Extraordinary Congress of July 14, 1981.

Pressure for renewal (Odnowa) was spreading not only from economic life to social and political practices, policies, and structures, but also caught the party in a similar whirlwind. Some 40 percent of the party's rank and file joined Solidarity. The party found itself in the crossfire of societal pressures for a total renewal. A relatively free press and the subsequent establishment of the Solidarnosc weekly (with a run of over 500,000 copies) left no subject unexplored, left practically no taboos in Polish politics (save some of the most sensitive topics dealing with Soviet-Polish relations and/or past tragic misdeeds in Soviet policies toward Poland).[28]

The party had to react to the powerful forces that resulted in the creation of Solidarity and left the government-controlled trade unions shattered. Although some three million workers remained in these unions (organized by trades),[29] Solidarity was undoubtedly more representative of the working class. Hence power pressures were exerted within the party to reform and thus be able to retain its self-proclaimed role of the vanguard of the proletariat in Poland. Although numerically still large (some three million), it had to cope with the unusual conditions, new not only to the Polish political system but to any ruling Communist party—the existence of the autonomous free union and the Catholic church, which represents some 85-90 percent of the nation. These facts, as well as the past accumulated misdeeds of the party now fully revealed by the press, resulted in the following popularity ranking of Polish public institutions: Church (1st of 14), Solidarity (2nd), the armed forces (3rd), government (6th), PUWP (13th), and the police (14th). Results of this survey were officially published by a leading Polish cultural weekly.[30]

The growing contrast between the spontaneous and widespread 1980-81 democratization of all institutions in Poland and the party only increased pressures for the democratization of the latter, grass root institutions undertaking creation of the so-called horizontal structures, which were to be linked together. This led to an even more glaring anomaly—a Torun meeting of party activists called outside official party channels to discuss internal reforms and new policy recommendations. The strength of such initiatives undertaken from below explains why one of

their main organizers, Zbigniew Iwanow, was able to attend the
Ninth Extraordinary Congress as a guest of the provincial Torun
delegation. [31] It is evident that the party was unable to prevent
the growing pressure for open discussion of structures and
policies, hitherto never discussed in public. At best, attempts
were made to control or check the main thrust of such pressures
by setting up orthodox-oriented, traditional groups openly
disagreeing with the democratization campaign within the party
(the so-called Katowice Forum and the Poznan Forum, the two
most publicized discussion groups that espoused the orthodox
line). Decreased openness of the press did not, however, create
a favorable atmosphere for such tactics since communist theorists
had to respond and defend past practices and, if not defend
the indefensible, at least rationalize past misdeeds.

The issue of responsibility for past mismanagement of the
economy, misuse of power, and outright abuses committed by
the high echelons of the authorities, or allowed to be covered
by the party, especially in the late 1970s, did not help the
party's tarnished image. Under the pressure of emerging public
opinion, now having at least fairly free access to the mass media,
thousands of party members (some 72,000) were accused of
such malpractices and their cases were brought to court. Huge
economic losses stemming from mismanagement prompted the
democratic opposition and semi-official groups outside the party
leadership to discuss the situation and plan for reforms. For
example, even prior to August 1980, the Experience and the
Future discussion group came forth with a detailed analysis of
the past and with policies needed for socioeconomic recovery. [32]

Although such discussions and planning had taken place
outside the mainstream of the party, its intellectual impact
challenged the party to open itself to similar developments.
Hence at least two sets of socioeconomic reforms were being
discussed openly. It is sufficient to say that the democratic
opposition planning entailed a de facto transformation of Poland's
socioeconomic relations and advocated construction of a Polish
model. That model would try to correlate such diverse elements
as the socialist framework and the geopolitical realities of Poland
(i.e., membership in the Warsaw Treaty Organization) with vast
societal liberalization (democratization, decentralization of
decision making, and subsequent social control of policymaking).

The heated and profuse debate of the above issues in the
mass media during 1980-81 was accompanied by the rapid growth
of Solidarity as an encompassing open and democratic national
force (more than three times larger than the party). During
that time, Solidarity was undertaking its basic programmatic

and structural development on all levels. The openness of these
processes also had an important impact on future developments
in the party. In order to understand the pressures resulting
in the Ninth Extraordinary Congress of July 1981 and its outcome, one has to understand the social and national context of
the discussions and actions taking place outside the party in
the nation at large.

Reformist elements, the revitalizers and/or Solidarity
members within the party (perhaps over 40 percent of its
membership at the time),[33] were thus prodded into discussions
about future reforms or used the outside context to pressure
for opening such dialogue. Thus, paradoxically enough, both
large-scale sociopolitical organizations—Solidarity and the party—
were not only simultaneously experiencing similar situations,
but also used or reacted to the activities on the other side.
Hence the painful and drawn-out programmatic formulations in
Solidarity, and its democratic, if not outright chaotic, modus
operandi were bound to result in rather similar mirror image
activities in the party, which was desperately trying to purge
itself of old sins, to stabilize and renew itself in order to be
able to remain credible in its role as a supposed vanguard of
the working class. In that context, the orthodox wing was
unable to stem the tide of grass-root changes sweeping the
party. They feared the resulting instabilities to be expected
from such a drastic departure from the old, comfortable and
safe practices of the past 37 years. The orthodox group would
have succeeded had it not been swamped by the chain reaction
caused by the revelation in the mass media of its sordid past.
Unable to prevent the congress, that faction put up a fierce
challenge to the reformers within the party before, during, and
after the Ninth Congress.

The party emerging from the congress was vastly changed
at the top (only four members of its new policymaking Politburo
were carry-overs) and in the Central Committee's composition.[34]
The orthodox group was considerably weakened but still remained prominently represented in both of these important bodies.
Furthermore, and much more important, the nomenklatura or
the personnel composition of the lower levels of bureaucracy
and the provincial control of the apparatus were then and still
are in the hands of the more rigid orthodox group. Even at
the top, Olszowski and Siwak were highly vocal and visible in
their quest to slow down, if not stall, any concrete results of
the reforms.

Regardless of their quest, it is evident that the Ninth
Congress resulted in the first democratic elections within the

PUWP. The rules adopted before the congress (i.e., free discussion, multiplicity of candidates, etc.), although carefully monitored and analyzed for their future impact, still resulted in such unforeseen situations as the change of the agenda to elect the first secretary at the beginning of the proceedings and the mode of election through direct open participation of all the delegates.

What emerged from the congress was billed by moderates as a new team, indeed, and debates over future policies of the party were likewise encouraged—in the words mindful of the national debates raging outside the party, "Let us cease to be afraid of thinking." Thus the outcome of the congress was presented as a positive step toward the reformist solution to Poland's economic and political problems. Indeed, the changes in the party's supreme authorities were radical. Only 16 members of the old Central Committee were reelected at the congress, and 90.5 percent of the new members had not previously performed any function as central authorities of the party.

It also should be noted that the socioprofessional composition of the new committee was also quite different from the old one. Whereas previously more than half of the committee was composed of party and government officials (and if all sociopolitical levels are included, they represented over 60 percent), they now accounted for only 3.5 percent,[35] and there was an increase in the representation of peasants, secretaries of the basic party organizations, and Army representatives. The most important changes were the great increase of workers, peasants, and the lower echelons of the activists (party, social, and professional) and the concomitant decrease of representatives of the upper party echelons and national government level. That stemmed from the partially implemented reforms aimed at separation of party/government functions previously centralized in the hands of the same men.

As for geographical distribution, the new Central Committee was heavily representative of the capital city, capitals of other provinces, and large cities. All 49 provinces but one (Ostroleka) were now represented in the committee. It was underlined in the press that in view of the more democratic (party) election procedures, many of the officials of the party apparatus and national government did not offer themselves as candidates for the new committee.

One should also observe the age structure of the top authorities, i.e., the Politburo. That body, as it emerged from the Ninth Congress, was dominated by men in their early fifties (only two were older—one 58 years old and the other 70—and one member was under 40). The average age of a Politburo member was 52 and that of the central authorities was 50.36 A woman, the first in the history of the PUWP, was elected to the Politburo (Mrs. Grzyb). She established another first by being simultaneously, at that time, a member of Solidarity, which membership she subsequently resigned in the fall of 1981.

The composition of the top authorities of the party had a distinct grass roots characteristic, but the leaders faced several problems that were to be expected. The fact that some had dual membership in the party and Solidarity did not augur well for the future in spite of its seemingly positive impact. They were bound to be caught up in every confrontation and theoretically could not reconcile such diverse memberships.

Furthermore, the internal renewal of the party leadership had built-in difficulties from the very outset, as it relegated all the former leaders and perennial members of these bodies to the ranks of the permanent opposition. The fact that those leaders now in opposition still had control of the lower apparatus and parts of the bureaucracy made for a relatively unstable situation and laid the foundation for a power struggle. Likewise, the new leaders' relative lack of experience and the rapidly approaching confrontation did not favor stability within the party. Any confrontation had to bring sharp differences of opinion in that now much more heterogeneous leadership body.

The new party leadership that emerged from the Ninth Congress was unable to control the situation in the country or to institute some basic reforms. It could not cope with the rapidly developing situation characterized by constant labor unrest that was prompted by sabotaging of the agreements arrived at by the party authorities with Solidarity at lower levels of the administration (if not at the top). The escalation of conflict throughout 1981 led to the inevitable confrontation between the party and Solidarity, which also was completing its organizational developments, culminating in the first national Solidarity congress in September 1981. The congress resulted in the election of Solidarity's permanent national authorities.

THE PARTY AND THE IMPOSITION OF MARTIAL LAW

Completion of the organizational stages by both the party and Solidarity ended the symbiotic rivalry in their implementation processes. The party's democratization, helped by the existence and early activities of Solidarity, had to be replaced by sharp polarization of positions and confrontation, especially after the conclusion by both organizations of their internal re-organization.[37] Thus the inability to compromise had to lead either to Soviet intervention or to the victory of Solidarity, either through actual sharing of powers with the party or by its collapse. The intervention option was changed to a military coup option, which saved the party from a complete debacle. That amended option was clearly outlined by a leading orthodox member of the Politburo, Siwak, as early as September 1981, but never really noted either by Solidarity or the outside world. He, in fact, set the deadline for martial law as early as November rather than mid-December 1981.[38]

The elevation of General Jaruzelski in September 1981 to the position of first secretary was a step in that direction, although it only formalized the basic inability of the party to play its leading role. The army had to prop up and in reality supplant the party through the medium of a state of war. However, it did not change the basic distribution of power in Poland in the triangular party-church-Solidarity relationship. In this relationship, the army had to play a direct role, for the first time in the history of the communist world, in taking over the country, contrary to all theoretical assumptions. The shifts and drastic changes in the party leadership within only a year, from Gierek to Kania to Jaruzelski, only reflected the rapidly declining fortunes of the PUWP in its moment of greatest challenge since the reestablishment of the Polish Communist Party in 1942.

Other forces on the Polish political scene also underwent some important changes that had and still might have wide political repercussions. The death of the Polish Catholic primate-statesman Stefan Cardinal Wyszynski in May 1981 and the eleva-tion of Jozef Glemp, his handpicked successor, reflected change in both the style and age of the leadership (he also is in his fifties, and the remaining three archbishops of Cracow, Wroclaw, and Poznan also are in their fifties and have assumed their offices within the last few years).

Finally, the September 1981 First National Congress of Solidarity brought to the surface a significant challenge to the meteoric rise of Lech Walesa, the charismatic leader of the first free labor union in the communist world. Walesa succeeded in stemming the challenge, but could not fully control or influence the decision-making process of the last fatal meetings of Solidarity before martial law was imposed.

It is worth observing that only a week before the state of war was announced, the moderate wing of the party was still talking about the possibility of a party-church-Solidarity compact that would restructure the Polish political system. A series of

councils, with mixed membership representing those three power
blocs, were described in the Polityka weekly in its last issues
before the martial law suspension of the press. [39]

Martial law thus opened a new chapter in the post-World
War II history of Poland. This solution was not anticipated and
when implemented caught the nation totally unprepared. Although the sending of military operational teams into each
commune (2,070) and each town and city (804) in the weeks
preceding the declaration of martial law [40] was the de facto
forerunner of the superimposing of military authorities over
the party structure, it generally was misread by the people as
an administrative measure designed to prevent further deterioration of the economy and to expose mismanagement, waste of
resources, and existence of unused or underutilized capacities.
It was not perceived as a dress rehearsal for the armed forces
takeover of the bureaucratic machinery and the national political
and economic structures.

That operation brought out the first confrontations between
the armed forces and the lower level apparatchiki resentful of
such a major interference with their prerogatives and complacent
practices. [41] Even if the direct clash was not discernible, enough
signs testified to the unusual characteristics of a situation in
which the army was moving into a position of dual power:
economic control and political decision making in areas hitherto
reserved for the party.

This was a precedent for any communist nation during
peacetime—the army superimposing itself on the party against
all the basic tenets of Marxism-Leninism pertaining to the relationship between both institutions. [42] It was, however, the near
collapse of the effectiveness, if not the very structure, of the
party that prompted such a move. Furthermore, the use of
the Polish armed forces in such an operation had a distinct
advantage since it preempted the need for military operations
on the part of the Soviet Union and other Warsaw Treaty Organization powers, [43] which could have proved dangerous and costly,
politically and militarily. The PUWP had lost its effectiveness
(if not legitimacy) in the eyes of that nation prior to martial
law. It also lost its members, not only to Solidarity but thousands
of disillusioned communists as well. [44] Hence the army takeover
from the party was all but inevitable.

The imposition of martial law was an extremely well-planned
operation. It totally closed down, so to speak, a nation of 36
million, the first such case in the history of modern Europe.
Especially effective was the impact of the total blockade of the
communication system, which prevented any potential large-scale

resistance on the part of Solidarity. The simultaneous internment of its leaders disorganized possible responses and limited
its effectiveness. The tragic desperate resistance at the Wujek
coal mine (in Katowice), in Wroclaw, Gdansk, and Cracow did
not minimize the military junta's success in saving the Polish
political system from obvious collapse. Suspension of telephone
and telegraph services, newspapers, and most of the radio and
television service for weeks added to the shock effect and had
guaranteed results for the martial law.

Although General Jaruzelski had previously accumulated
the powers of first secretary of the party, prime minister,
defense minister, and commander-in-chief of the armed forces,
his first martial law pronouncements did not refer to the party
or its primary structures. It was not until February 24-25,
1982, that the Polish Politburo and the Central Committee rubber-
stamped the decrees ex post facto. The martial law authority,
the Military Council of National Salvation (which used a rather
unfortunate acronym, WRON--or crow in Polish), also started
large-scale use of the militarized riot police ZOMO (or mecha-
nized units of the people's militia) and was effectively tested
in the takeover of the Firemen's Academy in Warsaw not quite
two weeks before imposition of martial law.

The widespread use of the hated and dreaded ZOMO,
largely recruited from alienated social elements and hard-core
opportunists and loyalists, has also prevented, so far, a clash
between the army and the resistance forces. Hence, regardless
of its cynical implications, it can be assessed as a considerably
successful measure. To this day the army has been largely
used for guard duty and thus insulated from dangerous confrontations with the people. This explains why the hatred
directed at ZOMO does not, by and large, affect the army, which
as a force composed of draftees and professionals still enjoys a
measure of public esteem in spite of its extremely difficult and
ambiguous position toward the repression of basic civil liberties.

Its commander-in-chief, however, has become an intensely
controversial person and has polarized public opinion. Attempts
by military authorities to cast him in the role of the Margrave
Wielopolski of the 1860s and a pragmatic politician have failed
to convince the public, which remembers Wielopolski's role in
precipitating the January Uprising of 1863! [45] To further secure
the army's posture, the authorities have decided to forego the
drafting of some 50,000 1982 recruits--for the first time in its
post-World War II history. Hence it further insulated its ranks
from the young men who would either be Solidarity members
themselves or brothers of such members.

The gradual restoration of communication links and the mass media brought about some measure of normalcy and resulted in a wearing off of the initial shock suffered by a population stunned by the martial law. Although military authorities generally have controlled the situation throughout 1982, in spite of a series of bloody confrontations and losses, it became painfully obvious that the initial success the military authorities had in curtailing any large-scale resistance simultaneously had a decidedly negative impact on any formulations of positive policies toward the society.

The security measures and siege mentality prevented rapprochement between the authorities, the Catholic church, and the working class throughout most of the year following imposition of martial law. The authorities, unable to propound any constructive new policies, resorted to continuous internment of Solidarity leaders and harassment of its activists who were still at large. This resulted in a situation of total stalemate precluding any compromise, if that is possible at all. Although the government has been able to control the country, it failed to prevent creation of an effective resistance with its impressive publications and elaborate contact system. The government, seemingly in control, is at the same time acutely conscious of the dimensions of the chasm dividing it from its own society.

Attempts to create new centers of public opinion (the government newspaper Rzeczpospolita [The Republic], seemingly somewhat outside the party mainstream) and the new structures (regional Committees of National Revival) as measures of tapping new sources of support for the martial law authorities have so far failed to bring any perceptible positive societal cooperation and/or support.

Even the censorship brought back after the 1980-81 hiatus is unable to hide the stalemate between the authorities and the society at large. Some papers (e.g., Tygodnik Powszechny, the prestigious Catholic weekly), although showing constant scars of the censor's cuts on each page, still convey an independent spirit so typical of the Polish scene.[46] Even more paradoxical is the fact that it was only under martial law (after some 38 years of communist rule) that the Polish parliament started publishing its equivalent of the Congressional Record— Diariusz Sejmowy (Parliamentary Diary),[47] containing for the first time uncensored speeches of parliament members, including those speakers against the martial law authorities.[48] The Diariusz Sejmowy (an annex of the Rzeczpospolita daily, 44,000 copies) is a sellout in martial law Poland.

The military law government has so far largely superimposed military personnel on all administrative areas. Some 18,000 NCOs and officers have been active in this endeavor in the decision-making capacities, on all levels of public life. The party, although officially publicized as active, is thus de facto ineffectual and/or absent on all lower levels. Government spokesmen freely admitted that many of these decision makers will not return to army service but will join the bureaucracy permanently.[49] Thus even after the lifting of martial law in July 1983 the role of the full return of the party to its decision-making role is far from clear.

The basic stalemate between the authorities and society at large has not been resolved in spite of the government's ability to prevent a general strike.[50] That measure of control, however, does not enable the regime authorities to prevent demonstrations of varying sizes and in various cities. It seems that this situation will prevail until some kind of compromise can be achieved, if possible at all, between authorities, Catholic church hierarchy, and the working class. Only then could social and economic harmony return to Poland. Although the release of Lech Walesa and the agreement for a return visit of Pope John Paul II were harbingers of such an accommodation,[51] continuing confrontations and deepening societal resentment make such possibilities more and more remote as time goes by.

In spite of all the uncertainties following the state of war, there is one axiom emerging in the Polish political situation. There is no alternative to the party (and the army) or some kind of future compact between the party and the working class (arrived at with the mediation of the church) with the tacit consensus of the Soviet Union. The reason for this is simply the geographic position of Poland and the role of the Soviet Union in upholding its vital strategic and political interests in Poland. Time will tell which solution will emerge.

NOTES

1. Heller Pick in The Guardian (London), June 12, 1979.
2. As privately admitted to the author by a high-ranking party official.
3. Z. A. Kruszewski, The Oder-Neisse Boundary and Poland's Modernization: The Socioeconomic and Political Impact (New York: Praeger, 1972), pp. 117-33.
4. Ibid., pp. 159-63.

5. Jan B. de Weydenthal, The Communists of Poland (Stanford, California: Hoover Institution Press, 1978), pp. 123-48, 167-69.

6. Polityka (Warsaw), "Spoleczenstwo w Podrozy," 40 (1179) Year 23, Warsaw, October 6, 1979.

7. Expressed openly in the press, e.g., Polityka, which runs a weekly column about shortages and price increases, called "Na rynku" (in the market place).

8. A prominent Polish social scientist summarized the situation succinctly by telling the author shortly before August 1980 that "all shortages can be traditionally endured by the Poles except . . . meat shortages, due to the psychological (or pathological) attachment to that product by the whole society." Some 35 years after the conclusion of World War II, public opinion (including even party members) could not condone these shortages, although Poles consumed almost three times more meat than in 1945.

9. Rocznik Statystyczny 1981 (Warsaw: GUS, 1981), Table 11 (825), p. 578.

10. The Week in Germany (New York: German Information Center), Oct. 5, 1979, p. 5.

11. Indirectly admitted by Polityka (Warsaw) in its analysis of the National Census of December 1978.

12. In 1980 alone, Poles bought $455.7 million worth of goods in U.S. currency. Maly Rocznik Statystyczny 1981 24 (Warsaw: GUS, 1981), Table 6 (212), p. 202.

13. de Weydenthal, op. cit., pp. 166-69.

14. See Tables 11.1 and 11.2.

15. David S. Mason, "Membership of the Polish United Workers' Party," The Polish Review 27 (1982):138-53.

16. See Table 11.3.

17. Polska 75 (Warsaw: PWN, 1975), pp. 195-215.

18. Polska 75, op. cit.

19. de Weydenthal, op. cit., pp. 180-81.

20. Ibid., pp. 85-86.

21. As reflected, for instance, in the issues of Opinia, the underground publication of the Movement for Defense of Human and Civil Rights (ROPCiO), published irregularly in Warsaw since 1977.

22. The rebuilding of the Warsaw Castle since 1971, after prohibition by the party from 1949-70, has been one of the most symbolic gestures of this kind.

23. See Table 11.3.

24. Adam Bromke, "Policy and Politics in Gierek's Poland," in Background to Crisis: Policy and Politics in Gierek's Poland,

Maurice D. Simon and Roger E. Kanet, eds. (Boulder, Colorado: Westview Press, 1981), pp. 6-10.

25. Zycie Warszawy, September 6-7, 1980, p. 3.

26. Ibid., p. 5.

27. Rocznik Statystyczny, 1980 (Warsaw: GUS, 1980), Table 7 (57), p. 35.

28. This affected a wide spectrum of the Polish press, including official party papers (all except army papers and those reflecting the most orthodox views).

29. To hide this fact, no figures for the trade unions were given for the first time in Maly Rocznik Statystyczny, 1981 (Warsaw: GUS, 1981), Table 3 (24), p. 20.

30. Published in Kultura (Warsaw) as reported by "Dziennik Zwiazkowy" (Chicago), June 22, 1981.

31. As reported by Polityka (Warsaw) in its coverage of the Ninth Congress of the PUWP.

32. Poland Today: The State of the Republic (Armonk, NY: M. E. Sharpe, 1981).

33. Mason, op. cit., p. 152.

34. Polityka, July 25, 1981.

35. Ibid.

36. Ibid.

37. Serwis Prasowy BIPS No. 261, November 10, 1981.

38. AS (Agencja Solidarnosci), No. 44, October 12, 1981, p. 205.

39. Polityka (Warsaw), November 21 and December 12, 1981.

40. This was accomplished after the assumption by General Jaruzelski of the position of the first secretary of the Polish United Workers' Party.

41. The Polish press, during two months preceding December 13, 1981, had carried full reports on the mismanagement, economic waste, and the incompetence of the officials in many areas of the country where the operational teams were assigned.

42. Roman Kolkowicz, The Soviet Military and the Communist Party (Princeton, New Jersey: Princeton University Press, 1967); Stephen S. Kaplan, Diplomacy of Power, Soviet Armed Forces as a Political Instrument (Washington, D.C.: Brookings Institute, 1981).

43. Soviet military intervention in both Hungary and Czechoslovakia has had negative repercussions on many communist parties in the world.

44. Polityka, December 4, 1981.

45. This is related to the positivist, pragmatic attitudes of a large part of the Polish leadership in the tsarist-ruled Poland, who saw advancement of some of the Polish national goals (economic as well as limited political ones) only in the context of Polish collaboration with the authorities of imperial Russia of the nineteenth century.

46. For example, Tygodnik Powszechny 25 (1721), June 20, 1982; Trybuna Opolska, June 1, 1982.

47. For example, Rzeczpospolita—Diariusz Sejmowy, March 26, 1982.

48. Op. cit., May 3-4, 1982.

49. As stated by Minister Jerzy Urban, the government spokesman in a meeting with the students of the Faculty of Political Science at the University of Warsaw, June 16, 1982.

50. Called for November 10, 1982, the second anniversary of the legalization of the Solidarity Labor Federation and admitted as a failure by its organizers.

51. Which closely corresponded with the change in the leadership of the USSR on November 10, 1982.

12.

The Polish Military and Politics

Paul C. Latawski

INTRODUCTION

The successive appointments of General Wojciech Jaruzelski leading to his martial law post of chairman of the Military Council of National Salvation (WRON) have underscored the growing political importance of the Polish military in the political life of Poland.

The immediate cause of Polish military rule lies in the erosion of the political importance of the Polish United Workers' Party (PUWP) during the course of the Polish renewal. In the face of irresistible popular pressures embodied by the Solidarity movement, the PUWP steadily lost both its members and the ability to govern Poland. The slow political demise of the Polish party meant that the generals increasingly held high posts in the party and in the government, which in turn culminated in a military regime. Nevertheless, the direct political role for the Polish military is only a recent development. In the Stalinist and Gomulka years, the Polish armed forces remained a closely controlled element of Polish society. The factional political struggles in the party in the late 1960s and the workers' riots of December 1970 and June 1976 granted the armed forces greater institutional autonomy and, albeit indirectly, a political role in the 1970s.

The political ambitions of the Polish generals provide the central impetus for Poland's military elite to seek power. The officers of WRON are relatively young men who share a common set of experiences: wartime service in the Soviet Union, the rigors of the Stalinist period, and career development during the rapid postwar modernization of the Warsaw Treaty Organization (WTO) armed forces. The Polish military elite represents a cohesive and homogeneous element on the Polish political scene. Furthermore, Poland's military leaders developed political influence while promoting the military establishment's interests with the PUWP civilian leadership and with their Soviet counterparts in the WTO command structure. For the Polish generals, political success meant rapid promotion, a bigger defense budget, and the latest Soviet weapon systems.[1] With tangible rewards to be derived from political activity, it is hardly surprising that Polish military leaders harbored wider political ambitions and proved capable of realizing them.

General Wojciech Jaruzelski, the leader of the military regime, typifies the ambitions and the characteristics of Poland's military elite. Alternately labeled a closet patriot or a Soviet stooge in the West, Jaruzelski has enjoyed a phenomenal career in the Polish army. His promotions have included the politically sensitive posts of chief of the Main Political Directorate and minister of National Defense. The first of these was held at the young age of 37. Considerable political reliability, ambition, and skill would be required to achieve such rapid advancement.[2] Jaruzelski thus represents an epitome of his generation's military elites.

The Polish generals control a formidable array of foreign and domestic assets that enhances the military's role as a political institution. The high-ranking Polish officers maintain regular contact with the Soviet military establishment on both a bilateral basis and in the multilateral context of the WTO.[3] This provides the Polish military with alternate channels of communication outside the official PUWP and government structure. However formal or informal these contacts may be, they help Poland's military elites to gauge the twists and turns of Soviet policy on Poland as well as to build Kremlin confidence in their ability to manage Poland's internal developments.[4] With Poland's internal affairs so dependent on relations with the Soviet Union, the ties between the Polish and Soviet military establishments assume great political importance.

Domestically, the most important strengths of the Polish armed forces lie in their disciplined and highly centralized structure, which possesses a virtual monopoly over the use of organized armed force in Polish society. Since the late 1960s, almost all important internal security formations have fallen, either directly or indirectly, under the control of the Polish Defense Ministry.[5] This change afforded the military the ability to deploy the bulk of the repressive forces at the disposal of the Polish state. When the infrastructure of bases, a logistic

network, communication, and headquarter facilities is counted,
then it becomes readily apparent that the Polish military has
the coercive means available to forward its political aims.

Up to the imposition of martial law, the Polish armed forces
were certainly a traditionally respected institution in Polish
society. The average Pole thought highly of the man in uniform
and associated the Polish army with the valiant struggles to
regain Polish independence from the time of the partitions.[6]
Whether this favorable view of the Polish military has continued
since the imposition of martial law, however, is debatable.

The Polish armed forces are not without serious liabilities.
In past domestic crises the military has acted as an instrument
of civilian political authority, while the rank and file has been
reluctant to follow. The limitations of the common soldier in
domestic police actions were clearly borne out by events of
June 1956 in Poznan and of December 1970 in Gdansk and in
the martial law deployments of December 1981 that avoided pitting
regular army units against workers. Unlike dedicated internal
security formations, an estimated 74 percent of the 207,000 men
in the present standing army are two-year conscripts.[7] These
men reflect the values and beliefs of the Polish population rather
than the outlook of the military establishment to which they
are temporarily assigned. Thus when civil disorders reach a
scale making the intervention of the regular army necessary,
a double reluctance sets in: that of the common soldier to fire
on his fellow countrymen and that of the military leadership to
commit unreliable formations in civil disorders.

The subsequent discussion of the political role of the Polish
military will analyze the military's role in light of the historical
events since 1945.

BACKGROUND

The origins of the postwar Polish army can be traced back
to the first and second Polish armies organized under the aegis
of the Soviet Union during World War II. Composed of Soviet
officers leading Polish enlisted ranks, these formations eventually
numbered 400,000 men and became the core of the Polish People's
Army in the postwar years.[8] At the outset of the postwar period,
the Polish armed forces were little more than a branch of the
Red Army. The death of Stalin and the Polish October dramatically altered the Polish military establishment, making it once
again a national force. In this startling transformation lies
the most important outcome of the years 1945-56: the emancipa-

tion of the Polish military from overt Soviet control. This important change opened the way for the development of a distinct Polish military elite and wider institutional autonomy.

At an early stage the Polish army showed clear indications of being unreliable in quelling civil disorders. The postwar anticommunist insurgency was suppressed through the efforts of the internal security forces with the army taking a distinctly secondary role. Because of the regime's doubts about the reliability of the Polish army it remained untested.[9] Later when regular army units were ordered to fire on protesting workers in June 1956 the soldiers balked. This Achilles' heel plagued the Polish army from the earliest years of Poland's communist regime.

In the late 1940s the Polish army acted in support of the internal security forces that waged a campaign against residual Western-oriented anticommunist resistance groups. The struggle between such groups including Zrzeszenie Wolnosc Niezawislosc (WIN) and the internal security forces approached the level of a civil war in the countryside. Because of concerns over the reliability of many formations, the Polish army's role was a supportive one. Only ultrareliable army cadres seconded to the security forces saw action.[10] By 1948, however, the authorities had succeeded in effectively suppressing the underground opposition.

Between 1948 and 1955, the Polish armed forces underwent a major transformation conforming them to the then current Soviet model. Soviet style uniforms, weapons, training methods, and doctrine were adopted. The Polish army expanded, and with the reintroduction of universal conscription in 1949, the army's strength approached 400,000 men.[11] The most significant change for the army was the importation of Soviet officers, who eventually made up half the entire officer corps. These officers occupied all the major commands of the Polish army and their influence extended to the small unit level in advisory capacities. The process was crowned with the appointment of Soviet Marshall Konstantin Rokossovsky to the dual positions of defense minister and commander-in-chief of the Polish military forces in November 1949.[12]

At the same time the Polish army officer corps was purged of elements deemed unreliable. In July-August 1951 a show trial of high-ranking Polish officers such as Generals Tatar and Kirchmayer resulted in life terms for alleged espionage for the West. Many of these officers had served in the West during World War II. In addition scores of lower-ranking Polish officers were secretly tried and executed.[13] As a result of these changes, the Polish army became an integral element of the Soviet army. This situation prevailed until March 1953 when the death of Stalin triggered an undercurrent of popular discontent in Eastern Europe, culminating three years later in Poland's first major domestic crisis.

The year 1956 saw a major change in PUWP leadership, a workers' rebellion, and a narrowly averted Soviet military intervention. The outbreak of labor unrest in Poznan in June provided the first test of the Polish army's reliability in a domestic disorder. A peaceful protest erupted into rioting, which quickly became unmanageable for the local security forces. Polish army units were called in, but soldiers reportedly refused to fire on the demonstrators and some of the soldiers actually sided with the crowds.[14] These events illustrated how the close association of conscripted soldiers with the general population debilitated the army's utility in this civil disorder. Eventually, troops from the elite Internal Security Corps (Korpus Bezpieczenstwa Wewnetrznego—KBW) restored order with many civilian casualties.[15]

By October 1956, the crisis in Poland reached a critical stage with Wladyslaw Gomulka becoming first secretary of the PUWP. Gomulka's election to the top position in the PUWP touched off a crisis in Polish-Soviet relations as the Soviets feared he would follow the liberalizing policies of the popular Imre Nagy in Hungary. The Soviet response was swift. Krushchev led an uninvited Soviet delegation to Warsaw on October 19 while Soviet troops began to move from their bases in Poland toward Warsaw. Heated discussions ensued in which Gomulka threatened armed resistance to any Soviet advance on Warsaw. To back his threat, he deployed General Komar's internal security formations around Warsaw. The Soviet leaders, beset with troubles in Hungary and faced with the unpleasant complication of Polish resistance, accepted Gomulka and agreed to tolerate a degree of domestic liberalization in Poland.[16]

The most important outcome of the events of 1956 concerned the level of direct Soviet military involvement in Poland. A new Polish-Soviet status of forces agreement greatly restricted, at least on paper, the size and deployment of Soviet forces in Poland.[17] The Polish army was renationalized with traditional Polish uniform styles and insignia restored and the officer corps similarly rebuilt along national lines. General Marian Spychalski succeeded Soviet Marshall Rokossovsky as defense minister who was, along with several thousand fellow Soviet officers, recalled to the Soviet Union.[18]

In the wake of the Polish October, the Polish armed forces evolved toward greater institutional autonomy while clearly

emulating new Soviet military doctrines. The Soviet revolution
in military doctrine restructured Soviet forces to conduct rapid
offensive operations with technically modernized formations.
With the new doctrine came a greater role for the East European
armed forces within the context of the Warsaw Pact Alliance.
The new direction in Soviet military policy prompted Polish
initiatives in military doctrine.[19]

Polish military theoreticians developed two parallel and
complementary doctrines: The first was a coalition doctrine that
envisioned the Polish forces being organized into a separate
Polish front where the army would fight as a unit. Soviet
acceptance of this was doubtful.[20] The second doctrine of
Defense of National Territory (Obrona terytorium kraju—OTK)
incorporated civil and internal defense organizations into an
integrated national command structure. The OTK was designed
to protect WTO northern tier lines of communication running
through Poland.[21]

The new military doctrines demanded the technological
sophistication of a highly professional officer corps. What
resulted was a contradiction between the need for party control
and the need for a competent military establishment. In a
communist state, the military traditionally has been kept strictly
subordinate to the dictates of the civilian political leadership.
The party has exercised its control in the armed forces through
the Main Political Administration (MPA) with the ubiquitous
political officer and with the Military Security Service (Wojska
Sluzby Wewnetrznej—WSW).[22] Throughout the 1960s, the PUWP
took measures to strengthen its position against the rising tide
of professionalism; however, the results did not match the level
of control enjoyed earlier.[23]

The technological modernization that accompanied the new
military doctrines greatly undermined the system of party control.
Not even political officers were spared technical training.[24]
Military professionalism superseded considerations based solely
on ideological reliability. With the lessening of party controls,
a professional officer corps began to emerge giving the Polish
military a distinct institutional character.

POLITICAL CRISES AND THE POLISH MILITARY 1967-76

Poland's cycle of domestic political crises extending from
the PUWP factional strife of 1967 to the workers' riots of 1976
made for profound changes in the military as an institution and
in its involvement in politics. The PUWP factional struggles in
1967-68 completed the professionalization of the officer corps

and marked the birth of a homogeneous military elite. Later, domestic upheaval influenced the military's role in politics. The participation of the military in the Baltic riots of 1970 demoralized the army to such an extent that, with renewed workers' riots in 1976, the military elite pressed for a political solution to avoid entangling the army. Overall, the workers' protests of 1970 and 1976 had the important effect of drawing the military more directly into the maelstrom of Polish politics.

1967-68

In 1967 the Gomulka-led PUWP leadership was challenged by the so-called Partisan faction, an ideologically orthodox group led by Mieczyslaw Moczar. The army became a battleground in this factional struggle. The defeat of the Soviet-supplied Arab armed forces following the Arab-Israeli conflict of June 1967 led to an extensive purge of the military under the guise of an anti-Zionist campaign. The first to be ousted were the air force generals who were critical of Soviet doctrine. Hundreds of officers from all branches of the military were sacked, with those of Jewish background being singled out.[25] The numerous vacancies created by this purge were filled by highly professional officers who were not in the political factions. By this means the incumbent political leadership deflected the Partisan challenge.[26]

The following year brought a major domestic crisis with the student protests of March 1968 and a renewed challenge from the Partisans. The students were quelled by the Citizens' Militia (Milicja Obywatelska—MO) in the streets of Warsaw while the failure of the Partisans to dislodge Gomulka decisively thwarted their attempt to control the PUWP. In April 1968 Lieutenant General Wojciech Jaruzelski was appointed minister of defense replacing the longtime Gomulka associate Marshall Marian Spychalski. The appointment of Jaruzelski over Lieutenant General Korczynski, the Partisans' candidate, considerably diminished the prospects of this faction gaining a dominant position in the military and thereafter it ceased to be a disruptive factor. Jaruzelski's appointment crowned the professionalization trend in the officer corps and signified the birth of a new military elite.[27] In August, Polish army units participated in the Soviet-led invasion of Czechoslovakia, which resulted in additional morale problems for the Polish armed forces.[28]

1970 and 1976

If the political infighting in the PUWP acted as a catalyst to the birth of a professional military elite, then the workers' riots in December 1970 and June 1976 prompted the military's initiation into Polish politics. The workers' riots in the coastal cities in December 1970 were met initially by local MO security units and, as the situation worsened, by local army units. Clashes in the streets of Gdansk were particularly fierce with the district PUWP headquarters set afire along with scores of police and military vehicles.[29] Both the MO and army units fired on the protestors and inflicted many casualties; official communiques put the figures at 45 dead and 1165 wounded.[30]

The order to use force was given by a close aide to Gomulka, Zenon Kliszko, who thought the situation counterrevolutionary. However the army leadership in Gdansk balked and appeared to resist irresponsible orders that it felt would lead to greater bloodshed. The Baltic coast events proved demoralizing for the army.[31] Because of its reluctance to use force, the Polish military participated in the PUWP leadership changes in 1970. The military leadership, at the very least, acted as a silent partner in the removal of Gomulka as first secretary of the PUWP and his replacement with Edward Gierek.[32]

In June 1976, the Gierek regime faced renewed worker unrest with riots at Ursus outside Warsaw and in the industrial city of Radom. The MO dealt with the workers in a tough manner with hundreds of arrests. Unlike 1970, the Polish government defused an explosive situation by quickly rescinding unpopular price increases. The military leadership was said to have counseled its political counterpart in the PUWP to exercise restraint and to seek a political solution. General Jaruzelski, then minister of defense, reportedly told the government that: "Polish soldiers will not fire on Polish workers."[33] In view of the demoralizing effect that the Baltic riots had on the army, Jaruzelski was wary of a possible recurrence. The generals avoided the uncomfortable position of being both an instrument and later a scapegoat for bloody oppression when, in the end, they would reap none of the political rewards associated with the restored domestic stability.

POLISH RENEWAL AUGUST 1980-DECEMBER 1981

The announcement of food price increases in the summer of 1980 unleashed latent unrest in Poland. The August 1980 crisis led to the creation of Solidarity and strong pressure for change. The phenomenal rise of Solidarity with its wide basis of national support posed a serious threat to Poland's communist regime. Parallel to the rise of Solidarity stood the growing political influence of the Polish military during the course of the Polish crisis. Most striking in this period was the gradual demise of the PUWP, thus creating a tempting political vacuum. As the PUWP faltered, more generals gained key political posts, with Jaruzelski in particular adding more government and party positions to his portfolio.

In the initial stages of the crisis, however, it is unclear exactly how the military leaders viewed both the question of employing force against striking workers and the leadership struggle that led to Gierek's ouster on September 2, 1980. Some observers have argued that the military exercised a veto over the use of force at that stage of the crisis and withdrew its support for Gierek in a manner similar to December 1970 and June 1976.[34] The tense days of August 1980 dictated restraint on the part of the authorities if a major domestic upheaval was to be averted. Furthermore, the signing of the Gdansk accord on August 31, 1980 represented for the PUWP an unprecedented catastrophe as it laid bare the political impotence of the Polish Communist Party.

The turning point for direct military involvement in the political life of Poland came in February 1981 with the appointment of General Jaruzelski to the premiership, making him the head of the Polish government. The Polish Communist Party had been under increasing pressure from Solidarity and it became clear that some unpopular and ineffectual figures must be replaced. Jaruzelski, who was seemingly divorced from the past errors of the Gierek years, offered the party a new face. He quickly took a tough stand and in a speech before the Sejm asked for and received a ninety-day moratorium on strikes. The moratorium soon collapsed, but it indicated a new style of leadership that sought to make use of the prestige and reverence of the military uniform in Poland as well as to project an image of authority. Subsequent speeches in the Polish Sejm nurtured this image although they were often tempered with conciliatory remarks.[35] In addition to firm policy line, Jaruzelski brought more military officers into party and government posts. These appointments placed military men at the head of key ministries controlling vital areas of the economy and administration.[36]

Despite the ominous implications of these appointments, the Polish army and indeed Jaruzelski himself enjoyed growing popularity with a wide section of Polish society. Jaruzelski often drew favorable comments from Lech Walesa, the leader of Solidarity, who publicly held him in esteem.[37] A public opinion poll on the most trusted political institutions held in May 1981 rated the military third. A similar poll held in September elevated it to second place. In both polls the PUWP took the last or next to last position on a long list of institutions. The military's popularity reflected a long-standing reverence that the Poles have had for the armed forces as a national institution.[38] Further reinforcing the popularity of the military in the public eye was the widespread belief that the army would offer resistance to a Soviet invasion of Poland. Short of an actual Soviet intervention, this popular notion remained untested.[39]

Some peculiar episodes of the Polish crisis stand in sharp contrast to the public popularity of the military. For example, the government-Solidarity clash over the beatings of Solidarity activists in the city of Bydgoszcz in March raised some questions over Jaruzelski's responsibility for the provocative police action. The timing of the March events, which came parallel to bloc media campaigns, WTO maneuvers, and bilateral and multilateral meetings, all suggest a concerted effort to confront Solidarity. It seems unlikely that the provocative beatings in Bydgoszcz could only be the work of PUWP hard-liners attempting to discredit a more moderate party line on Solidarity.[40] It is inconceivable that Jaruzelski did not know in advance about the Bydgoszcz provocation as well as its apparent coordination to other events. Jaruzelski may well have been testing the water for the subsequent imposition of martial law some eight months later.

The remaining months prior to martial law saw Jaruzelski elevated to first secretary of the PUWP on October 18 while retaining his previous positions. Following his unprecedented concentration of political offices, Jaruzelski stepped up more menacing government actions. In late October, he ordered squads of army personnel into rural villages and provincial towns, ostensibly to help clear up bottlenecks contributing to food shortages. As in the Bydgoszcz crisis in March, the deployment of small units around Poland may have been related to the subsequent martial law. Finally, in early December, the MO broke up an occupational strike of cadets at a fire fighter's academy.[41] This pattern of more forceful action marked the transition of Poland's generals away from a defensive posture toward a clear-cut offensive to check the power of Solidarity and formed the prelude to the declaration of martial law.

STATE OF WAR DECEMBER 1981-DECEMBER 1982

The declaration of martial law (stan wojenny—state of war) on December 13, 1981 decisively altered the shape of Poland's politics as it ushered in a new phase of direct military rule in Poland. A Military Council of National Salvation (Wojskowa Rada Ocalenia Narodowego—WRON), composed of 20 officers with Jaruzelski at its head, overnight became the supreme governing body in Poland. The Polish generals staged what may be considered the communist world's first successful military coup.[42]

When Jaruzelski announced the imposition of martial law, he declared that Poland was at the "edge of the abyss" and that the Council of National Salvation intended to save the nation from catastrophe.[43] He attempted to do this with a meticulously organized and swiftly executed operation that had been planned months in advance under a tight veil of secrecy. Issuing a flurry of martial law decrees, the military regime made public gatherings illegal, imposed restrictions on travel, introduced strict censorship, and militarized key elements of the state bureaucracy. All union activity including the right to strike was suspended.[44] Most important, the military rulers interned thousands of Solidarity activists, including virtually all of its top leaders. Many officials of the former Gierek regime were arrested in a cosmetic gesture of impartiality. The emergency powers conferred on WRON a wide latitude of powers designed to aid in the imposition of its authority in Poland.

The Solidarity leadership seemingly was caught unprepared for the state of war and only a fraction of its members escaped underground. Rank-and-file union members offered spontaneous but uncoordinated resistance to the imposition of martial law. Their protests took the form of scattered occupational strikes and street demonstrations that were broken up speedily by the martial law authorities. The clash between security forces and miners at the Wujek coal mine was typical of the ruthless use of force.[45] The military regime reacted quickly to strikes and demonstrations around the country so that it became impossible for Solidarity to organize a successful national strike, its most powerful weapon.

Despite the violent repression and mass internments, after Solidarity's initial setbacks some elements regrouped and formed an underground resistance. Well-known Solidarity advisors, such as Jacek Kuron, called for the organization of a mass resistance movement to oppose systematically the military regime.[46] A thriving samizdat press emerged together with clandestine radio broadcasts. Notwithstanding these successes, the Solidarity underground failed to channel effective opposition to the military regime. The underground's strategy of mass street demonstrations proved a dismal failure as the authorities crushed each one in turn. Security police arrests and the confiscation of printing supplies and radio equipment weakened the underground organization. The authorities felt strong enough to dissolve officially the Solidarity trade union.[47] By the end of 1982, with the suspension of martial law in sight, the Solidarity underground admitted its future seemed bleak and that it needed to rethink its strategy of opposition.[48]

Besides the Solidarity underground, the military rulers faced Poland's powerful Catholic church. The Polish episcopate, while denouncing violence and bloodshed, took a conciliatory and moderate stance.[49] The church advocated a social accord between the military rulers and Polish society. In April 1982, the church produced a white paper that sought to lay out conditions necessary to achieve national reconciliation.[50] Mixed with conciliatory efforts, however, there were tough statements of opposition to aspects of military rule. The Polish primate, Archbishop Glemp, followed an uncertain course that both demoralized and angered church supporters who had hoped for strong leadership and a tougher line.[51] The church, like Solidarity underground, failed to devise a strategy opposing military rule.

The year-long state of war was punctuated with civil disturbances that sorely tested WRON's internal security forces. Major protests, some national in scale, occurred at the beginning of May, the end of August, and in October with the official dissolution of the Solidarity organization. Smaller scale protests and riots took place so frequently as to defy a comprehensive list. The security forces, as the year progressed, became more adept at crowd control. Tear gas, water cannons, concussion grenades, and the baton charge were used most efficiently to sap the strength of pro-Solidarity protests. By December 1982, it was clear that WRON had won the battle for Poland's streets.[52]

The responsibility for the violent repression conducted in the course of the state of war rested on reliable internal security formations.[53] ZOMO typified these units. The regular army was excluded from acts of civil repression, and deployment patterns indicate that great pains were taken to preclude its use. Many army units simply remained in their barracks. Those employed manned checkpoints and roadblocks and occasionally paraded their armored vehicles in calculated displays of strength.[54] The Polish military leadership doubted the relia-

bility of the conscripted soldier in a civil disorder and planned
their unit dispositions accordingly (see Table 12.1). WRON
prevailed solely in its domestic police actions, with the internal
security assets of the Polish state. The integration of Poland's
security forces under a Defense Ministry command structure
gave the decisive advantage to WRON, which coordinated its
assets to maximum effect.[55]

During the state of war, the military regime made the
destruction of Solidarity and the pacification of the country its
primary goals.[56] The military rulers were uncompromising
against the underground opposition, street protestors, and on
the question of the revival of Solidarity. The trade union was
officially abolished in October 1982. The apparent failure of
the Solidarity underground to harness successfully the widespread opposition to the martial law regime must be considered
an important success for Poland's military rulers. Likewise,
the uncertain church policy aided the military regime.[57] In
the last months of 1982, the military rulers thought the situation
in Poland sufficiently normalized to offer some conciliatory
gestures. Lech Walesa, Solidarity's leader, was released from
internment and it was announced that the pope would visit
Poland in the new year. Finally, on the first anniversary of
martial law, Jaruzelski announced that it would be suspended
at the end of December 1982.[58]

Although the martial law regime counted some successes
in stifling its opponents, the political opposition in Poland is
far from dead. The military government's desire to smash
Solidarity and the heavy-handed police oppression have alienated
Polish society further from its rulers. For the long term, this
creates the basis for a greater opposition movement that will
sooner or later find a means of expression.[59] The regime's
nervousness is evident, for example, in the series of laws
passed by the Sejm making permanent the tough emergency
measures. Hence the end of martial law may mean little in
practice.[60]

Besides political problems, the period of martial law failed
to find any concrete solutions to Poland's grave economic difficulties. A much-lauded economic reform floundered for lack of
comprehensive application and political constraints placed on
the reformers. Apart from some successes in areas such as
increased coal production, the general economic dislocation
coupled with the massive foreign debt and trade problems resulted in the continued deterioration of the economy under
military rule.[61]

TABLE 12.1. Poland's Armed Forces

Category	Totals	Notes
Population	35,900,000	
Total regular forces	317,000	185,000 conscripts (58%)
Army		
Ground forces	207,000	154,000 conscripts (74%)
Number of divisions	15	
Tank	5	
Motorized rifle	8	
Airborne	1	
Amphibious	1	
Reserves	605,000	
Motorized rifle	1 or 2	
Air force	88,000	27,000 conscripts (31%)
Reserves	60,000	
Combat aircraft	679	
Navy	22,000	6,000 conscripts (27%)
Reserves	45,000	
Paramilitary		
Border troops	20,000	
Internal Security Corps	65,000	
MO	350,000	MO: Milicja Obywatelska (Citizens' Militia)
ORMO	250,000	ORMO: Ochotnicza Rezerwa Milicji Obywatelskiej (Citizens' Militia Volunteer Reserve)

Source: Data taken from The Military Balance 1982-1983 (London: The International Institute for Strategic Studies, 1982), and Friedrich Wiener, The Armies of the Warsaw Pact (Vienna: Carl Ueberreuter, 1974).

MILITARY RULE AND THE PARTY'S FUTURE

The imposition of martial law saw the eclipse of the ruling PUWP, and as a result the most pressing issue is the future of the party. Will the power of the PUWP be diminished permanently, usurped by the Polish generals, or at some later date will it regain its position of dominance? If the organizational features of martial law are any indication, then it is clear that the Polish generals are entrenching themselves for a long political siege. It is conceivable that military rule could become a permanent feature on the political landscape of Poland. Should the PUWP or its successor reemerge, it will be an organization completely rebuilt and cast in the image of Poland's military rulers.[62]

The political ambitions of Poland's military elite represent a crucial factor in the rise of the Polish armed forces to political power. Although critics of military rule in Poland have labeled the Polish generals as mere Soviet puppets or as stooges of the battered PUWP, such an analysis summarily dismisses the possibility of the Polish military elite harboring its own political ambitions.[63] Closer scrutiny, however, reveals a series of characteristics that contributed to the direct involvement of the military elite in politics.

The officers of WRON are relatively young men, with the average age of its highest ranking members in the late fifties. These senior officers share a common background of wartime service in the Soviet-sponsored Polish formations in World War II and participation in the subsequent postwar struggle against the right-wing resistance movement. Although the most junior officers may have missed the difficult Stalinist years, together the members of WRON enjoyed career development in the dynamic period of postwar modernization of WTO armed forces. It can safely be assumed that all WRON members belong to the party and have attended high-level military schools, with many receiving training at important Soviet academies (see Table 12.2). The backgrounds of these men do not suggest closet nationalism or total synchronism with Soviet desires. Rather, the members of Poland's military elite are best understood as products of and participants in the military section of the communist bureaucratic-state apparatus. They are loyal and successful participants in a system whose highest reward is the acquisition and retention of political power.[64]

Besides the martial law government replacing the civilian leaders of the PUWP, the Polish military regime has moved to consolidate its position in an organizational-bureaucratic sense. By virtue of the legal configuration of martial law, Jaruzelski and his colleagues are able to dominate the apparatchiki of the party's swollen bureaucracy. Through special Councils for the Defense of the Country (KOK) and military commissars, the country is ruled directly by the military, thus sidetracking the politically powerful PUWP bureaucratic apparatus.[65] This development not only indicates the level of control of the Polish military, but also the degree of institutional permanency being given to military rule.

Regarding the future of the PUWP, it is almost certain that the party will not keep its present form but it is unlikely to disappear completely. From the onset of martial law, the party underwent a purge affecting thousands of members. Not only Solidarity sympathizers were ousted but also hard-liners and corrupt individuals. Potential rivals to Jaruzelski, such as Stefan Olszowski, have been reshuffled to nonthreatening positions.[66] The obvious goal of such an extensive purge, covering a spectrum of political views, has been to build some sort of consensus in the PUWP. For Jaruzelski and his military colleagues to create a united party solely with the purpose of relinquishing their authority seems an unlikely proposition. The party may become a suitable facade for continued military rule in Poland.

WHITHER MILITARY RULE?

In February 1981, a Sunday Times (London) analysis of the involvement of the Polish military in politics asserted that "for General Jaruzelski and his military colleagues, anything like a takeover of the state would go very much against the grain."[67] Yet a little more than ten months later, a coup placed Jaruzelski and his colleagues in control of the Polish state. The subsequent twelve months of the state of war saw the party ousted from power and a crushing blow delivered to Solidarity. Such a scenario, considered unlikely in early 1981, became reality and one that raises questions on the future of military rule in Poland. Will the generals remain in power, and if so, what sort of solutions can they offer to the country's daunting political and economic problems?

Some observers of the Polish crisis have considered the beginning of military rule in Poland as something akin to a new ice age.[68] No doubt the violence surrounding the imposition of martial law goes a long way in setting this outlook of gloom and pessimism. However, there are those who have adopted a wait-and-see attitude toward martial law in a more optimistic vein.

TABLE 12.2. Poland's Military Elite: WRON

Name	Year of Birth	Wartime Service	Training	Branch	Rank	Pre-Martial Law Post
Wojciech Jaruzelski	1923	PSU PAP	SMS PMS	A	Army General	Head PUWP, Premier, Minister of Defense
Florian Siwicki	1925	RA PSU PAP	SMS	A	Lt. General	Deputy Minister of Defense Chief General Staff
Tadeusz Tuczapaki	1922	NA	SMS PMS	A	Lt. General	Deputy Minister of Defense
Eugeniusz Molczyk	1925	PSU PAP	SMS	A	Lt. General	Deputy Minister of Defense Chief Inspector Training
Lugwig Janczyszyn	1923	PSU PAP	SMS PMS	N	Admiral	Commander of Navy
Czeslaw Kiszczak	1925	NA	PMS	A	Major General	Military Intelligence
Tadeusz Hupalowski	1922	PSU	PMS	A	Major General	First Deputy Chief of General Staff
Czeslaw Piotrowski	1926	UND PSU	PMS	A	Major General	Chief of Military Research and Technology, Deputy Inspector of Technology
Jozef Baryla	1924	PSU	PMS	A	Major General	Chief of Main Political Board

284

Name		PSU	PMS		Rank	
Wlodzimierz Oliwa	NA	NA	PMS	A	Major General	Commander Warsaw Military District
Henryk Rapacewicz	NA	NA	NA	A	Major General	Commander Warsaw Garrison
Jozef Uzycki	NA	NA	NA	A	Major General	Commander Pomeranian Military District
Tadeusz Krepski	NA	NA	NA	AF	Major General	Commander Air Force
Longin Lozowicki	NA	NA	NA	AF	Major General	Commander of National Air Defense
Michal Janiszewski	1926	NA	PMS	A	General	Chief of Secretariat of Minister of Defense
Jerzy Jarosz	NA	NA	NA	A	General	Commander First Mechanical Division—Warsaw
Tadeusz Garbacik	NA	NA	NA	NA	Colonel	NA
Roman Les	NA	NA	NA	NA	Reserve Colonel	NA
Jerzy Klosinski	NA	NA	NA	NA	Lt. Colonel	NA
Miroslaw Hermaszewski	NA	NA	NA	AF	Lt. Colonel	NA
Tadeusz Makarewicz	NA	NA	NA	NA	Colonel	NA

PAP: Postwar Anti-Partisan
PMS: Polish Military Schools
PSU: Polish Forces, Soviet Union
NA: Not available

RA: Red Army
SMS: Soviet Military Schools
UND: WW II Underground

Source: B. Lewytzkyi and T. Stroynowski, Who's Who in the Socialist Countries (New York: K. G. Saur Publishing, 1978); Encyklopedia Powszechn PWN (Warsaw: PWN, 1973–1976); T. Wisniewski, Who's Who in Poland (Toronto: Professional Translators, 1981).

285

Adam Michnik, the well-known Solidarity advisor, while interned, smuggled out an essay entitled: Polish War. In it, Michnik argues that military rule in Poland is so unique to the annals of communism that it is unwise to judge it prematurely. He further notes that some coups have resulted in dictatorships, as in Chile, while others have led to greater democracy, as in Portugal.[69]

Because of the scale of Poland's political and economic problems, many in Poland think the only solution to the crisis lies in a national accord along the lines of the Catholic church's white paper of April 1982. Shortly after his release from internment, Walesa renewed his call for such an agreement.[70] Clearly a national accord enjoying the overwhelming support of Polish society means the participation of Solidarity and the church. On the surface, a military regime could provide the basis of an acceptable national accord as it is an attractive means of guaranteeing Soviet security interests toward Poland.[71] But the military government would have to want to seek a genuine rapprochement with Polish society.

However acute the need for a national accord in Poland may be, it is clear that the military intends to stay in power. The state of war has shown that the Polish generals are not eager to compromise. The very things that the military did to consolidate its position during martial law made a national accord more remote. The only alternative is rule by the bayonet. Given the strength of the political opposition in Poland, the future appears gloomy with the prospect of prolonged serious troubles.

POSTSCRIPT

The prognosis of a protracted impasse between Poland's military rulers and the political opposition has not been changed by the events of the first half of 1983. The Polish government has striven to place Lech Walesa, Solidarity's leader, into the political wilderness with a campaign designed to reduce his role in Poland to ordinary citizen Walesa. However, Walesa's ubiquitous cortege of police agents and the Western press along with his meetings with Solidarity's underground leadership and the pope belies the reality of citizen Walesa's actual political importance. Perhaps most of all, the papal visit in June highlighted the gulf that continues to divide Poland's military rulers and the people of Poland. While riot police stood poised to smother any outbreaks of pro-Solidarity demonstrations, immense

crowds heartily cheered Pope John Paul II when he offered
explicit condemnation of the Polish government for its failure
to live up to the August 1980 social accord. Although the papal
pronouncements may have provided some embarrassing moments
for Poland's military rulers, they did not prompt any major
shift in their policies. Indeed, the much-heralded lifting of
martial law on July 22 did not evoke much enthusiasm in Poland.
In practical terms, the change meant little as the temporary
regulations of martial law were replaced by more stringent
permanent legislation. In a most symbolic gesture, General
Jaruzelski was awarded the Order of Lenin by the Soviet Union
in honor of his contributions to building socialism. Jaruzelski's
distinction, above all, represented a vote of Soviet confidence
for the tough and uncompromising policies of Poland's military
rulers.

NOTES

1. Dale Herspring, "The Polish Military and the Policy
Process," in Background to Crisis: Policy and Politics in Poland,
eds. Maurice D. Simon and Roger E. Kanet (Boulder, Colorado:
Westview, 1980), pp. 222-24.

2. Ewa Celt, "Wojciech Jaruzelski: A Prime Minister in
Uniform," Radio Free Europe: Research 72 (March 13, 1981):1-4;
Andrzej Korbonski, "The Dilemmas of Civil-Military Relations
in Contemporary Poland: 1945-1981," Armed Forces and Society
8 (1981):4-8; Tadeusz Szafar, "The Party and the Army,"
International Review 1 (1982):15-16.

3. Herspring, "The Polish Military and the Policy
Process," pp. 222-24.

4. Michael Checinski, "The Military and Martial Law,"
International Review 1 (1982):21.

5. A. Ross Johnson, Robert W. Dean, and Alexander
Alexiev, East European Military Establishments: The Warsaw
Pact Northern Tier (Santa Monica: Rand Corporation, 1980),
pp. 34-35. Hence referred to as Rand.

6. Jerzy J. Wiatr, "The Public Image of the Polish
Military: Past and Present," in Political-Military Systems:
Comparative Perspectives, ed. Catherine McArdle Kelleher
(Beverly Hills: Sage, 1974), pp. 199-207.

7. Data taken from The Military Balance 1982-1983
(London: International Institute for Strategic Studies, 1982).

8. Stanislaw Gać, "The Polish People's Army (1943-1975),"
Historia Militaris Polonica 2 (1977):242; Rand, pp. 21-22.

9. Rand, p. 21.

10. Ibid. For more detailed summaries of the military's and security service's role in the anti-Partisan struggle see Ludowe Wojsko Polski 1943-1973 (Warszawa: MON, 1974), pp. 172-74 and W Walce ze zbrojnym podziemiem 1945-1947 (Warszawa: MON, 1972).

11. Rand, pp. 21-22.

12. One Polish publication put the total number of Soviet officers serving in the Polish army at 17,000 or half the entire officer corps: Zycie i Mysl 14 (1964):103. See also Ithiel de Sola Pool, Satellite Generals (Stanford: Stanford University Press, 1955), pp. 67-68; Mala Kronika Ludowego Wojska Polskiego 1943, 1973 (Warszawa: MON, 1975), p. 286.

13. Pool, Satellite Generals, pp. 60-65. For a partial list of the officers executed, see Kultura 3 (1981):150-51. For a detailed look at military justice in the 1950s, see Mieczyslaw Szerer, "Procesy przed Najwyzszym Sadem Wojskowym," Tygodnik Solidarnosc, November 20, 27, and December 4, 1981.

14. Richard Hiscocks, Poland: Bridge for the Abyss (London: Oxford University Press, 1963), p. 192.

15. Flora Lewis, Case History of Hope (New York: Doubleday, 1958), pp. 143-44.

16. For the political events of the Polish October see Zbigniew K. Brzezinski, The Soviet Bloc: Unity and Conflict (Cambridge: Harvard University Press, 1967), pp. 239-68. The possibility of Polish army resistance during the height of the crisis appears minimal because of the disruptive presence of large numbers of Soviet officers, although reportedly some Polish naval and air force units took steps to offer resistance. See Rand, p. 23.

17. For the text of the status of forces agreement of December 17, 1956 see: Stosunki Polsko-Radzieckie w latach 1945-1972 (Warszawa: KIW, 1974), pp. 338-44.

18. Rand, p. 24.

19. Rand, pp. 26-27.

20. For Polish doctrinal developments, see Rand, pp. 26-37. The Rand study expresses strong doubts about the possibility of a Polish front for political and operational reasons (Rand, p. 33). This position is reinforced in a recent article by Christopher Jones, "The Warsaw Pact: Military Exercises and Military Interventions," Armed Forces and Society 7 (1980): 5-30.

21. Rand, pp. 34-35. The OTK concept discussed in Boleslaw Chocha, Obrona terytorium kraju (Warszawa: MON, 1974).

22. The PUWP control mechanism in the Polish armed forces outlined in Rand, pp. 41-48. Concerning the WSW role, see Michael Checinski, "Ludowe wojsko polskie przed i po marcu 1968," Zeszyty Historyczny 44 (1978):30.

23. Rand, pp. 46-48.

24. Dale R. Herspring, "Technology and the Changing Political Officer in the Armed Forces: The Polish and East German Cases," Studies in Comparative Communism 10 (1977): 372-373.

25. Checinski, "Ludowe wojsko polskie przed i po marcu 1968," p. 24. For a general discussion of the events of 1967, see Wlodzimierz Rozenbaum, "The Anti-Zionist Campaign in Poland, June-December 1967," Canadian Slavonic Papers 20 (1978):218-36.

26. Radio Free Europe: Research, Situation Reports: Poland, 33 (April 17, 1968) and (October 11, 1968).

27. Radio Free Europe: Research, Situation Report: Poland, 33 (April 17, 1968).

28. Rand, pp. 58-59.

29. Mieczyslaw F. Rakowski, Przesilenie grudniowe (Warszawa: PIW, 1981), p. 47.

30. Ibid.

31. Michael Costello, "The Party and the Military in Poland," Radio Free Europe: Research 12 (April 26, 1971): 2, 6; Rand, p. 60.

32. Costello, "The Party and the Military in Poland," pp. 2-3.

33. Jaruzelski's alleged statement has been widely repeated in the Western press. For example, John Darnton, "Once Again, to whom and what is the Army Loyal," New York Times, February 1, 1981.

34. Korbonski, "The Dilemmas of Civil-Military Relations in Poland: 1945-1981," pp. 14-15.

35. John Darnton, "Polish Prime Minister Ousted: Defense Chief to Replace Him: Union Pressing its Walkouts," New York Times, February 10, 1981 and "Shift in Poland: Ominous Step or a Calming Move?" New York Times, February 11, 1981 and "Polish Union Chief Indicates that He Backs 90 Strike Free Days," New York Times, February 14, 1981.

36. For the appointments, see T. Hupalowski, C. Kiszczak, C. Piotrowski, and M. Janiszewski in Joseph Wisniewski, Who's Who in Poland (Toronto: Professional Translators, 1981).

37. For example, the interview by Italian journalist Oriana Fallaci, "Lech Walesa: The Man Who Drives the Kremlin Crazy," Washington Post, p. C5.

38. The information on the poll results taken from Michael Dobbs, "Polish Army Keep Country's Trust," Washington Post, November 14, 1981 and the later poll results from a lecture given by a noted Polish sociologist at Indiana University, 1981. For a historical perspective, see Wiatr, "The Public Image of the Polish Military: Past and Present," pp. 199-208.

39. On the resistance issue, see Darnton, "Once Again, to whom and to what is the Army Loyal," New York Times, February 1, 1981; Alex Alexiev et al., If the Soviets Invade Poland (Santa Monica: Rand Corporation, 1980); Elizabeth Pond, "Polish Army: how loyal--and to whom?" The Christian Science Monitor, March 10, 1981.

40. Korbonski, "The Dilemmas of Civil-Military Relations in Contemporary Poland: 1945-1981," p. 16.

41. John Darnton, "More Jostling on Poland's Well-Worn Tightrope," New York Times, December 13, 1981.

42. The only other coup attempt in a Soviet client state reportedly occurred in Bulgaria in 1965. See J. F. Brown, Bulgaria Under Communist Rule (New York: Praeger, 1970), pp. 173-84.

43. Jaruzelski speech declaring martial law in Trybuna Ludu, December 14, 1981, p. 1.

44. Martial law restrictions are listed in Trybuna Ludu, December 14, 1981, pp. 1-4.

45. For a vivid account of the events at the Wujek mine, see Committee in Support of Solidarity, Press Advisory, Special Edition January 10, 1982.

46. Jacek Kuron, "Tezy o wyjsciu z sytuacji bez wyjscia," Aneks 27 (1982):7.

47. Charles Gans, "War for Poland's Hearts and Minds," The Sunday Times (London), September 14, 1982; Roger Boyes, "How the legacy of Solidarity will be taken up," Times (London), October 7, 1982.

48. Roger Boyes, "Solidarity admits it has a bleak future," Times (London), November 18, 1982.

49. J. B. de Weydenthal, "The Church and the State of Emergency," Radio Free Europe: Research 49 (February 19, 1982):1-11.

50. Radio Free Europe: Research, Situation Report: Poland, 7 (April 26, 1982):2-4.

51. "Voice of the Church in Poland," Times (London), September 24, 1982.

52. Roger Boyes, "Deadly dance at nightmare 'disco'" The Sunday Times (London), October 17, 1982; Stephen Aris and Charles Gans, "End of Martial Law leaves masses cold," The Sunday Times (London), December 5, 1982.

53. J. B. de Weydenthal, "Anatomy of the Martial Law Regime: The Institutions," Radio Free Europe Research 32 (February 2, 1982):2-4.

54. de Weydenthal, "Anatomy of the Martial Law Regime: The Institutions," pp. 2-4; Spiegel interview with General Leon Dubicki. Der Spiegel, December 28, 1981, pp. 67, 68.

55. Rand, pp. 34-35.

56. Roger Boyes, "How the legacy of Solidarity will be taken up," Times (London), October 7, 1982.

57. Charles Gans, "War for Poland's Hearts and Minds," The Sunday Times (London), September 5, 1982 and "Voice of the Church in Poland," Times (London), September 24, 1982.

58. Hella Pick, "Jaruzelski suspends martial law," Guardian, December 13, 1982.

59. Roger Boyes, "How the legacy of Solidarity will be taken up," Times (London), October 7, 1982.

60. Charles Gans, "Counting the costs: muzzled, privatised, bound by laws . . ." The Sunday Times (London), December 19, 1982; Stephen Aris and Charles Gans, "End of Martial Law leaves masses cold," The Sunday Times (London), December 5, 1982.

61. Jacek Rostowski, "Economic reforms fail to revitalize Poland's industry," Times (London), September 21, 1982.

62. Zdzislaw M. Rurarz, "Possible Evolution of the Crisis," International Review 1 (1982):11; Roger Boyes, "How the legacy of Solidarity will be taken up," Times (London), October 7, 1982.

63. Adam Brumberg, "Poland: Operation Whitewash," The New Republic 186 (January 6 and 13, 1982):11-16; Tadeusz Szafar, "The Party and the Army," International Review 1 (1982): 16.

64. This point is one of the central themes in Adam B. Ulam, Titoism and the Cominform (Cambridge: Harvard University Press, 1952).

65. de Weydenthal, "Anatomy of the Martial Law Regime: The Institutions," pp. 5-8; Checinski, "The Military and Martial Law," p. 20.

66. Checinski, "The Military and Martial Law," p. 21 and "Shakeup in Polish Leadership," Times (London), July 17, 1982. For some purge statistics, see Trybuna Ludu, July 12, 1982, p. 3. For examples of some of the people purged in Poland, see Trybuna Ludu, December 24-27, 1981, p. 7.

67. Peter Calvocoressi, "Troubles push Army into Politics," The Sunday Times (London), February 15, 1982.

68. Brumberg, "Poland: Operation Whitewash," pp. 11-16; Szafar, "The Party and the Army," pp. 15-18.

69. Adam Michnik, "Polska Wojna," Aneks 27 (1982):21-22.

70. Thomas Netter, Roger Boyes, and Tana de Zulueto, "I'll talk, but not on my knees—Lech," Times (London), November 14, 1982. A letter dated December 4, 1982 is further evidence of Walesa's desire for a national accord: "Walesa presents workers' case," Guardian, December 13, 1982.

71. Stefan Bratkowski, "Wstepna ocena sytuacji," (Samizdat material) December 20, 1981, p. 7.

13.

Soviet Influence and the
September 1980 Succession

Howard E. Frost

Since the mid-1960s and especially since the advent of
detente, the relationships between the Soviet Union and its
East European allies have experienced a significant change.
Within the bounds of their alliance network with the Soviet
Union, most East European countries exercised more political
autonomy domestically and internationally than they had previously. The extent and dynamics of Moscow's control over these
initiatives have continued to interest Western analysts. To
examine the extent of Moscow's influence on the Polish succession
of September 1980, I have chosen to look at two particular
facets of the crisis. While influence, usually understood as a
continuing phenomenon, cannot neatly be discussed in terms
of specific issues, such separation provides virtually the only
means of assessing it with any amount of objectivity.

This examination of influence will of necessity overlook
dynamics of influence one could develop by examining a broad
range of Soviet-Polish foreign policy interactions over an extended period of time. The focus of this chapter is to investigate
the use of Soviet influence during a crisis when one might expect
Soviet influence to be extensive. Given the narrowness of this
focus, the results provide some interesting conclusions for the

*The views expressed in this paper are the author's and
do not necessarily reflect those of the Central Intelligence
Agency. The author wishes to thank Sarah Terry for her
comments on an earlier draft of this chapter.

Soviet-Polish relationship, although these conclusions cannot be taken as normative for the entire relationship.

In this analysis, I define influence to occur when one nation communicates to another objectives that are different from those of the target nation, and the target nation later assumes those objectives. To distinguish between influence and coercion, I assume influence may include threats of the use of force, either military or economic, but not the application of such force. The specific issues I selected for the 1980 crisis are Gierek's fall and the selection of Kania as his successor.* The basic conclusion I draw from this examination is that while the Soviet leadership did prefer certain outcomes for these problems, these preferences generally corresponded with those of the Polish leadership. Concerning Gierek's fall, it appears that the Soviets clearly communicated their lack of support for Gierek, particularly after the strike agreements, but that the Polish Politburo and Central Committee also supported Gierek's removal. There was also accord among principal Soviet and Polish leaders on the question of the successor, although Kania's attractiveness to the Soviets may have increased his appeal to Polish leaders. Therefore, while the Soviets communicated their preferences on these issues, successful Soviet influence cannot be assumed because of the basic agreement between the two sides on the issues. It is impossible to develop a precise perception of the operation of influence in Soviet-Polish relations during this period because of incomplete evidence. For the present discussion, however, I will draw impressions of influence from a series of events that indicate cause and effect relationships. Applying the definition of influence to the 1980 crisis, I offer two hypotheses. First, influence occurred if it can be proven that the Soviets successfully directed a changeover in the Polish government that would not have occurred or would not have occurred as quickly if the Soviets had not provided their input. Second, influence occurred if it can be shown that the Soviets were instrumental in bringing to power someone who was not earlier considered a prime candidate for the office he obtained.†

---

*This study is an extract from a larger unpublished piece, "The Bear and the Eagles: Soviet Influence and the Polish Succession Crises of 1970 and 1980," which examines the role of Soviet influence on a series of events in each crisis.

†I assume here that it makes a significant difference to the Soviets which particular candidate is chosen.

The basic criteria I use here to assess influence are policy statements and speeches by leaders of both countries, as well as newspaper articles from Polish and non-Polish periodicals. The policy positions presented in speeches and articles are analyzed for both their substantive content and the tone in which they were delivered. Commentaries in the Western press are examined because they provide information on dynamics of possible influence attempts.

DOMESTIC SUPPORT FOR GIEREK'S REMOVAL

To understand the Soviets' role in Gierek's fall, it is first necessary to understand the Polish leadership's perception of Gierek during the weeks prior to his resignation. This step is important in determining the level of their support for his continuation in office.

During the late 1970s, Gierek's popularity among party and nonparty members alike had been declining, primarily because of the country's major economic problems and widespread frustration with the managerial elite. Gierek had strengthened his position in the party, however, by the cabinet changes he had effected during the Eighth Party Congress in February 1980. In order to consolidate power among people who were both loyal and effective administrators, he had had Politburo member Stefan Olszowski, Premier Piotr Jaroszewicz, and several other officials dismissed. His plan at the time was to continue pursuing fiscally conservative policies necessary to improve the country's economic situation, in particular, the foreign debt. Poland's economic problems were his foremost challenge, and he knew that he would have to make major inroads against these problems to demonstrate the effectiveness of his policies.

Decreasing the subsidies for food prices was viewed as an important step in this process, as these subsidies were costing the government $3.3 billion annually.[1] In spite of the economic sense of this measure, the populace was no more inclined to accept the July 1, 1980 increases than they were those in 1976 or 1970. The prices of some meats increased 80 percent in the process of being moved from state to commercial shops in early July, but these measures did not affect the staple meats of the Polish diet. Moreover, the details of their implementation were left to local authorities. These steps were probably taken to calm objections to the changes, but the response from the populace was strongly negative. Such was the case not only because of the higher prices, but also because these measures were taken without the broad consultation that Premier Edward Babiuch suggested had occurred. Babiuch had indicated in an address before the Sejm in April 1980, as well as at other times, that food subsidies would eventually be lifted after consultation and discussion with the people about the optimum way to do so. Public announcement of the decision to implement these increases, however, occurred on July 2, the day after the increases had taken effect.[2]

For the next five weeks, strikes began in the central region of the country and spread, so that opposition to the increases had become nationwide by early August. While work stoppages in many factories were settled by the introduction of wage increases, the resentment against Gierek and his regime for the second unexpected price increase in five years (and the third within the last decade) grew.

The public reaction was initially misunderstood by the government, a problem increasing the people's sense of alienation from the government and leading to the erosion of popular support for the Gierek regime. On July 3, Interpress head Miroslaw Wojciechowski, characterizing the strikes as only heated discussions between management and labor, commented that economically sound policies may not always be popular. A week later, Gierek announced that the meat price increases would remain and that wage increases would not be possible except for low-income families.[3] Over the next few weeks, other political leaders as well as official journals expressed the same hard-line sentiment.[4]

Through mid-August, government officials and spokesmen remained generally adamant in their position on the increases; as the regime had already backed down in 1976 on the same issue, it could not politically afford to do so again. It was not until an August 12 news conference (for Western journalists only) that Politburo propaganda chief Jerzy Lukaszewicz for the first time used the word strike to refer to the work stoppages.[5] After the Gdansk workers struck on August 14, Babiuch, while apologizing for inadequately informing the public about the changes, stated that the increases would remain in effect until autumn 1981 and that additional pay raises would not be possible within the current budget. He concluded with a call to return to work to meet production schedules.[6] This speech, poorly received by the workers, was followed by additional exhortations in the media to return to work. Interpress, incidentally, announced on August 16 that the strikes were over but was forced to recant this statement several hours later.[7]

By the time the Gdansk Interfactory Strike Committee (MKS) was established on August 16, the number of striking workers in that city alone had grown to 50,000. Given the growth in the size and frequency of the job actions from early July through mid-August, the increasingly political nature of the strikers' demands, and the government's policy statements in response to these developments, it is clear that the all too familiar gap had developed between the perceptions of the problem held by the populace and by the government. Until Gierek's speech on August 18, government officials and the official media had clearly done little more than belatedly acknowledge the existence of the strikes and admonish workers to return to work.*

With Gierek's speech on August 18, the government sought to narrow this gap in perceptions, offering the populace a broader share in political decision making and admitting that the official unions should be more responsive to the workers.[8] Gierek offered to stabilize prices for staples and utility rates and to raise wages and family allowances. While stating that force would not be used to break the strikes, he enjoined workers to return to their jobs, warning that challenges to the foundations of Poland's socialist system would not be tolerated.[9] Although more conciliatory than previous remarks by government officials, Gierek's speech failed to address the objectives of the Gdansk MKS, which included genuinely representative trade unions and loosening of controls on freedom of speech and information.

On August 21, Gierek replaced the ineffective negotiator Deputy Premier Tadeusz Pyka with Deputy Premier and Politburo member Mieczyslaw Jagielski as head of the government's team meeting with the Gdansk strikers. During the ten days following this move, the government modified its intransigent position in order to bring popular discontent under control. Jagielski agreed to negotiate with the Gdansk MKS, on August 24 Gierek admitted the need for a radical change in the policies of the PZPR and the state, and a number of Politburo and government hard-liners were replaced by more moderate

---

*On July 18, a governmental commission headed by Deputy Premier and Politburo member Mieczyslaw Jagielski was sent to Lublin to negotiate with strikers there. Before the advent of the MKS, however, most strike settlements were negotiated by the management of the affected enterprises.

politicians. Additionally, the church was permitted greater access to the media, and official media published several commentaries and editorials presenting the MKS's objectives in a more favorable light.[10] Finally, the government agreed on August 30 and 31 to the primary demands of the Szczecin and Gdansk MKSs.

In spite of this more tolerant trend and the eventual settlements with the workers, the government had maintained basically the same unsympathetic position toward the work stoppages for a full month and a half, even though, as Lech Walesa commented on August 25, the populace anxiously sought major policy changes regardless of who was in power. Relating these developments to Gierek's tenure, it follows that his popular support had rapidly diminished from early July through late August. While some may have been willing to give him a second chance after the June 1976 price increases, he had become too closely identified with the government's unyielding position to maintain a strong base of support among the populace.

Many events during July and August manifested Gierek's dwindling support. By August 30 his government had acquiesced to a political movement he had earlier characterized as antisocialist, he eventually had to bring into the government people he had expelled less than a year previous, whose views he admitted he had not heeded (notably those of former Central Committee members Tadeusz Grabski and Stefan Olszowski), and he had to dismiss several of his associates (among the more important were Premier Babiuch and Radio and TV Committee Chairman Maciej Szczepanski). Adding to this erosion, particularly in the party sphere, were the criticism he undoubtedly received in the "sharp and painful" (Gierek's description) Central Committee meeting on August 24, during the presentation of grievances by the party rank and file in Gdansk and Szczecin on August 26, and during the work stoppages beginning in his home base of Katowice on August 30.[11]

If the political climate was ripe for Gierek to lose his position as first secretary, what timetable for his removal can one construct? As early as August 21, Gierek began encountering suggestions that he step down.[12] One party official on August 29 suggested that Gierek would likely leave in four to five months, and another official indicated to a Western journalist that Gierek would retire "soon, but 'with honor' and at a suitable moment when things were calmer."[13] Knowledgeable government officials in both West and East European capitals reportedly viewed Gierek's departure as inevitable as well.[14]

Gierek, too, apparently saw the handwriting on the wall. After his speech on August 18, he was reported as being surprised that workers failed to heed his advice to return to work. Subsequent to his speech on August 24, he allegedly commented that Poland's workers did not trust him and that their refusal to follow his advice was particularly disconcerting.[15]

Although the suggestions that he step down continued after August 21, interest in his removal very likely gained significant momentum after the strike settlements on August 30 (Szczecin) and August 31 (Gdansk).[16] The party considered the agreements at Gdansk and Szczecin to be the best they could obtain under the conditions, but Gierek's shortsighted approach to the events of the previous two months, as well as his unpopular management of the economy, made his continued tenure increasingly unlikely. His policies apparently encountered significant criticism in the September 5 meetings of the Sejm and Central Committee. It probably did not take very long for the Central Committee to vote on September 5 to dismiss him, especially if a consensus for this move had previously developed among the members of that body and the Politburo, as may well have been the case. In fact, a Polish journalist with reputedly close party contacts was quoted on September 5 prior to the Central Committee meeting as saying that Gierek "is totally isolated in the Politburo. He has no support left at all."[17]

It appears, then, that Gierek's slide in popularity during the last part of the 1970s because of the country's economic problems took a precipitous turn for the worse from mid-August to early September. While some Polish officials projected he would leave in late fall or early winter, others thought his departure would be much sooner. If the Polish journalist's comment that Gierek had little Politburo support left by September 5 can be taken at close to face value, it is likely that the majority of the Central Committee also envisioned his departure shortly after the announcement of the strike settlements. If this timetable is generally accurate, we can then assess the impact of the Polish-Soviet relationship on these events.

THE SOVIET FACTOR

Even though the Poles may have decided Gierek's fate during the week of September 1, what impact on this issue did the Soviets have? Did the Soviets want him out before September 5? Did they want him out at all? If they did want him dismissed, how may they have communicated this preference? The question of Soviet support for Gierek, or conversely, their interest in having him removed, is an issue closely tied with their interest in a conservative settlement of the strikes.

Clearly, any labor unrest in an East European country is problematic for the Soviet Union, but the July and August work stoppages in Poland were particularly so. Not only was the unrest taking place in a country where workers on other occasions had tasted their political potential, this unrest was also developing less than three months after the Soviets reportedly had their own bout with this problem on a much smaller scale in Togliatti and Gorkiy.

Prior to their August 19 reporting of Gierek's August 18 speech, Soviet media had not mentioned the strikes for either foreign or domestic consumption. The Soviets did, however, publicly imply their disapproval of the unrest in Poland on several occasions. On July 21, the Soviets downgraded their representation to Poland's National Day ceremonies at the Moscow embassy. Instead of sending at least one person from the Politburo, which had been the practice for several years, they sent a deputy chairman of the Supreme Soviet and a deputy premier.[18] On July 31 after Gierek's conference with Brezhnev in the Crimea, the TASS report from the meeting stated that the talks had been characterized by "cordiality and complete mutual understanding" instead of "cordiality and complete unity of views," the phrase used to describe both the talks between the two during the previous year and the 1980 talks between Brezhnev and most of the other Communist Party leaders.[19] While the TASS report of the Brezhnev-Gierek meeting commented only that the two had exchanged information about the "state of affairs in their respective countries," Brezhnev almost certainly discussed his apprehension about the Polish unrest with Gierek. Babiuch implied this topic was discussed when, during his speech on August 15—the eve of Gierek's return from the Soviet Union—he referred to Poland's "allies, who also worry about our troubles. . . ."[20]

Continuing from August 19, though, the Soviets followed basically a two-track policy in their media coverage of the developments. On the one hand, they called attention to the irresponsible, antisocialist elements operating in Poland and the need for strong action against the work stoppages that had been taking place. Most of the remarks that appeared during the rest of the week of August 18 were selectively emphasized commentaries taken from speeches by Gierek and from Polish media editorials.[21] Beginning on August 25 with a harsh commentary on Western subversion in Poland by Yuri Kornilov, followed

by similarly critical articles by "A. Petrov" on September 1
and Viktor Glazunov on September 2, Soviet media intensified
its coverage with analyses by its own commentators.[22] Furthermore, virtually all the reporting in the Soviet press was shorter
and less explicit in the versions for domestic than for international audiences. When Soviet media reprinted speeches of
the Polish leadership and Polish media commentaries that explicitly mentioned the strikes or measures suggested to resolve
them, these references were generally attenuated or dropped.[23]
The Soviets additionally emphasized their view that these events
were unpalatable for domestic audiences (and therefore a potential security threat) when they renewed their jamming of the
Voice of America, the British Broadcasting Company, and
Deutsche Welle on August 20.[24] As part of their detente policy,
the Soviets had not jammed these stations since 1973.

The second track consisted of Soviet attempts to indicate
that the Poles' problems were their own to handle. On August 22,
two Soviet officials told a Western journalist that the Soviet
leadership was taking a calm approach toward events in Poland
and was relying on Gierek to manage the crisis. On August 26,
a spokesman of the USSR's Ministry of Foreign Affairs stated
that the Polish unrest was "completely the internal affair of
that state" and that Soviet-Polish relations remained characterized by "full mutual cooperation in all spheres."[25] There were
also several indications that the Soviets took steps to signal
that neither "Brotherhood-in-Arms '80" (August 26-September 14)
nor the preparations for these exercises could be taken as pre-
cursors to an invasion of Poland.[26]

In keeping with their outwardly low-key approach to the
crisis, Soviet leaders during July and August maintained travel
schedules that frequently kept them away from Moscow. Brezhnev
was in the Crimea from July 24 to August 25, then spent only
one day in Moscow before traveling to Alma-Ata on August 27.
Chernenko joined him in the Crimea from July 24 through at
least August 18. Other Politburo members traveled extensively
during August as well, especially Shevardnadze, Aliyev, and
Rashidov. Furthermore, a large part of the Politburo was in
Alma-Ata from August 27 to August 31 for the Kazakh Republic's
anniversary celebrations. During this period in late August,
Kirilenko, another key Politburo member, was in the Russian
Republic's Belgorod oblast from August 28-30.[27] The Soviets
were probably indicating through their business as usual
schedules that the Polish events did not constitute a major
crisis requiring key decision makers to remain in Moscow. The
fact that most of the Politburo members were attending festivities

in Kazakhstan during the critical weekend of the strike settlement is an indication that the Soviet leadership wanted to
demonstrate a hands-off attitude toward the Polish problems.
To note that these leaders were frequently traveling during
the primary crisis periods is not, of course, to suggest that
they did not stay in contact with one another and Moscow—or
Warsaw—only that they wanted to give the appearance that the
Polish unrest did not necessitate an inordinate amount of attention on their part.

The growing severity of the Soviet media criticism of the
Polish situation as the number of strikers increased and the
MKSs continued to hold out for their demands indicated the
Soviet government's negative attitude toward the instability.
Although the Soviets were sending two different signals during
the latter part of August, the growing disapproval was clearly
the more important one. Calling the problem a Polish one, a
tactic basically for Western consumption, was an approach that
certainly would have been discarded had the situation severely
destabilized and the Soviets found it necessary to come to the
aid of "proletarian internationalism" again.

How much of this general criticism may also have been
particularly intended for Gierek is open to speculation. It
seems clear that the Soviets did support him throughout most
of the crisis. This support was suggested by their publication
of an anthology of his speeches in mid-August, by their prompt
reporting of his August 18 speech and August 24 announcement
of the cabinet changes, and by Yuri Kornilov's remarks in
his August 25 commentary that Gierek had "laid out a strategic
course" that could rectify the situation.[28]

This coverage, however, started to take a different course
after the settlements in Gdansk and Szczecin. On August 31,
instead of a report on the strike settlements, there appeared a
reprint of an article by American Communist Party Secretary
Gus Hall charging that Poland's problems occurred, not because
of defects in the socialist system, but because of weaknesses in
the Polish leadership.[29] Later that same day, TASS still ran
no news of the agreements, but instead broadcasted through
Radio Moscow a long commentary by the authoritative "A. Petrov"
that was especially critical of "antisocialist elements" and the
Polish workers' damaging "political demands."[30] East German
media, drawing on a Pravda commentary of September 1 that
stated that government negotiators had imprudently agreed to
examine the demands of "antisocialist elements," altered the
wording so that the sense was that Gierek had personally acceded
to the untenable demands of the workers. It is unlikely that

such an editorial change could have slipped by without Moscow's approval.[31] Most important, Gierek's name did not appear in the Soviet press from September 1 to September 6. Thus, the postsettlement coverage of Gierek indicates that the Soviets no longer considered Gierek's continued tenure desirable.

In addition to indicating through the media their indirect disapproval of Gierek, it is also possible, as suggested by Western journalists, that the Soviet leadership had been in contact with him at Bialowieza, in eastern Poland, during the week of September 1 and once several weeks previous.[32] While Polish party sources denied these rumors, they did indicate that Gierek continued to be in close contact with Moscow through the Soviet Union's Warsaw embassy.[33] Regardless of the channel, though, it is almost certain that Gierek was in contact with the Soviet leadership during the three weeks prior to his ouster. While they may not have used these opportunities to threaten Gierek with withdrawal of Soviet support, it is very likely that they would still have communicated their increased dissatisfaction with the strike developments. Furthermore, the Soviets could have communicated at other times to any number of Polish leaders their interest in having Gierek removed. While the Soviets were willing to give the Poles a fair amount of latitude in negotiating the strike settlements, it is clear from their reaction to the crisis, evidenced in the media and elsewhere, that they strongly disapproved of the agreements reached. Although Polish nego-tiators probably worked to frame agreements that the Soviets would not find objectionable, Soviet opposition to the agreements cannot but have redounded to Gierek's disfavor. Adding to the Soviet disappointment with Gierek was undoubtedly their realization during late August of his lack of support among the populace.

CONCLUSIONS ON GIEREK'S OUSTER

It is likely, then, that the Soviets wanted Gierek removed soon after August 31, primarily because of their ideological problems with the agreements in Gdansk and Szczecin and his lack of domestic political support, but also because of complica-tions involving an aid package the Poles and the Soviets had been discussing. The Soviets were probably not in favor of granting credits to an administration that was losing or had lost its popular (and party) support. Indeed, while a Soviet hard currency loan of $100 million (relatively small in light of Poland's needs) was publicized on September 3, talks concerning additional aid (foodstuffs and consumer goods) needed in the wake of the strikes did not begin until September 10, a week after Gierek's ouster.[34]

Given the Soviets' delay in publicizing the strike settlements and their criticism of them, their failure to mention Gierek's name during the week of September 1, and their quick publication of the news of Kania's succession, it is apparent that the Soviets decided a change was necessary in Warsaw. That they decided to send a get well message to Gierek later on September 6 detracts little from this conclusion. Whether they may have hoped Gierek would have been removed sooner is difficult to say.[35] If they had made Gierek's departure a precondition for the economic aid, it could be suggested that the Poles saw it in their own best interest to remove Gierek as soon as possible. Given the sum of the political and economic factors already in the picture, however, it is most likely that both the Soviets and the Poles wanted Gierek out quickly and reached that conclusion at approximately the same time.

As the Poles read the Soviet press during this period, the Polish leadership was particularly aware of Soviet sensitivities regarding the strike problem. References, oblique and otherwise, to a possible Soviet invasion frequently appeared in officials' speeches and media commentaries, and the specter of an invasion was surely a strong argument for conservatives and moderates alike to counsel against destabilizing change.[36] That these sensitivities could have contributed to support for Gierek's removal as well as for a conservative settlement to the strikes is certainly possible. However, while most of the Polish leadership was probably as much aware of Soviet sensitivities about Gierek during the week of September 1 as they were of Soviet sensitivities about strikes earlier, it does not seem that fear of an invasion provided the primary momentum for Gierek's removal. Moscow may have been advised about the impending change, but it is improbable that the actual decision to remove Gierek was imposed from Moscow.

DOMESTIC SUPPORT FOR KANIA'S ELECTION

Within the Polish Politburo, the principal candidates for the position of first secretary were Stanislaw Kania and Stefan Olszowski.* Olszowski was far better known outside the party,

---

*Politburo member Mieczyslaw Jagielski and newly installed Deputy Prime Minister and Central Committee member Tadeusz

but there were a number of reasons that Kania was more appealing to both the Poles and the Soviets.

Prior to his appointment as first secretary, Kania was not
a well-known politician, as he had rarely appeared in public.
Nevertheless, he had made a mark for himself in several important
areas. First, he had established for himself a reputation as a
political conservative. He took over the position as Central
Committee secretary for security and the military from Mieczyslaw
Moczar in early 1971, and by June of that year added to those
responsibilities the task of church affairs supervision. He also
reportedly had developed a reputation as a proponent of economic reform in spite of his political conservatism.[37] He allegedly
had opposed the pope's visit to Poland in 1979, but several
church administrators interviewed after the succession characterized him as tough but fair.[38] While Kania also had taken a
hard-line approach to the dissident intellectual movement, he
apparently counseled against using police force against striking
workers at a critical point early in the Gdansk negotiations.[39]
Kania's ability to manage the police force at Gdansk and at other
cities affected by the strikes brought him additional recognition
within the party; when the cabinet change occurred after the
Central Committee plenum on August 24, Kania received the
important Central Committee portfolio for supervision for the
trade union federation. Some American officials at this time
indicated that Kania was already being ranked in the Politburo
as second in line to Gierek.[40] One of the principal bases for
this observation was the fact that Kania, not Gierek, delivered
the main address at the plenum.

Olszowski, on the other hand, was viewed by Poles and
Western observers alike as a strong rival to Kania. As minister
of foreign affairs from late 1971 to 1976, he had developed broad
experience in international affairs at a time when Poland was
greatly expanding its foreign relations. Olszowski, who had
experience as an economist, was known as a major proponent
of economic changes during his 1976 to 1980 tenure as Central
Committee secretary responsible for economic policy. Although
known as well as an ideological hard-liner, he was also an initial
supporter of the reform-minded discussion group, "Experience
and the Future." His criticism of Gierek's economic policies,
however, led to his dismissal from the Politburo and the Central

---

Grabski were other possible alternatives. Jagielski's health
problems and Grabski's relative lack of national level government experience, however, made these two candidates unlikely.

Committee in February 1980 and to his appointment as ambassador to East Germany,[41] where he would be away from the centers of power in Warsaw.

In spite of the political momentum that Olszowski derived from his recall from the GDR to his old Central Committee secretaryship, his August 24 reappointment to the Politburo, and Gierek's public apology for not listening to critical opinions, there were a number of factors that may have tipped the scales in Kania's favor.

In addition to Kania's increased respect as a result of his careful management of the security forces during the Gdansk strike, he also had served nine consecutive years on the Secretariat (1971-1980), compared with Olszowski's four (1976-1980).* Although both had moved up within the central party apparatus, Kania probably had had a broader range of experience in domestic party affairs than Olszowski, whose primary areas of expertise were economics and international relations. Additionally, Kania may in fact have benefited from the infrequent publicity he had received because of the image he acquired during the succession crisis as a safe or compromise candidate. Olszowski, on the other hand, had a reputation as a particularly ambitious politician, a factor that undoubtedly created apprehensions among his Politburo colleagues.[42]

ACCEPTABILITY TO MOSCOW

For many of these same reasons, Kania, at the time, was probably also more acceptable to Moscow. In addition, although Olszowski was better known in Western diplomatic circles, Kania was better known to the Soviets. Because of his responsibilities for Poland's security apparatus, he probably had been in extensive contact with KGB chief Yuri Andropov and was therefore better known to other Soviet Politburo members as well.[43] Olszowski's March 1977 meeting with Brezhnev was assumed by many to suggest Soviet support of Olszowski, but Kania's party responsibilities had given him more consistent exposure to the Soviet leadership.[44] In any case, the Soviets at the time at least viewed Kania as the better prospect to press for a restrictive yet evenhanded interpretation of the agreements with the workers and to keep under control currents of political liberaliza-

---

*Olszowski had earlier served on the Secretariat from 1968-1971.

tion inspired by the agreements. Kania's comment in his September 6 speech to the Central Committee Plenum that the Soviets, particularly Brezhnev, had been understanding of Poland's problems during the current crisis suggests that he may have been in contact with Brezhnev during the week of August 31 about these issues.[45] Moscow's approval of Kania was well reflected in Brezhnev's congratulatory message that commented that Soviet Communists knew Kania as a "staunch" fighter for "strengthening the leading role of the Communist Party in Poland" and as a strong supporter of "proletarian internationalism and Soviet-Polish friendship."[46]

CONCLUSIONS ON THE SUCCESSOR QUESTION

Here again one finds Soviet and Polish accord on a crisis solution; Moscow probably did not pressure the PUWP Politburo and Central Committee into choosing a candidate that the latter did not desire. In the case of the choice of successor, the question remains of the extent to which Kania's appeal to the Soviets may have improved his appeal to his Polish colleagues over and above the other qualifications he demonstrated. It seems reasonable to conclude that Kania's close ties with Moscow, his antidissident attitude, and his affiliation with the internal security apparatus were several reasons that his election as first secretary may have been intended as a symbol to the Soviets of his colleagues' willingness to keep Soviet-Polish relations on an even keel. Regardless of Olszowski's popularity, foreign affairs experience, or interest in economic reform, he was probably not regarded by his Politburo colleagues as being as attractive to the Soviets as Kania was. Therefore, while the Soviets did not pressure the Polish leadership to accept Kania, the assumption that Kania's attractiveness to the Soviets was an important factor in his election leads to the conclusion that the Soviet viewpoint was given strong consideration, but that this influence was not determinative in Kania's selection.

Though the Soviets were willing to give the Poles some latitude in resolving the succession question and related problems during the August-September 1980 stage of the crisis, they have frequently manifested their grave concern for developments in Poland since then. As Solidarity grew to be an important political force and successfully challenged the government on a variety of issues, the Soviets, during the period prior to the imposition of martial law, often took the opportunity to communicate clearly their strong preferences for conservative resolutions

to the government-Solidarity confrontations.[47] Visi by high-
level Soviet officials for discussions with Polish leaders and
harsh Soviet media criticism of Solidarity were clear indications
of strong, almost desperate attempts by the Soviets to influence
the Poles to curtail the advance of liberalization.

While available evidence suggests little direct Soviet involvement in Kania's resignation as first secretary on October 18,
1981, the extent of the Soviet role in the imposition of martial
law is difficult to determine. Published Soviet commentaries
from late 1980 to October 1981 criticized Kania's administration
for concessions to Solidarity, but they in general did not single
out Kania for attack while sparing Jaruzelski and other administration officials. Furthermore, articles in the Polish press prior
to the October 16, 1981 Plenum of the PZPR Central Committee,
as well as the proceedings of the plenum itself, suggest that the
determinative groundswell of sentiment against Kania developed
as the plenum began and was not orchestrated by the Soviets.[48]

Evidence surrounding Jaruzelski's declaration of martial
law on December 13, 1981 presents a somewhat different picture.
The presence of Warsaw Pact Commander-in-Chief Viktor Kulikov
in Warsaw during the week prior to the declaration and the
support for Jaruzelski's move offered by official Soviet media
suggest that the Soviets may have provided encouragement and
assistance in planning this operation.[49] Conclusive evidence
on the extent of the Soviet role is currently lacking; U.S.
officials, however, on several different occasions strongly
implied Soviet complicity in the crackdown.[50] In the postmartial
law period, the Polish leadership will certainly maintain tight
control over political activity in order to preserve the party's
authority as well as to assuage the Soviets.[51] The extent to
which the Polish leadership will be able to accommodate the
Soviets without sacrificing its own political objectives or appearing too subservient to Moscow will continue to be an area of
major interest.

In both the 1970 and 1980 succession cases, the Soviets
demonstrated restraint in their approach to the crises. Although
a Soviet invasion was not clearly imminent in 1970, the threat
of one was certainly implied in statements by Polish officials in
August 1980. In the series of events surrounding both successions, though, Soviet forbearance in the decisions to let the
respective Polish governments handle the situations without
overt interference was an important factor in the resolutions of
the crises.[52]

In the 1970 succession, the Soviets had fewer opportunities
to exert influence than in the 1980 crisis because of the rapidity

of events involving Gomulka's ouster and Gierek's succession.* Additionally, the outbreak of violence during the 1970 crisis undoubtedly contributed an element of caution to considerations in the Soviet Politburo of alternatives for handling the Polish problem. In the 1980 crisis, the Soviets did have sufficient opportunities to communicate their preferences, yet again they chose not to intervene militarily though it was clear the situation was developing unfavorably. While specific reasons for non-intervention are clear in both cases, the fact that the Soviets did not intervene in either reflects their decision that the USSR's national interests and the security of the bloc would be better preserved by avoiding military action even though the political cost of nonintervention increased.

While the extent of Soviet involvement in the establishment of martial law is not clear, the Soviet policy thus far to avoid invading suggests that the Soviet approach to Polish politics will continue to be characterized more by influence attempts than by the direct military or economic coercion that the Soviets have used previously in Eastern Europe. While extensive Soviet involvement in Polish politics is certainly not a desirable status quo, the Soviet leadership's lessons from the 1970 and 1980 successions of the limits of their direct political control in Eastern Europe are of major significance for the evolving relationships between the USSR and its East European allies.

NOTES

1. John Darnton, "Meat-Price Rise in Poland Prompts Work Stoppages in Some Factories," New York Times, July 4, 1980, p. A2. For background on problems the Gierek regime encountered, see "Who Knew What," tr. Nika Krzeczunowicz, Przeglad Techniczny no. 23, 1981, Radio Free Europe Background Report no. 241, August 25, 1981; George Blazynski, Flashpoint Poland (New York: Pergamon, 1979); Experience and the Future Discussion Group, Poland Today, tr. Andrew Swidlicki, et al. (Armonk, NY: M. E. Sharpe, Inc., 1981).

Also informative are F. Stephen Larrabee, "Poland, the Permanent Crisis," Orbis 25 (Spring 1981):234-42; David Paul and Maurice Simon, "Poland Today and Czechoslovakia 1968,"

---

*The period from the initial signs of unrest to the succession was less than a week.

Problems of Communism 39 (September-October 1981):25-38;
Maurice Simon and Roger Kanet, eds., Background to Crisis:
Policy and Politics in Gierek's Poland (Boulder, Colorado:
Westview Press, 1981).

2. "More Meat, Poultry to be Sold in 'Higher-Class'
Shops," Warsaw PAP, July 3, 1980 (FBIS Daily Report on Eastern
Europe [hereafter FBIS Eastern Europe], July 3, 1980), p. G1;
"Official Interviewed on Change in Meat Pricing," Warsaw
Domestic Service, July 2, 1980 (FBIS Eastern Europe, July 3,
1980), pp. G1-2; "Babiuch Stresses Goals, Tasks in Eighth
Sejm Session," Warsaw Domestic Service, April 3, 1980 (FBIS
Eastern Europe, April 9, 1980), pp. G16-17.

3. "KSS-KOR Communique on Workers' Strike Reported,"
Dziennik Polski (London), July 5, 1980 (FBIS Eastern Europe,
July 11, 1980), pp. G1-2; William Robinson, ed., August 1980
The Strikes in Poland (Munich: Radio Free Europe Research),
p. 3 [hereafter Robinson]; and "Gierek, Ministers Discuss
Market Supplies, Meat Situation," Warsaw Domestic Service,
July 9, 1980 (FBIS Eastern Europe, July 10, 1980), pp. G7-10.

4. "Reportage, Comment on Work Stoppages in Lublin,"
Reuter, July 18, 1980 (FBIS Eastern Europe, July 21, 1980),
pp. G1-2; "Commentary on Stoppages," Warsaw Domestic Service,
July 19, 1980 (FBIS Eastern Europe, July 21, 1980), pp. G3-4;
"PAP Cites Zycie Warsawy on Work Stoppages, Wages, Prices,"
Warsaw PAP, July 24, 1980 (FBIS Eastern Europe, July 25,
1980), pp. G1-2; "Zycie Warsawy Explores Reasons for Labor
Unrest," Zycie Warsawy, July 24, 1980 (FBIS Eastern Europe,
July 30, 1980), pp. G4-9; "Trybuna Ludu Comments on Work
Stoppages, Economy," Warsaw Domestic Service, August 4,
1980 (FBIS Eastern Europe, August 5, 1980), p. G1.

5. "Lukaszewicz Holds Press Conference on Domestic,
Foreign Issues," Warsaw PAP, August 13, 1980 (FBIS Eastern
Europe, August 13, 1980), p. G1; Robinson, p. 9.

6. "Babiuch Addresses Nation on Socioeconomic Situation,"
Warsaw Domestic Television Service, August 15, 1980 (FBIS
Eastern Europe, August 18, 1980), pp. G1-5 [hereafter Babiuch].

7. "Trybuna Ludu Comments on Work Stoppages,"
Trybuna Ludu, August 15, 1980 (FBIS Eastern Europe,
August 18, 1980), pp. G23-24; "Warsaw Television Notes Losses
from Shipyard Stoppages," Warsaw Domestic Television Service,
August 18, 1980 (FBIS Eastern Europe, August 19, 1980), pp.
G10-11; "PAP Commentator Calls for Rebuff of Exploiting Forces,"
Warsaw PAP, August 21, 1980 (FBIS Eastern Europe, August 21,
1980), pp. G10-11; Robinson, p. 11.

8. Basically the only published expressions of concern
for the strikers' position until this speech were a July 5 com-

mentary by Polityka editor-in-chief Mieczyslaw Rakowski, which called for economic reforms, and a July 19 Radio Warsaw commentary by Jerzy Handbowski that closer cooperation between trade unions and party organizations could have averted some of the current unrest. See "Polityka's Rakowski Discusses Economic Problems," Warsaw Polityka, July 5, 1980 (FBIS Eastern Europe, July 17, 1980), p. G17; "Economic Problems Examined," Warsaw Domestic Service, July 19, 1980 (FBIS Eastern Europe, July 21, 1980), pp. G4-6.

9. "Gierek Addresses Nation Following Politburo Meeting," Warsaw Domestic Service, August 18, 1980 (FBIS Eastern Europe, August 25, 1980), pp. G1-5.

10. "Gdansk Radio Praises Changes for Greater Worker Participation," Gdansk Domestic Service, August 25, 1980 (FBIS Eastern Europe, August 25, 1980), pp. G14-15; "Decisions of the Fourth PZPR Central Committee Plenum Assessed," Warsaw Domestic Service, August 26, 1980 (FBIS Eastern Europe, August 26, 1980), p. G9; "Gdansk Report on Talks," Gdansk Domestic Service, August 26, 1980 (FBIS Eastern Europe, August 27, 1980), pp. G9-19; "Government Commission Report," Warsaw Domestic Television Service, August 28, 1980 (FBIS Eastern Europe, August 29, 1980), pp. G1-4.

11. John Darnton, "Poland's Premier is Dismissed in Sweeping Party Shake-Up: Gierek Pledges Union Ballot," New York Times, August 25, 1980, p. A7; "Gierek Addresses Closing Session of Central Committee Plenum," Warsaw Domestic Television Service, August 24, 1980 (FBIS Eastern Europe, August 25, 1980), p. G3; Robinson, pp. 17-21. Jan de Weydenthal, in "Workers and Party in Poland," Problems of Communism 29 (November-December 1980):1-10 [hereafter de Weydenthal] provides an excellent commentary on the Polish government's mistakes in handling the strikes.

12. Michael Dobbs, "Poland Fires Labor Chief, Launches Media Offensive," Washington Post, August 22, 1980, p. A20 [hereafter Dobbs].

13. Flora Lewis, "Vacillation in Warsaw: Government Uncertain How to Negotiate with Strikers," New York Times, August 30, 1980, p. A4 [hereafter Lewis]; Eric Bourne, "Poland: new leadership; old problems," Christian Science Monitor, September 8, 1980, p. 17.

14. Ronald Koven, "Western Europe Nations Uneasy Over New Polish Leader," Washington Post, September 7, 1980, p. A17; "Eastern Europeans React to Shift Briefly, According to Protocol," Washington Post, September 7, 1980, p. A18.

15. Dobbs, p. A20; "Kania Takes Over Poland," Newsweek, September 15, 1980, p. 47 [hereafter Newsweek].

16. Lewis, p. 4. For a good summary of the agreements and their significance, see de Weydenthal, pp. 10-22.

17. John Darnton, "Gierek Ousted from Post as Head of Polish Party; Security Chief Given Job," New York Times, September 6, 1980, p. 4 [hereafter Darnton]; and "Doctors Confirm Medical Diagnosis on Gierek," Warsaw Domestic Service, September 6, 1980 (FBIS Eastern Europe, September 8, 1980), p. G8. That Gierek's removal was due to politics rather than to illness, even if he indeed had been ill, is clear from several factors. The announcement of his removal did not indicate he had asked to resign for reasons of health, and the fact that he lost both his Central Committee secretaryship and his position on the Politburo so quickly after his alleged hospitalization make the report of illness almost too convenient. Furthermore, while there were rumors that he had checked into Emilii Plater Hospital in Warsaw on September 5, he had suffered no known health problems since a case of lumbago in 1978. He may have taken the reported two-week trip to a Czech spa in 1979 partly to aid his recovery from this illness. Finally, Ryszard Wojna and Andrzej Bilik, two Central Committee officials interviewed in early September by French and Italian news services, respectively, indicated that Gierek's illness was not the only cause for his dismissal. If the Politburo consensus for Gierek's removal had jelled before September 5, Gierek's illness, if it were indeed real, could have been precipitated by his awareness of the success of the move to unseat him.

18. "Kholov, Arkhipov Attend Polish Anniversary Meeting," Moscow Domestic Service, July 21, 1980 (FBIS Daily Report on the Soviet Union [hereafter FBIS Soviet Union], July 24, 1980), p. F1.

19. "Friendly Meeting," Pravda, August 1, 1980, p. 1; "Friendly Meeting," Pravda, August 5, 1979, p. 1.

20. Ibid.; Babiuch, p. G5.

21. "E. Gierek's Speech," Pravda, August 20, 1980, p. 4 (reported by TASS on August 19); "Article from Trybuna Ludu," Pravda, August 24, 1980, p. 4; "Labor Achievements Highlighted in Trybuna Ludu," TASS International Service, August 22, 1980 (FBIS Soviet Union, August 25, 1980), p. F4; "Polish Democratic Party Statement on Stoppages Cited," Moscow Domestic Service, August 24, 1980 (FBIS Soviet Union, August 25, 1980), pp. F3-4; "E. Gierek's Speech," Pravda, August 26, 1980, p. 4 (reported by TASS on August 25).

22. "Kornilov Scores 'Distorting Mirror of Bourgeois Propaganda,'" TASS International Service, August 25, 1980 (FBIS Soviet Union, August 26, 1980), pp. F4-6 [hereafter

Kornilov]; A. Petrov, "The Intrigues of the Enemies of Socialist Poland," Pravda, September 1, 1980, p. 5 [hereafter Petrov]; and Viktor Glazunov, "The Situation in Poland and the Machinations of its Enemies," Moscow in French, September 2, 1980 (FBIS Soviet Union, September 3, 1980), pp. F3-4. "A. Petrov" is a nom de plume for an article that reflects the views of high-level leadership.

23. See Lawrence Sherwin's summary of the Soviet media in Robinson, pp. 237-52.

24. Anthony Austin, "Soviet Jamming Western Radios; Fear of News About Poland Seen," New York Times, August 21, 1980, pp. A1, A12.

25. Anthony Austin, "Soviet Appears to Accept Polish Unrest Calmly So Far," New York Times, August 23, 1980, p. g; Anthony Austin, "Poles' Own Affair, Soviet Aide Affirms," New York Times, August 27, 1980, p. 6.

26. "Warsaw Pact Plans Exercises in Baltic," New York Times, August 24, 1980, p. A22; Dusko Doder, "Soviets End Silence on Poland, Cite Gierek Warning," Washington Post August 20, 1980, p. A20.

27. Central Intelligence Agency, Appearances of the Soviet Leadership, 1980 (Washington: Central Intelligence Agency, 1980 [draft version, chronological list]), pp. 208-33.

28. "Collection of E. Gierek's Speeches and Articles," Pravda, August 15, 1980, p. 4; Kornilov, p. F5.

29. Gus Hall, "Shameless Hypocrisy," Pravda, August 31, 1980, p. 5 (reported by TASS on August 30 and by East Germany's ADN on August 29).

30. Petrov, p. 5.

31. Ibid.; "ADN Cites Pravda, Trybuna Ludu Articles on Polish Crisis," ADN International Service, September 1, 1980 (FBIS Eastern Europe, September 3, 1980), p. E1; "The Situation in Poland," Pravda, September 2, 1980, p. 4 (reported by TASS on September 1).

32. Newsweek, p. 47; Darnton, p. A4. Some authors, such as Daniel Singer in The Road to Gdansk (New York: Monthly Review Press, 1981) suggest that the two Soviets who met with Gierek at Bialowieza were Andrei Kirilenko and Mikhail Suslov.

33. Darnton, p. A4.

34. "Jagielski: Soviet Union Supplying Additional Financial Aid," Warsaw Domestic Service, September 3, 1980 (FBIS Eastern Europe, September 4, 1980), pp. G1-2; and "Agreement on Food, Consumer Goods," Warsaw PAP, September 11, 1980 (FBIS Eastern Europe, September 12, 1980), p. G1.

35. "Gierek Illness, New Appointments," TASS, September 6, 1980 (FBIS Soviet Union, September 8, 1980), p. F5;

"Brezhnev Sends Gierek Get Well Wishes," Moscow World News Service, September 6, 1980 (FBIS Soviet Union, September 9, 1980), p. F1. It may have been the case that pressure from the Soviets helped create the aforementioned consensus in the Polish Politburo that Gierek had to be out very shortly after the strike settlement. It can be argued, on the basis of this assumption, that Gierek may have been able to fight off opposition to his continuing in office had not the Soviets pressured other Politburo members to vote him out. Information to evaluate this hypothesis, however, is not currently available.

36. See "Trybuna Ludu Editorial," Trybuna Ludu, August 18, 1980 (FBIS Eastern Europe, August 22, 1980), pp. G11-13; "Trybuna Ludu Condemns 'Antisocialist' Role in Strikes," Warsaw PAP, August 22, 1980 (FBIS Eastern Europe, August 26, 1980), pp. G21-22; "Rakowski Article Warns Against 'Uncontrollable Confrontations,'" Warsaw Polityka, August 23, 1980 (FBIS Eastern Europe, August 29, 1980), pp. G20-24; "Wojna Warns of 'Incalculable Consequences' of Excessive Demands," Warsaw Domestic Television Service, August 26, 1980 (FBIS Eastern Europe, August 27, 1980), pp. G1-3; "Trybuna Ludu Comments on Poland's Links with Socialist Community," Warsaw Domestic Service, August 29, 1980 (FBIS Eastern Europe, August 29, 1980), pp. G31-32.

37. Bradley Graham, "New Polish Chief Pledges to Honor Deal with Labor," Washington Post, September 7, 1980, p. A20 [hereafter Graham].

38. Ibid.; Darnton, p. A22.

39. Darnton, p. A22.

40. Ibid.; David Binder, "Stanislaw Kania," New York Times, September 6, 1980 [hereafter Binder], p. A5.

41. Robinson, pp. 335-37; Graham, p. A20.

42. Newsweek, p. 47.

43. Binder, p. A5.

44. Robin Herman, "A Pole Who Waits in the Wings," New York Times, August 27, 1980, p. A6. Soviet support for Olszowski's conservatism became much more apparent in the late spring and the summer of 1981 during the hard-liner-moderate confrontation in the PZPR.

45. "Kania Plenum Address" (read by announcer), Warsaw Domestic Television Service, September 6, 1980 (FBIS Eastern Europe, September 8, 1980), p. G4.

46. "To Comrade Stanislaw Kania, First Secretary of the Polish United Workers' Party Central Committee," Pravda, September 7, 1980, p. 1 (reported by TASS on September 6).

47. Particularly noteworthy articles on Polish political developments in 1981-82 and Soviet responses are William Schaufele, Polish Paradox, Foreign Policy Association Headline Series no. 256 (October 1981); Adam Bromke, "Poland's Upheaval—An Interim Report," World Today 37 (June 1981):211-18; Jiri Valenta, "Soviet Options in Poland," Survival 23 (March-April 1981):50-59; Richard Anderson, "Soviet Decision-making and Poland," Problems of Communism 31 (March-April 1982):22-36.

48. See "Zofia Grzyb 16 October Address to PZPR Fourth Plenum," Trybuna Ludu, October 17-18, 1981 (FBIS Eastern Europe, October 22, 1981), pp. G1-3; "PAP Summary of Plenum Speeches," Warsaw PAP, October 17, 1981 (FBIS Eastern Europe, October 19, 1981), pp. G36-38; "Zycie Warszawy on Change," Warsaw PAP, October 20, 1981 (FBIS Eastern Europe, October 20, 1981), p. G7. The initiative to unseat Kania may have been foreshadowed by speeches at the Warsaw PZPR Central Committee Plenum on October 13 and 14. See "Warsaw PZPR Committee Holds Plenum Session," Warsaw PAP, October 13, 1981 (FBIS Eastern Europe, October 15, 1981), pp. G15-16; "Warsaw Party Plenum Resolution Issued," Zycie Warszawy, October 16, 1981 (FBIS Eastern Europe, October 27, 1981), pp. G20-21; "Warsaw Party Aktiv is 'Fighting Alone,'" East Berlin ADN, October 15, 1981 (FBIS Eastern Europe, October 16, 1981), pp. E1-2. The June 5, 1981 letter, critical of the Polish leadership, that the Soviets sent to the PZPR Central Committee may have bolstered party hard-liners against Kania and contributed to anti-Kania sentiment that continued to grow over the following months. How instrumental this letter was in fostering and legitimizing this sentiment is difficult to determine with currently available information.

49. "Soviet Unit Said to Be Overseeing Poles," Los Angeles Times, December 18, 1981, p. 19; Neal Ascherson, "How Solidarity Was Murdered," London Observer, December 20, 1981, pp. 9-10; Dusko Doder, "Soviets Seem Satisfied with Course of Polish Crackdown," Washington Post, December 31, 1981, p. A16; Richard Spielman, "Crisis in Poland," Foreign Policy 49 (Winter 1982):27-33. Among the many commentaries in the Soviet media supporting the martial law declaration, see "TASS Statement on Poland: Soviet Response," Moscow TASS, December 14, 1981 (FBIS Soviet Union, December 14, 1981), pp. F8-9; "Commentary on Polish Events, Return to Calm," Moscow World Service, December 15, 1981 (FBIS Soviet Union, December 16, 1981), pp. F4-5; Vladimir Bolshakov, "Current Polish Normalization Measures Reported," Moscow Domestic Service, December 19, 1981 (FBIS Soviet Union, December 21, 1981), pp. F13-14.

50. "Text of Remarks by Reagan on the Suspension of Some Links with Poland," New York Times, December 24, 1981, p. A10; "Haig: A Misreading 'to Portray Situation in Poland as Resolved,'" Washington Post, December 27, 1981, p. A6; Don Oberdorfer and John Goshko, "Resistance Will Continue," Washington Post, December 27, 1981, pp. A1, A4; Max Kampelman (U.S. Ambassador to the Madrid Conference on Security and Cooperation in Europe), "Soviet Responsibility in Poland," World Affairs 144 (Spring 1982):502-5; Bruce Porter, "The USSR and Poland on the Road to Martial Law," Radio Liberty Research Bulletin 4/82 (December 30, 1981).

51. For a good summary of the roles of various political factions in Poland during martial law, see Casimir Garnysz, "Holding a Bear by the Tail," Encounter 54 (September-October 1982):73-86.

52. For other interesting insights concerning the 1970 and 1980 successions, see Adam Bromke, "Poland: The Cliff's Edge," Foreign Policy (Winter 1980-81):154-56; Bromke's "Socialism with a martial face," The World Today 38 (July-August 1982):264-68; Neal Ascherson, The Polish August (New York: Viking Press, 1981), pp. 229-59; Martin Myant, Poland: A Crisis for Socialism (London: Lawrence and Wishart, 1982).

14.

The Polish Crisis and Poland's "Allies": The Soviet and East European Response to Events in Poland

Roger E. Kanet

The imposition of martial law in Poland in December 1981 brought to an end one phase of the most recent Polish crisis. During the previous eighteen months that Solidarity pursued its efforts to create the foundations for a pluralist society in Poland, the Soviets and other East European allies of Poland voiced their growing concerns about the activities in Poland of counterrevolutionary forces and their imperialist supporters. In the West there existed serious concern that the Soviets would intervene militarily in Poland to prevent the collapse of the single-party dictatorship characteristic of Soviet-style communism. In November 1980 and again in late spring 1981 relations between Poland and its Warsaw Pact allies deteriorated, as the Soviets built up their military forces around the border of Poland and the Soviet and East European press expanded the condemnation of both the independent labor movement and the revisionist elements within the Polish United Workers' Party (PUWP).

Despite the relative calm that martial law brought to Poland and the fact that the government has recently seen fit to cancel martial law—without, however, eliminating some of the restrictions associated with it—the situation in that country has not been normalized. The underlying domestic causes of the crisis—

---

*This article was completed in August 1981; revised in August 1982 to cover events through the imposition of martial law; and revised slightly again in early 1983.

economic collapse, food shortages, incompetent and corrupt administration, and a host of other issues that built up pressure during the course of more than a third of a century of communist rule—have not been resolved. More important from the perspective of the present discussion is the fact that Poland's immediate neighbors have made clear their concern about domestic developments in Poland and their unwillingness to permit Polish events to undermine their own security. As Czechoslovak Politburo member Vasil Bilak noted already in October 1980: "We make no secret of the fact that what is happening in Poland is of deep concern to us politically, ideologically, and economically. . . . Our Polish comrades can therefore always rely on help from our party and our people."[1] This statement of concern and the implied threat of intervention is indicative of the response to events in Poland that occurred in Czechoslovakia, the German Democratic Republic (GDR), and the Soviet Union ever since the settlement of the strikes in Gdansk on August 31, 1980 that resulted in official recognition of an independent labor movement by the Polish government and party. Periodically during the next 15-1/2 months the level of criticism and of threats of intervention increased—e.g., during the buildup of Soviet forces along Poland's borders in late November and early December 1980.[2] Although the periods of growing tension were followed by periods of relative relaxation, the Soviets and their major allies in Eastern Europe continued their barrage of criticism of everything from the inability of the Polish regime to handle the situation in the country to the role of the papacy in stimulating "antisocialist counterrevolution" in Poland.[3]

    The purpose of this chapter is to examine the position of Poland within the alliance structure of the Warsaw Treaty Organization (WTO) and the Council for Mutual Economic Assistance (CMEA) and to assess the response of Poland's neighbors to events in that country from summer 1980 until the imposition of martial law on December 12-13, 1981. The East European Communist Party leaders, as a group, viewed the labor unrest in Poland and the challenges to the dominant position of the Polish United Workers' Party (PUWP)—as well as the democratization within the PUWP—as a threat to the foundations of socialism in Poland and, ultimately, to the very existence of the communist states themselves. Collectively they opposed these developments and exerted pressure on the Polish leadership to deal with the erosion of state power.

THE PLACE OF POLAND IN THE SOVIET
SECURITY SYSTEM

In a speech to the Sixth Congress of the PUWP in 1971, Soviet party leader Leonid Brezhnev stated that the Polish army represented the "outstanding military squadron of the international Communist movement."[4] Although Brezhnev may well have been exaggerating his view of the significance of Poland for Soviet and East European security for the sake of his Polish audience, the position of Poland within the Warsaw Treaty Organization and the Soviet security system is of great importance. Not only is Poland the most populous of the Soviets' East European allies and maintains the largest military forces, but the geographical location of the country places it in the very center of the Soviet security zone in Europe.[5] Access to the Soviet divisions stationed in East Germany runs through Poland and is, therefore, essential to the Soviet Union. Unrest in Poland that would jeopardize Soviet lines of communication is viewed as a major threat to Soviet security interests.[6]

Just as important for the Soviets as the direct military significance of Poland for the security of the USSR and the entire Warsaw Pact is the relevance of the Soviet-Polish relationship for the political position of the USSR. Traditionally, the Soviet leadership has pointed to the existence of socialist states in Eastern Europe as proof of the worldwide appeal of the Soviet variety of Marxism-Leninism and of the initial success of Marxism-Leninism in its inexorable march toward world dominance. The overthrow of the socialist regime in Poland would have represented a major setback for the Soviets—not only for their ability to control events in Eastern Europe, but also for the image of the Soviet Union as the leader of a vital and expanding system of communist states destined to replace the moribund international capitalist system. The collapse of a socialist state in Europe would challenge the theoretical underpinnings of the Soviet system, both within the area of Soviet control in Eastern Europe and in the Soviet Union itself.

On various occasions over the course of the past thirty years the Soviets have demonstrated that, once a state has undergone a socialist revolution and has been accepted into the community of Marxist-Leninist states, the process is considered irreversible. The invasions of Hungary (1956), Czechoslovakia (1968), and—in part, at least—Afghanistan (1979) were all responses to what the Soviets viewed as unacceptable potential reversals of the revolutionary process. The doctrine of limited sovereignty developed to justify the Soviet invasion of Czechoslovakia in 1968 maintained that no Communist Party has the right to modify the basic structure of an existing socialist state and that the Soviet Union had ultimate authority to determine what types of changes or reforms were acceptable within the context of Marxism-Leninism.[7] During the period from fall 1980 to December 1981 Soviet, East German, and Czechoslovak leaders referred to this doctrine on numerous occasions when they asserted that the "socialist community is indissolvable. Its defense is a matter, not only for every single state, but for the entire socialist community as well."[8]

Before turning to an examination of the reaction of the Soviet Union and its East European allies to developments in Poland during the Solidarity period, it is important to discuss briefly the background to those developments. Since other contributions to this volume treat this background in some detail, discussion here will be especially brief.

THE GIEREK ERA AND THE YEAR OF RENEWAL

Almost immediately after coming to power in late 1970 the Gierek regime decided that the solution to Poland's political and economic ills lay in a dual policy of expanded industrialization, based primarily on the import of new technology from the West, and a simultaneous raising of the real standard of living of the Polish people. Within a few short years this approach foundered and the economic situation began to deteriorate rapidly.[9] The political implication of the economic collapse of the mid- and late-1970s was the emergence of a political opposition after the riots of June 1976 and the laying of a foundation for the alliance between workers and dissident intellectuals that characterized the Solidarity movement of 1980-81. Soon after the outbreak of the strikes in the summer of 1980 the ties between the inchoate workers' organizations and the Committee for the Defense of Workers (KOR) became visible, as representatives of the dissident organization provided the workers with both advice and—possibly more important—a communications network that permitted workers' groups throughout Poland to keep in touch with one another and to get their message to the Western media.

When the strikes first broke out in June 1980 in response to an announced increase in the price of staple food items, they were dealt with on an ad hoc basis. By mid-August, however, the strikes took on a new character with the announcement of a full-scale general strike. The capitulation of the government

to the workers' demands and the signing of the Gdansk agreement on August 31 brought to an end the first wave of strike
activity. They also brought to an end the political career of
Edward Gierek one week later.

Throughout fall 1980 the appeal of the new Solidarity union
movement became evident; by early 1981 it was estimated ten
million Poles—three times the size of Communist Party membership—
had joined the union. Moreover, Solidarity demands continued—
demands for a restructuring of Polish society, the elimination
of corruption, a five-day work week, the recognition of a farmers'
union, etc. By spring virtually all of these demands had been
met and a new series of developments, important for the course
of the reform in Poland, became visible. Reform elements within
the Polish United Workers' Party became more open and more
assertive, and the party congress of July 1981 reaffirmed the
policy of reform within the PUWP.

After months of tension and virtual chaos—caused both
by developments within Poland and by the pressures exerted on
Poland by the USSR and several other communist neighbors—
the party had reaffirmed a policy of renewal. Poland at the
end of July 1981 had a far different sociopolitical system than
had existed only a year earlier. Workers had asserted their
influence and had apparently succeeded in institutionalizing
that influence through the independent union movement. The
party itself had undergone substantial renovation and was
seemingly committed to policies aimed at overcoming both the
inefficiencies and the inequities of the past. Moreover, the
USSR's apparent reluctant acceptance of the results of the PUWP
Congress brought to a close one phase of the Polish crisis.

Almost immediately, however, new sources of conflict arose—
an announcement by the government for the need to raise prices,
resolutions emanating from the Solidarity congress in September
that called for the establishment of independent unions elsewhere
in Eastern Europe, and a new wave of strikes during fall 1981.
In the two weeks immediately preceding the imposition of martial
law on the night of December 12-13, 1981, the level of confrontation between Solidarity and the government increased. The
final act in the confrontation was the proposal at the December 11-
12 meetings of the Solidarity leadership in Gdansk for a national
referendum "on public confidence in the government as well as
the possibility of free elections to the Sejm and the people's
councils."[10] The imposition of martial law cut off debate on
the resolutions prior to the registration of a vote.

SOVIET AND EAST EUROPEAN CRITICISM
OF EVENTS IN POLAND

During the Solidarity period from August 1980 to December
1981, Poland's allies reacted to developments within Poland with
growing concern and increasing hostility. The campaign of
vilification, which began soon after the Gdansk agreements of
August 31, 1980, was conducted primarily by the Soviets, the
East Germans, and the Czechoslovaks—although by summer
1981 the Hungarians and Bulgarians had joined in the chorus
of criticism. Romania took positions different from those of
the other WTO members—veiled criticism of actual developments
within Poland joined with assertions of Poland's responsibility
and right to deal with its own problems. In the following discussion of the Soviet-East European reaction to the revolutionary
developments within Poland, I shall trace the escalation of
hostile commentary concerning events, with primary focus on
the views of the three major critics—the USSR, the GDR, and
Czechoslovakia.

Not until the second half of August 1980—more than six
weeks after it began—did the press in the other communist states
refer to the worker unrest in Poland.[11] From the very beginning, however, two of the themes that characterized the criticism
of developments in Poland were enunciated: antisocialist elements
"are trying to knock Poland from the socialist path that it has
chosen, a path which answers the basic interests of the Polish
people,"[12] and Western imperialists were actively engaged in
attempts to undermine the socialist order in Poland.[13]

In the months immediately following the Gdansk agreements
the criticism aimed at Poland by the Soviets and their East
German and Czechoslovak allies focused on several issues.
First of all, the threat from counterrevolutionary, antisocialist
elements and Western interference in Poland's domestic affairs
continued as the major themes of this criticism. KOR, and
especially its leaders Jacek Kuron and Adam Michnik, came in
for strong condemnation. Throughout this period, however,
Poland's allies continued to express their confidence in the
ability of Poles to deal with their problems under the leadership
of the Polish United Workers' Party. Periodic promises of
support that could be interpreted as veiled threats to intervene
were voiced by commentators and government officials. For
example, already in mid-October the Czechoslovak press was
making allusions to the similarity of the tactics of foreign and
domestic reactionary forces to those used in Czechoslovakia in
1968. These tactics had allegedly been developed in training

sessions carried out under the auspices of the Flying Universities.[14] Reactionaries were warned that "the socialist countries will not allow counterrevolution to be exported to their lands. . . . [S]upport, cementing, and protection of these [socialist] achievements are a joint international obligation of all socialist countries."[15] Czechoslovak commentary throughout the fall was, if anything, even harsher than that of the Soviets. Already in November, on the very day when the Polish Supreme Court was considering the statutes of Solidarity, Rude Pravo carried an article that asserted: ". . . since inimical forces now dwell in the very womb of the new trade unions, one cannot expect the nearest future to bring about a substantial improvement in the situation . . . unless, of course, the Polish trade unionists themselves, and above all the communists, unmask these inimical forces before the entire society and unless they drive them out of the new trade unions."[16]

Throughout the fall criticism was generally restricted to "certain anti-socialist groups" within the labor movement; not until January 1981 were the criticisms broadened to include virtually the entire organization.[17] The purported role of Western intelligence agencies, Polish emigre groups, Western labor organizations, and assorted other reactionary opponents of socialism was emphasized.[18] In early December Pravda accused Zbigniew Brzezinski, President Carter's National Security advisor, of meeting with unnamed Polish political scientists to map out strategy and call upon "the forces of the Polish opposition to show militant resistance." Brezezinski's denial of the accusation was seen as additional evidence of the U.S. administration's "direct interference in Poland's internal affairs."[19]

Beginning in January there was a noticeable expansion of both the targets and the intensity of criticism from Poland's allies. It should be noted, however, that during the entire period after the August strikes much of the criticism leveled at foreign interference, antisocialist counterrevolutionaries, and revisionists echoed criticisms that were being made in Poland itself. On many occasions Soviet and other East European commentary cited with approval statements and articles that had appeared first in Poland.[20] In early January the attacks against Solidarity were stepped up. "Anti-socialist elements acting under the cover of the slogans of the 'Solidarity' trade union . . . are urging the trade-union organization to assume the role of a kind of counterweight to the official organs of power, to transform itself into an organ of political pressure."[21] By the end of the month not only certain groups—especially

KOR—but the very leadership of Solidarity was under attack: "The leadership of the new union, especially its right wing, in which anti-socialist forces are active, continued its call to the workers not to work. By this action, the leaders of the new trade union organization again confirmed that they are bringing about the disorganization of both the country's economic and social life."[22] This theme continued throughout the spring of 1981. Solidarity was accused of exploiting the "justified protest of the country's workers against the mistakes and miscalculations in economic development. All their activities in the period since August 1980 show that they subscribe to the principle: the worse things are in the economy, the better they are for the anti-socialist forces."[23]

A new theme entered the attacks of Poland's neighbors by early 1981—the danger of revisionism within the Polish United Workers' Party itself. Throughout the fall official statements and commentary in the USSR, the GDR, and Czechoslovakia— as well as in the other socialist states—had consistently voiced faith in the ability of the PUWP to turn things around in Poland and to restore political and social normalcy. By early 1981, however, the Polish party became the target of growing criticism for failing to act decisively to meet the attacks of "counter-revolutionary elements." In late January the press in both Czechoslovakia and the GDR noted that the overall situation in Poland was intolerable and that something had to be done to stop the deterioration.[24] The selection of General Jaruzelski to replace Pinkowski as prime minister in early February appears to have been viewed favorably in Moscow, Berlin, and Prague, for the criticism was cut back. However, developments in late March in Poland—e.g., the threatened strikes after the events in Bydgoszcz—elicited an escalation of criticism of the PUWP. The Warsaw party organization was condemned for not respond-ing to the "malicious anti-Soviet and anti-socialist trend" of a meeting held at Warsaw University in late March; "It has been observed here that no sort of ideological rebuff to the speakers at this meeting on the part of the Warsaw party organization was delivered."[25] Immediately after a visit of Soviet Politburo member Mikhail Suslov in April the Soviet press expanded its charges that "revisionist elements" in the PUWP were trying "to paralyze the party of Polish communists" and prevent it from carrying out its role "as the leading force in society."[26]

The culmination of the attack on the Polish party for its inaction came in early June with the publication of the criticisms of the "Katowice forum," positive support of these criticisms in the East European media, and, finally, the letter from the Soviet

leadership to their Polish counterparts. A TASS report of
June 1, 1981 asserted that "The leading organs of the state
administration are not undertaking a resolute and consistent
struggle against the opponents of socialism, so as to enable
the party to mobilize the Marxist-Leninist forces. Evasion of
resolute actions and adoption of decisions leading to conflicts
favor a situation in which the main blow, as before, is directed
against the party and leads to further division."[27] Soviet
commentary on the hard-line statement of the Katowice Forum
was strongly supportive.[28] TASS, on June 5, 1981, referred
to

> a campaign of attacks . . . on the decision of the
> Katowice party forum. It is initiated, first of all,
> by the right wing leaders of the trade union
> 'Solidarity.' The leaders of some party organiza-
> tions are acting in concert with them. . . . A
> massive campaign directed against the Katowice
> forum has unfolded in a number of organs of the
> mass media. As a rule, these are the newspapers
> that have already long been attacking the PUWP
> from revisionist positions.

What the TASS report failed to mention was the fact that First
Secretary Kania and other high-ranking officials also came out
against the resolutions of the Katowice party group. On the
very day of this TASS report the letter from the Soviet party
leadership also arrived in Warsaw. In response to the strong
accusations made against the Polish party in the letter, a
special session of the Central Committee of the PUWP was held
on June 9-10, 1981 that resulted in a reaffirmation of support
for Kania as leader and for the policy of reform within the
party.[29]

The Soviets were not impressed by the results of the
Central Committee session, as the failure of the Soviet media
to do more than merely mention its opening demonstrated. On
June 12, TASS noted: "notwithstanding the demand contained
in the resolution of the Eleventh PUWP Plenum to call to account
those spreading anti-Socialist and anti-Soviet subversive materials, these people are continuing, unpunished, to distribute
in Warsaw samizdat materials with dirty, slanderous fabrications
and attacks on the Soviet Union and the PUWP leadership."[30]
Not until the days immediately preceding the Polish party congress in mid-July did the attacks on the party abate.

Throughout this entire period the themes of Western interference and the relevance of the experience of Czechoslovakia

continued to appear in the East European press. At the Soviet
Party Congress in February, for example, General Secretary
Brezhnev asserted that "imperialist subversive activity" has
helped "stimulate elements hostile to socialism. . . . Opponents
of socialism supported by outside forces are, by stirring up
anarchy, seeking to channel events onto a counterrevolutionary
course."[31] Already in September 1980 Czechoslovak commentators
had claimed the existence of parallels between events in their
country in 1968 and the developments in Poland. Throughout
the fall and winter Czechoslovak officials reiterated this argument and pointed to the lessons of normalization in Czechoslovakia
in the period after the Soviet military intervention.[32] Speaking
at the Congress of the Czechoslovak Communist Party in April,
Brezhnev for the first time publicly compared events in Poland
with those that occurred thirteen years earlier in Czechoslovakia.[33]

September 1981 represented another peak in Soviet and
East European condemnation of Solidarity. After the call to
workers throughout the communist community to unite for a
truly free union movement made during the first session of the
Solidarity congress,[34] meetings were staged throughout the
communist states at which Solidarity and its leader Lech Walesa
were condemned for their "open call for a struggle against the
socialist system."[35] Throughout Eastern Europe the concern
was voiced that the attempts to bring about a counterrevolution
in Poland were "no longer the exclusive concern of Poland."[36]
Throughout fall 1981, as political and economic chaos in Poland
seemingly expanded, Soviet and East European commentary
continued to express concern for both the future of socialist
Poland and for the implications of developments in Poland for
the internal security of the other communist states, although
the replacement of Kania by General Jaruzelski as first secretary
of the PUWP in mid-October was generally welcomed.

Before turning to a discussion of the more concrete responses of the Soviets and their allies, brief mention should be
made of the verbal reaction to events in Poland by the three
East European countries not yet referred to—Hungary, Bulgaria,
and Romania. In many respects they stood back throughout
most of the year between the beginning of the strikes and the
PUWP Congress of July 1981 and permitted the Soviets, East
Germans, and Czechoslovaks to make the ideologically based
attacks on the growing danger to Polish socialism. The Bulgarians
gave only sporadic and limited coverage to events in Poland.
In general they refrained from commentary and relied on citations
from the Polish press or that of other East European countries.

Not until the end of May 1981 did they join with the East Germans
and Czechoslovaks in denouncing developments in Poland. [37]
In many respects the Hungarian response was similar. Throughout most of the year-long crisis the Hungarian press took a
rather mild approach to events in Poland. As was the case
with the Bulgarians, the Hungarians also relied on citations
from the Polish press rather than providing their own analysis
of the situation. By June 1981, however, after the issuance
of the Soviet letter to the Polish leadership, the Hungarians
joined in the criticism more fully. [38]

The position of Romania differed from that of all of the
other Warsaw Pact member states. While clearly not supporting
the gist of the developments within Poland, the Romanians stated
repeatedly that Poland's problems were its own and had to be
solved by the Poles themselves. In a speech to the Romanian
Central Committee on October 7, for example, President Ceausescu
criticized the PUWP for the serious mistakes that led to the crisis
and denounced the independent union as an instrument of reaction and imperialism. [39] In June, at a meeting of the Second
Congress of the Councils of Working People, Ceausescu reaffirmed the Romanian position against intervention. [40]

While the Soviets found almost universal support among
the East European Communist Parties—although somewhat muted
in some cases—for their criticism of the course of events in
Poland, they had much more difficulty in gaining the support
of other major Communist Parties. Among the ruling Communist
Parties, that of Yugoslavia was outspoken, both in support of
the process of democratic renewal within Poland itself and against
the possibility of intervention by other Warsaw Pact states. [41]
In late June, Milos Minic, a member of the Presidium of the
Yugoslav Communist League, stated that "the Polish people,
the Polish working class, and the PUWP alone are called upon
to find a solution for the difficulties . . . without interference
from any quarter whatsoever." [42]

It was from the major West European Communist Parties—
especially the Italian Communist Party—that the Soviets received
the most criticism for their policy toward Poland. Throughout
the entire period after the strikes of July-August 1980, the PCI
supported the reform elements within the Polish party. Shortly
after the outbreak of the strikes, the PCI daily blamed the
Polish crisis on the "pyramidal and totalitarian" political organization of Soviet-style socialism and called for the immediate
development of "democracy and participation." [43] Throughout
the fall of 1980 the Italian party made clear its support for
reform elements in the PUWP. When the prospects of Soviet

military intervention intensified, the PCI strongly opposed such a move.[44] By spring the Soviets and Italians were engaged in open polemics on the issue of Poland—with the Italians accusing the Soviets of interfering in Polish affairs.[45] Other West European Communist Parties joined in the support of political renewal within the Polish Communist Party and warned the Soviets against military intervention.[46]

The importance of the criticism from the West European parties becomes evident when one considers the attempts of the Soviets in recent years to hold the communist movement together and the likely political costs that military intervention would generate for the Soviets. For the Eurocommunists, developments in Poland were at least partial vindication for their own positions— e.g., the need for decentralization of the party apparatus, the necessity of greater sensitivity to different national needs, and the right of each party to determine its own course of development. The Soviet decision to intervene militarily in Czechoslovakia in 1968 was one of the crucial factors that stimulated the growth of Eurocommunism. A similar decision in Poland would likely have resulted in the complete break in relations between the Soviet party and many of those of the West.

CONCRETE SOVIET AND EAST EUROPEAN RESPONSES TO THE CHALLENGE OF POLAND

To this point we have surveyed merely the verbal reactions of the Soviet-line party-states to developments in Poland during 1980-81. However, the Soviets and their allies also reacted in more concrete ways both to curtail what they viewed as the erosion of communist orthodoxy and to limit the influence of developments in Poland elsewhere in Eastern Europe. The entire set of reactions is quite similar to the development of Soviet and East European responses to the liberalization of the Prague spring in 1968: strong, even vitriolic, criticisms; constant political pressures, including those exerted at a series of bilateral and multilateral meetings of high-level party and state officials; and military pressures stemming from troop buildups and extended military maneuvers.[47] We have already traced in some detail the evolution of criticism of Polish developments emanating from the other European communist capitals. As we have seen, this criticism was closely tied to specific events occurring in Poland and was used, in part, to attempt to coerce the Polish party-state leadership to assert control over domestic events. From at least the time of the Central

Committee Plenum called in late March 1981 the Soviets (as well
as some of the East Europeans) expanded their attack on revisionist elements within the PUWP and emphasized their continuing
support for healthy elements within the Polish party. On several
occasions Poland's allies attempted to intervene directly in the
policy and personnel debates that were raging within the PUWP.
For example, during the heated March plenum, when Stefan
Olszowski and Tadeusz Grabski, two of the most outspoken
conservative critics of Kania's policies, offered to resign from
their positions in the Politburo, a phone call from Brezhnev to
Kania reportedly played a role in the final decision not to accept
the resignations. 48 Later evidence is provided by the strong
support for the Katowice Party Forum, the efforts to oust Kania
from the leadership of the PUWP indicated by increasing attacks
on his policies that culminated in Brezhnev's harsh letter of
early June, and the campaign of vilification preceding the Polish
Communist Party Congress of the revisionists who were said to
be in the process of seizing control of the PUWP. 49

Closely related to the open criticism of Polish developments—
although the contents are not so easily documented—was the
series of meetings between Polish party and state officials and
their counterparts from the other communist countries. After
Gierek's fall from leadership of the party in September 1980
there were continuing streams of official visitors to and from
Warsaw. The party congresses in Moscow, Prague, and East
Berlin in early spring 1981 provided additional opportunities
for face-to-face consultation and the exertion of pressures on
the Poles. In the months preceding the Polish congress a series
of Soviet delegations visited the Polish capital. The late Mikhail
Suslov, the top Soviet ideologue and a long-term member of the
Politburo, arrived in late April, soon after the Polish party
plenum at which supporters and opponents of party renewal
had clashed. Obviously he was not impressed by the efforts of
the Poles to bring the situation under control, for immediately
after his return to Moscow the Soviet press expanded its charges
of revisionism within the Polish party. 50

In mid-May a delegation of unspecified heads of CPSU
Central Committee departments arrived in Poland where they
spent five days on a fact-finding tour of the country. 51 Soon
after their return came the support for the conservatives of
the Katowice Party Forum and the letter from the Soviet Politburo,
signed by Brezhnev, that in effect called for a replacement of
the current Polish leadership. The attempt to unseat Kania
failed, and he emerged from the emergency plenum held to
discuss the Soviet letter in a strengthened position. 52

The final high-ranking Soviet visitor to appear in Warsaw prior to the party congress was Andrei Gromyko, long-time foreign minister and member of the CPSU Politburo. The talks with the Polish leaders apparently resulted in Gromyko's returning to his colleagues in Moscow with the advice that the Polish congress and its results would have to be accepted. During the week between his return and the opening of the congress in Warsaw the Soviet press was noticeably reserved in its commentary about Poland.

What does emerge from this brief overview is the continuing effort on the part of the Soviets (as well as the East German and Czechoslovak leaders) to meet personally with the Poles in the attempt to influence the policies of the Polish party leadership. This is a pattern that parallels that which occurred in Czechoslovakia in 1968.

Another important aspect of the pressure placed on Poland was the almost constant threat of military intervention, if developments were to reach the point that Poland's allies considered totally unacceptable. As we have already noted, numerous East European officials and commentators asserted the indivisibility of the security of the entire socialist community and the commitment of Poland's allies to preventing "counter-revolution and Western interference" in Poland from challenging the Warsaw Pact's security. For example, in a statement that could hardly be misinterpreted, General Aleksandr Popotkhin, commander of Soviet troops in Poland, noted that his forces were ready to crush class enemies and that "the Warsaw Pact nations will guard the interest of their nations."[53]

Most important as a means of exerting pressure against both the Polish leadership and the population at large was the periodic buildup of Soviet forces both within and along the border of Poland. The first such buildup occurred in late November and early December 1980. Areas in the GDR along the Polish border were closed to Western visitors, and Soviet troops in western Belorussia and Ukraine were placed on alert.[54] Again in the spring a buildup of Soviet troops and the unexplained prolonging of Warsaw Pact military maneuvers on Polish soil were apparently used by the Soviets as a means to exert pressure on both the Polish government and its population.[55] In early August 1981, at the time of the resumption of political tensions in Poland in connection with the demonstrations related to the food shortage, uncommonly large-scale Soviet naval maneuvers in the Baltic—including amphibious landings in Soviet territory immediately adjacent to northern Poland—represented a renewed attempt to make the Poles cognizant of Soviet concern and of Soviet military capabilities.[56]

In addition to the various forms of pressure that the Soviets and their East European allies employed in dealing with the Poles, they also attempted to isolate Poland and to prevent the spread of the contagion affecting Poland itself. By late October 1980, the East German government had implemented policy changes aimed at reducing contacts between East Germans and both Poles and West Germans. On October 29 it was announced that all future private trips to or from Poland would require prior, police-approved invitations from specific individuals to be visited.[57] Two weeks earlier the East Germans had already doubled the mandatory exchange of currency for West Germans visiting the GDR. The effect was to reduce the number of West Germans applying for entry visas into the GDR.[58] In mid-November new restrictions on travel between Poland and Czechoslovakia were agreed upon by the two governments.[59] By mid-October the Soviets—who had never opened their borders to the free flow of Polish tourists as had the Czechoslovaks and East Germans—removed all Polish newspapers and magazines from sale in Latvia and Lithuania.[60]

All of these actions were aimed at preventing information concerning the demands of the Polish workers and the concessions of the Polish regime from reaching the people of the Soviet Union and Eastern Europe. Parallel to this attempt to isolate Poland and to prevent accurate new reports of developments in Poland from reaching their countries, the Soviet and other East European leaderships began efforts to forestall developments comparable to those that had occurred in Poland. Most important, in this respect, was the campaign to strengthen the official union movement in the various communist countries. Since fall 1980 the official propaganda organs throughout Eastern Europe were busy emphasizing the benefits gained by workers through the activities of the official union movement. In an article that appeared in Pravda in late December 1980, M. Baglai outlined the basic Soviet theory of the role of unions in a communist society:

> There are no social grounds or reasons for political confrontation between the trade unions and the state, and consequently the trade unions have no need to resort to strikes and other extreme measures to defend the interest of the working people. . . . Work stoppages at enterprises, whatever the reason for them—and the recent events in Poland convince us of this—play into the hands of anti-Socialist elements that are trying to impart

a totally different meaning to the economic protest,
to turn society away from the Socialist path of
development.[61]

Parallel to the ideological campaign to buttress the image
of the official unions was the effort to rejuvenate the unions
themselves. At the Twenty-Sixth Soviet Party Congress,
General Secretary Brezhnev stated: "At times the trade
unions lack initiative in exercising their extensive rights.
They are not always persistent in questions of fulfilling collective contracts and of labor protections, and they still react
only feebly to instances of the violation of labor legislation and
cases of bureaucracy and red tape."[62] Problems with union
work were the major topic of discussion at the Congress of the
Slovak Communist Party held in March 1981.[63]

The concern for the potential implications of developments
in Poland on the official labor organizations elsewhere in Eastern
Europe is not without foundation. Periodically during the 1970s
there occurred reports of strikes in the USSR; and in 1977
Romania faced large-scale strikes of miners.[64] In July 1981
strikes were reported in East Germany, in which the relationship to the events in Poland was clear, since illegal leaflets
were distributed supporting the activities of the Solidarity
union movement in Poland.[65] Hungary had already expanded
greatly the role of the unions in influencing management
decisions—in part before the outbreak of the strikes in Poland
in summer 1980. Moreover, the Hungarian government promised
a five-day work week by 1982 and increased both the minimum
and maximum wage scales.[66]

To this point we have emphasized the negative response
of Poland's allies to the developments of the past year—the
criticism, pressures, and attempts to isolate the Poles. There
was, however, another side of the Soviet-East European response;
namely, support of both a political and more concrete economic
nature. As we have already noted, throughout the months
immediately following the Gdansk settlement of August 31, 1980,
the Soviets and their allies repeatedly enunciated their confidence
in and support for the ability of the Polish leadership to resolve
the serious problems facing the Polish nation. In spite of the
growing criticism of the PUWP throughout 1981 for its inability
to deal with the situation, Poland's allies continued to voice
their commitment of political support.

In addition to this political support, however, the Soviets
and East Europeans also provided Poland with substantial amounts
of economic assistance. By far the most important source of

financial assistance to Poland after summer 1980 was the Soviet Union, which, according to Deputy Prime Minister Mieczyslaw Jagielski, committed a total of $4.2 billion of new credits, including $965 million in convertible currency, during the period August 1980 to mid-June 1981.[67] In addition, the Soviets granted a four-year moratorium on repayment of earlier credits from the period 1976-79 valued at 438 million transferable rubles.[68] Poland's smaller East European allies also provided assistance to Poland in dealing with its severe economic problems by sending additional supplies of food and consumer goods. Already in mid-September 1980, Radio Warsaw announced the delivery of extra food supplies from Czechoslovakia, Hungary, Romania, and Bulgaria.[69] During the first three months of 1981 the five East European states reportedly shipped food and consumer goods valued at 287.6 million exchange zlotys (approximately $88.6 million at the official exchange rate). Payment for these supplies was deferred until the period 1983-89.[70] A final area in which Poland's allies provided some support was in the supply of raw materials to Polish factories in return for the delivery of finished goods. At least two such agreements were signed prior to the imposition of martial law— one with the USSR and a second with the GDR—according to which additional supplies of raw materials were sent to Poland.[71]

However, economic relations between Poland and its CMEA partners were not characterized exclusively by such cordial assistance. The inability of the Poles to fulfill their export commitments to their trading partners resulted in cases of retaliation.[72] Already by the beginning of 1981, Polish officials had noted the importance of stepping up "exports so that Poland can fulfill its contract obligations toward foreign countries and repay her debts on time."[73]

THE IMPLICATIONS OF POLISH DEVELOPMENTS
FOR THE EUROPEAN COMMUNIST STATES

What should be clear by this point in our review of Soviet and East European responses to developments in Poland during the period prior to martial law is the continuing concern about Poland's future course and the variety of methods employed in the attempt to influence that course. However, in spite of Soviet and East European pressures, revolutionary change in both the structure of the Polish Communist Party and in the relationship between the party and the people continued. This change represented a serious challenge to the other communist states, for it exposed the fundamental weaknesses of the communist system and threatened the dictatorship of the party elite.[74]

Probably the major immediate political challenge represented by developments in Poland was that to continued party dominance. In Poland, in which the Communist Party has not been able to gain the type of control characteristic of the other European communist systems—witness the role of the Roman Catholic church—a pluralist sociopolitical system was, in effect, accepted by the party leadership. As the events of 1980-81 indicated, the party was no longer able to command obedience from society at large. The population, primarily through the means of the union movement, was able both to block government initiatives of which it disapproved and, in some cases, to force the political leadership to act on matters of concern to the workers. In addition, the workers' movement strengthened the forces of those within the Polish United Workers' Party who favored some form of devolution of political authority. This set of developments ran counter to the ideal of the Soviet-style communist state—as the numerous statements referred to above demonstrate. For the leaders of the Soviet Union and East Europe's other communist states the question arose of their ability to retain the centralized dictatorial system imposed by the Bolsheviks and their successors in the face of a developing—although limited—form of pluralism in Poland. Martial law and the arrest and imprisonment of Solidarity's leaders eliminated, for the time being at least, this challenge.

Closely related to the issue of party dominance was that of maintaining contact with the masses of the population. What communist leaders witnessed in Poland was the first effective workers' revolt against a so-called workers' party. In large part this resulted from the failure of the party to respond to the legitimate interests of the majority of the population. Throughout Eastern Europe the efforts to revitalize the official union movement and to maintain effective contact with and responsiveness to the demands of the workers indicated the awareness of party leaders of this fact. As Brezhnev stated at the Soviet party congress in February 1981, "The events in Poland convince one once again how important it is for the party to strengthen its guiding role by lending a sensitive ear to the voice of the masses and by struggling resolutely against all manifestations of bureaucratism and voluntarism."[75] Yet the demands of party dominance and centralized control contradict many of the concerns of the workers. Moreover, corruption of high-ranking and middle-level party and state officials—

which became an important political issue in Poland—is widespread elsewhere in the communist states. Reform and the elimination of the most blatant form of corruption would also reduce some of the important perquisites that have made official service attractive in the past.

Poland has also demonstrated—if demonstration was still needed—the bankruptcy of an economic system based on tight central control. Poland's economy is not alone in communist Europe in its inability to innovate or to meet the growing demands of the consumer. Elsewhere in Eastern Europe the recent past has witnessed growing scarcities of consumer goods, rapidly escalating foreign debts, and the inability to benefit fully from the expensive imported Western technology.

Throughout Eastern Europe the imposition of martial law in Poland on the night of December 12-13 was received with enthusiastic official approval. Not only did General Jaruzelski's seizure of state power result in the apparent destruction of the democratic movement in Poland, it also avoided the internecine struggle that most observers viewed as inevitable should Soviet and other Warsaw Pact troops have intervened in Poland. In their assessments of martial law, the East European leaders based their arguments on the same assertions that they had used in earlier condemnations of Solidarity: extremists in Solidarity had openly called for a seizure of power.[76] Solidarity had already organized shock troops that were to have attacked the party and government on December 17;[77] Western imperialist and revanchist support for the union movement had been aimed at undermining the socialist system in Poland and elsewhere in Eastern Europe.[78]

Although all of the official East European sources have agreed that the imposition of martial law was essential to prevent the total collapse of socialism in Poland, their assessments of the ease with which the situation would return to normal appeared to differ. For the East Germans and the Czechoslovaks the major issue appeared to be the rooting out of all antisocialist elements within the society. Continued vigilance remained necessary in order to prevent a resurgence of counterrevolutionary activity.[79]

More than two years after the imposition of martial law— and a year after it was rescinded—the situation in Poland has changed little. Even though there exist indications of some modest improvements in the economic situation and Solidarity and the reform movement no longer pose an immediate challenge to party hegemony, General Jaruzelski has not succeeded in reestablishing party and government legitimacy in Poland. The basic structural factors that caused the economic and political collapse of the late 1970s and early 1980s have not been modified, and the military regime during its year in power proved little more capable than was its civilian predecessor in providing effective leadership. The populace has been cowed; the basic problems remain.

NOTES

1. Rude Pravo, October 14, 1980, translated in Vladimir V. Kusin, "Vasil Bilak Implies Counterrevolution in Poland," Radio Free Europe Research (hereafter RFER), RAD Background Report (hereafter RAD BR)/247 (Czechoslovakia), October 20, 1980.

2. "Brezhnev Takes Aim at Poland," Newsweek, December 15, 1980, pp. 38-42, 47-48. In his speech at the Soviet Communist Party Congress on February 23, 1981, General Secretary Brezhnev stated: "And let no one doubt our common determination to secure our interests, and to defend the socialist gains of the peoples." New Times 9 (1981):21.

3. According to Radio Prague (January 28, 1981, 1830 hours) during the visit of Lech Walesa, the leader of Solidarity, to Rome, the Vatican had "given its instructions to Walesa, and the Catholic Fifth Column in Poland to help him implement these directions." Cited in Patrick Moore, "Tougher Line on Poland in Eastern Media," RFER, RAD BR/31 (Eastern Europe), February 5, 1981.

4. L. I. Brezhnev, O vneshnei politike KPSS i Sovetskogo Gosudarstva: Rechi i Stat'i (Moscow: Politizdat, 1978), p. 508.

5. For an excellent assessment of the military role of Poland within the Warsaw Pact see A. Ross Johnson, Robert W. Dean, and Alexander Alexiev, East European Military Establishments: The Warsaw Pact Northern Tier (Santa Monica: The Rand Corporation, 1980).

6. This point was made quite evident at the time of a threatened local railroad strike in November 1980. A Soviet commentary implied that this was to be a nationwide strike and noted that "the threat of a general transport strike, proclaimed by 'Solidarity,' could affect the national and defense interests of the country and disrupt rail transit links through Poland." TASS, November 24, 1980; published in Pravda, November 25, 1980.

7. The "Brezhnev doctrine," as this justification has been called in the West, was first expounded by Sergei Kovalev

in an article entitled "Suverenitet i internatsional'nye obiazannosti sotsialisticheskikh stran," Pravda, September 26, 1968, p. 4.

8. From the communique issued by PAP, the official Polish news agency, at the conclusion of the meeting of Polish and Soviet Party leaders after the Soviet Party Congress in Moscow. PAP, March 4, 1981, cited in New York Times, March 5, 1981, pp. 1, 6.

9. For more complete discussion of these points see Roger E. Kanet, "Le commerce exterieur polonais: les inter-relations entre la politique economique interne et exterieure," Revue d'Etudes Comparatives Est-Ouest 11 (1980):35-52; idem, "Poland, the Socialist Community, and East-West Relations," in Background to Crisis: Policy and Politics in Gierek's Poland, eds. Maurice D. Simon and Roger E. Kanet (Boulder, Colorado: Westview Press, 1981), pp. 371-401. The most detailed coverage of the Polish economy has been provided in the numerous articles of Zbigniew M. Fallenbuchl. Recent general overviews of the Polish economic situation are "Policy of the Polish Economic Relations," in Background to Crisis, eds. Simon and Kanet, pp. 329-70; "The Polish Economy at the Beginning of the 1980s," in East European Economic Assessment: Part I—Country Studies, 1980, a compendium of papers submitted to the Joint Economic Committee, Congress of the United States, ed. John P. Hardt (Washington: U.S. Government Printing Office, 1981), pp. 33-71; "Poland's Economic Crisis," Problems of Communism 31 (1981):1-21.

10. Radio Warsaw, December 12, 1981.

11. Pravda, August 20, 1981; Rude Pravo, August 23, 1980.

12. TASS and Radio Moscow-2, 1800 hours, August 27, 1980. See, also, the authoritative commentary by A. Petrov in Pravda, September 1, 1980. Without even referring to the strike settlement announced the day before, Petrov denounced the strike leaders for making political demands and for their ties with the Western media and with reactionary Polish emigres.

13. In a TASS commentary of September 9, 1980, it was claimed that "The August events in Poland . . . aroused hopes among the West German revanchists. It is not difficult to detect a recent upsurge of activity in such circles. Not only in the neo-Nazi press, but on television as well, maps with the frontiers of the pre-war German Reich have appeared." The theme of Western involvement is elaborated more fully by A. Petrov in Pravda articles of September 20, 27, and 29. Vasil Bilak, a member of the Czechoslovak Communist Party Presidium and the Central Committee secretary of interparty relations, condemned

of the Soviet position that "for the fraternal socialist countries, the weakening of Poland is also a threat to their joint interests and to their security," Trybuna Ludu, June 10, 1981.

30. Cited in Bruce Porter, "Initial Soviet Reactions to the eleventh plenum of the Polish Party's Central Committee," RLR, RL 233/81, June 16, 1981.

31. Pravda, February 24, 1981.

32. See, for example, the speech of First Secretary Gustav Husak at a district party conference in Kladno in Rude Pravo, February 16, 1981; translated in RFER, CZ.SR/4, February 14, 1981. In Husak's words, "Czechoslovak communists remember only too well what confusion, chaos and demagoguery they had to fight against and how they put a stop to it."

33. Radio Moscow, April 7, 1981. An article in the Ukrainian Communist Party journal, Pid praporem Leninizmu 3 (1981):23-37, discussed in some detail the role of revisionist groups in Hungary in 1956, as well as that of revisionist and bourgeois agents in Czechoslovakia in 1968. Although the author makes no explicit mention of Poland, he does note that "today forces that are hostile to socialism, including propaganda and intelligence centers of the capitalist states, have not abandoned their hope of weakening the leading role of the Marxist-Leninist parties that are in power, and do not refrain from attempts at direct intervention into the internal development of the socialist countries." Translated in Roman Solchanyk, "Ukrainian Party Journal Raises the Specter of Poland," RLR, RL 70/81, February 17, 1981.

34. PAP, September 9, 1981.

35. Rude Pravo, September 12, 1981.

36. Nepszabadsag, September 14, 1981; Rabotnichesko Delo, September 17, 1981; Izvestiia, September 22, 1981.

37. See Rabotnichesko Delo, May 31, 1981; cited in Patrick Moore, "Poland's Allies Keep up the Pressure," RFER, RAD BR/183 (Eastern Europe), June 30, 1981.

38. See, for example, Nepszadabsag, June 14, 1981; cited in Patrick Moore, "Still Sharper Eastern Criticism of Poland," RFER, RAD BR/176 (Eastern Europe), June 19, 1981. See, also, RFER, Hungarian Situation Report/10, July 15, 1981.

39. Scinteia, October 1980; cited in RFER, Romanian Situation Report/15, October 31, 1980.

40. Scinteia, June 29, 1981; cited in Patrick Moore, "Poland's Neighbors Remain Watchful," RFER, RAD BR/186 (Eastern Europe), July 1, 1981.

41. See, for example, Borba (Belgrade), January 25, 1981; cited in Zdenko Antic, "Yugoslavs Concerned Over Rising

Tension in Poland," RFER, RAD BR/25 (Yugoslavia), January 30, 1981.

42. Tanjug (Yugoslav Press Agency), June 25, 1981; cited in Slobodan Stankovic, "Yugoslav Leader Against Any Interference in Poland," RFER, RAD BR/190 (Yugoslavia), July 6, 1981.

43. L'Unita, August 19, 1980; cited in Joan Barth Urban, "The West European Communist Challenge to Soviet Foreign Policy," in Soviet Foreign Policy in the 1980s, ed. Roger E. Kanet (New York: Praeger, 1982), p. 179.

44. L'Unita, December 10, 1980, pp. 1, 15; cited in Urban, "The West European Communist Challenge," p. 174.

45. See Kevin Devlin, "Soviet-PCI Polemics over Poland," RFER, RAD BR/185 (World Communist Movement), June 30, 1981. See, also, Y. Samoilov, "Strange Position: Concerning an Article in the Italian Journal Rinascita About the Events in Poland," New Times 26 (1981), pp. 14-15.

46. Immediately following the initial publication of the Soviet letter to the Polish leadership, the British, Belgian, Italian, Dutch, and Japanese parties reaffirmed their support for the cause of democratic reform in Poland and against a repetition of the "errors made in relation to Czechoslovakia in 1968," in the words of Morning Star, the British Communist Party daily. See Kevin Devlin, "Western CPs Back Polish Renewal, Warn Against Intervention," RFER, RAD BR/178 (World Communist Movement), June 24, 1981; idem, "Japanese CP Warns Soviets on Poland," RFER, RAD BR/203 (World Communist Movement), July 15, 1981.

47. For excellent discussions of the reactions of the USSR and its allies to events in Czechoslovakia, see H. Gordon Skilling, Czechoslovakia's Interrupted Revolution (Princeton: Princeton University Press, 1976), pp. 658-712; Jiri Valenta, Soviet Intervention in Czechoslovakia, 1968: Anatomy of a Decision (Baltimore: The Johns Hopkins University Press, 1979), passim. For comparisons of events in Poland with those in Czechoslovakia, especially a comparison of Soviet and East European reactions, see Jiri Valenta, "Soviet Options in Poland," Survival 22 (1981): 50-59.

48. For a discussion of the plenum see J. B. de Weydenthal, "The Polish CC Plenum Reveals Division in the Leadership," RFER, RAD BR/109 (Poland), April 23, 1981. The phone call is reported, without a source, in "Soviet 'Occupation by Osmosis' Perils Democratization Process in Poland," Studium News Abstracts (The North American Study Center for Polish Affairs) 5 (1981):3.

49. Immediately prior to the Polish congress the official GDR news agency published a purported third statement of the Katowice forum in which the legality of the election of some delegates to the congress was questioned. ADN, July 4, 1981, Neues Deutschland, July 6, 1981, p. 2.

50. Pravda, April 26, 1981.

51. Pravda, May 24, 1981.

52. For an interesting assessment of these events see Elizabeth Pond, "Kremlin's Maneuvering on Poland Backfires," The Christian Science Monitor, June 16, 1981, pp. 1, 8.

53. Cited in a UPI report by Robert Kaylor, "Poland Leaders Leave for Soviet Conferences," published in Champaign-Urbana (Illinois) News-Gazette, February 22, 1981.

54. See Eric Bourne, "Polish Leader Warns Radicals, Soothes Jittery East-bloc Allies," The Christian Science Monitor, December 3, 1980, p. 6; see, also, "Brezhnev Takes Aim at Poland," Newsweek, December 15, 1980, pp. 38-42, 47-48.

55. The maneuvers, which lasted three weeks, ended on April 7, 1981. See New York Times, April 8, 1981. For a discussion of the political implications of the maneuvers see Bruce Porter, "Warsaw Pact Maneuvers and Poland: The Political Implications," RLR, RL 118/81, March 17, 1981. For a comparison of the use of military maneuvers vis-à-vis Poland with those in Czechoslovakia in 1968, see Vladimir V. Kusin, "Warsaw Pact Military Maneuvers in Czechoslovakia 1968: A Look Back," RFER, RAD BR/79 (Czechoslovakia), March 23, 1981.

56. See Ted Nemko, "Lull Ends, Soviets Renew Pressure on Poles," The Christian Science Monitor, August 10, 1981, p. 9. Soviet maneuvers lasted until September 12, 1981.

57. Neues Deutschland, October 29, 1980.

58. The Christian Science Monitor, October 19, 1980.

59. PAP, November 18, 1980, Rude Pravo, November 21, 1980; cited in RFER CZ.SR/28, November 28, 1980.

60. See David K. Willis, The Christian Science Monitor November 17, 1980, p. 1.

61. M. Baglai, "Profsoiuzy v usloviiach sotsialistecheskogo obshchestva," Pravda, December 26, 1980, pp. 2, 3. For a similar argument against the acceptability of free unions, see the speech of Karel Hoffmann, a member of the Czechoslovak Communist Party Presidium and the head of the Czechoslovak Labor Union Organization, at the Tenth Plenum of the Czechoslovak Central Trade Union Council, October 29, 1980; printed in Rude Pravo, November 13, 1980 and cited in Vladimir V. Kusin, "Prague Continues to Read Strictures to Warsaw." RFER, RAD BR/278 (Czechoslovakia), November 10, 1980.

62. Pravda, February 24, 1981.

63. See the speech of Ladislav Abraham, Slovak Communist Party Presidium member and chairman of the Slovak Labor Union Council, Pravda (Bratislava), March 24, 1981; at the Czecho-slovak party congress the next month Karel Hoffmann, the head of the Czechoslovak Labor Union Organization, noted that "the events and the development of the labor union movement in Poland have sharply focused attention on the problems of the socialist trade unions and have prompted a broad debate even among our working people. . . ." Rude Pravo, April 9, 1981, p. 5. Both citations are taken from RFER, CZ.SR/7, April 30, 1981.

64. For a recent discussion of the role of workers in Romania see Daniel N. Nelson, "Workers in a Workers' State," in Romania in the 1980s, ed. Nelson (Boulder, Colorado: West-view Press, 1981), pp. 174-97.

65. Der Spiegel, July 17, 1981; see also The Christian Science Monitor, July 29, 198, p. 2.

66. Eric Bourne, "Hungary Tiptoes Behind Poland with Own Cautious Reform Program," The Christian Science Monitor, February 17, 1981, p. 5. The introduction of the 40-hour work week in Poland in early 1981 meant that Polish workers had the shortest work week of any of the workers in the communist countries of Eastern Europe. See Eric Bourne, "Poland's Workers Win Best Deal Yet in East Europe," The Christian Science Monitor, February 2, 1981, p. 8.

67. PAP, in Russian, June 20, 1981; cited in Cam Hudson, "The Inconclusive 35th CMEA Council Session in Sofia," RFER, RAD BR/201 (Eastern Europe), July 15, 1981. This figure agrees with earlier Western estimates. See Yakov Samoilev, "Soviet Economic Aid for Poland," RLR, RL 49/81, February 2, 1981.

68. Washington Post, February 23, 1981, pp. A1, A6. See also, Hudson, "The Inconclusive 35th CMEA Council Session in Sofia." According to a recent estimate, economic assistance received by Poland from its Eastern allies totaled $4.5 billion in 1980 (of which $4.3 billion came from the USSR). The following year the amount increased to $5.9 (of which $5.6 was from the Soviet Union). See Elizabeth Ann Goldstein, "Soviet Economic Assistance to Poland, 1980-81," in U.S. Congress, Joint Economic Committee, Soviet Economy in the 1980's: Problems and Prospects (Washington: U.S. Government Printing Office, 1983), II, 567.

69. Radio Warsaw, domestic service, September 19, 1980, 2200; cited in RFER, Polish Situation Report/23, December 20, 1980.

70. <u>PAP</u>, in English, June 23, 1981; cited in Hudson, "The Inconclusive 35th CMEA Council Session in Sofia."

71. Radio Warsaw, domestic service, June 11, 1981 and <u>PAP</u>, in English, June 19, 1981; cited in Hudson, "The Inconclusive 35th CMEA Council Session in Sofia."

72. During the first six months of 1981 coal exports dropped to 8.5 million metric tons (down from 19.5 million tons a year earlier). Since coal is one of the crucial exports from Poland to both the GDR and Czechoslovakia, the drop had a serious impact on the two countries, Washington <u>Post</u>, July 29, 1981. See also, Richard M. Farkas and Cecil M. Regner, "The East European Response to Polish Change," unpublished paper presented at the annual meetings of the International Studies Association, Cincinnati, Ohio, March 24-27, 1982.

73. Statement of Prime Minister Jaruzelski after a government meeting dealing with foreign trade, <u>PAP</u>, February 18, 1981.

74. For a discussion of the implications of Polish events for Eastern Europe, see Adam Bromke, "Communism at the Watershed," <u>Toronto Star</u>, May 17, 1981. See, also, Bruce Porter, "The Repercussions of Gdansk: Poland's Crisis and the Socialist Community," <u>RLR</u> RL 163/81, April 16, 1981.

75. <u>Pravda</u>, February 24, 1981.

76. <u>Zemedelske Noviny</u>, January 7, 1982, p. 2.

77. <u>Rude Pravo</u>, January 13, 1981, p. 6.

78. <u>Neues Deutschland</u>, December 23, 1981, p. 1.

79. <u>Pravda</u> (Bratislava), January 16, 1982.

15.

Martial Law and Beyond: Jaruzelski's
Poland in the Post-December 1981 Period

Maurice D. Simon

The turbulent summer of 1980 witnessed the emergence of a genuine workers' movement in communist Poland that sought fundamental economic, political, and social policy reforms. The demands formally accepted by the governing authorities in the Gdansk, Szczecin, and Jastrzebie agreements were intended to guarantee a variety of citizens' rights that had been neglected and abused throughout the postwar period. The subsequent establishment of the Independent Self-Governing Trade Union, Solidarity, whose membership swelled to nearly ten million, paved the way for the transformation of the workers' movement into a movement for national renewal. For more than sixteen months, the challenges presented by a mobilized civil society desiring deep changes threatened the governing order. The mounting internal and external pressures prompted General Wojciech Jaruzelski's declaration of a state of war and the enactment of martial law.[1]

The Military Council for National Salvation (WRON) stated that its main objectives were "to secure conditions for the effective protection of peace and public order, . . . to restore social discipline, which has been violated, . . . [and] to secure the conditions for the efficient functioning of the government, the state administration, and the national economy." Its major steps involved the suspension of civil liberties, especially those associated with the activities of the trade unions and the public organizations that had flourished during the previous sixteen months, and the militarization of critical units of the national economy and the state administration.[2] Through such measures, a process of normalization would occur, eventually culminating in the reinstitution of civilian government. From Solidarity's and society's perspective, however, martial law was seen as an extraordinary abnormalization process—a renunciation of promises made throughout the 1980-81 period. A collective state of emotional depression was experienced by a majority of citizens, with passive and active resistance manifested on a widespread scale.[3] Thus, the formal lifting of martial law on July 22, 1983 (a national holiday commemorating the thirty-ninth anniversary of the establishment of communist rule in Poland) did not signify a return to social stability and order. While General Jaruzelski claimed that the termination of the state of war was "proof of the good will of the authorities," the Polish Sejm (parliament) displayed the authorities' defensiveness by adopting a series of precautionary legislative acts, including, notably, a constitutional amendment facilitating the declaration of a state of emergency by the Chairman of the Council of State in the face of internal threats. General Jaruzelski explicitly warned, "Any attempts at antisocialist activities will be muzzled no less decisively than before."[4]

What, then, has martial law in Poland accomplished. In this brief concluding chapter, I will offer some perspectives on martial law and its aftermath. I shall begin by discussing the authorities' overall efforts to consolidate central political control. Then I will describe the main political actors and their goals during the post-1981 period. Finally, I will consider the political direction of post-martial law Poland.

CONSOLIDATING CENTRAL POLITICAL CONTROL

The primary objective of martial law in Poland was to prevent the emergence of a system of dual (or shared) political power by eliminating or severely restricting the organizational potential of the perceived opposition. By late 1981, it had become evident that a process of polarization was taking place within Solidarity. A visible split occurred between radicals advocating a form of confrontation politics and moderates favoring negotiations and compromises with the governing authorities. On a number of occasions and on a variety of issues, heated debates indicated that the militants (figures such as Jacek Kuron, Andrzej Gwiazda, and Zbigniew Bujak) favored direct political challenges to the regime. They emphasized the necessity of self-management (workers' control) in enterprises, the use of active or general strikes, and the independent organization of referenda and elections free from communist interference. The moderates (figures such as Lech Walesa, Tadeusz Mazowiecki, and Wladyslaw Sila-Nowicki) were predisposed toward parliamentary over direct democracy, supported extensive consultations and bargaining with the communist authorities, and showed a distaste for mobilizational rhetoric and activities.[5] While it is beyond the scope of this analysis to evaluate either the validity or sincerity of the authorities' claims that Solidarity (particularly the radicals) had overstepped the boundaries of permissible political behavior by aspiring to supplant the Communist Party, it cannot be denied that martial law measures were designed to eliminate or severely curtail the power potential of the opposition and critics.

The widespread use of internments and arrests throughout the entire period of martial law was the most overt and effective method of reestablishing state authority. Such coercive actions were designed as political shock therapy for Polish society, serving to impress upon citizens the penalties for challenging the existing order. Solidarity officials and activists were the primary victims of this coercion, but internments and arrests were applied against activists and members of leading independent organizations (the Independent Students' Union and the Independent Farmers' Solidarity Union), oppositional and dissident groups (KSS "KOR", KPN), prominent intellectuals, and a cross section of all occupational groups. Throughout the martial law period, recurrent releases, internments, and arrests were manipulated for political purposes—to intimidate citizens and to break the spirit of resistance.[6] Despite the fact that most internees and prisoners were released after the suspension of martial law in December 1982 and the lifting of martial law in July 1983, prominent members of the political opposition (such as Kuron, Michnik, Wujec, and Romaszewski) remain in prison and will undoubtedly be prosecuted and sentenced as negative examples for Polish society. Repression in the workplace is another form of coercive power that has been widely utilized. Accurate statistics are unavailable, but it is likely that thousands of employees have been dismissed from their jobs based upon political criteria.[7]

A second major method of consolidation of state power was the dissolution of organizations that had posed a threat to the authorities. Following a strategy of peeling back the layers of organizational opposition, the martial law authorities dissolved such important organizations as the Independent Students' Union; the Polish Journalists' Association; the Association of Polish Theater, Television, and Film Actors; the Polish Writers' Union; the Independent Farmers' Solidarity Union; and, most

notably, the independent self-governing trade union, Solidarity.
The new trade union law enacted on October 8, 1982 effectively
banned independent trade unions such as Solidarity and Rural
Solidarity—one of the central pillars of the 1980-81 renewal
process. While this legislation was framed in democratic language
emphasizing labor's right to self-government, it was very clear
that the formation of unions, the nature of their organization,
their right to strike, and their access to the mass media would
all be tightly controlled by the state authorities.[8] Henceforth,
the organizational autonomy that facilitated interest articulation
during the Solidarity period will be severely restricted.

The third key element in reasserting state authority was
the framing of special legislation. Throughout the martial law
period, the Polish Sejm has been especially active in developing
legislation that enhances the power of the state. Law and order
legislation, including bills designed to combat social parasitism,
juvenile delinquency, and alcoholism, gave wide administrative
discretion to the authorities, raising the possibility of abuses.
Similarly, higher education legislation provided for close scrutiny
of academic institutions by the administrative authorities.
Legislation amending the penal code and the censorship law
considerably strengthened the state's repressive potential.[9]
These legislative trends (including the trade union law) indicate
that, even with the lifting of martial law, the authorities fully
intend to maintain strict controls over Polish society.

A fourth element of political control must be mentioned.
Since the declaration of martial law, the officially controlled
mass media have waged an unremitting campaign against Solidarity
and its leadership, prominent dissidents, and independent critics
of the reconsolidated political order. In doing so, they have
leveled personal attacks against such popular figures as Lech
Walesa and have thereby confirmed public suspicions that they
are inflexible and do not seek compromises. Although communist
ideology has been discredited by events, the authorities seem
bent upon waging an ideological struggle.

KEY POLITICAL ACTORS

The constellation of political forces that currently exists
in Poland is exceedingly difficult to analyze. The main political
groupings are often divided over both strategy and tactics.
Every policy decision and event seems to precipitate shifts in
political orientations, thereby lending a kaleidoscopic quality
to the pattern of politics.[10] The following actors are of central
importance.

The Jaruzelski Team

General Jaruzelski has governed Poland with the combined backing of the top military command and the moderate wing of the Communist Party leadership. This group's strategy has been based upon a carrot and stick approach. As described above, the Jaruzelski team has made extensive efforts to strengthen central political authority by removing the opposition's organizational potential. The development of tough legislation has been designed to prove the firmness of the authorities and their unwillingness over the long haul to permit the Solidarity phenomenon to reoccur.

On the other hand, they have held out the possibility of a Hungarian (Kadarist) evolution of the system. Over time, with the stabilization and reform of the economy, they promise that national reconciliation will be achieved in the political sphere. Here, they point to their realistic course in suspending martial law in December 1982, in permitting the summer 1983 visit of Pope John Paul II, the July 1983 lifting of martial law, and the release and amnesty of most of those who have been interned and arrested. Moreover, they hail the creation of the Patriotic Movement for National Rebirth (PRON) as a new political mechanism for promoting national unity and continually reemphasize their commitment to effective trade unions and to self-management. Adam Bromke, who sees the Jaruzelski team as realists, states, "Jaruzelski's position, thus, resembles that of Margrave Wielopolski, who in 1863 proceeded to introduce reform in Poland in a similarly autocratic fashion."[11]

The Hard-Line Communists

The most doctrinaire and Soviet-oriented elements of the Polish United Workers' Party have persisted in advocating a neo-Stalinist solution to the crisis. They would unflinchingly tighten the political screws on Polish society, proposing more than the mere neutralization of the opposition; instead, they seek its permanent liquidation. They would be more willing to employ police repression (and draw support from these elements); to go slowly in instituting economic reforms and rapidly in pursuing closer economic integration with the bloc; and they would avoid policies of reconciliation with critics of the order. Their approach is not one of gradually overcoming the opposition, but of assaulting it and introducing a Czech (Husak) type solution for Poland.

The hard-liners are primarily representatives of the party apparatus. They dislike and distrust the ascendancy of the military that occurred during martial law and persists in its aftermath. They would like to see the military consigned to its traditional role. In their view, the Communist Party has been systematically sapped of its strength. In fact, this is true given the massive expulsions and resignations of party members since the summer of 1980. Thus, they are suspicious of promised efforts to rid the party of internal corruption. Efforts to strengthen the power of the state without clearly emphasizing the party's dominant role are also viewed quite negatively.[12]

Solidarity and Society

Despite the trauma of martial law, including the overt repression and the frontal attack on organizational opposition, few analysts would deny that the Solidarity ideal is still cherished by the overwhelming majority of Polish citizens. While the size and intensity of open demonstrations of support for Solidarity diminished as martial law wore on, the manifestations of popular backing during Pope John Paul II's summer visit were visible proof of continued resistance to the regime.[13] General Jaruzelski has employed a strategy of attrition, counting on the carrot and the stick process to break down open opposition to the authorities as weariness of struggle set in. In a sense, he has been successful in quelling direct action. Yet he has not been able to generate support for the authorities. Citizens have boycotted and ridiculed the mass media, the majority of workers have shunned the new labor unions, and economic productivity has been notably low. A mood of frustration and resentment prevails, which cannot be overcome in the near future.[14]

Forced underground and effectively banned by legislation, the Solidarity organization persists. Circumstances have generated a continuing debate among the activists on how to continue the struggle from an underground position. Strategic and tactical divisions reflect differing orientations characterized by dichotomies such as pragmatists versus radicals. Among the Solidarity leaders, there have been differences over whether to operate on a centralized or decentralized organizational basis; over whether to mount open demonstrations and strikes or to exercise various forms of passive resistance; and over whether Solidarity supporters should seek to penetrate the new trade unions and councils or boycott them.[15] Since the release of Lech Walesa in

November 1982, the Solidarity underground has a visible champion of its cause who remains a powerful symbol and resource despite the obvious tight restrictions on his activities. While it is beyond the scope of this analysis to delineate the various streams of thought within the Solidarity movement, it is probably safe to predict that it will persist in a variety of forms and will practice diverse modes of opposition. Moreover, while support in terms of membership and direct action may decline, a considerable segment of the population will remain loyal and available for mobilization under the proper circumstances.

The Catholic Church

As Pope John Paul II's summer visit to martial law Poland indicated, the Catholic church continues to exercise its traditional role as the repository of national values and arbiter of conflicts during periods of crisis.[16] While church strategy and tactics since 1980 have been complex and controversial, it obviously remains the most effective institution for the promotion of social peace and stability in Poland. For example, Pope John Paul II was able to serve as the spokesman for the vast majority of Poles in his meetings with General Jaruzelski. At their first meeting, he argued for the opening up of a dialogue "to solve social conflicts and search for the common good." In particular, he emphasized:

> Taking into account the interests of various groups, it is possible to arrive at a peaceful settlement through dialogue, through democratic observance of freedom, through everyone fulfilling his duties, through structures which ensure the people's participation, together with all kinds of arbitration institutions—for instance, to deal with conflicts between employers and employees—and through due respect for cultural, ethnic, and religious groups that make up a nation, thus linking them together.
> In cases where dialogue between government and nation unfortunately ceases to exist, social peace becomes threatened and even disappears altogether and there arises, so to speak, a state of war.[17]

While it cannot be claimed that the pope's visit prompted General Jaruzelski's ending of martial law, it is undeniable that the moral spirit of the nation was lifted. Mass expressions of support for the pope, the church, Solidarity, and the nation intermingled, thus reaffirming the need for some authentic process of normalization.

Although the pope's presence in Poland served to boost society's morale, it should not be assumed that the church will become an active and open advocate of Solidarity's cause. Indeed, the pope's private meeting with Lech Walesa generated concerns that the church was encouraging a deactivation of Solidarity's struggle. On the other hand, in the months following the visit, Cardinal Jozef Glemp has been vocally critical of the authorities' failure to foster a "genuine dialogue" with the "authentic representatives" of the people (those associated with the Solidarity movement) and has expressed his dismay over governmental foot-dragging in the legalization of a church-sponsored development fund designed to assist Polish private farmers.[18] The maneuverings of the church indicate that it clearly sympathizes with Solidarity's cause, but that it will not jeopardize its own long-term interests by becoming too closely linked with the movement. Instead, it will retain its own independence and will seek to play a mediating role between Solidarity and the state in an effort to achieve a viable national reconciliation.[19]

The Superpowers and Their Allies

Martial law and normalization have served the interests of the Soviet Union and the Warsaw Treaty Organization allies who feared the collapse of communist power and the potential costs of military intervention.[20] Since December 1981, the Soviets and members of the bloc have maintained close surveillance over the Polish scene, both praising Jaruzelski for his firmness and applying political pressure when disruption occurred. Troubled by the negative political and economic consequences of the Polish crisis on their own societies, bloc leaders have moved to reintegrate Poland more tightly into the communist fold.[21]

The United States and its West European allies have continued to mount criticism against the Jaruzelski regime for its violations of civil liberties and its deviation from the promised policies of 1980-81. Moreover, they indicated a willingness to cooperate with Poland in resolving its enormous economic problems if domestic progress was achieved. Yet it must be emphasized that the economic and political penalties imposed on Poland have been rather mild and ineffective. Moreover, the allies (both governments and banks) have squabbled over such issues as the Soviet gas pipeline and debt rescheduling.[22] In the wake of the lifting of martial law, one may expect that it will be difficult to maintain a common front. There will be active diplomatic maneuvering by all states concerned, as Poland seeks to regain its international credibility.

WHITHER POLAND?

The preceding discussion did not focus on one crucial factor influencing Poland's future—the performance of the Polish economy. The imposition of martial law occurred at a moment when Poland was in desperate economic straits. The militarization of the economy was meant to impose discipline in key areas of production, guaranteeing that workers and managers alike would fulfill governmental plans for the achievement of stabilization. At the same time, a logically contradictory policy of economic reform has been partially followed, providing for increased managerial autonomy at the enterprise level. For example, factory managers have been given more latitude in setting prices and wages. The authorities continue to express a commitment to long-term reform and decentralization, including a role for workers' councils, but Jaruzelski himself has admitted that so far the reform is "a prematurely born child, with all its peculiar weaknesses."[23]

Despite some slight signs of recovery, most economic indicators show that progress will be exceedingly slow. While the overall deterioration of the economy has been arrested—national income declined 12 percent in 1981, 8 percent in 1982—Poland's national income in early 1983 was 25 percent lower than in 1978.[24] The inflation rate has been estimated at the 30 percent level and it is believed that the real incomes of low wage earners and those on pensions have dropped some 10 to 15 percent.[25] Shortages continue to plague most areas of the consumer economy. Food products remain in scarce supply, while food prices continue to soar. During the first half of 1983, there was minor improvement in the foreign trade sector, as Poland has cut back on its Western imports while intensifying its interaction with the Eastern bloc. Finally, there was some easing of the debt repayment problems in the short term, but long-term solutions still remain to be discovered.[26]

The economic problems that bedevil the Jaruzelski regime are a major stumbling block to the resolution of the political

crisis. Unlike Kadar's Hungary in the post-1956 period, Poland
will not be able to win public support by focusing society's
attention on economic successes. All that the present leadership
can promise is an arduous and frustrating climb back to the
standards of living that existed in the pre-1979 period. Most
of Polish society is skeptical and pessimistic about the prospects
for economic recovery. Their experience with immobile party-
state bureaucracies affords little reason to believe that the
present authorities will prove to be rational, efficient, and
just in their supervision of the economy.

The political legacy of the post-1980 period is also negative.
Although the Jaruzelski team may be conceived by some sectors
of the population as relatively moderate (this, in itself, is a
controversial assertion), society will continue to view it as the
group that destroyed the independent trade union movement.
Repressive actions taken during martial law and the enactment
of severe legislation that can be employed to block criticism
and dissent are in stark contrast to the civil society model
that society embraced during the Solidarity period. The
Jaruzelski government's refusal to enter into negotiations with
Walesa or other Solidarity leaders, in combination with their
pursuit of criminal penalties for former KSS "KOR" and Solidarity
activists, serves to stiffen resistance to the current regime.

The internal divisions within both the Polish United Workers'
Party and the Solidarity movement also weaken the prospects
for stabilization. The hard-line factions within the Communist
Party, sometimes supported by similar groupings in the Soviet
Union and the rest of the bloc, will act as a brake on the
process of national reconciliation. Fearful of the resurgence
of another popular mass movement in Poland, they will carefully
scrutinize all efforts to promote political change in a direction
reminiscent of 1980-81. The splits within Solidarity over
strategy and tactics will mean that there will be less political
leverage applied on the authorities to pursue change. It is
even possible that actions taken by the more radical or militant
segments of Solidarity will prompt reaction and backpedaling
by the authorities. Thus, the political situation will remain
fluid and unpredictable.

Polish nationalism is another complicating factor. The
Solidarity movement unleashed Polish national emotions that
have had a permanent impact upon society. For the foreseeable
future, Solidarity will be identified as one of the symbols of
the desire for a free and independent Poland. The current
leadership and the Communist Party will be indelibly associated
with the Soviet Union and its interests: a compliant and quiescent

Poland. Such a situation means that it will take much time and unusual efforts to build political support for the existing order.

Speculation about Poland's future is an intriguing, but often misleading process. As we have seen, Polish politics are complex and volatile. The hopefulness of the Solidarity period was transformed into the fearfulness of martial law. Poland at this time has stabilized to some extent but it is far from a state of normalcy and social peace. The Polish crisis will remain with us for some time to come.

NOTES

1. Most of the relevant literature on Poland in the late 1970s and early 1980s has been cited in this volume. Two recent volumes that deserve mention are: Abraham Brumberg, ed., Poland: Genesis of a Revolution (New York: Vintage Books, 1983) and Jean Woodall, ed., Policy and Politics in Contemporary Poland (New York: St. Martin's Press, 1982). A recent, perceptive article summarizing political trends is Oliver MacDonald, "The Polish Vortex: Solidarity and Socialism," New Left Review 139 (May-June 1983):5-48.

2. See "December 13, 1981: The Announcement of the State of War" and "The Decree of the State of War," Bulletin Solidarnosc 2 (March 1982):10-11.

3. A perceptive journalistic account of the moods of Polish society can be found in Lawrence Weschler, "A Reporter at Large—A State of War," The New Yorker, Part 1 (April 11, 1983), pp. 45-102 and Part 2 (April 18, 1983), pp. 52-123.

4. New York Times, July 22, 1983, pp. 1 and 6.

5. For example, see the documents on "Civil Society Versus the State" and "Towards Workers' Self-Management" in an excellent collection of Solidarity materials, Stan Persky and Henry Flam, eds., The Solidarity Sourcebook (Vancouver: New Star Books, 1982), pp. 109-240. Also, see Adam Bromke, "The Revival of Political Idealism in Poland," Canadian Slavonic Papers 4 (December 1982), especially pp. 341-344 and Casimir Garnysz, "Holding a Bear by the Tail: The Polish Crisis," Encounter (September-October 1982), especially pp. 79-82. As might be expected, there is some controversy among analysts over what is radical/militant/romantic or moderate/realist and over whom to assign to these categories.

6. For fuller information, see Anita Wasilewska, "War and Justice," Poland Watch 1 (Fall 1982):29-40; George S. White, "Political Trials Under Martial Law," Poland Watch 2

(Winter 1982-1983):23-32; Piotr Niklewicz, "Political Trials Since the Suspension of Martial Law," Poland Watch 3 (Spring-Summer 1983):11-20.

7. See Jane Cave, "Repression in the Workplace," Poland Watch 3 (Spring-Summer 1983):21-28.

8. See "A Trade Union Law?", Bulletin Solidarnosc 4 (January 1983):16-19. Also, Jane Cave, "The Banning of Solidarity," Poland Watch 2 (Winter 1982-1983):1-9.

9. See Anna Swidlicka, "Legislation Perpetuates Martial Law Restrictions," Radio Free Europe Research, Polish Situation Report no. 11, July 18, 1983, pp. 2-8; Anna Swidlicka, "After Martial Law: Repression Written into the Law," Radio Free Europe Research, Polish Situation Report no. 12, August 4, 1983, pp. 5-14.

10. One of the best accounts of the various actors is Garnysz, op. cit., pp. 73-86. See, also, Jadwiga Staniszkis, "Martial Law in Poland," Telos 54 (Winter 1982-1983), pp. 87-100, and the articles included in "Poland Under Jaruzelski," Survey 3-4 (Summer and Autumn 1982).

11. Bromke, op. cit., p. 356.

12. See, for example, Garnysz, op. cit., p. 78; John Kifner, "Polish Party Loses Members, but Not Control," New York Times, August 21, 1983, p. 4E. A brief, perceptive, and provocative interpretation of Jaruzelski's efforts at building a strong state authority (and deemphasizing the party) may be found in correspondence by Richard Spielman, Foreign Policy 51 (Summer 1983):182-88.

13. On the pope's visit, see Ewa Celt, "Papal Pilgrimage: The Spiritual Dimension," Radio Free Europe Research, Polish Situation Report no. 10, July 5, 1983, pp. 2-13; RAD Polish Section, "The Pope's Sociopolitical Comments during his 16-23 June 1983 Visit," Radio Free Europe Research, RAD Background Report 153, June 30, 1983, pp. 1-14; J. B. de Weydenthal, "The Pope's Pilgrimage to Poland," Radio Free Europe Research, RAD Background Report 158, July 8, 1983, pp. 1-12; Tadeusz Walendowski, "The Pope in Poland," Poland Watch 3 (Spring-Summer 1983):1-10.

14. See Weschler, op. cit.; also, Jane Cave and Marsha Sosnowska, "Protest and Resistance," Poland Watch 1 (Fall 1982):63-74.

15. See Andrzej Tymowski, "The Underground Debate on Strategy and Tactics," Poland Watch 1 (Fall 1982):75-87; Andrzej Tymowski, "Solidarity or a Political Program?", Poland Watch 3 (Spring-Summer 1983):95-108; Stefan Malski, "Political Groups in the Polish Underground," Radio Free Europe Research, RAD

Background Report 215, September 8, 1983, pp. 1-9; the
articles in "Poland Under Jaruzelski," Survey 3 (Summer 1982):
48-86, 128-164, and 4 (Autumn 1982):77-109.

16. Discussions of the role of the church can be found
in Dieter Bingen's chapter in this volume and Michael D. Kennedy
and Maurice D. Simon, "Church and Nation in Socialist Poland,"
in eds. Peter H. Merkl and Ninian Smart, Religion and Politics
in the Modern World (New York: New York University Press,
1983), pp. 121-154. Also, see the items in note 13.

17. Quoted in Walendowski, op. cit., p. 6.

18. For example, see Ewa Celt, "Cardinal Glemp Addresses
Farmers in Czestochowa," Radio Free Europe Research, Polish
Situation Report no. 14, September 21, 1983, pp. 2-4.

19. See Garnysz, op. cit., pp. 82-83; Casimir Garnysz,
"Warsaw's Wary Welcome for John Paul," The New Leader 11
(May 30, 1983):6-7; and Daniel Singer, "How Many Masses is
Poland Worth?", The Nation 6 (September 3-10, 1983):173-176.

20. See the chapter by Roger Kanet in this volume; also,
Jiri Valenta, "The Explosive Soviet Periphery," Foreign Policy
51 (Summer 1983), especially pp. 91-93.

21. See Christoph Royen, "Polish Perspectives after the
Suspension of "Martial Law,'" Aussen Politik 2 (1983), especially
pp. 163-165 and 167-170.

22. Recent accounts include Charles Gati, "Polish Futures,
Western Options," Foreign Affairs 2 (Winter 1982-1983), pp.
292-308; Valenta, op. cit., pp. 84-100.

23. Quoted from John Kifner, "Poland's Abundance of
Scarcity," New York Times, March 6, 1983, p. 4E.

24. Ibid.; Royen, op. cit., p. 163.

25. Royen, op. cit., p. 163; R. S., "Poland's Economy:
Stagnation Rather than Progress," Radio Free Europe Research,
Polish Situation Report 13, August 26, 1983, pp. 6-8. Some
other economic trends can be found in Jean-Yves Potel, "A
Year of Martial Law in Poland," Labour Focus on Eastern Europe
5-6 (Winter 1982-1983), especially pp. 18-19.

26. Royen, op. cit.; also Kifner, "Poland's Abundance of
Scarcity," op. cit.

The author would like to thank the Research Council of
the University of North Carolina at Greensboro which supported
this project. Also, Richard Rodriguia who assisted in final
preparations.

Index

Agriculture: collectivization, 31, 82; food prices, 81, 83, 86-88, 91-92, 295-96, 353; pre-1980 policy, 35, 78-83; production and output, 36-37, 46-47, 244; rural public opinion of agricultural policy, 153-54
Andropov, Yuri, 306
"Appeal to the People of Eastern Europe" (by Solidarity), 228
Association of Polish Journalists, 201, 205, 347
Association of Polish Theater, Television, and Film Actors, 347

Babiuch, Edward, 121, 150, 253, 296, 298, 300
Baglai, M., 331
Barcikowski, Kazimierz, 133, 222
Believers' Self-Defense Committees, 194
Bierut, Boleslaw, 31
Bilak, Vasil, 318
Biuletyn Informacyjny (Information Bulletin), 193
Bojarski, Wlodzimierz, 65
Bozyk, Pawel, 62
Brezhnev, Leonid, 300, 301, 306, 319, 326, 329, 332, 334; Brezhnev Doctrine, 319-20
Bromke, Adam, 349
Brzezinski, Zbigniew, 323
Bujak, Zbigniew, 346

Bureaucratic/technocratic rule, 73, 201-2
Bydgoszcz confrontation, 173, 224, 277, 324

Catholic church: church-state relations 1944-70, 212-14, 252; and confrontation of 1981, 227-29; and crisis of 1976, 214; and crisis of 1980, 217-21; and KOR (KSS-KOR), 215, 222, 224; and martial law, 229-36, 279, 286-87, 351-52; and PAX group, 213; and Solidarity, 221-25, 228-29, 352; and strikes, 218-19; and ZNAK group, 198, 213, 231
Catholic Intellectual Clubs, 201
Catholic Social Council, 234
Ceausescu, Nicolae, 327
Center for Public Opinion Studies of Polish Radio and Television, 150
Center for Social and Labor Tasks, 123
Central Council of Trade Unions (CCTU), 99, 110
Chernenko, Konstanin, 301
Chief Technical Organization, 102, 113
Citizen's Militia (Milicja Obywatelska-MO), 274, 275
Committee of Cultural Associations, 203

Katowice Forum, 256, 324-25, 329
Khrushchev, Nikita, 139
Kirilenko, Andrei, 301
Kliszko, Zenon, 275
Kornilov, Yuri, 300, 302
Kuberski, Jerzy, 233
Kukolowicz, Romuald, 219, 231
Kulaj, Jan, 85, 89
Kulikov, Viktor, 308
Kulpinska, J., 102
Kurczewski, Jacek, 127, 128
Kuron, Jacek, 193, 194, 205, 224, 278, 322, 346, 347

Labor code of 1975, 106
Large Economic Organization (WOG), 36-37, 61
Lay Left, 193, 194
Lipinski, Edward, 101
Lipski, Jan Jozef, 205, 347
Lis, Bogdan, 109, 227
Lublin Manifesto of July 1944, 212
Lukaszewicz, Jerzy, 296

Macharski, Franciszek (Cardinal), 222, 223
Main Political Administration (MPA), 273
Malinowski, Roman, 89
Martial law ("State of War"): 23, 41, 113-15, 261-62; 264, 277-80, 321, 335, 345, 346; and the Catholic church, 182, 229-36, 279, 286-87, 351-52; and control legislation, 348; and dissolution of organizations, 347-48; economic reforms during, 42-45, 47, 353; effects on foreign economic policy, 74; and intellectuals, 204-7; and internments/arrests, 77, 204-5, 347; and military, 179-82, 278-80; and peasants, 88-92; and Polish United Workers' Party, 259-64, 282-87; Soviet involvement in, 309; suspension of Solidarity, 77, 113, 114, 348
Mazowiecki, Tadeusz, 219, 347
Michnik, Adam, 286, 322, 347
Military (Polish): 179-82, 260, 261-64, 268-70, 282-87; composition of, 281, 282-85; and crises 1967-1976, 272-75; development of, 270-73; and martial law, 179-82, 278-82; public confidence in, 150-52; reliability, 271-72, 275; and "Renewal", 275-77
Military Council of National Salvation (WRON), 180, 262, 268, 278, 280, 282, 284-85, 345
Military Security Service (Wojska Sluzby Wewnetrnej-WSW), 273
Millenium of Polish State (1966), 213-14
Minic, Milos, 327
Ministry of Labor, Wages, and Social Affairs, 106
Moczar, Mieczyslaw, 274
Movement for the Defense of Human and Civil Rights (ROPCiO), 194-95, 197

National Consultative Commission of Solidarity (KKP), 123, 177, 178
National Unity Front (FJN), 59
Nestorowicz, Tadeusz, 69

[Soviet Union]
responses to Polish events
post-December 1981, 352-
53; role of Poland in Soviet
security system, 319-20;
and Polish succession of
1970, 308-9
Spychalski, Marian, 272, 274
Stalinism: 2, 115, 170; and
public opinion research,
138-39
State Land Fund, 81
Stomma, Stanislaw, 231
Strikes (Polish): 1956, 3, 31,
100, 272; 1970, 6, 34, 61,
104-5, 242, 275; 1976, 9-
10, 37, 106, 171-72, 193,
275; 1980-81, 13-17, 59,
109-11, 253, 296-97, 320-
21; and the Catholic church,
218-19; organization and
tactics, 14-15, 109-10;
public opinion about, 141-43
Supreme Chamber of Control,
59
Supreme Court (Polish), 85,
124
Swiecicki, Andrzej, 219
Szczecin agreements, 122, 124,
129, 131, 220, 299, 302, 303
Szczepanski, Maciej, 132, 298
Szydlak, Jan, 110

TASS, 234, 300, 325
Trade unions: Free Trade
Union Movement, 10, 105,
107-8, 109-10, 146, 192-93;
and martial law, 113-14,
348; official trade unions,
108-9, 110, 255; reform of
trade union law (1980),
111-13
Trybuna Ludu, 122, 131
Tygodnik Powszechny, 224,
263

Tygodnik Solidarnosc, 123,
220, 255

United Peasants' Party
(UPP), 59, 83, 85, 89,
144
United States and Western
allies: response to post-
December 1981 Polish
events, 89, 352-53

Wages: 353; differentials,
121-24, 128-29; reforms
of, 5-6, 35, 45, 100
Walentynowicz, Anna, 109,
227
Walesa, Lech, 109, 111, 176-
77, 223, 224, 227, 229,
230, 236, 260, 264, 280,
298, 347, 348, 350-51,
354
Warsaw Pact allies (WTO
allies): concrete pres-
sures on Poland, 328-33;
domestic implications of
Polish events, 333-36;
economic assistance to
Poland, 332-33; response
to Polish events post-
December 1981, 352-53;
verbal responses to 1980-
81 crisis, 317-18, 322-28
Wielopolska, Margrave, 262,
349
Wielowiejski, Andrzej, 219,
231
Wiez, 220
Wojiechowski, Miroslaw, 296
Workers: activism/opposition,
10, 106-15; and factory
councils, 98-99; and self-
management, 3, 21-22,
45, 96-98, 102, 112-13
Workers Councils, 3, 22, 48,
98-103

About the Contributors

DAVID BEALMEAR is a Ph.D. candidate in Sociology at the University of North Carolina at Chapel Hill and is engaged in a study of the welfare state in Poland and Great Britain.

JACK BIELASIAK is Associate Professor of Political Science and member of the Russian-East European Institute at Indiana University. He obtained the Ph.D. at Cornell University. He has written on political elites and workers' issues in East Europe, and on the political crisis in Poland. He is editor of Poland Today and contributor to Poland: Genesis of a Revolution, and Communism and the Politics of Inequalities.

DIETER BINGEN is a member of the research staff at the Bundesinstitut für ostwissenschaftliche und internationale Studien in Cologne. He holds the Ph.D. from the Friedrich Wilhelms University, Bonn. He is the author of a number of articles on the Polish church and Solidarity published in Osteuropa, Aus Politik und Zeitgeschichte, and Herder-Korrespondenz.

JANE LEFTWICH CURRY is Assistant Professor of Political Science at Manhattanville College and Senior Consultant to the Rand Corporation. She received the Ph.D. from Columbia University and is the author of The Black Book of Polish Censorship and editor of Dissent in Eastern Europe.

HOWARD E. FROST is a Soviet affairs analyst with the Central Intelligence Agency and a Ph.D. candidate at M.I.T. He has written on Soviet and East European military and political affairs for scholarly edited volumes.

T. ANTHONY JONES is Assistant Professor of Sociology at the University of North Carolina at Chapel Hill. He has written on education and on workers in the USSR, on modernization theory, and on patterns of change in socialist societies. He is currently working on a study of technology and social relations in the Soviet factory.

ROGER E. KANET is Professor of Political Science and a member of the Russian and East European Center at the University of Illinois at Urbana-Champaign. He received the Ph.D. from Princeton University. He is the author of numerous articles on Soviet and East European foreign and domestic politics and is editor of Soviet Foreign Policy in the 1980s, Soviet Foreign Policy and East-West Relations, and (with Maurice D. Simon) Background to Crisis: Policy and Politics in Gierek's Poland.

DAVID M. KEMME is Assistant Professor of Economics at the University of North Carolina at Greensboro. He has authored several articles on the Polish economy and central planning in Soviet-type economies. Dr. Kemme was a Fulbright lecturer at the Central School of Planning and Statistics in Warsaw during the 1981-82 academic year.

MICHAEL D. KENNEDY is a Ph.D. candidate in Sociology at the University of North Carolina at Chapel Hill and is doing research on changes in occupational structures in Poland and the responses of the professions to those changes.

ANDRZEJ KORBONSKI is Professor of Political Science and Director of the Center for Russian and East European Studies at the University of California, Los Angeles. He is the author of numerous articles on political and economic developments in the Soviet Union and Eastern Europe in a variety of scholarly journals and books. Among his works is Politics of Agriculture in Poland, 1945-1960.

Z. ANTHONY KRUSZEWSKI is Professor of Political Science at the University of Texas, El Paso. He holds the Ph.D. from the University of Chicago, and is the author of The Oder-Neisse Boundary and Poland's Modernization.

PAUL C. LATAWSKI is a Ph.D. candidate in History at Indiana University, Bloomington. In the 1982-83 academic year he was in Poland on an IREX grant to study Polish foreign policy.

DAVID S. MASON is Assistant Professor of Political Science at Butler University in Indianapolis. He received his Ph.D. from Indiana University and has published articles on Poland in The Polish Review, The Journal of Politics, and Soviet Studies. He spent the first half of 1982 in Warsaw on the exchange sponsored by IREX.

BARBARA A. MISZTAL is a Post-Doctoral Fellow at the University of California, Riverside. She holds a Ph.D. in Sociology from the Academy of Sciences, Warsaw. She has written several articles and is coauthor of Attitudes Towards Work.

BRONISLAW MISZTAL is Visiting Professor of Sociology at Pitzer College in Clarmont, California. He received the Ph.D. from the Academy of Sciences, Warsaw. He is the author of Peer-Groups in the Structure of Socialist Society, Problems of Participation and Cooperation, and Urban Sociology. He was a Senior Fulbright Scholar at the University of Chicago in 1980-81.

JOANNA PREIBISZ is a graduate student in International Affairs at Columbia University. She is the compiler and editor of Polish Dissident Publications: An Annotated Bibliography

CHRISTINE M. SADOWSKI is a Visiting Scholar at the Hoover Institution, conducting research on Poland's Solidarity movement. She received the Ph.D. from the University of Michigan and has taught at Trinity College and Loyola Marymount University. She was the recipient of a Kosciuszko Foundation scholarship for Krakow in 1970-71 and a Fulbright Scholar at Warsaw University in 1976-77.

MARCIN SAR is a Visiting Research Fellow at the Rockefeller Foundation. He has taught in the Department of Political Science at Warsaw University and was an exchange Professor at the University of Kansas. He has written several articles on East-West relations and foreign economic policy.

MAURICE D. SIMON is Associate Professor of Political Science at the University of North Carolina, Greensboro. He obtained the Ph.D. from Stanford University and has written extensively on political developments in Poland. He is the coeditor of Background to Crisis: Policy and Politics in Gierek's Poland and Developed Socialism in the Soviet Bloc.